# "SAY... DIDN'T YOU USED TO BE GEORGE MURPHY?"

# "SAY... DIDN'T YOU USED TO BE GEORGE MURPHY?"

BY U.S. SENATOR GEORGE MURPHY
WITH VICTOR LASKY

BARTHOLOMEW HOUSE, LTD.

BARTHOLOMEW HOUSE, LTD.
First Printing . . . July 1970

© 1970 by George Murphy

Library of Congress
Catalog Card Number: 76-110744
Standard Book Number 87794-024-X

Manufactured in the U.S.A.

# CONTENTS

Photography sections follow pages 63, 172, and 346

To
my patient, understanding, loving
and helpful wife Julie,
who is the finest lady
I've ever known

# "SAY... DIDN'T YOU USED TO BE GEORGE MURPHY?"

# CHAPTER 1

### *"That nice young man*
### *who once danced with Shirley Temple"*

It used to happen all the time. Usually at airports. I'd be get-ting off a plane and suddenly I'd notice a little old lady staring at me. It was obvious she had half-recognized me but she wasn't too certain who I was.

"Don't I know him?" she would ask someone standing close by.

"Oh," was the usual reply, "he's a United States Senator."

The little old lady would still be confused. Then, as I'd walk by, she'd remember. "Say," she'd ask politely, "didn't you used to be George Murphy?"

And I'd say, "Madam, I still am."

It hasn't happened as often lately. Perhaps it's because I am no longer primarily known as that nice young man who once danced with Shirley Temple. After five years in the rough-and-tumble of high-level Washington politics, it has finally become established in the public mind that I am, indeed, the senior Senator from California, the most populous state of the union, and am sitting on committees that are concerned with the most momentous issues confronting our nation.

What always amused me when I first ran for office and even after I began serving in the Senate were the constant references to me in the press or on television as "the former song-and-dance man." Invariably, there was a belittling note in such a description.

To be candid, I didn't mind one bit. The statement, after all, was accurate. I had been a song-and-dance man, one of the best in the business. As Arthur Krock, then the prestigious colum-nist of the *New York Times* (and one whose wisdom we have sorely missed since his retirement), put it following my election in 1964: " . . . like George M. Cohan, Fred Astaire, George Burns, Danny Kaye, Jack Donahue and others past and present who developed this form of clean entertainment into an art, (Murphy) sang and danced to the delight of children and adults alike. . . "

But if I didn't feel the need to beat my breast, crying out *mea culpa,* over having made a living in show business, I did resent any implication that I was just an ex-hoofer and nothing more. The fact is that I probably had more kinds of experience than most aspirants to important political office. There aren't many politicians who can lay claim to having worked in a coal mine, as a bouncer in a dance hall and as a runner on Wall Street. And there aren't too many, if any at all, who can say his career encompassed the leadership of a labor union as well as front-office duties as a business executive.

Most everything I've ever done in my varied careers ties in closely with what I'm doing now in the United States Senate. Even my motion picture background. For example, there were a lot of quiet chuckles on the Senate floor and in the press gallery when "the former song-and-dance man" first arose to discuss a particularly complicated subject of special concern back home: letting migrant farm workers from Mexico—"braceros" —into the United States.

There were a few colleagues, I'm sure, who were impatiently waiting for me to fall flat on my face. I think I disappointed them because, as Willard Edwards reported in the *Chicago Tribune,* I "quickly revealed an impressive mastery of the subject." Also, while I have always believed that there is no business like show business, I refrained—as I always have in public life—from indulging in histrionics.

When I began to speak on the subject that day, Senator Harrison Williams interrupted me and said it was a shame that I had no real knowledge of the farm labor problem. I told the distinguished Senator from New Jersey that it was a shame the Senator did not know that I had been concerned with farm labor problems in California since about the time he was in high school.

When I made my maiden speech in the Senate I already knew a great deal about the braceros. They were the subject of a film I had appeared in fifteen years before at Metro-Goldwyn-Mayer entitled *Border Incident.* Ricardo Montalban and I played the roles of Mexican and American immigration agents respectively. For eight weeks we lived on location close to the Mexican border, and it was there that I first became fully aware of the magnitude and complexity of the problem.

In the course of a crowded lifetime, I have fought gangsters and Communists, and my life has been threatened on a few occasions. So the present wave of hoodlumism, both criminal and ideological, sweeping the country is nothing new to me. I've seen it firsthand and I know that if my fellow legislators are willing to do battle and pass the needed legislation to assist our harassed law enforcement officials, we will eventually succeed in curbing these forces of evil. It won't be easy. I learned long ago that few things in life come easy. But it will have to be done, the sooner the better.

Anyway, I'm still George Murphy—and proud of it. Call me a "former song-and-dance man" if you will. I'm proud of that, too. Whether I've been a good Senator—and I think I have—is up to the people of California to decide. At any rate, here is my story.

# CHAPTER 2

## *"The flags were waving"*

Believe it or not, the flags were waving and firecrackers exploding throughout the nation about the time I was born. Everyone was enjoying it except my poor mother. To be honest, the celebration had nothing to do with my coming into the world. It happened quite fortuitously that I was born on a July 4, the birthday of our great nation—and therein lies a tale.

For it has been said—disparagingly for the most part—that I am a superpatriot, whatever that means. I suppose it means that I have an excessive love of country. I plead guilty. I see no reason to apologize, even in these days of cynicism and doubt, for our heritage and our national purpose. This country has been good to me and my forebears. It has provided opportunity and incentive and has permitted more progress than any other nation on earth. Call it flag-waving if you will, but that's the way I feel. And if you don't feel the same way about it, that's your privilege as a free American.

At any rate, I was born on Independence Day, 1902, in New Haven, Connecticut, the youngest child of Michael and Nora Long Murphy. There were two other children. The first was my sister Mabel; then came my older brother, Charles Thorne Murphy, whom for some forgotten reason I called Bob. We were a close-knit family, dominated by a loving father who constantly demanded the best of us.

My father, better known as Mike Murphy, is a legendary figure in the world of sports. He trained more world record holders and Olympic champions in track than any other athletic trainer, and his teams won more intercollegiate championships. Among those he trained were John Owen, Alvin Kraenzlein, Bernie Wefers, Jim Thorpe, Don Lippincott and Ted Meredith.

He could quickly analyze any track performance. For example, Arthur Duffy was once credited with running the hundred-yard dash in nine-and-four-tenths seconds. Dad said he didn't do it. When asked how he knew, Dad said simply, "I've seen him run." They measured the track. He was right; the track was short.

Dad was always ahead of his time. Over sixty years ago he told us that, given the same training opportunities, Negroes would one day hold all the records up to a half-mile. He believed they had a slight physical advantage. Today we call it "the will to win," or "desire."

When I was born, my father was the track coach and trainer at Yale University, where he worked sometimes in tandem with the world-famous football coach, Walter Camp. Camp was quite a man. It was he who, several years before my birth, initiated the practice of honoring the eleven best college football players of each season by naming them to Walter Camp's All-American Team of the year.

Both Camp and Dad were men of strong opinions. Though friends, they frequently clashed over what was best for Yale athletics. Dad left Yale to take over similar duties at the University of Pennsylvania and took his talents with him, as the record books will attest.

My father died in 1913 when I was eleven years old, but today, over half a century after his passing, I still have vivid memories of him. He was a dedicated man, dedicated to a clean mind and a healthy body, and he insisted on discipline. Like any good sportsman, he wanted his boys to win—but not at any price. There were times when he didn't mind if the other team triumphed.

For a long time and for reasons I don't recall, Dad had a strong dislike for Jack Moakley, the Cornell coach. They hadn't spoken in years. But once during an indoor track meet, Dad realized that John Paul Jones, the famous Cornell miler, had a chance to break the world's record. Forgetting his animosity momentarily, Dad slapped Moakley on the back and shouted, "Get over there and take him down the back stretch and I'll bring him on home." Moakley was so startled that he did what he was told and Jones set a new record. Dad went right back to being mad at Moakley again.

Oh, the stories I could tell about Mike Murphy. He was a slight man with a brush mustache and a twinkling eye who spent his life taking care of everyone but himself.

Dad was one of the most respected and most influential men in Philadelphia. I remember some politicians coming out to the house to ask him for his endorsement, for which they offered to build him a health institute on a two-hundred-acre piece of land on the Main Line. Dad rejected the proposition out of hand simply because he didn't want to be beholden to the "boys."

I first became aware of the esteem in which Dad was held the night the Penn team left to play Michigan in football. The students lifted him onto a newspaper kiosk in the railroad station and insisted that he deliver one of his famous between-the-halves inspirational speeches. He did and the crowd went wild. That was also when I first realized the power of the spoken word. One of Dad's famous lines is engraved on a plaque at the entrance to Franklin Field at the University. It reads: "You can't lick a team that won't be licked."

By this time Dad had developed a deserved reputation as one of the best physical conditioners in the nation. Among those whose infirmities he treated was Theodore Roosevelt, who became a good friend of the family. Both men were hard-of-hearing, and when my Dad would visit at Oyster Bay, the neighbors said they could be heard shouting at each other clear across Long Island Sound.

Dad's intensive studies of anatomy and surgery at the University of Pennsylvania helped him originate many new types of athletic equipment. He invented the "crouch" start for sprinters, designed running shoes with football ankle supports and developed the prototypes of much of the protective equipment now worn by football players.

My father was a great believer in massage. In those days rub-downs were pretty much hit-and-miss, but not with my father. He recognized the importance of properly kneading out the aches and pains that often beset athletes. At the University of Pennsylvania Dad had a Negro assistant, Billy Maurice, who, though he couldn't read or write, was in my Dad's eyes the best rubber in the business. Billy was the only masseur Dad would permit to use his "golden hands" on his sprinters.

While Dad worried about everyone else's physical condition, he rarely bothered to take care of himself. We often felt that in getting the best out of his boys, he was killing himself.

He was always working. When he wasn't at the university, he would sit at a desk in the sitting room of our home in West Philadelphia. There, under a gas light, he kept up an extensive correspondence with other coaches and trainers across the country. Many of these people were boyhood pals whom he'd trained to be great coaches, like Pouch Donovan at Harvard, Keene Fitzpatrick at Princeton, Steve Farrell at Michigan, Johnny Mack at Yale and others. A whole cycle of amateur athletics was developed under my father's leadership.

We three children have often recalled the enormous respect that we had for him. He never had to scold or spank us for misbehaving. His parental approach was quite different. "I don't think that would be the right thing to do," he would say, and he had a way of saying it that convinced us we had better do the right thing. When he said it, you believed it.

We lived in an interesting old house, one of a row of four sitting on a terrace on Chestnut Street. It contained a parlor which was used only when a boy came calling on my sister. The family really congregated in the sitting room on the second floor where my father had his desk. The room had a large bay window with cushions where you could sit and keep track of everything going on in the street.

And there was always something interesting going on. For instance, we could see members of the famed Barrymore family taking their walks. The Barrymores had a home not far from us. Mabel, in fact, can remember seeing young John Barrymore, who had not yet made his mark as an actor, going to the neighborhood saloon to load up the family beer can. We called it "rushing the growler."

In 1910 Dad was assigned by the Philadelphia *North American,* a great newspaper in those days, to cover one of the most exciting sports events of the time, the world's championship heavyweight fight between the champ, James Jeffries, and Jack Johnson, the Negro challenger whose life was recently dramatized—and somewhat romanticized—in *The Great White Hope.*

The big fight was to take place in Reno, Nevada. When my father arrived at Jeffries' training camp, the champion's manager wouldn't let Dad watch him work out. This made Dad suspicious. He told my brother Thorne, then sixteen years old, to buy a bicycle, hide in the bushes near the camp and follow Jeffries whenever he did his road work.

Thorne discovered that the champ's road work consisted of jogging about a mile, then being driven to the Truckee River where he would fish for a while. When enough time had elapsed, Jeffries would ride back most of the way, and then about half a mile from his training camp he would begin to run, working up a slight sweat for the benefit of the onlookers.

That was all Dad needed to know. He sat down and wrote a story reporting that Jeffries was in such bad condition that he should not be allowed to fight. The story, when published in the *North American,* was headlined: THEY CAN'T COME BACK.

Somehow, even before Dad mailed in the story, the fight promoter, Tex Rickard, heard he had written it. The infuriated Rickard offered Dad a substantial sum of money not to send it to Philadelphia. In the room with Dad at the time was Pudge Heffelfinger, the former great Yale football star. Dad turned to him and said, "How do you feel, Pudge?"

"Fine, Mike," was the good-natured reply.

"Then," said Dad, "throw this crooked son-of-a-bitch out the window."

Whereupon Pudge lifted Rickard up by the seat of his pants and heaved him out. Fortunately they were on the ground floor, and the only damage done was to Rickard's dignity.

Dad was welcomed royally at Jack Johnson's training camp, and there never was any question in his mind as to the outcome of the bout. As a matter of fact, Johnson told Dad that he intended to carry Jeffries for a couple of rounds in order to make it look like a good fight and not embarrass his opponent.

There was one newspaperman who had been mean to Johnson. "Mr. Mike," Johnson said, "when I get ready to knock him out, I'll knock him right into that newspaperman's lap." And he would have done precisely that, except for the lamentable fact that as Jeffries was sailing out of the ring, his leg got caught on the lower rope.

Johnson remained a great favorite with the Murphy family. When, in 1915, he lost the championship to Jess Willard in Havana, Cuba, after being knocked out in the twenty-sixth round, none of the Murphys could believe it and we don't to this day.

Probably the greatest all-around athlete my father ever coached was Jim Thorpe. During the 1912 Olympic Games in Stockholm, Dad shepherded the American track and field team of which Thorpe was a member. A full-blooded American Indian, Thorpe had already achieved a nationwide reputation as one of the greatest football players of all time. As a halfback for the Carlisle Indian School, he had been named an All-American.

But it was as a member of Mike Murphy's track and field squad at the Olympics that Thorpe achieved worldwide fame. At first, on the ship sailing to Sweden, Dad had difficulty getting Thorpe out of his stateroom. A track had been laid down around the deck of the ship, and everyone in the squad turned out for practice except Thorpe. Dad was furious, but he kept his cool.

When he encountered Thorpe, he decided to goad him by seeming to forget his name. "There's no need for you to train too much, Tom," he said. "We all know you're a great athlete. I don't want you to overtrain."

"My name is Jim," Thorpe answered somewhat sullenly.

"Oh, yes, Jim."

But the next day it was "Tom" again. On the third day Thorpe took the hint. In fact, he got so mad he started to practice with the marathon runners. When the team sat down to dinner that evening, Thorpe was still running around the deck.

His brilliant performance at Stockholm was unforgettable. King Gustaf V of Sweden rightfully called Thorpe "the greatest athlete in the world" when he became the first person ever to win both the grueling decathlon and the pentathlon. He may well have been the greatest athlete in recorded history.

There was a poignant ending to the triumphant Thorpe saga. In 1913 the Amateur Athletic Union, having learned that one summer Thorpe had played semiprofessional baseball in North Carolina, disallowed his Olympiad victories and forced him to return his gold medals and trophies.

I have always believed this was a bad rap. There has never been any doubt in my mind that Thorpe was unaware of the proscription against playing ball for money. The money itself was a pittance. And the fact that he played under his own name is proof enough, for me at least, that Thorpe never intended to deceive anyone.

Thorpe, in my opinion, was treated badly by the nation he served so well, and the time has come to make amends. One way to accomplish this would be to restore Jim Thorpe's records to the Olympic books—a symbolic gesture, perhaps, but a significant one. At the same time, Jim's medals and trophies should be restored to his family.

I know Mike Murphy would have liked that.

When I was six or seven years old, I came down with an awful case of diphtheria. I had the bug so bad that for a time all hope for my survival was gone. Fortunately, an antitoxin had recently been discovered, and in desperation I was given a double dose. It worked; I finally got well.

I also wound up cross-eyed.

Again I was fortunate, because one of the most famous eye doctors of the time took me as his patient. Somehow he straightened out my eyes without an operation. How he did it I still don't know, but I will always be grateful to that good Philadelphia doctor. Had he failed, I'm sure I would never have made it in show business, unless maybe as a trainer for the cross-eyed lion in "Daktari."

The weakness in my right eye served me well when I played baseball. I always hit from the left side because I could see better that way. And anybody who knows the fine points of baseball knows that when you hit from the left side you can beat out more bunts and slow rollers than from the right side.

Need I mention that I am of Irish stock and that my grandparents on both sides came from the auld sod. My father's parents, the Murphys, were hard-working farmers in Massachusetts. Unlike some Massachusetts families of similar origins, we all worked hard for whatever we got. And we were all thankful for the opportunities this country provided.

My mother, Nora, was a quiet woman who worked hard keeping a home for her husband and three hell-raising kids. One thing she made sure of—we were always ready for church on time.

Though we were devout Catholics, Mabel, Thorne and I went to Philadelphia public schools. My parents wanted it that way. The school was located at 36th and Chestnut Streets. The Catholic school was at 38th and Chestnut. And we lived at 44th and Chestnut. So we had to pass through the enemy lines every day to get to school and back home.

In those days school rivalries often took the form of fisticuffs. Quite often Thorne and I literally had to fight our way past the parochial school. Yet on Sundays we went to church with the very same kids we fought with during the week. On Sundays we were friends; on weekdays we were enemies.

There is one basic difference in the school situation today. In my day, the kids fought as an exercise, rarely in anger. Today, in some metropolitan areas, the schools have literally developed into "blackboard jungles" with the presence of policemen constantly required to prevent bloody warfare. Sometimes even the police, let alone the teachers, have been physically assaulted.

At the risk of being dubbed backward in pedagogical techniques, may I say that the public schools of my time, and even long after that, were far more successful in inculcating discipline than they are today. Now discipline seems to have gone by the board. Some schools, in fact, seem to be specializing in turning out malcontents whose sole purpose in life appears to be disrupting our social institutions, attacking all established authority and generally rehearsing for the coming revolution—all in the name of a spurious academic freedom.

We had gangs in those days in Philadelphia, but as I recall, the main purpose of the gang was to get ready for a big bonfire on Election Night. We used to go through the neighborhood and grab all the wooden boxes and wooden barrels we could find and hide them to get them ready for the Election Night bonfire. The other gangs would do the same. There was the Carlton Avenue gang, the Lancaster Avenue gang and we were in the Walnut Street mob. In any event, the trick was to try to find out where the other fellows had stored their barrels and then steal them. We would then pile them in an empty lot and set fire to them. This was my first contact with the election process. I must say it was pretty exciting and more fun than sitting around listening to Huntley and Brinkley analyze the whole thing for you.

Not all education takes place at school. I believe I learned some of my most valuable lessons in the company of my father, around Franklin Field at the university. I got to meet all sorts of people and as I grew older, people became more and more important in my life.

One of my best friends in this period was an elderly Negro man whom I knew simply as "Tom." He was the assistant grounds-keeper at Franklin Field, and occasionally he would come out to do odd jobs for my mother. Every now and then he would live at our house.

During the track meets, Tom had one special job—rolling the track for middle distance events. To do this he used a roller five or six feet high pulled by an old gray horse. Tom would always honor me by permitting me to sit next to him as we rode majestically in the performance of this most essential task.

What a horse! Invariably, as we passed the Pennsylvania cheering section, the horse would be inspired and would raise his tail in reaction to the excitement. But Tom was always prepared. He had armed himself with a very large cigar box at the end of a broomstick. As everyone watched with bated breath, Tom would shove his makeshift receptacle under the horse's rear, always just in time. The inevitable cheers were deafening. Tom would acknowledge his feat by tipping his hat and flashing a smile that was something to see. It was my first experience with the joy of reflected glory.

There was rarely a dull day at the Murphy household. Just before the 1912 Olympics, a tall handsome fellow from the University of Southern California came to call on my sister Mabel. Fred Kelly, a fine athlete, was a member of my father's Stockholm-bound contingent. But this wasn't enough for my brother Thorne, who apparently felt that Kelly should have got his permission before stepping foot into our home.

While Fred and Mabel were sitting in the first floor parlor, Thorne went to the attic on the third floor. He picked up a basket containing inexpensive flat tableware that we used to take on picnics and dropped the full basket down the stairwell. It sounded like a bomb. The silverware went flying in all directions and spoons, knives and forks seemed to be dropping for the next five minutes.

Mabel was so mad she would have killed Thorne if she'd been able to catch him. Poor Fred was in shock. He didn't know what to make of it.

Fred managed to recover from this experience, and returned to our home many times. We all—including Thorne—became the best of friends. After the Olympics, Fred went on to become a pioneer in commercial aviation and had an enviable record in World War I. The first pilot Western Airlines hired, he wound up as the line's Chief Pilot. He only recently retired.

Summers were always great fun for the Murphys. Dad had bought a farm in Westboro, Massachusetts, not far from Southboro, where he was born. An uncle who lived across the road did the farming.

We lived in the old farmhouse, a wonderful place reputedly built by a retired pirate named Kelly. The house was standing when oxen pulled the cannons through the snow from Boston to the battle of Princeton. Legend had it that Kelly had frequent difficulties with the Indians, which, according to the same legend, was why he had constructed an unusual reservoir system to provide himself with a safe supply of water in case the Indians harassed his place.

Kelly drew his water from a spring about two hundred yards away, through wooden pipes carefully concealed underground. That was the way it still was when we lived in the old Kelly place. Plenty of pure, clean, spring water was always available. In addition, we had a primitive refrigeration system. Mother kept her perishables in heavy iron pots sunk in the basement pool of ice-cold spring water.

We used to have great times playing at the far end of the cow

pasture that sloped off down into a swamp. This was the famous
Cedar Swamp were Tecumseh and his band of fugitive Indians,
fleeing from the United States Cavalry, were supposed to have
hidden out for an entire year. Whether there was any historical
validity to the story was not important to us kids. We thought it
was true and that was all that counted. Many were the times we
played Indians and Cavalrymen down at the swamp. It was
always very exciting and a little scary. We always made sure we
got out of the area before sundown. In the backs of our minds
we secretly thought that some of Tecumseh's descendants might
still be hiding out there.

An old gravel road ran in front of our farmhouse. I was assigned the job of keeping the road in good shape in case any
athletes should come by for a workout under my father's watch-
ful eye. Every day I would rake the road and remove rocks and
pebbles. My father pleased me no end when he once described
the road as the fastest quarter-mile of track in the world.

All sorts of people visited my father in Westboro, including
that colorful Boston pol, John F. "Honey Fitz" Fitzgerald. Little did I dream as I listened to big, red-faced "Honey Fitz" sing
"Sweet Adeline," which as far as I know was the extent of his
repertoire, that one day I would serve in the United States
Senate with two of his grandsons.

"Honey Fitz" and Dad were good friends, and Dad took him
and his daughter Rose to the Olympic Games in London in
1908, along with my sister Mabel and my mother, who
chaperoned the two girls.

After the Games, they visited Sir Thomas Lipton in Ireland,
and he entertained them on his yacht, the Shamrock V. After
two glasses of sherry, "Honey Fitz" and my Dad decided it
might be a good idea to marry Rose to Sir Thomas Lipton so
they would always have a boat to use when they wanted to go
fishing.

As a child I could dance fairly well and I wasn't shy about

demonstrating my talents. On Saturday nights the family would invite the neighbors over and have a dance in the kitchen of our farmhouse. Sometimes we would go to a pavilion at nearby Lake Chauncey where every two weeks there was a real, live orchestra. The town barber, Slip Sullivan, a pal of my Dad's, had three pretty teen-age daughters who were kind enough to ask me to dance with them. I was all of six or so and thought I was the hottest thing in town.

One night Dad took me aside. "You know, Georgie," he said, "I don't know whether you ought to go out there and dance like that anymore. Some people might think you're trying to show off." I took the hint, and after that refused the entreaties of the charming Sullivan girls. My first romance was ended. My luck didn't improve even when I went to Hollywood—I was always the nice guy who seldom got the girl.

What Dr. Benjamin Spock might make of our childhood discipline I don't know. I can only say that the Murphy kids never rebelled against their family or society and I think they have lived normal, sometimes even useful lives.

Our childhood was dominated, of course, by sports. Thanks to Dad's tutelage, Thorne and I became quite proficient on the track and pretty good at baseball. Dad spent considerable time at Westboro teaching us how to use the bat properly. He stood us in front of the barn door and threw curves at us with a tennis ball until we learned to hit, and he spent hours knocking flies out into the pasture for us to learn to catch.

On his return from Stockholm and the 1912 Olympics, the doctors warned my father to take a year off for health reasons. He had literally worn himself out in the cause of amateur athletics. But he refused to take his doctors' advice. He returned to the University of Pennsylvania and his track and field team won the 1913 intercollegiates.

It was then that Dad suffered a breakdown. He was very sick for a long period, and during the last eight or nine hours he was in a semicoma. For much of that time I sat by his bed, holding his hand. He knew he was going to die and he said he wanted to tell me some things. Much of what he told me I have long since forgotten. But the one thing that has remained with me all these years was his statement that making lots of money had never really mattered to him. He said the most important thing was your self-respect and then if you were really lucky, you would have five good friends.

He rambled on about the many famous people he had known in his crowded lifetime, about the Vanderbilts and the Whitneys and his friend Teddy Roosevelt. He grasped my hand tightly as he spoke of a man named Gaston B. Means. Means was evil incarnate, my father said, a man to be avoided at all costs. To me, a boy of eleven, the name meant nothing, but it remained in my memory. When the famous Lindbergh kidnapping case was in the news, I remembered Dad's warning about Gaston B. Means. How my father became acquainted with him still puzzles me, but Dad knew all kinds of people, and he was a great judge of character.

Word of Dad's death spread quickly and by the next day the house on Chestnut Street was literally jammed with relatives and friends who had come from almost everywhere to bid farewell to Mike Murphy.

That evening one of my uncles decided to take me for a walk. Mother thought it a good idea for me to get out of the house and get a little air. When we passed the neighborhood saloon several blocks away, my uncle told me to wait outside while he went in to get a cigar. I waited and waited and waited. Finally I got worried and went home. I did not see my uncle again until the day of the funeral. That was, I guess, my first real brush with bars and booze.

A well-attended memorial service was held at the University of Pennsylvania, where nearly the whole student body marched. The body was taken by train to Boston, where more crowds appeared. Finally Michael Murphy was buried in a cemetery in Hopkinton, next to his good friend George Brown, whose son started the Celtics. The spot is about fifty yards from where the Boston Marathon begins each spring.

The final rites were attended by people from all over the area. All available horse-drawn funeral hacks from miles around were pressed into service. As Mabel, Thorne and I rode in one vehicle on an old country road going from Westboro to Hopkinton, the bottom fell out.

"Dad surely would have laughed if he had seen what just happened," my sister said.

"He probably did," my brother replied. And as I think back on it, I'm sure Dad was right with us, as he had always been.

# CHAPTER 3

## *Yale: "The wrong attitude"*

I was not what you would call an intellectual kid. I was much more interested in what was happening outside the school than inside. My earliest brush with the written word came when my beloved Aunt Nance read to me from the adventures of "Billy Whiskers," a story of a goat. Aunt Nance was something special in my young life because she not only read to me, but she had a boy friend who would bring me a box of Huyler's candy whenever he came visiting. I was too young in those days to recognize a bribe.

Later I read the usual things—Nick Carter, Tom Swift, Frank Merriwell and the Rover Boys. My reading was usually confined to rainy days or when I wasn't feeling well. I preferred outdoor activities. Of course, there was always school work. But I had a fairly quick mind, absorbed lessons easily, and could ad-lib well enough to pass, so that wasn't too much of a chore.

After my father's death, the family returned to New Haven. We traded at Mr. Weiss's grocery there. In later years his son George, who was my brother's age, became the genius of the New York Yankee farm and scouting system.

George and I shared at least one juvenile adventure. One Thanksgiving week we "borrowed" a jug of apple cider and hid it in a nearby barn. The jug froze overnight. After we got up nerve enough to visit the scene of our crime, we drank what liquid was in the center. We never knew what hit us.

On Sundays a group of us would go out to the city pig farm. The big sport of the afternoon was to enter the pigsties with the big boars and make believe we were having bullfights. This was great fun until the farm superintendent discovered us. He chased us out with the threat that he would fill us with rock salt from his shotgun if we ever came back. We took him at his word.

After nearly two years in New Haven, we moved to Detroit to live with my mother's parents, the Longs. We lived in a house so tiny that how we all managed to squeeze inside remains one of the unanswered mysteries of my life.

The action centered in the sitting room where there was a big potbellied stove that we filled with coal three times a day in winter. Saturday nights we took our baths in a big copper tub in the kitchen, youngest first. Why we weren't asphyxiated by the coal gas on winter nights remains another wonder.

We lived in a part of Detroit right back of the ball park. It was called Corktown, because so many of the inhabitants came from County Cork in good old Ireland. If there was considerable bigotry against the Irish in those days we weren't aware of it. We were aware that there were some imbeciles outside of Corktown who didn't have the proper affection for the royal blood of the Irish kings, but we felt that was their hard luck.

We Irish have done well in the worlds of commerce and entertainment, and some have even succeeded in politics—one of us got to be President. I have done a lot of traveling in my lifetime, and what I say now is based on considerable personal observation. Our nation, made up of so many different peoples, is the only one in the entire world where those of lowly backgrounds have the opportunity to rise to the top of the economic and social ladders—that is, if they have the talent, the capability and the dedication to work for it. In the final analysis, there is no other way.

Grandfather Long, who came to this country at the age of eleven by jumping ship, worked hard for most of his life. He lived to be ninety-eight, and I believe he would still have kept going but for the fact that his eyesight was failing. When he could no longer see the pretty girls, he lost interest.

He was a wonderful, gay, happy man, who used to boast about being the youngest member of the famous Massachusetts Regiment during the Civil War. He never claimed to have been a hero. He went into the Army because someone paid him to take his place. He served in the Michigan Legislature and had been in charge of Customs between Detroit and Windsor for so long that they were afraid to retire him.

One of the few pleasures of his last years was to tipple a bit. His tippling was mainly an excuse to meet his friends and enjoy the camaraderie of the bar. His limit was generally two drinks, but occasionally he'd return home having had an extra drink or two, his hat askew over one eye, speaking politely to neighbors on their porches even when they weren't there.

One of his favorite haunts was Long's saloon, the heartbeat of Corktown. The Longs probably were related to our family in some fashion, and Grandfather always insisted that Mrs. Long was the prettiest colleen ever to leave County Cork. Of course, by the time I got to know her, Mrs. Long was far from being a maiden. But she was a very nice lady who always managed to find cookies and milk whenever I entered her establishment. And she raised four strong sons who could fight like hell.

One of the more hilarious episodes that I remember during the time we lived at Grandpa's occurred when Tim Sullivan's cousin disappeared. Word came from the police that a man's body had been picked up near the railroad tracks. The body had been so badly mangled that the face was battered beyond recognition. Everyone assumed immediately that the body was that of Tim's cousin and his bereaved relatives made arrangements for the funeral.

While the ladies were in the parlor bemoaning the loss of a dear cousin and the gentlemen were in the kitchen warming up for a first-class Irish wake, Tim's cousin walked through the front door. I'll never forget the resulting pandemonium. People were leaping through the windows. It turned out that Tim's cousin had not been hit by a train at all but had been arrested and held for intoxication. That was the last Irish wake I ever attended.

Four years after Dad's death, Mother died too. It was Mabel, just twenty years old, who took charge of what was left of the family. We moved to a house on Oregon Avenue in northwest Detroit. How Mabel managed to keep us together I'll never know. Not that Thorne and I were wild boys, but we were young and exuberant and not always willing to listen to sisterly admonitions. Fortunately she had Dad's ability to make us understand.

Eventually Mabel married a gracious gentleman, Urban Fisher, whose family was in the automobile business. Today she lives in Grand Rapids, Michigan, and has fourteen grandchildren and four great-grandchildren, out of which she guarantees a couple of Jim Thorpes and a Johnny Unitas. Mabel has taken a great interest in my career. She has always been my biggest fan. You'd better not say anything against me in her presence—she's very biased.

My brother Thorne went to Peddie Institute and then to the Sheffield Scientific School at Yale University. At both schools he did well in sports. He played quarterback on the Yale football team and shortstop on the baseball team, carrying on the Murphy name in a way that would have pleased Dad. He was a great dropkicker. And in his last Yale-Harvard baseball game, with the great Eddie Mahan pitching for Harvard, he stole second, third and home on three pitched balls. The Mahans have hated the Murphys ever since.

Midway through Yale, Thorne enlisted in the U.S. Ambulance Corps (the United States had intervened in "the war to end war") and later he transferred to the Army Air Corps, where he was commissioned a second lieutenant.

In 1917 I was enrolled at the University of Detroit High School, but my mind wasn't on my studies. The nation was at war and so was my brother Thorne. My school chum, Frank Nolan, and I talked things over, and we decided we'd enlist. We chose the Canadian Air Force because they had the fanciest uniforms—a Smokey-the-bear hat with a white band, and puttees, considered very dashing in those days. The only problem was that we were each fifteen years of age. We took the ferry over to Windsor, Ontario, where we signed up, claiming to be eighteen. Then we went home to await induction.

Three weeks later, someone told Mabel what we had done. She immediately notified the Canadian authorities of our true ages, and our dreams of becoming war heroes were cut short. We were discharged with an angry reprimand.

I stayed in high school largely because a Jesuit priest, Father Walsh, who had been a chaplain at Sing Sing Prison, took me aside and said, "Young man, you're going to be able to influence a lot of people some day for good or evil. It's time you made up your mind which it's going to be."

I didn't realize it then, but this was probably one of the most important pieces of advice I have ever received.

One of my high school friends was big Frank Hogan, who played tackle on the varsity team. Saturday nights Frank and I would regularly participate in the waltz contests at the Palais Dance Hall out on Jefferson Avenue. Our partners were the young ladies—all good dancers—whom we would meet at the hall. Hogan invariably would win first prize. Second prize usually went to a young fellow I got to know later in New York—Tony DeMarco. And I would generally win third prize, which meant that I would be admitted free the following week.

A year or so later, I went to Peddie Institute on a partial athletic scholarship. This is a fine Baptist school located near Hightstown, New Jersey, from which Thorne had graduated some years before. I had a little pocket money which my dear sister somehow arranged, and to help pay for my tuition I did all sorts of odd jobs around the school, including waiting on tables for my meals. Consequently I ate better than most of my fellow students. I made sure I drank nothing but cream and always got the outside cut of the roast beef.

Like my brother Thorne before me, I was a good athlete. I am still somewhat of a hero at Peddie Institute because I was on the first Peddie football team that ever beat the Lawrenceville team, our deadly rival. We had an exceptional squad, since five of my teammates were older men who had served in the armed forces for two years. In fact, one of the ex-doughboys was baldheaded.

We played a practice game against the Princeton varsity one afternoon, and at the end of the first half the score was fourteen to nothing in our favor. I had scored the two touchdowns by picking up fumbles on a dead run. As I crossed the goal line the second time, Frank Gilroy, the famous Princeton player, tackled me from behind with such force that I did a double somersault in the air, landed on my head and broke my shoulder. I went from there right to the hospital. At the time I thought it was unnecessary roughness, but then knowing the Irish I wasn't surprised.

That spring, in the last baseball game between Princeton and Yale, my brother tagged Gilroy as he slid into second. He tagged him right on the top of the head with the ball, and said, "Frank, that's for my little brother George!" A Murphy never forgets.

Somehow my scholarly attainments failed to satisfy the headmaster. He considered them somewhat below the high standards required of Peddie men, and he told me so repeatedly. One day this venerable gentleman was so aroused by my chronic inability to get better grades that he irately informed me I was on the verge of being expelled.

I got a reprieve, however. One day there was a big fire downtown which threatened to set all of Hightstown ablaze. That being more interesting than my studies, I raced to town to do my bit as a volunteer fire fighter. Climbing the steeple of the Baptist Church with a hose, I kept the fire from spreading to that ancient edifice. After hearing of my youthful burst of ecumenical heroism, the headmaster decided to let me remain at Peddie, with a warning to apply more diligence to my scholarly endeavors. He was probably afraid to expel me—I was the town hero for about two weeks.

Some Peddie boys had "rescued" several cases of liquor from a burning roadhouse and hidden them in the woods. On Sunday a group of us went over to sample the goods. After a few drinks I turned green, and I thought my insides would erupt. They did. From that day on, my intake of alcoholic beverages has rarely been excessive.

The next year, having received an athletic scholarship, I transferred to the Pawling School in Pawling, New York. Here again I played on all the teams. One day, after playing third base in a tough baseball game against the Taft School in Watertown, Connecticut, Bertie Thomas, our coach, said, "Murph, one of my track team members is sick. Would you go over and run in the 100-yard dash just to fill out the roster?" I said I'd be glad to.

I took off my baseball suit and got a very lucky start and, more to my surprise than anybody else's, I won the 100-yard dash. Bertie Thomas was so amused that he said, "Why don't you go in the 220?" I did, and I won that. "Would you care to go for the 440?" he asked. I tried that too, and got another first place. Then came the high hurdles and the broad jump, which I also won.

To wind up the afternoon I tied for second in the high jump. The referee suggested that my opponent and I jump off to see who would get the points. I had to beg off—I was just too tired. But I proposed that we split the points, and flip a coin for the medal. I won the flip and got the medal and half the points.

It was at Pawling that I met a tall, handsome young man named Robert Montgomery. Bob got into show business before

I did and had some success on the Broadway stage before going on to Hollywood, where he deservedly achieved fame and fortune. He was one of the leaders in forming the Screen Actors Guild. He and I were successive presidents of the Guild and, still following the same pattern, became active in Republican politics during the Willkie campaign.

After Pawling, however, I didn't see Bob for at least a decade. One night while Julie and I were doing our act at the old Olsen Club I heard a gasp from ringside, "My God, it's Murph!" I glanced up and it was none other than Bob Montgomery. We resumed our friendship and we've been more than good friends ever since.

Another character I met at Pawling was Horace Stoneham Jr., who today is the president of the San Francisco Giants. One weekend Horace decided we should go to New York. It was my first visit to the big town and, as it turned out, a memorable one.

Despite his tender years, Horace knew Manhattan—or at least its night spots—like a book. We began our evening with dinner at Delmonico's and then went on to Ziegfeld's Midnight Frolic atop the New Amsterdam Theater on Forty-second Street.

I know it will be hard for many New Yorkers to believe it, but Forty-second Street in those days was one of the most glamorous thoroughfares in the theatrical district—with legitimate theaters and fine restaurants lined up all the way from Eighth Avenue to Broadway. It breaks my heart to see what has happened to Forty-second Street in recent years. The street has degenerated into a human cesspool. I hope that when they rebuild the inner cities some great genius will rehabilitate the whole Times Square area.

Anyway, Horace got a ringside table at the Midnight Frolic by phoning for a reservation in the name of his well-known father, Horace Stoneham Sr., then president of the New York Giants.

As I recall, the attractions included Will Rogers, Joe Frisco and the most beautiful chorus girls in the world. The setting was one of absolute splendor.

After the show we went to Reisenweber's for supper, where Sophie Tucker was the headliner. Reisenweber's, a huge barn of a cabaret at Eighth Avenue and Fifty-eighth Street, eventually succumbed to the Volstead Act. But these were still the early days of Prohibition and Horace had come well-fortified with several small bottles of something potent—too potent for my taste.

After a few drinks, he accidentally dropped one of the bottles. A heavyset bouncer came over to remonstrate. Words were exchanged and Horace threw the first punch. The bouncer hit Horace and I hit the bouncer. Half a dozen waiters—"the Flying Squad"—grabbed us and threw us down the stairs, which thank God were heavily carpeted. Waiting for us were two detectives who took us to the police station.

But Horace was not without influence, and I soon discovered the importance of political clout. Horace telephoned a business associate of his father's, a Judge McQuade, who came rushing to the station. He spoke quietly to the desk sergeant, who then told us we could leave.

The plainclothesmen, who had been amused by our predicament, suggested that if we really wanted to see New York we should meet them the next night, which was their night off. We didn't have to be asked twice. We began in Chinatown and kept traveling uptown in an unmarked car, finally winding up having coffee at a place called Healey's Golden Glades. Horace and I learned things from these detectives they don't teach at places like Pawling.

It was at Pawling School that I first became audience-conscious. At the insistence of Dr. Gamage, the headmaster, I competed for the Chauncey Depew Award. This called for writing and orating a three-minute speech. I chose Theodore Roosevelt as my subject.

It chanced that Chauncey Depew himself was in the audience. After the celebrated attorney and former U.S. Senator from the state of New York congratulated me on my victory, he asked to see my paper. I was forced to tell him that I hadn't followed the paper at all, that when I saw all those faces in front of me I got some better ideas and began to ad-lib. Depew, who was renowned as an orator and after-dinner speaker, laughed and laughed. "Son," he said, "there's no law against thinking on your feet."

When he learned that I was Mike Murphy's son, and therefore an orphan, Depew graciously offered to send me through college and later to Harvard Law School. I thanked him profusely, but refused his offer. Even in those days I never wanted to feel obligated to anyone. I have always wanted to do things on my own.

Little did I know when I met the former Senator that I would one day be sitting in the same chamber in which he had served with such distinction. In those days I had little interest in politics. Whatever aspirations I had were to become a mining engineer, the career my brother Thorne had chosen. Like my brother, I decided to enroll in the Sheffield Scientific School at Yale, better known as "Shef."

To get into Yale, I had to take the College Boards Examination. I was five credits short, so to make up my credits I spent two weeks at the famous Rosenbaum Tutoring School in Milford, Connecticut, where I crammed day and night for the college entrance examinations. They could do the impossible when it came to getting you into college. It's true you couldn't remember a thing a month afterward, but the Rosenbaum people filled you with enough information to pass the Boards. All you had to do was remember it for a week.

So in the fall of 1921 I managed to get myself admitted to the scholarly environs of Yale University. Frankly, it was not a day that will go down in academic history.

I'll never forget my first few days at Yale. My roommates

included Hay Adams, who later twice became captain of the football team, an unheard-of achievement; Jimmy Richey of New York, whose dad made all the lithographs for the motion picture industry, and George Smith from Locust Valley, Long Island, who under my tutelage became a great baseball player and later was a vice-president of the Chase Manhattan Bank.

Our first night in Durfee Hall was not a happy one. We found ourselves on the top floor of the oldest dormitory at Yale University on a very dismal fall night without any furniture or even kindling wood to start a fire in the fireplace. By some miracle, while rummaging through an upstairs cupboard I discovered an old bottle of whiskey which must have been collecting dust for at least fifteen years. We built a fire with wood from the crates in which we'd brought our clothes and books and managed to overcome our loneliness—at least for awhile.

A few days later our furniture arrived, the famous Whiffenpoofs came onto the campus and sang for an hour and finally we began to get the feeling of what Yale was all about. We began to feel we belonged.

During my first year, I made the freshman football team and played baseball as well. Somehow I got through my studies and managed to become a sophomore. It was then I ran into a major problem. I had been in the common freshman class. In previous years, the Sheffield Scientific School had been a three-year course, but the year I decided to go to Yale it was expanded to four years. Since I wanted to be in the scientific school, I was now forced to take extra courses in mathematics, chemistry and physics. The Dean decided that I couldn't study and at the same time play football, so he disqualified me from the team. That broke my heart and eventually led to my quitting Yale the following year.

When I remonstrated with the Dean, he asked me bluntly whether I had come to Yale to play football or to study. I told him that of course I wanted to study, but that if I played football there would be certain advantages when I left college that I wouldn't have otherwise.

The Dean said rather brusquely that I had the wrong attitude and that he had no choice but to place me on probation to
make sure that I would concentrate on my studies and not get
any more wild ideas about competing on the gridiron. In my
judgement, this was not the kind of man who should have been
in charge of a boys' school. He didn't understand. As the kids
say today, he just wasn't with it.

While I was at Yale I got my first taste of show business.
Somehow I discovered that a wonderful Negro band was coming up from Georgia to play at the school prom. I also learned
that for $250 we could get the band to come up a day earlier
and play for us in New York. Two other student entrepreneurs
and I joined forces to raise the money and enough besides to
travel to New York, where we rented the ballroom of the old
Delmonico's. We had enough money left over to launch a modest promotion campaign aimed at the college and post-college
crowd. There were no other expenses.

On the big night we were ready for business—at five dollars a
couple. And the couples came streaming in. The place was soon
packed and jumping. About eleven o'clock someone had the
not-so-bright idea of feeding copious quantities of gin to the
musicians with the mistaken notion that they would play better.
They did—for about twenty minutes—and then two of them
passed out.

Fortunately, the great banjo player Sleepy Hall was present.
We explained our misfortune and he graciously consented to
entertain the restless crowd with a borrowed instrument. We
also recruited the talented Virginia Riggs, who could sing and
dance. Between Hall and Miss Riggs the audience got an unexpected forty-five-minute show. Meanwhile, I was downstairs
forcing the musicians to drink black coffee like it was the end of
time. Then I hustled them back upstairs where, praise the Lord
and pass the black coffee, they did a commendable job for the
rest of the evening.

For our first venture into show business, the three of us did pretty well. We netted several hundred dollars each. Fortunately we had had the foresight to get rid of the checkroom concession. Somehow a big oak door was broken and about a dozen raccoon coats disappeared. But, as we told the manager, the concessionaire was responsible, not us. We took our profits and fled back to New Haven.

Despite the limited funds at my disposal, I always managed to be one of the better-dressed Yalies. The reason was that, thanks to my brother before me, I was shilling for the best tailor shop in New Haven. Owned by Abe Alderman and his brother, the shop was located just across the street from the famous Shubert Theater where so many plays have had their pre-Broadway tryouts. My job was to lure students into the shop. For this I was handsomely clothed at no cost (I thought) by the Alderman brothers. In the language of those years I always looked "sharp," even though there were times when I didn't have a dollar to my name.

Several years later, when I was in a show called *Hold Everything* in New York, I was getting made up for a matinee when a sheriff showed up in my room with a bill from the Alderman brothers for seven hundred and fifty dollars they claimed I owed them for clothes. The sheriff said either to pay up or go to jail. I couldn't pay.

As I was being taken through the stage door, I happened to see Eddie Branigan, a detective who had been Mayor Jimmy Walker's bodyguard. I called him over and explained my predicament. "Eddie," I pleaded, "do something about this guy."

Branigan flashed his badge and informed the sheriff that the Mayor owned half the show (which he didn't) and that if I were taken away there would be no show and the sheriff would wake up the next morning without a job. The sheriff let me go that day, but later on, under protest, I was forced to pay the seven hundred and fifty dollars.

To help pay for my education I worked summer vacations in auto plants around Detroit. Getting a job was no problem, particularly if you could play baseball. All you had to do was go see Harry Jewett, the president of the Page Detroit Motor Car Company, or John Kelsey, the head of the Kelsey Wheel Company, both of whom were ardent supporters of an industrial baseball league that used to play out in Clark's Park. The teams were made up of workers from the different factories and rivalries were intense.

In addition to playing baseball, I was employed on the assembly line at the old Page Detroit Company, working on the rear axles. The company went out of business two years later and I have often wondered whether I was responsible. In those days it was all piecework, and there was one big riveter at the end of the line who made sure we kept on our toes. The more work we turned out, the more money we all made, and that big man wasn't above threatening you if he felt you were goofing off. It was not easy work but I was a big kid myself, and I liked that weekly paycheck.

On Sunday nights my high school chum Herb Guiney would take me to the Harmony Club, a German singing group that served the finest food and beer. The orchestra, all fine musicians from the old country, played beautiful music while we sang and sang. The grown-ups guzzled stein after stein of beer brewed by the club's own brewmaster, and the young folks were allowed a small glass or two.

Then came Prohibition—the Great Experiment which was supposed to have heralded the death of John Barleycorn. The reports of his death were greatly exaggerated. Because of the extraordinary number of parched throats in the United States, smuggling liquor became a big business. Detroit, facing Canada across a mile-wide river, became the liquor capital of the world, thanks to wholesale smuggling by speedboat.

About a mile down the river, where the Ford plant is now located, I first observed the brand-new phenomenon of rum-running. A little town there called Ecorse was a convenient haven into which the smugglers could race their boats at high speeds. A dozen or so men would unload about fifty cases of whiskey in a matter of minutes, loading them onto waiting trucks that would be gone by the time the police arrived.

One night a friend and I were driving by Ecorse and saw that one of the houseboats that lined the river bank was on fire. We rescued a lady and removed some furniture and trunks from the burning boat. A German shepherd puppy remained cut off on the river end of the houseboat. Taking off my shoes and socks, I swam out and grabbed the frightened animal and brought him to shore. There I began squeezing the dog's lungs in an effort to get rid of the smoke he had inhaled. As I was working on the dog, a man's voice said, "Stay here. I want to talk to you."

The voice belonged to the boss of the smugglers. He lived on the houseboat and directed the smuggling operations from there. We got to know each other fairly well. He was an interesting person, having once been a leading man in burlesque. Far from being a gangster type, he had organized this colony of rumrunners to make big money fast. He certainly was successful in his new career.

The rumrunners had organized their own club which they called the Down River Gun Club, and they honored me by making me a lay member, entitled to bring guests. Among other social advantages, the club boasted a fine Chinese cook who claimed to have been with Admiral Peary when he reached the North Pole in 1909. The cook told fabulous stories about the northern lights, a luminous atmospheric phenomenon which I never expected to see. But I have since seen them several times, most recently when I traveled to Alaska with Senator Ted Kennedy in the spring of 1969, on what was then believed to be one of his early Presidential campaign starts.

My friendship with the chief rumrunner permitted me to move freely along the waterfront. I got to know many of his accomplices. Some were not much older than I was. All of them seemed to enjoy their new profession. They particularly enjoyed dreaming up new schemes to outwit the law. Now it must be emphasized that in the early days of Prohibition many of these lawbreakers were amateurs. Only later did organized crime lay its heavy hand on this most lucrative of endeavors.

Several times I inspected the boats on which the booze was brought in from Canada. You could hardly believe that these dirty, decrepit-looking craft could out-race the more modern-looking police boats. But when you went below the deck you could see why. They were often equipped with two Liberty engines and could beat out anything in the water, with the possible exception of Gar Wood's famous *Miss America IV*.

One bitterly cold winter the Detroit River froze. This normally would have cut the stateward flow of liquor down to a trickle. But ingenuity prevailed. The rumrunners loaded up their big Army surplus trucks on the Canadian side and drove across the ice. One night we heard that one of the trucks hit a soft spot and went through the ice down near Grosse Isle. The driver managed to scramble to safety but the precious cargo was lost.

When the ice thawed in the spring, Herb Guiney, Jack Adams and I found the truck submerged in the water close to shore. We dived in and removed five cases of whiskey. We gave the stuff to Herb's father who, as I recall, was most appreciative.

My Detroit vacations were highlighted by invitations to some of the smartest parties in town. How I began to get invited to these affairs I'll never know. But at one of them I danced with a lady named Sadie Burnham who asked who I was and what I was doing. Only later did I learn that Miss Burnham was the social arbiter of Detroit. It was she who put me down on her list as an unattached Yale man available for dancing with the young ladies. As a result, I went everywhere first class and got to know almost everyone of importance in town.

One of these parties was a truly fabulous affair. One of several held to celebrate the opening of the Book-Cadillac Hotel, it was hosted by auto magnate Horace Dodge, who never spared any expense in having a good time. Dodge had the Grand Ballroom decorated to simulate the tropics. A lot of foliage, including orange trees, had been shipped in from Florida. Adding to the gaiety were monkeys cavorting in cages and parrots making cheerful noises.

It was at the Dodge party that I really got to know a young lady named Julie Henkel. I had met her before and thought she was mighty cute, but I didn't fully realize how attractive and intelligent she was until the Dodge party. We got to talking and found we had many mutual interests. Of course, the glamor of the evening didn't do any harm. The music was superbly romantic, and I discovered that Julie was an excellent dancing partner.

The party ended beautifully, too, in the wee hours of the morning. Mr. Dodge graciously presented Julie with one of the parrots he had imported from Florida, and I escorted both Julie and the screeching bird to her home.

From then on I began to see a great deal of Julie Henkel. You might say I had become addicted. One day she asked me whether I liked horses. Even though I knew next to nothing about the equestrian life, I had the feeling I had better reply in the affirmative. I told her I was crazy about horses.

"Then why don't you come out to the farm and ride with me?" she asked.

The fact was that I was scared to death of horses. But I could hardly back away from her invitation now. So I went to an Army surplus store and purchased a pair of riding breeches. Also a pair of boots so tight that later I had to cut them off.

Julie, of course, had her own horse, and I rented one from a nearby stable. We took off riding in what was real country in those days—down the Ten Mile Road outside Detroit. At first everything went fine. I managed to hold on fairly well, though I suspected that my horse was trying to brush me off on every big tree he saw.

When it came time to turn homeward, Julie's nag took off at full gallop and mine began chasing hers. Then Julie left the trail to ride in what looked to me like absolute wilderness. The next thing I knew she was sloshing through a swamp. As my horse and I were directly behind, we got hit with mud—but good.

By the time we returned to the stable, we were completely plastered with mud. The man who had rented me the horse took one look at me and demanded, "Where the hell have you been with my animal?"

Embarrassed, I said, "We just took a ride in the woods."

"You're a lousy rider," the man told me angrily, "and don't ever come back here for a horse."

"Don't worry," I replied. "I won't be back."

Actually I never did ride again until we went to California. Then Julie trapped me once more, and finally I really got to enjoy riding.

But I'll never forget that ride through the mud on a fall afternoon. It nearly ended a great romance.

Julie and I corresponded when I went back to college. As I have already noted, I had some difficulty convincing Yale authorities—or at least one of them—that I could combine the academic life with playing football. One day I got so fed up arguing the matter that I packed up and went to New York, resolved never to return to New Haven.

In New York I walked the streets looking for a job. But jobs were not plentiful and, at most, the ones I was offered paid somewhere between twelve and twenty dollars a week. Finally I ran into a bandleader I had known, Ray Miller, whose band almost rivaled Paul Whiteman's in popularity.

Ray told me he was opening a dance hall in Newark and that he was looking for a floor manager. I assured him that I was the best floor manager he could possibly find. He hired me at the incredible wage of fifty dollars a week. And that's how I wound up as the floor manager of the Paradise Dance Hall in Newark, New Jersey, on the second floor of a building right across the street from City Hall. I had no idea of what I was getting into, but by the time the place opened, I did realize that the title of floor manager was a fancy name for bouncer.

In addition to physical dexterity, this job required diplomacy. The Paradise clientele consisted largely of college kids who were called "cake eaters" and a tougher element called the "sharpshooters." As a rule, I had very little trouble with the "cake eaters" for the simple reason that many of them thought I was Mickey Walker's brother. I did look a little like the prize fighter and I made no effort to correct their misapprehension.

The "sharpshooters" were the guys I was worried about. One night five of them, a bit tanked up, came in and made no secret of their intention to wreck the dance hall. Ever the diplomat, I cautiously approached them and in a quiet, firm voice suggested that while they might succeed in their effort temporarily, they inevitably would get into trouble with the Newark Police Department.

I will never forget the response of one of them. "I got an idea I'm goin' to punch you right in your big fat nose," he said, getting up from his chair to perform the horrendous deed.

"Nobody is going to punch nobody in the nose," a voice behind me said.

The voice was that of authority, and very timely too. I had never seen him before, but I learned that he was Ernie Krieger, a real tough guy himself, who bossed the "Down-the-Neck" gang, a Newark group that I was told specialized in hijacking silk trucks that traveled the New Jersey highways.

Taking the hint, the "sharpshooters" quickly left the premises and the word spread that I was Ernie's pal. I never had any trouble with them again.

Krieger and I became friends. He arranged to have his car take me nightly to the "tubes," the train bound for Manhattan, and I have never forgotten his care and courtesy. He saved me many lumps, I'm sure. After I quit the Paradise, I lost track of him. But I was reminded of Ernie at the 1968 Republican Convention in Miami Beach when I ran into Phil Napoleon, the great trumpeter, who had also known him in Newark. "What ever happened to Ernie?" I asked.

Phil didn't know. "He just kinda disappeared," he said. The terrible thought then crossed my mind that Ernie might have disappeared as so many other tough guys did, somewhere out in the Jersey meadows beyond Kennedy's Abattoir. That name, Kennedy's Abattoir, has always fascinated me.

Though I had announced to all and sundry my irrevocable resolution not to return to Yale, some of my friends in New Haven believed I could be persuaded to give the university another chance. So they assigned Ted Weicker Jr. to convince me. Ted came down to New York and accompanied me one night to the Paradise Dance Hall. He had so much fun he decided to stay over.

At that time I was residing—if that's the correct word for it—in a fleabag of a rooming house located above a Nedick's stand at 50th Street and Broadway, opposite the entrance to the Montmartre nightclub. But Ted, who had been reared in more genteel circumstances, didn't seem to mind. This was a life he had never known before and, to say the least, it was different.

Back at Yale, Ted's failure to return aroused consternation among our friends. So another fellow, Louis Bott of Cincinnati, came down to get the two of us back. Louis had so much fun that he decided to stay. Then Mike Gaines of Chicago arrived. He also stayed. He was followed by Charlie Cooper of Gloucester, Massachusetts, who stayed too. Then came Joe Knowles from San Francisco. Finally there were seven of us living in this tiny room, eating hamburgers when we ate, and drinking phony orange juice from Nedick's. We slept on the floor, on the couch, just all over the place, but having the time of our young lives.

Down the hall from us lived a bootlegger who sold some terrible-tasting stuff he called gin for about thirty dollars a case. My roommates would get cartons of orange juice from Nedick's downstairs, shake it up with the "gin," and it was orange blossom time.

But all good times must eventually come to an end, and the boys reluctantly agreed they had better go back to school. Their mission to get me to return to Yale with them looked like a failure until the night I went to work and Ray Miller, my boss, asked, "How many people did we have last night?"

"We had a big night, boss, about five hundred people," I said.

"Well," he said, "there were only four hundred checked in at the front door."

"Oh, I thought you knew—"

"Knew what?"

"Well," I said, "your brother is letting them in the fire escape at fifty cents a head."

He got so mad because I told him how his brother had been fleecing him that he fired me on the spot.

As things worked out, I guess he did me a big favor, because the last thing I would want to be today is a grown-old bouncer from a defunct nightclub dance hall in Newark, New Jersey.

A couple of years ago, driving through Newark with the Governor of the state and the Mayor of Newark, I said, "Stop the car."

They asked, "What for?"

"I used to work over there," I said. "Upstairs."

"When?"

"When it was the Paradise Dance Hall," I told them.

The Governor was too young to remember, but the Mayor remembered very well and he said, "My God, how did you ever survive?"

"I don't know yet myself," I said.

At any rate, I returned to Yale to resume my interrupted studies.

One summer vacation my brother decided I should work in the coal mines to learn the more practical side of mine engineering. Thorne was now a mining engineer working in the Pennsylvania coal mines. After the war, he had returned to Yale and obtained his degree. He eventually returned to Detroit and wound up in the steel business, getting married to a lovely girl named Louise Vhey in the process. Several years ago he retired as vice-president of the McClouth Steel Company.

At any rate, Thorne got me a job as a coal loader in Portage, Pennsylvania. Loading coal was not the easiest job around the mines. For my efforts I received eighty-six cents a ton.

To get to the room in which I worked I had to walk through about thirty yards of flooded mine. To get the coal cars in I had to blast out eighteen inches of bottom rock. If my brother hadn't gotten me the job, I would have walked out at the first sight of that chamber of horrors.

The miners were great practical jokers. If you put your lunch box down in a dark place, they would be apt to wire it to a power line, so that when you picked up the box you'd get a shock that would knock you clear across the passageway. Or if you happened to fall asleep, they would pour oil all over you—putting it on your face last so that you would be well-covered before you woke up.

They were a pretty rough crowd, but they really were not bad guys once you got to know them and they got to know you. Having a gift of gab, I would tell them stories at lunchtime that fascinated them. Gradually I would lead them into an argument as to who among them was the fastest coal loader. I would arrange a contest, the first prize being a pack of cigarettes which I would donate. You'd be surprised how often the boys would load a whole car of coal for me for a package of cigarettes. My brother finally got wise and tipped off the miners. From then on, I had to do all that hard work myself.

It was during this period that I joined my first union, the United Mine Workers of America. Let me put it this way: I was forced to join. When I got a paycheck for my first two weeks of work, the check was ten dollars short. I brought the discrepancy to the attention of the management and they said they could do nothing about it. The ten dollars were my union dues. Being a little naive about such matters, I said I didn't know whether or not I wanted to join the union. The management put it to me bluntly—either I joined the union or the next day three hundred and fifty men would decide not to work with me. That meant they would have to get somebody else for my job. I joined the union.

Later on, of course, I held membership in several other labor unions and even helped launch a couple—including the Screen Actors Guild, the American Federation of Radio Artists and the American Federation of Television Artists. That's why I am so amused when some of those who would find reason to criticize me try to pin an "antilabor" label on me. Not that I always agree with the unions. But I have always sought to defend the interests of the rank-and-file worker.

One day, while I was working in the coal mine, a railroad car flipped off the track and the spilling coal pinned me against a wall. Fortunately I wasn't too badly hurt, but it was the beginning of the end of my interest in mining engineering.

During my junior year I finally decided I had had enough of Yale. I thought the time had come to make my fortune. And where were fortunes being made in those days? In New York, of course.

# CHAPTER 4

### *Julie: "Those bells began to ring"*

My arrival in New York was quite inauspicious. In fact it was dismal. As I recall, it was a Sunday afternoon in the fall of 1924 and I was nearly broke. Despite my memorable stay above the Nedick's stand and numerous weekend visits as a student, I did not know many New Yorkers. And there is nothing more lonesome than being in the Big City without anyone to call up.

I spent the first few days making the rounds looking for a job. I had no idea what I wanted to do and didn't care. I just wanted a job, any job.

One day I ran into an acquaintance, John Wilde, to whom I confided my need for employment. I was then down to my last seven dollars. Wilde, a nephew of Jules Bache and the youngest broker on the New York Stock Exchange, arranged to get me a job as a runner with his uncle's company at twelve dollars a week. A runner was a sort of glorified messenger boy, who carried bonds, stock certificates and sales orders from one brokerage house to another. It was a job. I could eat. I took it. At the time the brokerage business seemed to be as good as any other in which to launch a career.

Someone in the Bache organization must have been impressed by my ability to run around the financial district delivering and picking up envelopes without getting lost too often. Within a week I was appointed head runner with a five-dollar boost in salary. This meant I was now making seventeen dollars a week, and by working after five o'clock I was entitled to fifty cents extra in supper money. Naturally I arranged to work late almost every day. You could eat pretty well for four bits in those days.

For a new boy in town I had few complaints. Then who

should come back not only into my life but into New York City—Julie Henkel! Those bells began to ring again. Though we had kept in touch, I had not expected to see her so soon. But Julie had her mind set on a career in show business and New York obviously was the place for the launching.

How do you romance a girl on seventeen dollars a week? It was tough. You can only ask a girl to enjoy the view of the Hudson at Ninety-seventh Street a certain number of times before she gets fed up. However, Julie didn't seem to mind too much, and her patience has lasted amazingly well. After forty-three years of marriage she's still understanding.

Julie was busy learning to dance. Under her professional name, Julie Johnson, she was taking lessons at the Ned Wayburn School on Columbus Circle. This was a popular institution with a fine reputation. Many a successful star, soubrette and showgirl got her training at Wayburn's school. But I have to laugh every time I think of how the school managed to extract every loose coin from its students. Before each session, for instance, the pupils were required to weigh themselves. In those days you could get weighed anywhere for a penny. Not at Wayburn's—there it cost five cents. During practice, only Wayburn rompers and dancing shoes could be worn. Apparently old Ned thought you couldn't learn to dance unless you bought your outfit from him.

One of the prettiest gals around, Julie was small and lithe, with an engaging smile. She moved with such grace that I didn't see any need for her to take lessons. I thought she was great. I found myself spending more and more of my spare time hanging around Wayburn's waiting to take her home or out for a bite. She was getting used to having me around, too. At least, I hoped so. I was really stuck on her.

Julie lived uptown in a large apartment with the family of McCall Lanham, a noted music teacher. Lanham's stepdaughter Fay Kimbro and Julie were good friends. Fay, who hailed from Tennessee, later married my dear friend Henry J. Taylor, the distinguished journalist-diplomat who over the years has been helpful to me in so many ways.

To be closer to Julie, I rented a room at Mrs. Wolfe's Boarding House on Ninety-third Street and Broadway, which was just across the areaway from the Lanham apartment. This was an ideal arrangement since Julie and I could signal to each other and talk back and forth, sometimes to the dismay of the other tenants.

To help with the rent of seven dollars a week, I shared my room, which was not much bigger than a large-sized closet, with a young fellow my age, Henry Alexander, who had known Fay Kimbro from his Tennessee days. Henry had studied law and was working as a clerk in the John W. Davis office at the wild rate of fifteen dollars a week. Eventually he became president and board chairman of the Morgan Guaranty Trust Company.

All this time, Julie was being pursued relentlessly by my former roommate Ted Weicker, who had a few advantages going for him. Ted had the use of his father's Rolls Royce, and he could buy orchids for Julie. Orchids were a big item in the romance department in those days. As far as I was concerned, if I could scrape up a buck to take Julie to the movies and buy her an ice cream soda afterwards I was doing fine. But I had an edge—I was a better dancer.

It was a friendly rivalry. In retrospect, I had another overwhelming advantage—I was living in New York. Ted, on the other hand, had returned to Yale and conducted his courtship more intermittently. Finally, as they used to say in the movies, I got the girl. We all remained good friends through the years. Six months after Julie became my wife, Ted found himself a bride—the first of three.

In the early Thirties Ted founded his own brokerage firm, Weicker & Co. In fact, he asked me to join the firm as a partner. I was tempted, particularly when he told me that I would share in the profits at the end of the year. But, I asked, what about losses? Ah, said Ted, everyone in the firm would have to share those. That was when I decided to remain in show business.

My entrance into show business was purely accidental. It was not the result of an overwhelming urge to demonstrate my talent as a performer. I didn't consider myself extraordinarily talented in any way. My one experience on stage had not been a momentous event. That was back in my Yale days when, while on vacation in Detroit, I got to know Fred Waring who was then leading his band at a downtown club.

One night Fred asked me whether I would like to travel with his group to Jackson Prison, where he was scheduled to entertain the prisoners. I was delighted to go. I was on the bandstand when Fred, full of hijinks, asked me to dance. I put on the drummer's gold derby and performed what they called in those days a "Frisco dance." I didn't know what I was doing, but I did it very quickly, and everyone seemed to like it. I can't say that I shook the world. Every time I met the great Joe Frisco afterward in New York and Hollywood, I was embarrassed.

Looking back over these many years I can see now that I had always been intrigued by show business. While working at Bache, I spent many evenings at places such as the Palais Royal where I was admitted gratis, thanks to a friend at the door.

I was fascinated by the big orchestras and the ballroom dancers. I could watch them for hours as they gracefully twisted and turned. My favorite couple was Maurice and Hughes. Of course there were other great teams—Moss and Fontana, Durant and Bennett (Joan's sister), Tony and Renee DeMarco, Ramon and Rosita, and my close friend who was the finest tango dancer of them all, Medrano of Medrano and Donna.

Medrano had come to New York as a prize fighter, but in his first fight he got hit in the nose and quickly decided that there must be an easier way to make a living. His partner, Donna, looked more Spanish than Medrano, but actually she was the daughter of the man who owned the Holland Furnace Company in Holland, Michigan.

Later on, all of us dance teams would occasionally meet Sunday nights at John Perona's place where we would eat, drink, gossip and sometimes put on our own show. I especially remember one night when Medrano showed up without Donna. He had had a few drinks and was feeling pretty good. He walked in and, without saying a word, took a tablecloth and threw it around his shoulders like a gaucho, and began to dance. He danced with an imaginary girl for over an hour. It was an unbelievable performance.

Another good friend of that period was Cesar (Butch) Romero, who also started out as a dancer. In those early days he danced with a girl named Elizabeth Higgins on the Park Central Roof. We've been friends ever since. Once Cesar saw me doing a dance by myself. He announced, "If Murph can do a solo, so can I." He perfected a routine that involved jumping over a cane. As Cesar is pretty tall, it took a lot of jumping.

I recall the day Fred Astaire and I went to see Buck and Bubbles do their tap-dancing act in a vaudeville show in one of Broadway's bigger motion picture theaters. When John Bubbles saw the great stage dancer sitting in the audience, he could hardly refrain from demonstrating some extra special—almost impossible—dances. Finally the theater manager came over to us and whispered, "Won't you guys please get out of here? We're twenty minutes overtime as is."

Florence Hughes of Maurice and Hughes was a perfectly gorgeous creature with a style and presence never to be forgotten. I always felt she didn't need to dance to communicate with her audience—she had that sort of magnetism. She had the same rapport with an audience that Helen Morgan had as a singer. Helen wasn't really that good a singer, but when she sat on a piano and gave forth with "Can't Help Loving That Man," well, strong men wept. We used to call it personality. The new word is charisma.

A couple of gentlemen named Thompson and Salvin operated the Palais Royal, which later became the Latin Quarter. Thompson was a handsome, well-groomed fellow, while Salvin looked like a gargoyle that had fallen off the Notre Dame roof and gotten damaged on the way down. He was so ugly that his partner tried to keep him out of sight. I still remember Salvin standing in the cigar store on the corner of Forty-seventh Street and Broadway, smoking a big, black stogie and receiving hourly reports on how good business was.

I was at the Palais Royal the night Paul Whiteman played "Rhapsody in Blue" for the first time. Oh yes, I'm aware that the books say the Whiteman band first performed this immortal George Gershwin composition at Aeolian Hall on February 12, 1924. That was the official occasion. But the band actually tried out the number before a group of invited friends at the Palais Royal after hours several nights before. It was an exciting performance and Whiteman, who had commissioned young Gershwin to write "Rhapsody," gave credit to Ferde Grofe for orchestrating it so beautifully.

I'd been fascinated by show business for a long time, but I only got into it myself because Julie informed me she had been offered a job in a show called *Ziegfeld Palm Beach Girl.* The trouble—for me, at least—was that the job required her to spend the winter season in Florida. I was upset and told her so. I did not want her to leave New York. Julie said this was the break she had been waiting for and, anyway, she was going.

I was desperate—I just couldn't let her leave New York. "Look," I finally blurted out, "I can dance as well as any of those clowns. We should be a team. If I can get us a job as a dance team, will you stay?"

"Well," she replied, "if you can get us a job before the show leaves for Florida, it's a deal." Then she added, "On second thought, who told you you could dance?"

The thing was that I actually believed I could dance as well as any of the professionals I had been seeing around town. It looked easy and I was too stuck on Julie to let a little thing like talent get in my way. However, naive as I was in many respects, I still knew we had to practice.

But where? That was the big question for a pair of nobodies trying to break into show business. Of course you could rent a rehearsal hall for five dollars an hour and hire a pianist for another five. But my hangup was that I didn't have the money. I had to find a place for free. As for an accompanist, I decided I could whistle.

Suddenly I had an inspiration. I thought of a chop suey joint at Ninety-sixth Street and Broadway, downstairs, where I occasionally took Julie to eat. Unlike other Chinese restaurants, this place had a three-piece orchestra. I made a deal with the somewhat dubious proprietor. The idea was for us to use his dance floor to rehearse during the day, and at night we would put on a free show for his customers.

That first night, as you can imagine, we were dreadful. I was prepared then and there to give up show business. But our Chinese friend thought we were wonderful. So wonderful, in fact, that he said that starting the following night we could dine on the house. Julie and I were overjoyed. Maybe we weren't so bad after all. Anyhow we were in business at the rate of two chow mein dinners per performance. Whenever I go to Ah Fong's in Beverly Hills for Chinese food, I think of my pal in New York and what he got me into.

After a few nights, Julie and I felt that we were good enough to exhibit our wares in a more appropriate setting. It was Julie who got the bright idea we ought to make our formal debut at a place called Ten East Sixtieth Street which was the name as well as the address of the place just east of Fifth Avenue. This was a lovely room which specialized in tea dancing and attracted a collegiate crowd. We knew many of the youngsters who frequented the room and we also knew Emil Coleman, the ultra suave society-type band leader who played at Ten East Sixtieth. I had first met Emil when I lived in the rooming house across the street from the Montmartre, where he was the headliner.

Emil liked the idea of brightening up the show with a youthful dance team. His problem was trying to sell the idea to the owner of the place, Charles Bellak, who was about as miserable a character it was ever my misfortune to encounter. Bellak made it quite clear to Coleman that he didn't want to spend a nickel on live entertainment. He didn't like entertainers and particularly *verstunkiner* ballroom dancers.

We had an ace in the hole, though. An elderly, genial gentleman, a Mr. Seligman of the banking family, who lived upstairs in the Bellak-owned hotel, had taken a liking to us. He argued long and hard with Bellak about giving us a chance. Finally Bellak capitulated. He would let us audition for him at two o'clock the next day.

At this point in my life I was living rent-free in a room that had been part of the magnificent Dodge townhouse off Fifth Avenue near St. Patrick's Cathedral. The townhouse was now a speakeasy, the first really glorified "speak" in town, owned by Billy Wilkerson, who later went on to become publisher of the *Hollywood Reporter*. Billy was good enough to let me live in an empty top-floor room over his "speak," and it was there I bedded down all excited about my two o'clock audition for Mr. Bellak the next day.

But I couldn't sleep. I had developed a terrible toothache. I tossed and turned. Finally, at wit's end, I got up and went to an all-night drug store where I purchased two little boxes of Red Cross toothache medicine. The contents were supposed to ease the pain. I kept dabbing the stuff on my aching tooth (which proved to be ulcerated) and finally whatever was in it—pure chloroform, I think—put me to sleep about five in the morning.

I slept in a sort of stupor and didn't awaken until it was a quarter to two—fifteen minutes before my scheduled audition. Panic-stricken, I leaped out of bed, dressed hurriedly and rushed to Ten East Sixtieth. It was too late. Bellak, looking disgusted, was leaving as I arrived. I tried to explain, but he wouldn't listen. He just stalked out, leaving me to the tender mercies of Miss Julie.

Miss Julie was furious. You can't imagine a girl as mad as my partner. A how-can-you-do-this-to-me expression was all over her pretty face. She was on the verge of tears, but she was too infuriated to cry. I tried to explain what had happened. "Don't you ever dare speak to me again!" she said. "This is the end."

For a while I thought it was. I went to see Mr. Seligman, a compassionate soul. He listened to my story and began to laugh. "That's the funniest thing I ever heard," he said.

I didn't think it was *that* funny. But Mr. Seligman said he would see what he could do in my behalf, and whatever clout he had with Bellak he used to our advantage. Bellak gave us another chance.

I suppose I ought to be grateful to Bellak. That miserable man hired us on a trial basis—for one week. But at least it was a start.

Julie was all excited. She had a beautiful gown for the opening. She had saved her allowance for two months to get it. But I was flat broke and could not afford to buy a tailcoat, an article of clothing *de rigueur* for a ballroom dancer.

I did the next best thing under the circumstances. I "borrowed" a tailcoat from one of the finest shops on Fifth Avenue. First I had the garment fitted. As impoverished as I was, I still wanted to look good. After my measurements were taken, I arranged for the final fitting to take place on the eve of my debut.

On the big day I walked into the shop, tried on the finished product and complained about the fit of the shoulders. The proprietor went to the back to fetch the tailor. I dashed out with the coat and probably broke the half-mile record running up Fifth Avenue. I left a note explaining I wasn't a thief and that I had a job and would pay him back the following week. I will never forget the relief I felt when, dancing with Julie the second night, I looked up and saw the proprietor standing in a doorway with a big smile on his face, nodding in friendly fashion. He was letting me understand that everything would be all right. As soon as I had the money, I paid what I owed him. And I became a longtime patron of his establishment.

Emil Coleman had been exceptionally helpful to us during rehearsals. He taught us things like how to walk on and off the floor gracefully. He arranged our music. He taught me more about ballroom routines than anyone, and I have been forever grateful to this wonderful man.

As a result of his help, we did fairly well on opening night. Even Bellak was impressed—so much so that he agreed to keep us on at one hundred dollars a week on a week-to-week basis.

Bellak was displaying no newfound magnanimity. We began to bring in business and, as long as we were doing so, he was willing to part with some of the additional profits he was reaping.

The tea dances, of course, were continued. But when teatime was finished at six o'clock, he ordered the waiters to open all the windows. The wintry blasts would clear the room of lingerers—everybody was out by 6:05 and then the dinner business began.

Now remember, I was still working downtown for Bache during the day. I could make it because I was finished at the firm by 3:45. Later on, when we were working at Barney Gallant's club, my boss at Bache heard of it and informed me that no respectable firm could permit one of its employees to perform in a supper club. He was rather stuffy about it.

"You mean," I said, "that you want me to give up my half—fifty a week—for seventeen bucks a week? That makes no sense financially. I'm quitting Wall Street." And that was the end of my being a son of a Bache.

Meanwhile, word of our successful New York engagement reached Detroit and, much to our surprise, Julie and I received an offer from the Wertheimer brothers to appear at the Addison Hotel. Mert, Lou and Al Wertheimer ran a hotel which included a gambling operation on the side, but we didn't know about that. Mert offered to double our salaries and pay all our expenses. We gladly accepted the deal.

Bellak hit the ceiling when we gave him a week's notice, but we had no contract and summer would soon end the tea dance season. So off we went, and there was nothing he could do about it.

Incidentally, Bellak got over his dislike for entertainment. At considerable cost, he built a nightclub by literally carving it out of the entire basement of Ten East Sixtieth. Eventually he hired another Yale man, Rudy Vallee, and renamed the club the Villa Vallee. But this time Bellak made certain that he had Vallee under contract. Poor Rudy, who has since learned a good deal about these matters, found himself, at a peak period in his career, working for the Hungarian impresario at the barest minimum under a ruinous contract.

Today, what was Ten East Sixtieth and later the Villa Vallee is the site of what is probably the most famous night club in the world—the Copacabana. Whenever I pass through East Sixtieth Street I stop and tip my hat. I can't help but think of how my entire life and my career in show business hung in the balance because of Charles Bellak and how, if he hadn't given us a job, Miss Julie might well have given me the air.

Opening night at the Addison Hotel in Detroit was an overwhelming success. Lou Wertheimer had bet one of my friends, Charles Sullivan, that less than two hundred people would show up. Lou lost one hundred bucks on that wager, but he didn't mind at all. Over three hundred and fifty people packed the place. Lou came over to me, gave me his keys, and said, "Here, you can run the joint for a week. I'm going away on vacation."

It was a great week. Julie's friends from high society, as well as my friends from not-so-high-society, came every night. After three weeks of this kind of reception we returned to New York where, unfortunately, we found no clamor for our services. Nevertheless, we knew now we had something going for us. What we had been getting by with was a vague soft-shoe routine as well as an all-out Charleston. We decided to improve our act.

I began to report faithfully to Michael's Dancing School where for one dollar you could practice every day as long as you wanted and get a towel and a locker thrown in. Instructors were available at cut-rate prices and one of the most helpful was a young guy with a charming smile who would teach you a step now and then for free. He could tap, do soft-shoe and ballet, but he always seemed restless and about to go somewhere. He did. He went West to become one of Hollywood's best-loved actors and most brilliant stars. He was James Cagney.

James was to precede me as one of the presidents of the Screen Actors Guild. I'll always recall the night a few of us were talking in Dave Chasen's restaurant about building the Motion Picture Home. Jimmy, who by that time owned most of the real estate in Beverly Hills, asked, "How would a fellow get into this Home?"

I said, "If he were you, Jim, he could buy the place and pick out the room he liked." Jim was one of the moving spirits in this wonderful project, as he was in so many other good works.

The team of Murphy and Johnson next got a job at Barney Gallant's in Greenwich Village. This was a fabulous speakeasy on West Third Street, one that was particularly "in" for the theatrical, newspaper and literary set. As a college student I had visited the Club Gallant and had gotten to know the genial Barney himself.

Barney was a celebrity's celebrity—a more literate Toots Shor. A short, round man of Russian origin, he was one of the most charming and wisest people I have ever met. He had achieved a reputation as a foreign correspondent covering the Mexican troubles during the Pancho Villa days and he often boasted of having been a paid press agent for the revolutionaries below the border.

I recall his telling of some of his hijinks at a time when Pancho Villa was taking it easy and, as a consequence, there was little hard news out of Mexico. In order to scare up some headlines, Gallant arranged for the "kidnapping" of two American newsmen, hiding them away in a house on the Mexican side of the border and supplying them with food, tequila and a couple of senoritas to keep them company. By the time the story had been milked of all its drama, the "kidnapped" newsmen refused to be "rescued," they were having so much fun.

Barney had another claim to fame. He often boasted about being the first speakeasy operator to be arrested and jailed—for thirty days—on a charge of violating the Volstead Act. Most people who counted in those days felt such repugnance towards the Act that Gallant emerged from the hoosegow a hero. On another occasion, prohibition agents threatened to raid him, but his good pal "Two Gun" Murphy, the famous narcotics agent, guarded the door all evening. There was no raid.

I had no hesitation about asking Barney for a job. He was the kind of guy who gave everyone a hearing. But he was astonished at my claim to being a dancer.

"You're not a dancer," he said. "You're a halfback."

"Maybe you're right," I responded somewhat lamely, "but I have a girl who dances and I sort of keep out of her way."

Barney laughed and put us to work that night without an audition. The money wasn't big but at least we could eat properly. And we were appearing before important audiences. Sometimes that means just as much to entertainers, particularly newcomers, as money.

Now it would be nice to say that Julie and I soon became the toast of the town, but the facts were otherwise. We were just two kids trying to get ahead in a tough business. We did have one thing going for us—a clean-cut appearance which was in vivid contrast to most of the Latin-type dance teams then so much in vogue. I believe we were the first team to take stage dancing and accommodate it to the ballroom or nightclub floor. Instead of the customary lifts and spins performed by our competitors, we concentrated most of the time on soft-shoe dancing in tandem, fox trots, and of course later on the Varsity Drag.

Whatever it was we were doing, we must have been doing it right, since we slowly developed a following. Nothing big, mind

you, but big enough to keep Barney Gallant happy. And when
Barney was happy, we were happy. As the weeks went by, he
generously increased our salaries.

Barney was a very smart showman. He taught me a lesson
which I have never forgotten. One night Julie and I had performed better than usual and the audience kept insisting that
we do more. But we had run through our routines and had
nothing different to offer. On the spur of the moment, I dashed
across the floor and slid into the bandstand like a baseball
player stealing home. I nearly injured myself but I got a big
hand.

I thought I was sensational, but Barney didn't think so. He
really let me have it. "Right now, tonight," he said, sternly,
"you're going to learn the hardest lesson there is in show business. You're going to learn when to get offstage. From now on,
no matter what reactions you get from the audience, you are going to do two numbers and one encore. Nothing more. You understand?"

I understood, and all through the years I've tried to follow
Barney's instructions.

It was at Gallant's that I first began to meet some of the
leading celebrities of the era—people like Mayor Jimmy
Walker, columnist Heywood Broun (who often would write his
column at a corner table), cartoonist Peter Arno and such newspapermen (most of them long since gone) as O. O. McIntyre,
Herbert Bayard Swope, Frazier Hunt, Walter Winchell and
Mark Hellinger. When these people began greeting me like an
old friend, I knew I had arrived—I was becoming part of the
New York scene. And that was important to me in those days.

As soon as it seemed that we had a steady job at the Club
Gallant, Julie and I decided to get married. The date was
December 28, 1926, and the place was the Little Church
Around the Corner, where so many theatrical people—for some
reason lost to memory—preferred to tie the knot during the

Twenties. It was a private ceremony, and Julie's parents, who had come to New York for the Christmas holidays, were present.

Barney gave us a reception and a lot of our friends showed up. The band played and the champagne (illicit) flowed and, believe it or not, Julie and I were still scheduled to perform that night. The crowd was so big that Barney insisted we do two shows. After the first show Julie begged off—she was too tired. She went home while I carried on solo. I love to perform, but that was one time I wished the show didn't have to go on.

Slowly but surely we were developing a fairly good reputation. We were tagged as a "Westchester act" and began to dance at coming-out parties. More important, we had become seasoned performers, learning and improvising all the time. We were both what I guess would be called "natural" dancers and worked well together.

Financially, we were just about making it. One big drain on our expenses was costuming for Julie. She always had to be well-dressed, and custom-made clothes were exceedingly expensive. We finally made a deal with the well-known theatrical costumer, Kiviette, to provide Julie with gowns at about one hundred and twenty-five dollars each—an awful lot of money in those days.

Me? All I needed was a full-dress suit and I was in business.

Incidentally, one of my old suits is now the property of a village chief down in Panama. My son Dennis took it down there several years ago and wore it as a gag while fishing for black marlin. That night the chief from up the river saw the tailcoat and admired it so much that Dennis presented it to him as a gift from "my father, the Senator." He also gave the witch doctor my old opera hat.

After Julie and I were married, we lived in fairly modest digs in what had once been an old mansion on Thirty-Seventh Street near Madison Avenue. It would have been very nice except we soon became a *ménage à trois*. I found myself competing with a monkey—a wedding gift from a Detroit friend. As far as I was concerned there was no living with the creature, and as far as the monkey was concerned there was no living with me. But he loved Julie, who was forever protecting him from me.

Once, after looking for a job most of the day, I came home and wearily went into the bathroom to wash up before dinner. I took off my wristwatch and placed it on top of the washbasin. Unbeknownst to me the little creature from the jungle was observing every move I made. At the right moment he dropped down from the chandelier, grabbed the wristwatch, threw it into the toilet and then flushed. I could have strangled him, but Julie, ever understanding of the foibles of the animal kingdom, rescued him from my angry clutches.

She thought that the monkey's antics, while occasionally deplorable, were cute. When Julie's mother came to visit with us for a while, however, the monkey just about drove her crazy. The animal knew Julie's mother was a little frightened of him, and he would purposely try to scare her to death. He would sit above the doorways and suddenly drop on her when she walked underneath. Then he would scoot away like the wind when I tried to catch and punish him.

Every once in a while I would make an effort to grab him and give him a couple of whacks on his backside. He would screech like a banshee before I touched him, and Julie would take out after me. His wailings were enough to wake up the neighbors so even then I was thwarted.

And there was the Grand Central Station episode. Julie was planning to visit her mother. Rather than leave the monkey with me, she decided to take him with her to Detroit. She bought a papier-mache box and put him in it. By the time we arrived at the station, the monkey had managed to widen the air hole, get himself loose, and escape into the milling crowd. I chased him all over that cavernous depot. He knew what was in store for him so he kept eluding me. Finally Julie managed to corner him. After she talked quietly to him, the monkey meekly surrendered. She put him under her coat.

"What are you going to do now?" I asked.

"This is the way I'm going to take him to Detroit," she said.

And that's the way she took him aboard the Detroiter, the crack train that got her there the next morning. She had absolutely no trouble—the monkey, for once, not acting like a monkey.

We next had a wire-haired terrier, a beautiful specimen but possessed of one of the meanest dispositions I've ever encountered in a dog. He particularly disliked the doormen along Park and Fifth Avenues or anyone wearing white gloves. Whenever one of these white-gloved gentlemen would reach over to pet him, the terrier would bite him. I myself was frightened of him.

Once, while Julie was combing the dog, he turned around and bit her just above the eye. I grabbed at the beast and she ran into the bathroom. Shutting the door, she refused to let me in. She wanted to see how much damage was done to her face. It wasn't too bad. Even then she wouldn't let me get rid of the dog. Fortunately, he decided to run away. A while later, someone reported that he had seen the dog riding, next to a chauffeur, in the front seat of a Rolls Royce town car. He looked happy.

Julie wanted him back. "Forget it," I said, "we can't afford a town car."

But don't get the idea that I don't like animals. I've had no choice after four decades of married life with a dedicated animal-lover. Wherever we have lived, our household has been arranged more to accommodate animals than us. We've had collies, Kerry blues, Siamese cats, standard-size and miniature poodles, several ducks and a goat. We even had a fighting rooster. The rooster started out as a tiny yellow Easter chick and developed into the biggest, most beautiful fighting cock I have ever seen. In addition he was a superb "watchdog"—he wouldn't let anyone into the house except members of the family. When we knew guests were coming we would have to cage him.

One day he was guarding the front of the house when a strange dog came by. "Quonk" chased him into the street and unfortunately got hit by a passing car. The veterinarian said his leg was broken and he should be killed, but Julie would have none of it. With two small wooden sticks we made a splint, and after three weeks he was as good as new. Better, in fact, because he now walked with sort of swing, like Fred Astaire.

Today, in our Beverly Hills home, Julie and I live with two beagles, Revel and Mr. Biggs, both of whom are getting along in years and require a great deal of attention and care which they are getting. Because our children, Missie and Dennis, have grown up and are raising their own families, Revel and Mr. Biggs are the most important "people" in the household. And don't kid yourselves. After you live with dogs for a while, they become "people." You love them almost as much as if they were your own flesh and blood.

The author's father, Mike Murphy,
famous trainer of athletic champions

George Murphy on Yale's championship football team (front row center)

*(Brandenburg Studio)*

Julie Henkel inspired George Murphy to become a dancer

The Murphys enjoyed costume parties at home, too

George and Julie became the hit team of Murphy and Johnson

Julie put aside her own career to make a home for the Murphy family

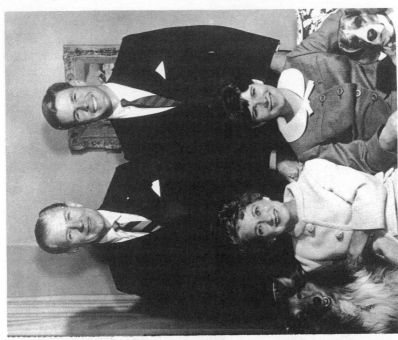

The Murphy family, with their popular dogs Revel and Mr. Biggs

George became the busiest actor in Hollywood, but Dennis and Melissa could always corner him with

# CHAPTER 5

### The Nightclub Circuit

Shortly after our marriage, Julie and I decided that we were ready for bigger things. Barney Gallant agreed. He told us he would have no objection to our leaving if we could do better elsewhere. It wasn't long before we joined forces with George Olsen, the band leader who also packaged a variety show for the nightclub circuit.

The first room we worked with Olsen was Peter's Blue Hour on West Forty-ninth Street. Small and intimate, it was an ideal place to perform. We had only one difficulty. Though Olsen had a pleasant personality and a smile that revealed more teeth than any one man has a right to, he just couldn't keep a strict tempo.

We were annoyed, but we didn't dare say anything. Then we bought a new routine from the great choreographer Buddy Pierce. For the period, it was pretty advanced stuff and involved tricky rhythms. If the music wasn't played exactly right, Julie and I could wind up stepping on each other's feet. That might have been a funny bit, but we were not comedians—we were for real.

We had no alternative but to ask Olsen if he would mind letting Eddie, his pianist, direct the band while we were performing this intricate number. George didn't mind at all. "Anything to make you happy," he said. George may not have been the greatest musician in the world, but he certainly was one of the most successful, and he had a thorough knowledge of show business. His orchestra played in the nation's leading spots. He made records and was one of the first big attractions on radio, particularly on the Stromberg Carlson Hour. And he had a magnificent girl singer and comedienne who later became his wife—Ethel Shutta.

It was at Peter's Blue Hour that I first worked with a young crooner, Harry Lillis Crosby, better known today to the world at large as "Bing." Crosby, along with Harry Banas and Al Rinker, had appeared as a trio with the Paul Whiteman orchestra. They were known as the Rhythm Boys and I liked them. When Olsen needed an act, I recommended them.

Bing was a mild-mannered lad from Tacoma, Washington, who never seemed to take life too seriously. In those days he was inclined to imbibe a little flagrantly. As a consequence, he was carefree, loose and relaxed like his singing and he sometimes failed to show up for performances. In fact, he failed to appear his first night at the Blue Hour. This upset me because I really wanted to hear him sing. The same thing happened when he was hired to sing over the Columbia Broadcasting System. When Bill Paley or some other big shot called Bing's brother and business-manager to complain, Everett Crosby responded, "Well, Bing can sing pretty good for two hundred dollars a week, but for one thousand five hundred he gets very nervous."

Of course, Bing resolved his problem and became one of the greatest entertainers in history. He is a very wealthy man, deserves all his success and he still is as relaxed as ever. If you don't think so, watch his back swing—on the golf course, that is.

The Olsen entourage was so successful at Peter's Blue Hour that it moved to larger quarters, the Club Richman on West Fifty-sixth Street which was launched by Harry Richman as a showcase for his singing talents. Richman was a big star on Broadway, one of the biggest, and if there was ever a real ladies' man, he was it. He made many millions. The last I heard of him, he had a ranch near Las Vegas, but in his book he says he blew it all and wound up scrounging for vegetables in a supermarket.

Our Club Richman show was an enormous success. For at least twelve weeks, the place was so packed on Friday and Saturday nights that the tables were jammed right up to the bandstand. This meant Julie and I had no place to dance. When we were introduced, I would lift Julie up and set her down, and then the master of ceremonies, Genial George, would say, "That's a rough idea of what the Murphys do, ladies and gentlemen. If you want to see them dance, please come back Monday night."

On the bill with us at the Club Richman was a gay young Irish lad who had started out as a news butcher on the New York, New Haven & Hartford Railroad—Morton Downey. Within a few years he became Mr. Big of the radio networks with his theme song "Carolina Moon." Mort also made a fortune. Unlike Richman, he not only kept it but considerably increased it. One of his closest friends was the late Joseph P. Kennedy, the multimillionaire founder of The Dynasty, and I suspect old Joe advised Morton of an investment here and there that helped. He also married a very rich girl.

One night Downey was interrupted in the middle of his act by an extremely obnoxious drunk. He was not only obnoxious, he was so loaded you couldn't shut him up. Morton was a past master at quieting ringside drunks, yet try as he would, he couldn't persuade the man to keep quiet. Nor could the waiters, who obviously were intimidated by the sheer size of this particular drunk. Downey cut his act short, walked off in disgust, and whispered to me, "Did you ever see anyone get a Mickey Finn?"

"No," I said.

"Well, you're going to see it tonight."

With that he led Julie and me upstairs to a small balcony and we watched as the waiter served the victim the doctored drink. After the drunk gulped it down, an extraordinary thing occurred. This fellow, who had been so belligerent and willing to fight anyone in the house, suddenly became so weak that the waiters had no difficulty whatsoever in leading him out of the room. Moreover, he never came back. I think we may have cured him for all time. I hope so.

In those days, every experienced bartender kept a Mickey

Finn close by just for occasions like this. It was much quicker and quieter than repairing a smashed nightclub. It was also against the law.

As part of the Olsen show, I did a deadpan knockabout comedy act with Jack Shutta, Ethel's brother. Olsen had heard us playing harmonicas together and thought we would do well as a comedy team. Jack was a giant of a fellow and, though in those days I weighed in at one hundred and seventy-five pounds, he would pick me up with one hand and carry me around at the finish. I looked so different in this act that some of the patrons failed to recognize me as Julie's partner of the preceding act. Some, in fact, thought I was my own brother. I remember Sam Goldwyn coming in one night, watching the whole show, and then asking me which one was the older brother. It was my first introduction to the brilliant motion picture producer who was later to take me to Hollywood.

We used to have trouble with one guest who came in regularly once a week. Until he had his third drink, he was a perfect gentleman. After the third drink, he would try to trip the dancers as they performed their routines or badger the singers. He did this one night to Jack Shutta. Jack lost his temper and asked this clown what he was trying to prove. He said he wanted to fight, so Jack said, "Come on, we can do it in the men's room or out in the street. We're not allowed to fight inside the club. My brother-in-law doesn't like it, and it disturbs the other guests." He chose the street and as he stepped out the door Jack whacked him and he fell right into my arms.

We carried the man upstairs and put ice on his forehead and his darkening eye. When he regained consciousness, he demanded, "Who hit me?"

"I did," Jack said.

Looking at me, he said, "You must have hit me from behind."

I declined the honor, and Jack finally convinced the gentleman that he was hit fair and square. Somewhat chastened, he asked if he would be permitted to return to the club. "Of course," we said, "if you agree to take only two drinks and then leave." He agreed with the proviso that if he ordered a third drink he be escorted outside to a cab. We never had any trouble with him again, and he used to be a regular customer.

Nor did we have any trouble with the racketeers who infested the nightclub business (as I understand they still do) in the Twenties. Anyone in show business with half a brain could easily recognize the denizens of the underworld who were carving out fortunes peddling illegal spirits in this era of Prohibition. Some of these gentlemen actually owned the clubs in which some of the biggest names in entertainment were starring, even though these establishments frequently were "fronted" by respectable-appearing businessmen.

They were rough guys, these racketeers, yet in a curious way they had their own code of morality. They did not take easily to the idea of cheap hoods messing around in their backyard. Once a former tap dancer named Billy, who had lost a leg and was selling jewelry to make a living, came into the Club Richman and reported that everything he owned had been taken away from him in a holdup.

"Did you call the police?" I asked. When he said he hadn't, I was horrified. "What are you going to do about it?"

Billy didn't seem to be anguished. "Oh," he casually responded, "the boys will take care of it."

And "the boys" did. Within an hour, "the boys" had uncovered the identities of the culprits and forced them to return their ill-gotten gains to Billy.

Not all racketeer stories were that pleasant, however. None of us in the business could forget the time that the great comic Joe E. Lewis hovered between life and death after being viciously knifed by a couple of Chicago mobsters. As I remember, it was all because Lewis did not want to appear at one nightclub, preferring to work at another. A friend of mine once said of a gangster who had killed three people, "He was always kind of headstrong."

During this period of our lives Julie and I traveled with George Olsen to Florida, across the country and back, playing class spots and picking up much-needed experience and polish.

In 1930 we went to California with Olsen to open a big, beautiful nightclub in Culver City called The Plantation. It was an absolutely fantastic place. Olsen had eighty-five spotlights and he used to play them like a console on an organ—a pretty good idea because it kept him off the bandstand. As I have noted, George's rhythm wasn't as good as it should have been.

The Plantation was an enormously successful place, and Julie and I found ourselves an increasingly popular attraction. We did routine after routine until we ran out of ideas. So one night we borrowed a number from the famous dance team of Moss and Fontana called *Tango Tragico,* a pretty macabre sort of dance with, however, sensational music. The "story" was about a French apache who finds his girl fooling around with another man and chokes her to death. When the police arrive, he picks up the dead girl and dances with her.

One night, in the middle of this emotional scene, some fellow made a loud rude remark. When the dance was over, I went over to his table and told him, "Sir, you're wanted on the telephone." He got up and asked where the phone was. "Right out here," I said, leading him to the front porch where I belted him with my left hand, knocking him into the shrubbery. I'm not sure whether he ever got up again and I couldn't have cared less.

I also continued to do my comedy knockabout act with Jack Shutta at The Plantation. People said we were funnier than ever.

One night who should walk into the club but a man who had been widely publicized for having killed two people and who was then out on bail. The alleged killer had brought two girls with him and was demanding a table. The headwaiter, who immediately recognized him, did not know what to do.

Jack and I had no choice but to take over. We approached

the man, who looked as tough and mean as they came, and asked him if he had a reservation.

"Naw," he said in a surly tone, "I don't need no reservation."

"Sir, would you be so kind as to wait for a moment," Jack told him, "and I'll see about getting you a table."

"Keep talking to him," Jack whispered to me. "I'll be right back."

So I kept talking to the man and his two ladies, and they began to get impatient waiting for a table. I was getting more nervous by the second.

Finally the tough guy said, "Where's my table? If I don't get a table right now, I'll blow this joint right off the street."

At that moment Jack came through the kitchen door on the run, just in time to hear the outburst. He said, "Okay, buster, if you start blowing I'll blow it right with you."

Jack had raced across the street to his tiny apartment and had returned with an old Civil War type pistol with which he chased this tough guy right out of the lobby. As this bum got into his car, he shouted, "I'll leave now, boys, but I'll be back. Don't you worry about that."

Well, we did worry about it for several weeks. Every night when Jack and I showed up for work we wondered whether this guy would come back and try to square the account. But we never saw him again.

Deep in his heart, Jack Shutta resented his brother-in-law, George Olsen—why, I never knew. One night Jack had had a few drinks and decided the time had come to take care of Olsen. He let out a yell. "Tonight's the night!" he shouted, and took off after the bandleader.

Realizing his danger, Olsen began to run down the long hall of The Plantation's second floor. I took off after Jack, catching him at the top of the stairs with a flying tackle and holding him long enough so that Olsen could get through the front door and into his car and away. When I finally let Jack up, I must say he recognized the humor of the situation and began to laugh. But

I'm afraid that if Jack had caught George that night, that would have been the end of Olsen and Shutta. And what was more important, Julie and I would have been out of work.

Summertimes were frequently reserved for the Ross-Fenton Farms in Spring Lake on the New Jersey coast. This was probably the most glamorous roadhouse in the country. It had the entire summer colony from the whole Jersey coast for a clientele. Not more than an hour's drive from Manhattan, it also attracted well-heeled New Yorkers who had no better place to go during hot weather. Very few places were open in Manhattan in the summer, as this was before air conditioning, and most New York night spots closed for the summer.

Mabel Ross and Frank Fenton, who launched the roadhouse, were ex-vaudevillians of exceptional taste. They actually started it as a boarding house for actors, where they began giving impromptu shows on the front porch. Almost from the beginning they had a hit on their hands. It was finally expanded to include a beautiful pavilion on the lake that seated twelve hundred people. Weekend nights the place was absolutely packed with more than a thousand people to hear such outstanding entertainers as Helen Morgan, Helen (boop-boop-a-doop) Kane, Ethel Merman, Morton Downey and Eddy Duchin and his orchestra.

Julie and I always did well at Ross-Fenton, and we look back at our summers there as among the happiest in our lives.

With the passing of the years, Ross-Fenton changed its management. At one time, one of the major partners was Meyer Davis, who has made a fortune supplying orchestras to hotel rooms, debutante parties, Presidential and other balls. An associate was Ralph Maurice who also did well operating hatcheck and other concessions in night spots around New York. It was Maurice who paid us for the coat room concession at the promotion my Yale partners and I had staged at Delmonico's several years previously. On that occasion he had lost money, as he ruefully and repeatedly would remind me.

One night early in the season, Maurice and I were listening to a young girl singer whom Davis had hired for fifty dollars a night. "My God, she's lousy," Maurice said. "Tell her she's fired."

"I don't think she's bad at all," I said. "Anyway, I'm not going to tell her anything of the sort. It will break the kid's heart."

"Heart, smart," Maurice continued. "In this business, you've got to be tough. This ain't amateur night, you know."

Maurice was tough. He went to the girl's manager, Anna Sosenko, and told her that her protégée was through. Not only that but in his inimitable fashion he suggested that the girl consider a career as a waitress.

Years later, Julie and I went to the Persian Room at the Hotel Plaza in New York. This was—and still is—one of the classiest rooms in town. And who should be the star attraction that evening but the very girl Maurice had brutally fired at Ross-Fenton. The girl's name was Hildegarde. She had become, and deservedly so, one of the nation's leading nightclub entertainers.

I must say Hildegarde really seemed pleased to see us. She introduced us to the audience and presented Julie with one of the roses that had become her trademark. She told how she had worked with the Murphys at the Ross-Fenton Farms, but she did not go into any of the bitter details which, incidentally, included the fact that she had never been paid the fifty dollars for her one night's work. As I think back, they clipped me once for two hundred dollars, too.

While working summers at the shore, we rented a six-bedroom house near the beach for three hundred dollars a season. The season began when you arrived and ended when you left. The house was always loaded with chums from New York and elsewhere. There were no formal invitations. If you were a friend of ours and the house wasn't too crowded, you could always be our guest. One of our friends, Teddy Bassett, a New York socialite, occupied one of the bedrooms for three weeks before we even knew he was there, and big Eddie McCarthy spent the entire summer.

Breakfast was the only meal we served our guests, and some never showed up for breakfast. The arrangement was to get your own lunch down at the beach and dinner elsewhere.

Brother, did we keep busy! On a typical day I'd play eighteen holes of golf, take a swim, then play four or five sets of tennis, take another swim, then another nine holes of golf, another swim, then dine with Julie, after which we'd get ready to work at the Farms. I can't ever remember being tired. In fact, I don't recall ever getting really tired until I was in my mid-fifties. Then I got into a doubles match for the championship of the old West Side Tennis Club in Hollywood. The match lasted five hours and when it was over, for the first time in my life I was really fatigued.

It's obvious I was a sports nut. One summer on the New Jersey coast I organized a softball league. This may have been the first time softball was played outdoors—previously the game had been played inside gymnasia. Every town up the coast got a team together and we played every Sunday on the lawn of the Monmouth Hotel.

My team was composed of college kids who lived or worked in and around Spring Lake. Not only did I play with my team, but I was the pitcher—no speed but great control. We were pretty good, if I say so myself.

One day a famous stock trader named Joe Higgins watched us play. Higgins was without question the biggest trader in Wall Street, and he suggested he could bring a team that could beat us.

We accepted the challenge and the date was set. My team was ready for the big game. Then I discovered that Higgins had begun to bet heavily with members of my team. I begged him to lay off, pointing out that most of the kids were betting way beyond their means and when too much money gets involved, the fun may be destroyed. But Higgins was what Dad would have called a "thick neck" and he disregarded my plea and continued betting.

The night before the game I ran into Joe Bannon, a partner of Moe Annenberg's in the newspaper business. Bannon was a long-time admirer of the dancing Murphys and he knew me well enough to recognize that something was troubling me. I told him how Higgins refused to stop betting with the kids, and my concern about the results.

He took a certified check for fifty thousand dollars out of his pocket, handed it to me and said, "If Higgins wants to bet, tell him to cover this." It was the biggest check I had ever seen.

Higgins wanted to know where I had got the check. "I won't embarrass you by asking where you get your money," I said. "I expect you to pay me the same courtesy. Just cover it or shut up."

He didn't press the point. Nor did he want to bet the fifty thousand. But he was willing to go for ten thousand, which still was the most money I had ever bet in my life. To say I was nervous about the whole business is an understatement.

I was even more nervous the next day when I learned that Higgins had brought down a group of professional ballplayers on leave from the Boston Red Sox and the New York Giants to play against our kids.

But once the game got underway I relaxed. Softball is not like baseball; it's a different game. Higgins' pros never got a man past second base. My kids won going away, and poor Higgins looked as though he would have a stroke on the sidelines, he was that angry.


In the winters we were very fortunate to be able to work at the Montmartre with Emil Coleman who at that time had by far the best dance orchestra in New York. The headwaiter was a Frenchman named Charlie Journal whom I had known for several years and who became one of the best friends Julie and I ever had.

The Montmartre was located in the Winter Garden Building at Fiftieth Street and Broadway. When it was first opened, nobody knew about it and there were no reservations. But Charlie Journal opened all the windows on the third floor where the club was located and kept the orchestra playing all night. People who happened to drop by at the Fifty-first Street entrance found the door closed. The doorman would open the door slightly and ask if they had a reservation. When they said they had none, the doorman would say, "Sorry, the place is full," and shut the door in their faces.

The word spread like wildfire around New York that there was a new nightclub you couldn't get into. That did it. Everyone wanted admittance. By the fourth night, Charlie opened with one of the most select groups ever to attend a nightclub opening in New York. Mrs. John Wanamaker came in from Philadelphia. Mrs. William Randolph Hearst was there, and Otto Kahn, the banker, and many of the town's other social leaders.

To this day I think I am one of the few people who know that for the first three nights of the Montmartre's existence the lights were on and the music played but there wasn't a single paying customer in the place.

The Montmartre may well have been the most successful nightclub in New York. It lasted for seventeen years and was a very gracious and orderly place. For dancers it was an excellent place to work. We did one show consisting of four numbers at midnight. Then Julie and I would have supper with Charlie and return to our tiny apartment on West Fifty-fifth Street.

In all the time I spent there I don't recall ever seeing any trouble or anything like a fight. But one night the inevitable happened. It was the night of the Dempsey-Carpentier fight and one of Jack Dempsey's sparring partners, Joe Benjamin, got angry with some college kid. A bunch of college kids rushed to the defense of their chum. The result was one of the great donnybrooks of nightclub history.

My friend Charles Boetcher, whose father owned the Brown Palace Hotel in Denver, was in the gentlemen's room upstairs when the fight started. He hadn't the slightest idea of what was going on downstairs, but he happened to walk back in through the curtained doorway just as Benjamin threw a right hook and missed the fellow he was aiming at. He hit Boetcher right smack in the nose. My friend was revived twenty minutes later with a broken nose, still not knowing what had happened.

By the time the ruckus was over, there were at least eight collegiate bodies stretched out cold in the coat room. That was the last and only fight ever to mar the quiet of the sedate Montmartre, at least as far as I know.

Charlie Journal ran the room with an iron hand. He knew most of his customers personally. He would never accept a tip, but at Christmas time the gifts would pour in. I couldn't say for sure, but I'm certain his mail in those few weeks was worth anywhere from one hundred and fifty thousand to two hundred thousand dollars a year.

One night Otto Kahn, probably the most famous banker in New York, came in and asked to sit at a particular table.

"Mr. Kahn," said Charlie, "I have your table all arranged. I don't interfere with your bank. So please don't interfere with my restaurant."

Julie and I got to love Charlie Journal. He was a lonely man and apparently had an unhappy home life. We enjoyed talking to him.

Weekends, Charlie would take Julie and me riding in his car. Invariably he would drive to a little place in New Jersey called Twin Rivers, probably because two rivers came together at that point. Charlie seemed interested in a country restaurant near the twin rivers. One Sunday I asked him to stop the car. I went inside the restaurant and asked the owner what he wanted for his place. I told Charlie the price and he wrote out a check and bought it then and there. He always loved this place because, he said, it reminded him of his home in France. Years later, when he retired, Charlie and two Montmartre chefs ran the resttaurant and had the best French cuisine for miles around.

The Montmartre went out of business while Julie and I were in London doing a musical show called *Good News*. When we returned to New York we decided to do something about reopening the Montmartre. All it needed was a good cleaning and a coat of paint and it would be ready to go.

But even that cost money and we didn't have any. We went to the Shuberts and they agreed to come up with the financing if we could get a high-calibre band. George Olsen was available and he was willing to take a chance with us. Charlie Journal wanted to get back into action, so our team was complete.

I put the package together and as it worked out, after all expenses were paid, Olsen was to get two shares, Charlie one, and Julie and I would take a single share. The Shuberts took a percentage as rent and, despite their reputation, were very fair, I must say.

Opening night was sensational. The Montmartre was jammed with our friends. Olsen and his orchestra were tip-top and Julie and I had new routines for the occasion. When Olsen began to introduce celebrities in the audience, most of them got up to entertain. It was that sort of evening.

Bing Crosby, already a star, crooned a tune. So did Morton Downey, then at the height of his fame. Several comedians, getting into the spirit of the occasion, did their *shtik*.

The show was absolutely sensational—until a young comic named Jackie Osterman was introduced. Jackie, who could have been a great monologist, just couldn't resist telling dirty stories. Sure enough, he ran true to form that night. He told two funny stories and had the audience in hysterics. Then he began to use four-letter words. We signalled him to knock it off, but once he got going there was no stopping him. We knew we had a crisis on our hands.

Finally I got a bright idea. I tipped off three waiters and ran into the kitchen, where I pulled the master switch that shut off all the lights. By the time the lights went on, the three waiters had hustled Osterman halfway into a taxicab. But unfortunately, the damage had been done. At least half of the customers had asked for their checks, and it looked as if our initial effort as entrepreneurs was doomed to failure.

I guess the stories Osterman was telling would be considered mild today. That's how much times have changed. I must say that much of what goes on today in the name of entertainment I find absolutely incredible. This is one former performer who can't comprehend some of the material that is being used in public places, and I'm not sure that any of it is any great improvement over what we used to do years ago. Judging from my mail in the United States Senate, many other people in this country are developing a deep-seated revulsion toward the entertainment excesses which are now being taken for granted, excesses which are protected by the courts as involving freedom of expression. Freedom of expression, my foot!

Despite Osterman, our night club venture caught on and we began to do business. We were making good money and we thought we had it made. But then about two weeks after the opening, George Olsen announced he was not pleased with the financial arrangement. He said that since he was the main attraction he ought to get the bulk of the profits while Julie and I—and of course Charlie Journal—ought to be paid salaries. Julie and I walked out of the venture and within a week the Montmartre was again closed.

Some time later the newspapers carried stories about how Jackie Osterman got hit by his wife with a champagne bottle, which raised a big lump on his head. A few nights after the story appeared, Osterman showed up at a benefit. He told a few jokes and then asked his usual question: "What do you want little Jackie to do, folks? Just tell little Jackie what you want him to do."

Someone yelled out, "Take off your hat, you bum, and show the folks the bump on your head!"

I've encountered many a quarrelling couple in show business. One of the most fascinating was the Humphrey Bogarts. At this time he was married to Mayo Methot, a very fine actress from New York. And did they use to battle! Privately and publicly they were apt to square off at any moment. The amazing thing was that Miss Methot, weighing in at one hundred and twenty pounds soaking wet, could lick the great tough guy, and usually did. It was always a source of wonderment to me that Humphrey Bogart's movie image was that of the toughest guy in creation.

It's been my experience, too, that dance teams are prone to quarrel. There's something about the nervous tension on stage and doing those complicated steps with a partner that causes great emotional strain. Our good friends, Medrano and Donna, a fine pair of ballroom dancers, once gave vent to their emotions publicly in a scene I'll never forget.

They were appearing at the Academy of Music on Fourteenth Street with the Fred Waring orchestra and were into their third number—a paso doble—when Donna somehow missed a step. No one in the audience noticed it, but Medrano did and he was furious. As the curtain was coming down, they gracefully took their bows. And as the curtain went up for a second bow, obviously Donna had slapped Medrano in the face.

Once again the curtain came down. The audience applauded wildly. As the curtain rose, it caught Medrano in the act of kicking Donna in her derrière. Down came the curtain—again great applause—and up went the curtain as Medrano and Donna battled it out all over the stage. The audience kept yelling for more. It was one of the funniest scenes ever. The only time I have seen funnier bows was when a second-rate comedienne grabbed the curtain and went up with it.

Then there were the DeMarcos, one of the finest dance teams in the business. Renee and Tony DeMarco were just fabulous on the floor. They were a joy to watch. Julie and I never missed a chance to watch them perform. But even with their magnificent skill and grace, there was temperamental tension.

One night while they were appearing in the Persian Room of

the Hotel Plaza, Tony got so angry at Renee that when their act was finished he rushed upstairs and ripped up all her dresses. This was a silly thing to do because, after all, he was paying the bills. Moreover, as Renee later chortled, "I got myself a whole new wardrobe."

I think we were one of the few dance teams around that got along both on and offstage, the reason being that neither Julie nor I ever were very temperamental and we were more inclined to find humor in our mistakes. Like most married couples, we had an occasional argument. But when we argued it was at home and out of public view, and it was never really very serious. Each of us has a happy facility for eventually seeing the other's point of view. That's why we have been together more than four decades.

# CHAPTER 6

## "By special request of Her Majesty"

One brisk sunny morning I was walking down Broadway, looking for a job as usual, when my pal in the box office at the Chanin Theater yelled at me.

"Hey, Murph, they're looking for a leading man at the Cohan Theater," he said.

I was off like a shot.

Arriving at the George M. Cohan Theater, I learned that a young leading man was indeed being sought for a new show whose producer happened to be none other than the veteran comedian Lew Fields, of Weber and Fields fame. Waiting to audition were several young hopefuls. When my turn came, Fields asked whether I could dance. Yes, I replied, that was the way I made my living. I demonstrated a few steps. Could I sing? Yes, I could. Fields seemed impressed. But someone with him said, "I bet he can't act."

"We'll see," said Fields, who handed me a copy of the manuscript.

He called one of the stagehands to sit on a bench with me. The idea was for me to read from a love scene between a boy and a girl. As I read (the boy's part, of course), I glanced at the stagehand. He was without question one of the ugliest creatures I ever had the misfortune to lay eyes on, and I was to play a love scene with him. This was too much even for a guy who needed a job real bad.

"Mr. Fields," I finally said, "this is a little too much for me. Thank you very much for listening. I'll come back later."

As I left Fields said, "Don't be discouraged. You dance and sing well."

I never went back.

On another occasion I received a telephone call from the
Shubert Casting offices. I was asked to report to a gentleman
referred to as "Ma" Simmons, who cast bit players and chorus
boys for the various Shubert productions. The reason they
called him "Ma" was soon obvious. He was gracefully effeminate in his mannerisms and always wore a long white silk scarf.
There was a singing part available and "Ma," looking me over
more than casually, asked me whether I had brought an accompanist. I said I hadn't.

With a girlish toss of the head, "Ma" said, "Well, I will accompany you myself." As he passed behind me on his way to the
piano, he gave me a gentle pat on my wallet—what the boys at
The Lambs club would call a "keister touch." That was more
than I could take. Once again the track conditions were too
rough for me and once again I left hurriedly before the humor
of the situation forced me to burst out laughing. I was beginning to find out how difficult it was to get started on the stage.

When Julie ·and I were appearing with George Olsen at
Peter's Blue Hour, we often attended rehearsals of a new Broadway musical called *Good News*. This was a rah-rah college-type
show which featured the Olsen band. After the show each night,
the band would rush over to the Blue Hour for its engagement
there. While watching the rehearsals, Julie and I learned to do
a new dance staged by my friend Bobby Connolly, the "Varsity
Drag," which was to become the sensation of the season. We
adapted it for use in our nightclub act and did extremely well
with it.

So well that when the London producer, Herbert Morrison,
came over to cast the London company of *Good News*—one of
the biggest hits of the Broadway season—he hired us to do the
Varsity Drag number as well as to play several other roles in the
musical. We grabbed the job primarily because we wanted to
get some experience in the theater, and it seemed pretty exciting to be going to England. Neither of us had ever been there.

The company took off on a small Cunard ship, the *Samaria*. None of us had ever been on an ocean voyage before and we all had the time of our lives.

As we crossed the Atlantic we learned that the *Samaria* would make a stop in Ireland to permit three hundred Irish pilgrims from the Bronx and Brooklyn to disembark for a visit to the old country. We arrived at the tiny port of Galway and there a lighter came out to pick up the pilgrims.

I got to know the captain of the lighter, Michael Folan, who generously agreed to take me ashore and return me to the *Samaria*, despite the fact that I had no visa to visit Ireland. Folan, it seems, had enough influence with the British customs official to make it possible for his newfound buddy from America, Georgie Murphy, to see Galway. For several hours I visited this delightful little town and met some of its people.

When I returned to the *Samaria*, I wanted to do something in return for Folan. I asked him what he would like to have as a token of our newly-born friendship. He thought for a while and then suggested that he would like to have two cups and a teapot, as well as half a dozen white breakfast rolls. Apparently the people of Galway at that time hadn't had any white bread for about two years.

My first trip to Ireland was most enjoyable, even though it was slightly illegal.

Prior to the London run, *Good News* was given a tryout in Birmingham. The story was about a football player who had to pass an examination in order to play in the big game. The audiences were receptive despite the fact that the British didn't know too much about football or the rules of the game. But they loved the singing and dancing and the comedy.

I had a wonderful series of parts. I was kept busy running on and off the stage, asking or answering a question. I must have had fifteen entrances and exits in the first act alone. Each time I appeared, however, I had put on a different-colored sweater.

For example, I would dash onto the stage and, in an agitated voice, ask, "Anyone here seen Tom?" Someone would respond to the question and I'd rush off to don another sweater and make another entrance. "Do you think Tom is going to pass the examination?" I would ask. Again I would rush offstage, put on another sweater, and charge back saying, "Spread the word—it looks as if Tom may pass the examination!" And I'd run off and come back with still another sweater, saying, "We're not sure whether Tom is going to pass."

I was the busiest actor doing nothing in the history of the theater.

Julie, meanwhile, was playing a far more important role. She was one of the coeds and what used to be called the soubrette of the show. She not only was having a wonderful time but was getting good stage experience as well. She had two numbers to do besides the number we danced together later on in the show, the Varsity Drag.

Such is the unpredictable nature of show business that within a few days I was handed the leading role in *Good News*. What happened was that the producer felt that the actor originally recruited to carry on the college romance had failed to give even his second best for good old Tate University.

And all this occurred within twenty-four hours of our arrival in London. I was called in and asked whether I could play the lead. Since I was the understudy, I had followed the rehearsals carefully and did know the part to some extent. I asked when I should go on in the new role. The boss said, "Tomorrow night."

Aghast, I said, "Couldn't you make it Wednesday?"

"The other man has been sacked," he told me. "Hot or cold, you play the part tomorrow night."

I was in a panic and the poor leading lady nearly died of fright.

Not only did I have to memorize the script, but I had to have a new wardrobe. I was built differently from the actor I succeeded. But those London tailors, Morris Angel & Sons, were magnificent. They came through with a brand-new wardrobe for me by the time the curtain went up.

While they made the suits, Julie and I stayed up all night going over the script, the songs and dances. Frankly, I thought I would never be able to do it, but when you're young nothing is impossible. Then there's something I've heard about fools rushing in.

The London production of *Good News* opened as scheduled at the spanking new Carlton Theater on Shaftesbury Avenue near Piccadilly Circus. It was one of those glamorous first nights of prewar London, with the ladies all beautifully gowned and the gentlemen in their evening clothes.

They may have enjoyed it. I couldn't be sure, I was too scared. All I can recall of our debut was that the curtain went up and then sometime later it came down. What went on in between I could never remember—I was that much in a daze.

But we couldn't have done too badly because the first-night audience did bring us out for several curtain calls. Even more important to me was the fact that the producer told me after the show, a big smile on his face, that the lead role was mine for the rest of the London run.

At Julie's urging, I did have the presence of mind to inquire about a raise in salary. "What salary raise?" the producer asked.

I was surprised by his response. "After all," I said, "I'm playing the lead role, a much larger and more important part."

Then came the awful truth. The fact that we were playing leads was, in his opinion, payment enough, since it would help us get our next show at better prices. Apparently that was the British system at the time, or so I was told. Maybe it was just Herb Morrison's way of making a good deal for himself. I do hope that things have improved for the acting profession in England since I was there.

To say that *Good News* was the biggest thing ever to hit the boards in London would be an exaggeration. For about eight weeks we drew the West End crowd and things went well.

Though most Londoners knew next to nothing about American football and its glorious traditions, the costumes worn by the chorus in the football scenes were terrific, and Julie and I always managed to bring a big round of applause with our rendition of the Varsity Drag. Londoners as a rule have always been very respectful to American musicals, no matter how far-fetched the book.

The queerest part of the show—and I do mean queer—was the chorus. Those British lads, all selected to depict tough American football players, constituted the gayest group I have ever encountered in all my years in show business. The manner in which they lisped their lines—particularly in the scene where the coach, played by Ray Lloyd, is giving them a pep talk between halves—was enough to make Jim Thorpe turn over in his grave.

Then there was a comic in the show, Pat West, who played the part of the trainer. He should have stayed in burlesque. One piece of business called for him to keep shaking salt over his shoulder for good luck. He thought the more salt he shook, the more they would laugh. To make sure the salt was visible to the audience, he used ten-penny nails to enlarge the holes in the shaker.

This created a problem for Julie and me because we had to follow him with the Varsity Drag. Every night the stage was covered with the white stuff, making it difficult for us to move with any degree of safety. I begged Pat to limit the area of his salt-shaking, since sooner or later one of us was going to slip.

Pat ignored my admonition. Sure enough, one night I not only lost my footing, I flipped in the air and landed seated in the footlights with my legs dangling into the orchestra pit. The audience, of course, exploded with laughter. Even my darling Julie could hardly contain herself. In fact I don't think she tried. She laughed so hard that tears began flowing down her cheeks.

Try as I might, I found it almost impossible to extricate

myself from my awkward position. After what seemed like a lifetime, with Julie's help, I struggled to my feet. Making the best
of the situation, I pretended I was picking footlight glass out of
the seat of my pants. The audience continued to laugh hysterically, so I milked it for all it was worth.

After the show, the manager said it was the funniest bit he
had ever seen on any stage. Would I care to repeat it every
performance?

"You must be out of your mind. I nearly broke my neck," I
retorted. "But for an extra ten quid I'll try it."

On another night we arrived at the Carlton to learn that the
Prince of Wales was expected to attend that evening's
performance. The news electrified the entire company. Prince
Edward had that kind of personality. He was without question
the most popular figure in the British Isles and was greatly admired in America as well. Just as important, if he liked the
show it wouldn't do us any harm at the box office.

Typically, the Prince arrived with his party just as the curtain went up. Julie was miffed. "What kept him so long?" she
asked, half-kiddingly. But she, like all of us, was happy he was
there. Although a bit uptight, as they say, we tried to do our
best.

All through the first act we kept getting reports from the
ushers on the Prince's reactions. We got word he wasn't reacting
at all. To our horror we learned that the Prince appeared to be
dozing towards the close of the act. That really got us nervous.
If the word spread that His Highness didn't like the show, we
had had it.

Fortunately, during intermission the Prince fortified himself
with several drinks and appeared to be having a wonderful time
during the second act. He laughed and applauded and seemed
to enjoy himself, shall I say, royally. When Julie and I finished
our version of the Varsity Drag the Prince rose to his feet. He
may even have whistled, I'm not sure. But he liked it and from
then on we loved him!

The fact that the Prince had remained for the final curtain apparently was the tip-off that he liked the entire show. That was the word that quickly got out to the general public, and *Good News* was assured of a long run. We were in.

There was one other performance at the Carlton that I'll never forget. While doing a number with Julie, I looked up and saw what looked like smoke seeping through the doors in the back of the theater. Turning away from the audience, I whispered to Julie that I thought the place was on fire and to keep her cool and just keep on doing what we were doing, lest we alarm the audience. By the middle of the number it was so thick that we could barely see the audience—but there was no panic. I couldn't understand it.

Once offstage, however, we learned the truth. What was coming through the doors was one of those heavy fogs for which London is famous. By now it was coming in so heavily that literally we could barely see each other. But because of the lighting on the stage, the audience could see us, though we couldn't see a thing beyond the footlights. It was a weird experience indeed.

What was even more weird was leaving the theater and discovering that because of the thick pea-souper, no taxis were available. I had heard of London fogs (after all, I was a Sherlock Holmes fan), but you really have to experience one to believe it. You couldn't see a foot ahead of you. Julie and I had two guests that night—Morton Downey and Mark Hellinger—and we had no alternative but to walk, or rather grope, all the way home to Grosvenor House on Park Lane, which suddenly seemed to be a hundred miles away.

The Grosvenor House was pretty posh digs for a couple of youngsters who didn't make too much money. It was brand-new; in fact, only one wing had been finished. But we managed to pay our bills.

One of the problems of London accomodations, at least in our time, was that our British cousins don't value heat as much as Americans do. By the time we got home the place would be near the freezing point. I think the engineer used to go in the boiler room in the morning, turn the valves and give the radiators a little squirt of steam, and that was it for the day.

Consequently I arranged with the head porter, the sergeant major, a gracious elderly man, to prepare a hot toddy for me every night before bed. The toddies were delightfully warming and relaxing, but when I got the bill for our first two weeks at the hotel, my eyes nearly popped out. The cost of the toddies was astronomical. The concoctions I had been drinking and enjoying so much were made with Napoleon brandy, imported limes, and I'm sure the sugar was mixed with a little diamond dust, judging from the price.

I chided the porter, "You shouldn't have done that."

He seemed somewhat hurt. "Nothing but the best for you, sir," he said. "You're one of my favorite people."

Needless to say, I was embarrassed. His great heart made up for my lack of head. But I must confess that after drinking those toddies I did sleep like Napoleon.

Also stopping at the Grosvenor were Fred and Adele Astaire. This fine brother-and-sister team was starring in the London company of the hit they had appeared in on Broadway, *Funny Face.* We became great friends and spent a good deal of time together. There was a store in Mayfair that specialized in American canned goods. The girls would display their culinary skills by cooking such gourmet delights as hot dogs and baked beans and spaghetti and meat balls. Many were the nights the four of us wished for a Reuben,s Special sandwich. I'm sure had Arnold Reuben known, he would have sent them over.

There was another American in the show, who was not as at home in London. He was Ed Gargan, actor Bill Gargan's brother, who must have played New York cops in a thousand Hollywood films. Naturally, he played a cop in our show.

Ed was as Irish as Paddy's pig. He hated the British with a vengeance before he even met them. To him, everything in

England was horrible. The food was bad (about which there could be little argument) and the weather was bad (about which there could be less argument). In short, Ed Gargan was constantly looking for a reason to defend Ireland's honor and right the wrongs of six hundred years of history.

One matinee day, Ed came to the theater blowing his top. He said he had had it up to his ears. His hotel accomodations were execrable—except he used another word. His room was filthy, and the housekeeper refused to change his sheets and towels more than once a week.

"If there's one thing an Irishman must insist upon, it's clean linens," he shouted. I suspected a trace of brandy on his breath.

"Since when?" someone asked.

"Who's the dirty no-good so-and-so who said that?" he demanded, looking around angrily. In his mood, no one dared to confess.

Finally, I couldn't resist the temptation and I took Ed aside. "Look," I said, "as a protest, why don't you move all your furniture out into the hall? Then they'll have to pay attention to you."

He did just that.

That did it. The hotel manager, accompanied by the sergeant major, came flying up the stairs to ask what in the name of His Majesty's bad health this crazy American thought he was doing. Ed told them where they could go. The manager had a long beard and Gargan likened him to von Tirpitz, the Hun submarine commander. That, as they say, broke the game wide open. There was so much yelling and screaming that the cause of Anglo-American unity must have been set back a decade. Even the arrival of the bobbies failed to dissuade Gargan from shouting his intense dislike of all things British, starting with the King and ending with the manager.

That evening he quit the show, sold his return ticket to the States, and went to Paris on the proceeds.

After *Good News* ended its run in London, we returned to

the States by ship. We embarked at Southampton and crossed the English Channel to pick up passengers at Le Havre, before crossing the Atlantic for home. As I watched the loading of the ship at the French port, I saw Ed Gargan walk up the third class gangplank. His clothes looked well-worn and he obviously had run out of money. He was no longer the fearsome fighter for freedom who only a week or two before had challenged the entire British constabulary.

"Hey, Ed," I yelled. "Look—up here." Ed's Irish countenance beamed as he waved hello.

"Ed," I went on at the top of my lungs, "the manager of the hotel sends his regards."

Ed's smile vanished. The royal blood rushed to his head and once more he was ready for battle. I have a feeling he would have killed me if he could have managed to leap the several decks that separated us.

While in *Good News,* Julie and I were given permission to make nightclub appearances after the show. We first went to work at the Cafe de Paris, where the star attraction was our old friend from home, Morton Downey. After the first performance our reception was so cool that Julie and I thought we were through. We had given our all, but the applause was perfunctory. The nightclub owner, however, said he liked us very much and we were fine.

Maybe we were, but we couldn't understand the lack of enthusiasm on the part of the patrons.

"You just didn't take care of the boys," said Downey, explaining that it was customary in London for entertainers to slip five quid to the headwaiter who would arrange for his waiters, hiding behind posts around the balcony and elsewhere, to whip up a storm of applause after each number—a sort of claque. Thanks to Morton and the waiters there was plenty of enthusiasm the next night.

After the Cafe, we appeared in another of the London smart

places, the Kit Kat Club in Haymarket, which went in big for American entertainers. One of the problems for Americans working in London in those days was the orchestras. They generally were not quite up to the American dance bands, and their rhythm and beat were a little sluggish for ambitious young folks like Julie and me.

Our big London break came when we ran into Sir Francis Towle at a Sunday afternoon tea party. Julie and I had absolutely no idea who Sir Francis was when we engaged him in a lively discussion of the nightclub business. He seemed to know a good deal about the clubs in New York, and when we said we had worked with George Olsen and Emil Coleman he asked, "How would you like to work for me?"

"Do you have a nightclub?" I asked.

"Yes," he said, "I'm the managing director of the Mayfair Hotel."

Julie and I didn't have to be asked twice. We leaped at the offer. The Mayfair, after all, was the finest supper room in town and had by far the best dance orchestra.

"When can you come to work?" Sir Francis asked.

"As soon as I can get my suit pressed," I facetiously replied.

Sir Francis took us at our word and we immediately drove to the Mayfair where he introduced us to Bert Ambrose who, as I have said, led the best orchestra in London. Bert was an American who had decided to stay in England. He became one of the British nation's top recording artists and, as he told me, he was doing much better in England than he might have back home. Besides, he loved London and the British.

This was Sunday evening, and of course there was no dancing on Sunday in those days, so we really had no chance to rehearse. The orchestra played a concert on Sunday, and between numbers we sort of talked over our routines. There was another slight problem—we didn't have any orchestrations of our own.

Bert was patient and understanding and, sure enough, at 11:45 the following night, Murphy and Johnson appeared at the Mayfair Hotel with Bert Ambrose's Orchestra.

Somehow we managed to get through two numbers, a waltz and a schottische, but our third routine was something else again. We hadn't rehearsed and we forgot the routine. We had to stop. That evening I learned an important lesson—that singly you can ad-lib, but when you're dancing with a partner both of you had better know what you're doing.

Deciding to take the bull by the horns, I addressed the smartly-dressed Mayfair audience. "Ladies and gentlemen," I said, "I'm extremely sorry about our performance. My dancing partner Miss Johnson and I met Mr. Ambrose for the first time last night. Since it was a Sunday, we couldn't rehearse, and we have forgotten our routine.

"So forgive us," I went on. "We will expose you tonight to a brand-new experience. We are going to let you see how a dance team rehearses."

There was laughter and a burst of handclapping. Julie and I started again and this time, thank God, remembered the routine. We got off to a great deal of applause.

My impromptu remarks had made such a hit that each night as we finished our second number, the audience would insist on a speech. From then on I would usually comment humorously on something in the newspaper headlines, and little by little I began talking almost as much as dancing.

We had a wonderful engagement at the Mayfair. We had been hired for two weeks, but after we broke all records for attendance, Sir Francis extended us to eight weeks. We literally performed before the crowned heads of Europe. Regular guests were the King of Greece, the Queens of Spain and Romania, and lesser royalty. The ubiquitous Prince of Wales was there almost every night, dancing into the wee hours with some of the more beautiful ladies and then walking home alone to his palace, while all the bobbies on the way turned their backs so as to appear not to notice him. Some nights he even "swayed" a little, but on him it looked good.

The Prince's mother, Queen Mary, was most kind to us on

one occasion. Julie and I had been asked to appear at a ball, the proceeds of which would go to a charity in which Her Majesty was interested. When our turn came to perform, we were brusquely informed that our services were not required that evening. Upon inquiring, we learned that some society lady had got herself a professional partner, prepared a routine or two, and they wanted to exhibit their dancing talents before the Queen. They weren't about to have any transient American kids get in the way.

The Queen, believing this to be a display of bad manners to American visitors, dispatched an equerry with a message asking us not to leave the premises. Naturally, we were pleased and obeyed the royal order. We remained. The regular show went on and then came supper. During the meal, the master of ceremonies announced that "by special request of Her Majesty, the brilliant dance team of Murphy and Johnson" would perform. That night, I think it is fair to say, we deserved the accolade "brilliant."

The Queen's courtesy and kindness will never be forgotten.

Sir Francis turned out to be not only a fine employer but a good friend. He loved Americans and went out of his way to be nice to them. Once, at a luncheon for the American Ambassador, he had Morton Downey, the visiting columnist Mark Hellinger and me as his guests. The one thing I recall about the luncheon—aside from the good-natured joshing at our table— was the anguished orchestra leader who, after playing "God Save the King," didn't know what to play for the Ambassador of the United States. So, while everyone stood at attention, the band played "Ol' Man River." No one seemed to mind, least of all the visiting Americans who thought it all quite amusing.

We were in the closing days of *Good News* when we received a cable from George Olsen:

HAVE SIGNED CONTRACT TO REOPEN ZIEGFELD ROOF. JULIE AND YOU ARE IN SHOW OPENING CHRISTMAS WEEK. HURRY HOME.

This was great news. Until then we had had no idea what we were going to do next. We had been offered a tour of the Riviera and another engagement at the Mayfair, but we were homesick and missed New York. Olsen's wire did the trick. We cabled Olsen we would be back in time.

We arrived in New York on Christmas Eve. A message was waiting for us from Olsen, but it was not exactly cheerful news. He reported that he had had a fight with Flo Ziegfeld and the deal to open the Ziegfeld Roof was off. So we were without a job and we had little money. It was not a very merry Christmas for us at all.

# CHAPTER 7

*Broadway*

Our first big break on Broadway came in the summer of 1929 when we were hired to replace the two leads in the long-running musical *Hold Everything* at the Broadhurst Theater. We were hired by the producers, Alex A. Aarons and Vinton Freedley, both of whom had been in a quandary over who was to take over for their stars, Jack Whiting and Betty Compton.

The show was really a big hit, not so much because of the presence of Whiting and Miss Compton, though they were very good, but largely because of the inspired tomfoolery of Bert Lahr. He was described by one critic as "the most promising low comedian the stage has discovered since Ed Wynn bought his first pair of shell-rimmed glasses." Also in the cast was that genial, gentle comic Victor Moore, and the friendly joshing between Moore and Lahr was a joy to behold.

The story line was nothing extraordinary. It was about a young prize fighter who nearly was fed knockout drops on the eve of the big fight but somehow managed to avoid all sorts of perfidies to emerge victorious in the ring.

Jack Whiting played the young boxer "Sonny Jim" Brooks, who loved a sweet girl played by Ona Munson. But another girl—socialite Norine Lloyd (Miss Compton)—took a fancy to him. . .

Not much by today's standards, but with its songs, dances, girls and general exuberance *Hold Everything* became a smash hit. The show had opened in October 1928 to generally excellent reviews. By the following summer, however, Jack Whiting and Miss Compton had other engagements. Miss Compton, who was being ardently courted by New York's dapper Mayor Jimmy Walker, went on to appear with Billy Gaxton in *Fifty Million Frenchmen*.

Bert Lahr did a great deal to bolster the show. His was not the kind of humor that can easily be described. He had a face seemingly made of India rubber and he was given to sudden explosions of weird sounds. In *Hold Everything* he played a bellowing punch-drunk fighter. One of his scenes was so ludicrous that it invariably dissolved audiences into deep-throated laughter. This was a dressing room bit in which Lahr would shadowbox with himself and finally knock himself down. When picked up from the floor, he would say, "Don't bother me—I'm winning."

This was our first Broadway show, and Julie and I were thrilled to be replacing such stars as Betty Compton and Jack Whiting. They were indeed names to be reckoned with in the late Twenties. Fame is fleeting in the theater, however. Today these once-vibrant actors have long been forgotten. Except perhaps for Miss Compton, who is probably better remembered as the paramour and later the wife of Jimmy Walker.

We played at the Broadhurst Theater for eight weeks and then went on the road, performing in such cities as Chicago and Detroit. Needless to say, we did extremely well in Detroit where our friends and relatives packed the theater. Our personal reviews in the newspapers were good, and Julie and I felt that at last we were on our way to fame and fortune.

But, alas, the Great Depression was upon us. Things were bad all over, but they were particularly bad in show business. Fortunately Julie and I kept busy, always managing to make a living. Others in our profession were not doing as well. We were, after all, in a luxury business, one that catered to affluence. People had less money and were more careful about spending it.

In the summer of 1931, while the country was deep in the throes of economic crisis, Julie and I got our next important opportunity. This was in a Broadway revue called *Shoot the Works* which was the brainchild of that iconoclastic columnist and friend of ours from Barney Gallant days, Heywood Broun.

What Broun sought to do with *Shoot the Works* was to shake Broadway out of its doldrums. The show was conceived on the notion that actors could be self-supporting if only they banded together. The few backers whom Broun induced to help finance the show were warned that the most they could expect was to get their money back—which, in those depression days, wasn't too bad a prospect. I rather suspect that the chief angel was Broun himself.

As a matter of fact, we had practically no scenery, no props, and the sketches and music were donated. Broun was a pretty fair promoter.

Of course, Broun had something else going for him. He knew almost everybody who was anybody and did not hesitate to put the arm on some well-known literary figure or songwriter for a sketch or a song. Those who contributed sketches to *Shoot the Works* included Dorothy Parker, Harry Hershfield, Nunnally Johnson, Peter Arno, E.B. White and Broun himself. Music and lyrics were by people like Irving Berlin, E.Y. Harburg, Ira Gershwin, Dorothy Fields and Jimmy McHugh.

Nevertheless, Broun did achieve a record of sorts when he brought the show in on opening night for less than six thousand dollars. Today that kind of money would about pay for the electricity. Broun had made a deal with the various theatrical unions whereby they wouldn't hit him too hard. Only the chorus girls were guaranteed a weekly income. The rest of us were supposed to divide up what was left.

Production costs, as a consequence, were kept to the barest minimum. One chorus number was specially constructed around some large Mexican straw hats which had been left in the theater basement from a previous production. The idea was for the girls to cavort around the hats on stage. There was one drawback—the straw was infested with biting insects.

The choreographer was Johnny Boyle, who in my book was possibly the greatest dancer of all time. He also appeared in

*Shoot the Works.*  Most critics agreed he had one of the best-looking chorus lines in town. And why not? Heywood Broun, who had an eye for pulchritude, picked the girls himself. One girl he personally selected, a small, black-haired beauty named Connie Madison, he later married.

The star of the show was none other than Heywood Broun, a big, shaggy hulk of a man who conceded he was a frustrated ham. Outside of Broun there were no big names in the cast—it consisted mostly of young, little-known people. Some of us went on to achieve greater prominence. A waif-like creature who sang a plaintive song in the show years later became an outstanding television star. Her name was Imogene Coca.

The night before the show opened Broun called Julie and me into his office. He informed us that Irving Berlin had just donated a song to the show, something called "Begging for Love."

"This will be your number," Broun said. "Do with it what you want, but don't spend any money." We had twenty-four hours to get a number together, because as Heywood said, "We mustn't disappoint Irving."

We came up with a simple production routine. I stood downstage and sang the song while Julie sat upstage on top of a stepladder. The curtains covered all of her except for her face, which was illuminated by a pin spot. After I finished the first chorus, the pin spot faded out. Then I sang another eight bars of the melody, giving Julie time to climb down the ladder and suddenly appear out of darkness to join me for the dance.

We didn't have too much time to rehearse the Berlin tune, but we did it well. At least the first-night audience thought so. The reviews were excellent. What we didn't know until several years later was that our performance had been observed by Otto Harbach and Jerome Kern. They were writing *Roberta* at the time and they liked the way Julie and I looked on the stage. So much so that we were the first two people signed when they began casting *Roberta*.

*Shoot the Works* opened on July 21, 1931 on a night that turned out to be the hottest of the year. This was before air conditioning and to get some air into the theater all the doors were kept open. The cast had to compete with the street noises. Somehow we managed.

Despite the heat, the theater was packed with Broun aficionados who had come to watch their writer-hero perform. Even Broun's mortal enemy, Mayor Walker, whom the columnist was excoriating in print almost daily, could not resist the unusual spectacle. When the final curtain came down, Broun made a little speech.

"Just begin your review," he advised Walter Winchell, who was sitting front row center, "by saying that *Shoot the Works* is swell, and go on from there."

Actually the reviews were only so-so, but despite them we managed to do eight weeks at the George M. Cohan Theater. And I can't tell you how important those eight weeks were to the Murphys.

Like most revues, the show had a very thin story line. In the first scene I was a song plugger trying to sell various tunes to Broun, who played a newcomer about to produce a show. As I was doing the fast-talking supersalesman, Broun kept fortifying his judgment from a flask. The more he drank, the more enthusiastic he became about the songs, until he finally bought them all—blackout—and the show was off to a flying start.

The rest of *Shoot the Works* consisted of sketches built around the songs I had "sold" Broun. The whole thing was kind of an audition—only the audition became the show.

Many were the occasions when I wondered whether Broun wasn't drinking the real stuff from that flask. That the columnist liked to tipple a bit was no secret to anyone in the know. On several occasions when he began his famous column with, "As I walked briskly through the crisp fall air on the way to my office—" I happened to know he hadn't been out of bed, much less out of his apartment.

One night he arrived at the theater just before curtain time and quite seriously said, "George, I've had too much to drink and I don't know whether I can go on tonight." I've never seen a more honestly contrite character and he did indeed look as if he was about to topple over. I dispatched a chorus boy to the drugstore on the corner for some spirits of ammonia. Broun sniffed the stuff for a while, brightened up like a spring sunrise and said he felt fine. So fine that no sooner had I gone back to my dressing room than he took another drink. Then he sniffed the spirits again. Another drink. Need I say more?

He somehow managed to get through the first act, but at intermission he collapsed. He had definitely overtrained.

No one knew what to do. We were still trying to find the answer when the curtain went up for the second act. I was in the opening number and as I scanned the audience I saw the answer—seated in the third row was the famous monologist Julius Tannen. Julius could do five, ten or fifty minutes on a moment's notice, and he was good, too. So I stopped my scene, walked to the front of the stage and, peering over the footlights, said, "Excuse me, ladies and gentlemen. Mr. Tannen, would you please come backstage quickly? You won't believe the message I have for you."

One of the finest performers of his day, Tannen was a forerunner of Bob Hope, Milton Berle and even Henny Youngman, the self-styled King of the One-Liners. Besides his great wit, Tannen was a gentleman. Realizing that something was amiss, he rushed backstage and readily agreed to appear as a substitute for Broun who, by this time, was lost to the world.

Tannen more than filled the bill. For about half an hour he let loose a string of gags which had the audience in stitches. He opened up with something like this: "Pardon me, ladies and gentlemen, for being so late—I squeezed out too much toothpaste and couldn't get it back."

By the close of the show that night, Heywood was back on spirits of ammonia and on his feet again. In a typical gesture, he insisted that the entire cast be called on stage whereupon he made a full confession, a full apology, and fulsomely thanked Tannen and everyone for carrying on. Then he took off for the Stork Club to start training for the next performance.

Salaries were an on-and-off thing in *Shoot the Works*. They varied from week to week. It was a sort of cooperative venture where everyone shared the take. It was understood that as a team Julie and I were entitled to only a single share in the venture, but Broun didn't agree. Nor did the cast, which held a special meeting and voted that we were each entitled to a separate share, since we not only worked as a dance team, but also did individual sketches and numbers.

We did well the weeks when Broun did well in his traditional Saturday night poker games. These were famous high-stake sessions out on Long Island, and the players included such monied notables as Bernard Baruch, Herbert Bayard Swope and George Gershwin. When Broun did well at poker, our salaries were usually very good, but when he lost we were in trouble. Heywood had a lot of people pulling for him in those Saturday night games.

One night Broun got really ill and could not appear. His doctor ordered him to bed for an extended rest. The cast decided that without Broun there should be no show. Broun, after all, was the chief attraction and his name was bringing in the people. And so ended *Shoot the Works*, which in retrospect was an extraordinary venture in the American theater. I must say it was a very pleasant engagement.

Julie and I really felt we'd made the grade when we were engaged to perform at the Central Park Casino. This was the top spot in New York. The Casino, located just inside the park about one hundred feet west of Fifth Avenue near Seventy-second Street, was probably the most beautiful nightclub in the world. It attracted a nightly patronage that could only be described as a veritable Who's Who In New York. The clientele was the finest, the food the best, the atmosphere perfect, and dress, of course, was formal. Barbara Hutton, Jules Bache, Harry Content, Mrs. William Randolph Hearst, and the Jim Farleys were some of the regulars.

The proprietor of this establishment was Sidney Solomon, who had been a ready-to-wear dress salesman and fancied himself a gourmet, having traveled widely through the kitchens of Europe. He had obtained the lease for this city-owned property from his buddy, Mayor Jimmy Walker, and had then spent about a quarter of a million dollars—a huge sum of money in those days—to refurbish and decorate the sixty-year-old building. Nothing but the best was Solomon's credo. Sidney had dreamed of this club for years, and when Jim Walker was elected it became a reality.

To decorate the premises, Solomon hired a Viennese named Joseph Urban, probably the best scenic designer of the period, who had gained his pre-eminent reputation designing sets and costumes for the great Ziegfeld. Joe Urban outdid even himself at the Casino. There were to be two ballrooms plus a separate dining room and a beautiful terrace, open in summer and glassed in during the winter, which was truly the talk of the town.

Walker had his own private retreat upstairs—a spectacular room, ostensibly Sid Solomon's office, with walls covered with green silk, furniture upholstered in green, a gold leaf ceiling and a blue tiled bath and shower. From here the business of the great metropolis was often conducted, and there were sometimes complaints that the Mayor of the City of New York spent more time here than he did at City Hall. Looking over the record of some other mayors, I think New York might like to have Jim Walker back. He did a fine job for New York, even if he did spend a lot of time uptown.

The Casino was surrounded by stonework and was kept cool in the summer months by a fountain that played on the roof. In the wintertime, with snow piled up around it, it had a Currier and Ives look. You almost expected sleighs to pull up at the door.

As for the interior, Joe Urban provided the press with the following description before the opening: "The moods of each room are established through rhythmic line and sensuous color, and in the whole composition each room plays up to the next room. In the main dining room, broad surfaces of silver give a living neutral background to a pulsating rhythm of maroon and green. In the ballroom, the line of mural composition is like the wave of a conductor's baton beginning the dance music. . . . In the pavilion the freshness of spring flowers and joyousness of a wind among young leaves inspires the decorations. . . ."

As they used to say in those days, the Casino was a "classy joint" and Sid Solomon kept it that way. Only the finest entertainment was provided. He had two bands going at one time. One was Emil Coleman's, the most famous dance orchestra in New York, while in another room Leo Reisman played the melodic, society-styled dance music that appealed to everyone, young and old. Sid Solomon soon found out that sometimes one band is better than two and he wound up with Leo Reisman. Emil went back to the Waldorf where he became a regular fixture.

Reisman, incidentally, featured two piano players, Nat Brandwynne and a youngster named Eddy Duchin. Brandwynne undoubtedly was the better musician, but Duchin had a far more pleasing personality and a musical style that was never matched. He did to a keyboard what Fred Astaire does with a dance floor. Some I've heard have come close, but no one has ever equalled him. He was very handsome and well-mannered, and when he played, the ladies were completely mesmerized.

Solomon and Reisman had a personality problem. Reisman, a fairly wild-looking honcho, took to staring at some of the ladies and they didn't like it. Neither did Solomon.

Being no dope, Solomon knew he had something big going with Duchin. So one night when Reisman threatened to quit in a huff, Sidney took him at his word, paid him off, and told Duchin the band was his. From then on there was rarely an empty table at the Casino. (Incidentally, one of the relief pianists was a black-haired youngster, Carmen Cavallaro. When *The Eddy Duchin Story* was filmed in Hollywood in the early fifties, the part of Eddy was played by Tyrone Power and the music for the picture was recorded by Cavallaro.)

These being the waning days of Prohibition, no liquor was sold on the Casino premises. The general practice was that patrons would bring their own liquor. Soda water, however, cost three dollars a bottle and there was a three-dollar cover charge for each customer. Somehow Jimmy Walker always managed to have a bottle of properly chilled champagne waiting at his table. But the Mayor was a special customer and he deserved special treatment. I was told once that his refreshments were kept stashed in an automobile parked near the Casino driveway. Maybe so.

Solomon was his own admissions committee and he kept out undesirables. My old friend Louis Sobol, who was always kind to me in his Broadway column, has since reported this episode in his book of reminiscences. *The Longest Street:* "I recall a night in the early thirties when Sidney Solomon . . . stared coldly as three couples entered, the men immaculate in dinner suits, the girls, all blondes, in evening gowns right from Paris. It was an opening night for a couple of attractive ballroom dancers— George and Julie Murphy . . . Solomon didn't think these couples seeking admission were his type of people, and when his headwaiter demurred at his command to order them to leave, he stalked over himself, and addressing himself to the obvious leader of the group, said, 'Sorry, there isn't a table left in the place—we're sold out.'

"And though the girls pouted and two of the men glowered, the chap to whom Solomon had made his address merely smirked and without any further protest led the little company out. It was absolutely unbelievable to some of us who watched and had overheard, and I saw a potential page one story leave with them. For the leader of the unwelcome group was the ruthless murderer and mob chief, 'Dutch' Schultz!"

Gangsters were not the only people the imperious proprietor barred from his ornate palace. For some undisclosed reason, Solomon had a hate on for one of the city's most prominent public officials, Robert Moses. And he kept him from entering his establishment. In turn Moses vowed that, once Jimmy Walker left City Hall, he would "plow the Casino under." That's pretty much what happened when Fiorello LaGuardia became Mayor. As the city's Park Commissioner, Bob Moses ordered the demolition of Solomon's pride and joy, and so passed the city's finest nightclub and, as far as I'm concerned, the finest I've seen anywhere in the world.

Solomon had another set rule—no Broadway producers were welcome. Sid's explanation was that if he allowed a producer into the Casino he would bring some of his "cuties" with him and some of the gentlemen customers would be eyeing the girls and this would cause trouble and would be bad for business. He also barred newspapermen after one had written a bad column about him.

Solomon was an oddball in other ways. He dressed peculiarly, at least for the times. He always wore tight pants, jackets with very tight sleeves and vests with precisely eleven buttons. As he talked to you he continually shot his cuffs and kept looking over his shoulder like a racetrack tout making a fast pitch.

He liked to tipple, but when he had too much to drink he would sometimes do things for which he would be very sorry later. One New Year's Eve, an inebriated Solomon for some unknown reason got so angry with Eddy Duchin and his band that he fired them all and ordered them off the premises—this despite the fact that it was about 11:30 P.M. and the Casino was crowded with people who had paid forty dollars a plate to ring in the New Year with Eddy Duchin and the Casino crowd.

Duchin appealed to me for help. "The guy's *meshugge*," he said. "He doesn't know what he's doing."

"Well, let me take care of it," I told him, although I didn't know quite what to do.

It was about fifteen minutes before midnight. The crowd was growing restless. The band had been off the bandstand longer than usual and the customers wanted to dance. They wanted to be on the dance floor, arms around their favorite lady, when the clock struck twelve o'clock.

Suddenly I had an inspiration. "Come with me," I told Duchin. I took him into the back room and sent for the still-angry Solomon. I then let loose a string of insults the likes of which you wouldn't believe. I called Solomon every name in the book. I referred to his parentage, his looks, his manners and every other thing I could think of. Solomon couldn't say a word—he was in shock. I gave Eddy the high sign to take off and start playing.

By the time Sid got his wits back, Eddy was back on the bandstand and the floor was crowded. That wonderful magic moment of midnight, New Year's Eve, had arrived.

While Eddy played "Auld Lang Syne," Solomon was still telling me, in various ways, what a no-good ingrate I was and why he should never have hired me in the first place. I wished him a very happy new year and walked out, leaving him sputtering in a by now somewhat diminished rage.

Eddy Duchin and I became very good friends in the three years Julie and I appeared at the Casino. Eventually he married one of the young socialites who frequented the club, the lovely Marjorie Oelrichs. Tragedy hit hard when Eddy's wife died giving birth to Peter Duchin, who himself has become a most popular society orchestra leader. I don't know young Peter well, but I hope he has his dad's gentle charm as well as his talent.

There was one occasion when a feud arose between Solomon and Jules Glaenzer, the distinguished man-about-town and vice-president of Cartier Inc. Glaenzer, who liked to give big parties and entertain pretty girls at the Casino, was an insatiable tango dancer. One Sunday night he asked Duchin to play Latin-type music. But the other guests obviously preferred to do two-steps and waltzes. This annoyed Solomon, who was always a little jealous of Glaenzer anyway because he couldn't dance. "Don't play any more tangos," he ordered Duchin.

Glaenzer was offended, thinking this was a personal attack on him. I guess today we would call it an invasion of his civil rights. One word led to a real argument, and Duchin and I suggested that the proper way to settle a matter of honor was a duel.

We told a few newspaper columnists that Glaenzer had issued the challenge and Solomon had accepted, and that the choice of weapons was undecided and might take some time. Solomon and Glaenzer, both slight figures physically, took the well-advertised feud seriously, but you never saw two guys less anxious for the fatal day. They even went to separate gymnasia to prepare for the big event. It became the talk of Broadway, and on Wall Street the odds would shift back and forth according to the latest rumors.

For weeks they argued about weapons. When Eddy and I thought the nonsense had been played out, we announced that they would battle it out with bows and arrows at one hundred paces, and everyone knew that the whole thing was a big joke since neither Jules nor Sid could see a hundred yards. The would-be combatants, relieved, shook hands and forgot their feud.

I was present at the Casino when a real feud had unpleasant consequences. This was the night of a big birthday party for William Gaxton, then starring in *Of Thee I Sing*. Notables of all kinds were present—probably the finest and most select gathering of Broadway and Park Avenue since the old Mayfair Club closed.

Everyone seemed to be having a glorious time. Love was in the air. Sam Harris and George White, who had been feuding for years, made up. They even did a little dance together to demonstrate the end of their quarrel. What the quarrel was about I can't remember, but to them it was important. Morton Downey sang. Ethel Merman sang. The DeMarcos danced. Crosby sang. Ed Wynn entertained.

Producer Earl Carroll was there, accompanied as usual by two beautiful showgirls. A few tables away sat Walter Winchell. Several years before, the columnist had testified in federal court about a party at which a bathtub contained champagne and a very nude young lady. Winchell had testified that the host of the party was Earl Carroll, and the producer was sent to Atlanta for one year. At the time, Carroll publicly vowed that one day he would embarrass Winchell as much as Winchell had embarrassed him.

When Carroll was introduced at the Gaxton party, he rose up like a great dignified gray ghost. "Walter Winchell," Carroll said, his voice as cold as a Vermont icicle. "Walter Winchell," he repeated, "if you have one spark of decency in your makeup, which I doubt very much, you will realize that you are not fit to sit in the same room with ladies and gentlemen such as are gathered here tonight and you will get your hat and coat and leave."

The room was hushed. No one said a word. The seconds ticked away. Winchell, who was sitting next to Mayor Walker, did not make a move. In fact, no one moved. Finally, Carroll motioned to his guests. Accompanied by the girls, he stalked out.

That was the end of Billy Gaxton's party. The festive air had disappeared. A group of us repaired to Reuben's, a favorite after-midnight eating spot for notables. There we ran into Ed Sullivan, Winchell's competitor on the New York Daily News. They were more than competitors. Their dislike of each other was legendary. Someone told Sullivan of Carroll's outburst. Sullivan's exclusive story the next morning was headlined something like this: GAXTON BIRTHDAY PARTY BREAKS UP

IN BRAWL. When Gaxton read that, he wanted to belt Sullivan. Oh, it was a memorable evening!

Whatever else may be said of Winchell, he was a powerful influence in New York. A man with that kind of power can't always be loved. My own relations with the columnist were always of the best, so I don't have any particular axe to grind. But it should be noted that, in getting to the top of his profession, Winchell undoubtedly hurt some people. On the other hand, his "orchids"—as he described his plaudits—helped considerably in furthering a lot of careers. And his public feud with Ben Bernie, the famous bandleader, was without question one of the finest public relations jobs ever.

In recent years, Walter has mellowed considerably. He has gone out of his way to restore good personal relations with people with whom he had feuded for years. In this spirit, he even extended the olive branch to Ed Sullivan, who also decided to let bygones be bygones.

For the most part, Julie and I had a wonderful time working for the Central Park Casino. As Mort Downey would say, "The pay wasn't so great, but it was the best place to book out of." We did have one problem. For all the money he was making, Sid Solomon rarely had enough in the bank to cover his checks.

One night Ethel Merman threatened to make a scene because one of Solomon's checks had bounced. That had become an old story with Julie and me. I tried to calm her down.

"Now, Ethel," I said, "don't get mad at Uncle Sidney. He doesn't mean any harm. He's just got lots of problems."

"Yeah," she replied, "one of them is this rotten check."

"Well, I'll see what I can do."

I walked over to the table where Solomon was sitting with a Wall Street character and explained the situation. Solomon, who had heard it all before, just said, "Tell Ethel to be patient." I explained that Ethel was at the end of her patience and was threatening not to sing that night.

With a shrug of boredom, Solomon turned to his stockbroker friend and said, "Make out a check, Harry." Harry did so. I gave the check to Ethel. The next night Miss Merman was doubly furious. Harry's check had bounced.

One reason that Solomon was always broke was that he was a compulsive gambler—and loser. He always had about twenty thousand dollars (a considerable fortune in those days) in bad checks floating in midair between the Casino and his debtors. For a while, the milkman and the grocers would unload only when the cash was at the door.

But in spite of his idiosyncrasies, Solomon had the finest nightclub ever.

When Julie and I finally ended our three wonderful, never-to-be-forgotten years at the Casino, Uncle Sidney owed us about seven thousand dollars. We had the bad checks to prove it. After a great deal of bellowing on my part, Solomon promised to pay us off on April 5, 1933. I remember the date because that was the day Prohibition finally expired.

That night Julie and I were at a big party at the Plaza Hotel celebrating the end of the Great Experiment. The party was being given by May and Wadell Ketchings and it was a lulu, with plenty of bubbly at hand. I was having a good time when Julie nudged me at the stroke of midnight. She reminded me that I was supposed to get our seven thousand bucks from Solomon.

"Oh, honey," I said, "let's wait until the party is over."

"Nothing doing," Julie replied. "You go up there right now and get it. If you don't get it, just don't come back."

Handed such an ultimatum, I grabbed a cab and drove uptown to the Casino. For once I didn't have to argue with Solomon. He took me into the kitchen, opened the cash register, and handed me a wad of bills that totalled what he owed us. I was so astonished that I forgot to return his bad checks and he forgot to ask for them.

I had them framed and sent them to him the following Christmas.

# CHAPTER 8

## *The Joints of Old New York*

Mention New York and I think not only of one of the great cities of the world but of a city that was very good to me, a city that took me in when I was alone and gave me the opportunity to do what I wanted to do, a city that provided me with a wealth of experience and many a laugh, as well as a few heartbreaks.

This is a city where even today I can walk down the street and a cab driver will yell out, "Hey, Murph, how's it going?" And a policeman will give me a big smile as though I hadn't been away. When I was there last year to receive the Irish Historical Society medal, I was more honored by the old friends who showed up, like Jim Farley, Ed Hogan, Joe Sullivan and others, than by the fine words of the toastmaster.

It's a city where I am still welcomed not only by cabbies and policemen, but by waiters and doormen, and even the little old ladies who question politely, "Didn't you used to be George Murphy?"

It fills me with sadness when I hear of the old haunts going out of business. One of these places was Dinty Moore's, the citadel of corned beef-and-cabbage made famous by George McManus' *Maggie & Jiggs* cartoon strip. Now, as I understand it, Moore's has been taken over by a real estate combine and is being continued under a new management.

I spent many happy hours at Moore's in the heart of the theatrical world on West Forty-sixth Street. It was a restaurant renowned for its corned beef hash, oxtail ragout, kosher-liver-cum-Irish-bacon and a superb gefilte fish made every Friday by a matronly Jewish lady from the Bronx, which attracted more Irish than Jews.

Until he died, the restaurant was also famed for its founder-proprietor, Jim (Dinty) Moore. Jim was a breed unto himself. He almost patented the gift of blarney, invariably dominating any conversation in his restaurant. His tales, particularly of the old days and the athletes he knew, were wondrous indeed.

Jim Moore kept his lobsters alive by feeding them oatmeal. His steaks were great. And if you liked the Broadway atmosphere, you had to love Moore's. I would guess that more big theatrical deals were consummated in Moore's than in all the offices on Broadway. All the inside news of the town was exchanged there daily, or should I say nightly.

Once old Jim told us of a chap called "Rats" McGowan, whom he described as the toughest man who ever lived in Hells Kitchen. According to Moore, "Rats" got his name because of his penchant for biting off the heads of live rats in saloons for drinks. "Rats" was also the catcher on the baseball team. He never wore a catcher's glove and half the time he wouldn't even bother to catch a ball. Instead, he would let the ball hit his midsection and then flip it back to the pitcher with his belly. The prettiest part of the whole thing, according to Jim, was that "Rats" smoked a pipe through the entire game. He had endless stories of the old days, and it's a shame we didn't have tape recorders to record those wonderful stories.

The night before the Notre Dame-Army football game, a group of us—including the original "Four Horsemen" from South Bend—sat around a table at Moore's. I saw Jim coming and suggested that as a joke we not allow him to get into the conversation. He sat down as was his wont, and tried to open his mouth. We ignored him and talked right over him and around him and by him. He got angrier and angrier.

Finally he blurted out that Frankie Frisch was the greatest base runner ever to play in baseball. As far as I was concerned, this was too good to let pass by. I said that was nonsense. But Jim insisted that Frisch could slide in from thirty feet off the bag right on his wishbone.

"Show us how he did it," I challenged him. Jim was so steamed up at this point he ran across the marble floor of his restaurant and slid right into a table. We had to rush him to Bellevue Hospital. Thank God he was not injured. He would do anything to get the spotlight.

Usually I would drop in at Moore's for late breakfast. This would be about eleven o'clock and I would be allowed to have my bacon and eggs in the back room with a lot of other late-rising Broadway habitués, including a few of questionable character like Larry Fay, Johnny Irish and Tough Willie McCabe. These were the sort of people who provided Damon Runyon with some of his choicer stories.

Larry Fay was one of the funniest men I've ever listened to and a remarkable mathematician besides. He broke an early building trades strike in the Bronx by putting in more tough guys then the union could muster. He also owned a night hawk cab business, and at one point is reputed to have jumped into one of his own cabs about two a.m. and told the driver, said to be George Raft, "Take me to Hollywood."

"Where is that, boss—in Brooklyn?" Raft asked.

"No, you dope—it's in California," Fay reportedly said. And that's how George Raft is supposed to have first made the scene on the Coast.

In the back room at Moore's, Jim would show us how he prepared what he claimed to be "the greatest hamburger in the world." He would put an enormous amount of chopped meat into a huge bowl, then about two inches of salt and pepper, then a big layer of onions, more meat, more salt and pepper, and more onions—then he would mix it all up.

After watching him perform this daily ritual, I asked him, "Don't you think you're using a lot of salt?"

"You're damned right I am," Moore replied. "You'll have to have at least three glasses of beer with every hamburger."

Jim Moore had other gimmicks with which to promote his wares. In wintertime he would place freshly-baked mince pies in convenient locations around his restaurant. "Once they smell that mincemeat pie," he said, "they won't be able to resist ordering a piece." As usual, he knew what he was doing.

I'll never forget one morning when Jim suggested I try a new dish, a strawberry omelette. While I was eating it, he came over and asked, "How do you like it?"

"Pretty good," I replied.

Whereupon he called a waiter over and said, "Get me a menu." Using his pen, he marked the price of the omelette up from seventy-five cents to one dollar—and I was only half finished.

There was another happening at Moore's I'll never forget. A well-known agent on Broadway, Billy Grady, was a regular; he had had his dinner in Moore's every night for at least ten years. He and Jim Moore were close pals. But one night Grady ordered hamburger without onions and Moore had him ejected bodily and refused to let him back until Billy Gaxton and I had a petition signed by every celebrity in town to please let him back before he starved to death.

Later on Grady went to Hollywood and was the head of the casting office at M-G-M for many years. He had a lot to do with bringing the great Spencer Tracy to Metro-Goldwyn-Mayer.

There were hundreds of other fantastic characters who came into my life during the late Twenties and the early Thirties, including Walter Batchelor, Leo "Deep Dish" Fitzgerald, Johnny Boyle, Hymie Miller, Broadway Rose, Billy LaHiff, King Levinsky—oh, I could go on and on.

Texas Guinan, for example. Miss Guinan looked like an old-time Western showgirl should look—big, gusty and busty. She ran two or three late spots which were very popular, particularly with the "butter and eggs" men who came to the big town from the Middle West to have a fling. These "suckers," as Miss Guinan affectionately dubbed them to their face, always brought money. She managed to extract as much of it as possible from them. They loved it.

They bought grape juice spiked with alcohol, made in Jersey, at $25 a pitcher and paid $5 a seat for the privilege. They saw the lovely Ruby Keeler dance, watched the classic antics of Clayton, Jackson & Durante and if they stayed late, they could watch George Raft, the greatest Charleston dancer of all time. Who knows, on a clear night they might even get to see His Honor the Mayor at ringside.

Once Texas had a night spot in the Hotel Abbey off Seventh Avenue. I was coming from the Madrid Club with Louie Schwartz when we heard shots. It sounded as if World War I had broken out all over again. Louie and I leaped into a doorway as the siege continued. When it was all over, I learned that three men had been killed in what was tabbed by the next morning's tabloids as an outbreak of a gang war.

One of Miss Guinan's underlings at the time was a big handsome guy from Philadelphia who went under the name of Toots Shor. He was supposed to be the doorman, but some people suspected he would rather give you a hit in the head than let you into the joint, especially if he didn't like you. He had a heart as big as Times Square and a smile brighter than the lights on the old Chesterfield sign. He also had the fastest right hand I ever saw.

Toots made a lot of friends as he moved from one night spot to another. It was inevitable that he would one day become the genial host of his own establishment. If you haven't been to Toots' watering place on West Fifty-second Street, you haven't been to New York.

At Texas Guinan's I first saw the sensational trio of Clayton, Jackson & (Jimmy) Durante. They were far and away the hottest group around. At the time a young lady friend of mine, Lois Long, wrote a column for the *New Yorker* which was signed "Lipstick." Lois was married to Peter Arno, the great cartoonist, and had a tremendous amount of influence. If you got your name in her column, it was even better than going on the Ed Sullivan show today. You were well-launched in show business if "Lipstick" gave you a plug. One night I took Miss Long to see Clayton, Jackson & Durante. I thought they were funnier than ever, but Miss Long didn't seem to be amused. She just didn't think they were funny.

I got so mad that I made her come back four nights in a row. And on the fourth night the act finally got to her. By the fifth night she was really "with it" and from then on you could always find Lois and Peter at the El Fey Club—that is, until the club got padlocked.

Many years later, I appeared in a film with Durante. In the picture, Jimmy did a piece where he cross-examined himself in a courtroom—he was both the witness and the examining attorney. As far as I was concerned it was hilarious, but apparently it was too fast for the audience. They didn't understand it. Nobody laughed, nobody applauded, just nothing happened. So Darryl Zanuck cut the scene out of the film. Three years later Durante caught on in pictures and is still one of the great entertainers of all time.

The film Durante and I appeared in was *Little Miss Broadway*, in which I starred opposite one of my favorite leading ladies, Miss Shirley Temple. It's still playing on the late show, and I hope they'll be showing it in California when I run for reelection. It won me a lot of votes during my 1964 campaign against Pierre Salinger. During that campaign, about ten old pictures that I appeared in were playing on the "late late show." I figured that seventy-five percent of the audience was in bed, and I claimed that I had the most intimate approach to my constituents of any candidate who ever ran for office. It didn't hurt any—I won.

My favorite hangout was—and still is—the Twenty One Club. Whenever I am in New York, that is my address. To me it has always been home away from home and whenever I am there, I cannot help recalling the many happy moments I've spent in its environs.

But when I first came into contact with this now famous establishment, it was not yet the Twenty One Club. It was not located on West Fifty-second Street either. It was at 47 West Forty-ninth Street and had been founded by two cousins, Jack Kriendler and Charlie Berns.

My introduction to Jack and Charlie's, as are so many pleasant things in life, was purely accidental. I was taking my morning constitutional one Saturday when I heard a girl's voice say, "Hello, Murph." Looking around, I recognized an extremely pretty girl who had appeared in a number of motion pictures and was visiting in New York between films.

"Hi," I said, "how are you?"

"I'm having a birthday party and I wish you would join us," she responded.

I had nothing to do, so I thanked her and said I'd be delighted. The next thing I knew, I was in a speakeasy I had never heard of before. It was fairly dark but rather attractive. I was taken to an upstairs dining room in which about fifteen people were gathered and I must say champagne was being served as if it were going out of style. The food was as good as the wine and the birthday cake was a beautiful production.

It occurred to me that the bill for this birthday party was mounting to the point that if this turned out to be a Dutch treat affair I would be unable to pay my share. I have always made it a point never to accept hospitality that I couldn't return. Deciding I had better find out whether this was Dutch treat, I turned to the beautiful birthday girl and asked her, "Who is paying for all this? I mean, who is the host?"

"Oh, don't worry about it," she said. "Everything has been taken care of."

It was a gay party and the company was pleasant, but I'm not much of an afternoon drinker and I left long before the apogee, as we say in moon talk.

Later I learned that a very rich man, enamored of this young lady, had done a gentlemanly thing. He had gone to Florida for the weekend but arranged an unlimited charge account for her at "47". That weekend bill, I'm told, came to over twelve hundred dollars. Our host should have married the girl and taken her with him. She was very cute.

The Forty-ninth Street club soon began to prosper, unquestionably because they always served the finest of food and drink and they insisted on a very select clientele. In early 1930, Kriendler and Berns moved their establishment to 21 West Fifty-second Street, the address that gave the Twenty One Club its name. The club became known for its wrought-iron grillwork and painted iron jockeys on the outside and for its highly selective policy of admittance inside.

At its new quarters, the Twenty One Club became the most difficult place in New York to get into. Berns and Kriendler laid down stringent rules as to the type of lady and gentleman who would be granted permission to enter, and the way you behaved if you ever wanted to come back. You would ring a bell outside and Jimmy, the man at the door, would give you the once-over. How he determined the select few who gained admittance I never knew. But Twenty One was invariably filled with the so-called "top" people of New York and elsewhere. Jimmy made very few mistakes and never the same one twice.

And those "top" people had to behave. Drunkenness was not tolerated, which is one reason why Berns and Kriendler rarely got into trouble. I recall one well-known society lady being informed that her luncheon companion, a lady who had become a bit noisy, would no longer be welcomed. And furthermore the lady herself would not be admitted if she brought any more like that. You could get into the Social Register easier than "21".

In its new location, the club consisted of two old brownstone houses. The interior of one was decorated in a manner befitting the most attractive restaurant of the Prohibition era. The brownstone located at 21 West Fifty-second Street became the restaurant and the house next door, spoken of as the Judge's house, was the storehouse for possibly the most valuable collection of fine wines and liquors anywhere in the world. A series of passageways connected the basements of the two houses.

The reason for all this, of course, was Prohibition. Protective devices were developed to forestall the police from discovering the illegal possession of alcoholic beverages. To get from one building to the other was almost impossible unless you knew the secret techniques. One door was opened by the insertion of a silver dollar, another by fitting a very long wire into an almost invisible hole in the brickwork. To gain entrance through another door, you would have to take a teaspoon and make a connection between two electrical outlets. The door then would swing open. It was by far the most ingenious set of precautions ever imagined and if you get to know dear old Gus, the steward of the club, he might show you how the whole thing used to work.

But the *pièce de résistance,* as far as mechanical devices were concerned, was the manner in which the liquors on the back bar could be disposed of in a hurry. The bar, which at that time was located along the west wall of the downstairs dining room, could be triggered from several vantage points. All the bottles would be dumped at one time onto a bed of jagged rocks in the cellar, breaking them into smithereens. A stream of water then would be activated, washing away all the alcoholic content and the evidence would be long gone before any official could even get through the front door.

I remember having my lunch at the club one day and observing a police raid at first hand. It was not anything like the raids in the movies. Nobody smashed doors down. The Prohibition agents did not rush in blowing whistles or brandishing axes. Instead they entered quietly and the guests continued to eat. But they'd barely gotten past Jimmy at the door when the bar was triggered, dumping the illicit bottles into the basement. It probably would have killed my grandfather, Jerry Long, if he had been forced to witness the destruction of so much fine stuff.

I finished my lunch and left for a matinee performance of the musical I was then appearing in, and afterward walked back to the club for a bite of supper with Julie. The officers were just leaving. They had been there most of the day, searching the premises, but were unable to discover any evidence of illegality.

In the early years, Twenty One had a policy of closing at one o'clock at night no matter who might be lingering over a drink And for very good reason—it was a fine, orderly restaurant. The white work-light went on and that was the signal for everyone to clear out. Of course, there were special nights when Charlie Berns would whisper to a few couples, "Let's have a party." Then we would sneak upstairs and wait until the place was closed officially. When all the other guests had gone, "the family" would gather. We had wonderful times. Lillian and Hubie Boskowitz would be there, and Frank Hunter, Ben Finney and his beautiful spouse, Eddie and Edwina Sutherland, and once in a while we'd be honored by the royal presence of His Highness, Prince Michael Romanoff.

The lights would be turned back up, sandwiches and drinks would be brought in, and the party would begin. Nothing wild, but fun. Our greatest treat was when Charlie's wife Mollie, one of the prettiest girls I have ever seen, would sit up on the bar and sing Yiddish and Hebrew songs as I have never heard them sung before or since. There were many such moments which made us feel as if we were part of the family. We still feel that way.

When the Prohibition era finally ended, the Twenty One management was left with enormous stocks of whiskeys and wines which they could not sell for the simple reason that they did not have Government stamps on the bottles. Julie and I were among the favored few who were presented with some of these bottles, which again made us feel like part of the family.

Now that the Judge's house was no longer needed, the two buildings became one and the place was twice as big and twice as attractive.

On Election Day in 1952 I was in New York, having finished my work in the campaign for President Eisenhower. I had been in charge of all the rallies and big gatherings and was tired of crowds, bands, speeches, and people. So I walked over to Twenty One to see my good friend Pete Kriendler. The bars are closed in New York on Election Day, but Pete said it was okay for a fellow to entertain a few friends in his private office. So before lunch we enjoyed a drink as we assessed the political situation and the probabilities of the day. The company included Mr. and Mrs. James Farley, Pete Kriendler, Charlie and Molly Berns and me, and we all guessed the outcome of that one correctly.

One of the great joys I've had was taking my son Dennis and my daughter Melissa into the Twenty One Club to see a little of the kind of places their parents used to frequent before they were born. It was difficult to tell the children about the nightclubs we performed in, since most of them are long gone.

The only places that have retained their character and style, I guess, are the Persian Room in the Plaza Hotel in New York and the Coconut Grove at the Ambassador Hotel in Los Angeles. I hope they never change.

Most of the clubs today are too noisy for sanity, too smoky for safety, and resemble upholstered sewers too closely for my taste. And what happened to dancing? The whole thing now seems routined by St. Vitus, if you get my meaning.

Speaking of those Twenty One days, I remember the day that great singer Chauncy Allcott passed away. Next to John McCormack, Allcott was probably the most popular Irish tenor in the world, particularly among the Irish cooks and maids who always flocked to his concerts. At the time I was appearing in *Of Thee I Sing,* and I was among a group of entertainers who were asked to assist at the funeral services at St. Patrick's Cathedral. I was assigned to be an usher in the center aisle.

Some of the most prominent people in town, both high and low, came to bid Chauncy farewell. For example Harry Sinclair, the oil man, and George Bull, who headed the racing at Saratoga, arrived shortly before the services were to begin. I took them down the aisle and seated them in the third or fourth pew.

By now the church was full and the service began. I was given orders not to allow anyone else down the center aisle. But I hadn't counted on a woman who arrived sobbing bitter tears and hysterically insisting that she be permitted down the aisle I was to guard.

You have never seen such an exhibition of grief, and I felt sure the poor soul must have been a close relative or at least a dear friend of the deceased, but my orders were clear—no one down the aisle.

"Madam," I said, in my most understanding voice, "I'm sorry, but you can't enter now. The services have started. I'll find you a seat elsewhere."

As I turned around, the woman scooted down the middle aisle. I could have chased her and gotten her out, but that would have created a scene and I thought it the better part of wisdom just to ignore the episode. But I did notice that she had pushed herself between Harry Sinclair and George Bull.

When the services ended, I encountered these two gentlemen in front of the cathedral and we exchanged the usual niceties about how well the ceremony had gone.

I suggested we go to Jack and Charlie's, adding, "You would do me a great honor by permitting me to be your host at lunch." They agreed that Twenty One was a splendid suggestion, but each insisted he would be the host. I remonstrated a little.

"Don't be silly," said Sinclair. "Let me get this one." He reached into his pocket. With a look of dismay on his face, he blurted out, "My God! I've been robbed—my wallet's gone."

"Harry, don't worry about it," Bull said. "I have more than enough to take care of the bill and I insist on the pleasure." Then he checked his wallet, and it was gone, too.

What obviously had happened was that the hysterically tearful sob sister had fleeced the two of them of their wallets during the funeral ceremony.

I don't know whether or not the lady made funerals her usual place of operations, but I'll bet she never caught a finer pair than Harry Sinclair and George Bull at one sitting—or should I say laying out.

# CHAPTER 9

## *Of Thee I Sing*

The biggest hit Broadway show I ever worked in was *Of Thee I Sing*, which ran eighty-six weeks at the Music Box Theater, won a Pulitzer prize and constituted a major breakthrough as a satirical thrust at something we now call the Establishment. Except that *Of Thee I Sing* was purely good-humored and did not contain the meanness and bitterness found in most of the anti-Establishment theatrical efforts today. Our show was for entertainment; this new type today is for destruction.

I got into the show by accident, which pretty much sums up the nature of show business. It's not an easy life, and you've got to wait for the breaks and be ready when they come. This is not to say talent isn't important. It helps a lot. But a little bit of luck doesn't hurt either.

My big break came when I met William Gaxton in Florida. Billy and his wife Madeline had come to watch Julie and me perform and had taken a fancy to us. At the time he told us he intended to get us into his next show, something called *Of Thee I Sing*. That a musical comedy star like Billy had taken such an interest in our future pleased us no end. Billy had played the lead in such major attractions as *A Connecticut Yankee* and *Fifty Million Frenchmen*. And he had broken all records playing ten consecutive weeks in a vaudeville act at the famous Palace Theater.

When we returned to New York, I received a telephone call from Louis "Doc" Shurr. "Don't ask me any questions," Shurr said. "Come right over to my office."

Shurr was one of the biggest agents in show business. I mean in importance. He was actually only about five feet six inches tall. Everyone called him "Doc," and when he ordered you to rush over to his office, you rushed over. I'd hardly had time to say hello when Doc grabbed me by the arm and led me out to the street where he hailed a cab. Along with three girls and another man I was shoved into it. Shurr gave an address on Riverside Drive. On the way he said we were going to George Gershwin's apartment. But he didn't say what it was all about.

The apartment was crowded with people and I soon realized that Gershwin was auditioning all of them, presumably for his new show. Someone told me to make myself comfortable. I walked out on the terrace and played with the composer's dog, a frisky Airedale. Finally I was called in to meet the noted Gershwin. Everyone else had left and there were just Gershwin, Shurr and me. It was a thrilling moment for me. This was the brilliant young man who was literally rocking the world of music with his genius. He had added rhythm and a beat to great musical sounds and was revolutionizing the entire field.

Gershwin couldn't have been nicer. "I'd like to hear you sing something," he told me. Then he sat down at his piano and started to play something from one of his previous shows which fortunately I happened to know. Apparently my rendition was acceptable.

"You'll do fine," Gershwin said.

I was too flattered, scared and impressed to ask, "What for?"

The diminutive Doc Shurr grabbed me by the arm and led me to the street where he hailed another cab. He said nothing, and I didn't want to ask.

Finally I couldn't stand it any longer. "Where are we going?" I asked almost desperately.

"Never mind," he said. "Just don't ask so damned many questions."

I was taken to the office of Sam Harris, another notable figure in the world of the theater. Harris was the most respected producer on Broadway and had achieved considerable success as the partner in numerous theatrical ventures of George M. Cohan, the song-and-dance man for whom I had the utmost admiration.

After Shurr introduced me to Harris, the producer got to the point quickly.

"I talked with Gershwin—he says you're okay. Do you want the job?" he asked.

"What job?"

"The job in the show."

For the life of me I had no idea of what show he was talking about. But I was in no position to argue. These were depression years—I would have taken any job in any show.

"The job pays two hundred and seventy-five dollars a week," Harris continued, "and if you want it I'll make it three hundred and fifty dollars."

"I'll take it," I said quickly. "I'll take it. And thank you very much!"

"Do you want a contract?" he asked.

"Not unless you do," I replied.

"I'd rather shake hands," he said.

We shook hands and then he told me that I was to play the part of Sam Jenkins, a political press agent, in his forthcoming production Of Thee I Sing. I left his office knowing that I was one of the few actors who ever got a raise even before going into rehearsal. It was a pretty good feeling in those grim days when jobs—particularly in the theater—were few and far between.

Once rehearsals were under way we rarely saw Harris. On the night of the dress rehearsal, however, he did show up at the Music Box Theater and asked to see Billy Gaxton, Victor Moore and me backstage. "Well, fellows," he said in his quiet voice, "I've got the whole bankroll including the house in Great Neck riding on this show. So please, do the best you can." Then he walked away.

Of Thee I Sing was the biggest thing to hit Broadway in years. The reviews were sensational. One of the yellowed clippings still in my possession shows that the theater critic of the New York World-Telegram, Robert Garland, concluded his rave review as follows: "For the time being, suffice it to say that

*Of Thee I Sing* is an event in the history of the American theater. I must remember to tell my grandchildren that I was
present at its opening."

Sam Harris did not have to worry about his house in Great
Neck.

Harris was one of the finest people I ever worked for—and I
have worked for a lot of nice people in my time. He was a gentleman in the truest sense of the word. If he had faith in you, he
hired you. And if he hired you, he left you alone.

When he died, someone in one of the eulogies observed that
Harris never cut corners. Sam was the kind of man who would
walk clear out to the curb to give people who were interested in
shortcuts plenty of room to walk by him. There wasn't a mean
bone in his body. He cared about the people who worked for
him.

One little incident that will always remain in my memory was
the time Sam had left town for an Easter vacation. While he was
away, the play manager announced a ten percent cut in everybody's salary. This was not an unusual practice in those grim
days of economic despair, but we were playing in a smash hit
with the house sold out almost every night. The cut didn't make
sense.

It didn't make sense to Sam Harris either. When he returned
from his much-needed vacation, Sam called the cast together to
announce he had restored the salary cuts. He also got a new
manager.

"If I can't run a show on the salaries the contracts call for, I'll
close the show," he said.

When newly-elected Franklin D. Roosevelt closed the banks,
Harris, who had friends almost everywhere, had been tipped off
about this possibility. The producer arranged well in advance
to pay us off in cash. In fact, we were the only show in town that
was paid off with real, honest-to-goodness money.

From the first note of George Gershwin's overture to the
dropping of the final curtain, *Of Thee I Sing* succeeded in

cramming as much gaiety into an evening of good-natured spoofing as any evening has the right to hold. In retrospect the story line may seem silly, but back in 1931 it won almost unanimous praise as the first major show to make hilariously satiric use of the American scene in general and Washington politics in particular. It came at the right time—at a time when depression-ridden America was in need of a good laugh.

Of course, Gershwin's music didn't do the show any harm. But too little credit has been given to George's brother Ira, who wrote lyrics as good as the music. And this is not to overlook the book itself, which was written by two superb craftsmen, George S. Kaufman and Morrie Ryskind. Morrie, incidentally, now lives in Beverly Hills and has long been one of my most loyal political supporters. His humor is still irrepressible, as demonstrated in the column he writes regularly for a newspaper syndicate. He and his Mary are two of the finest people I know and I value their friendship greatly.

The star of the show, of course, was Billy Gaxton. In his inimitable fashion, Billy played the role of John P. Wintergreen, who campaigned for the Presidency of the United States on a platform of Love. As the Gershwins' lilting tune had it, "Love is Sweeping the Country." Wintergreen's major campaign pledge was to marry the winner of an Atlantic City beauty contest.

Or as the Gershwin lyrics have it:

> *If a girl is sexy*
> *She may be Mrs. Prexy.*

But love, real love, intruded just as the judges of the beauty pageant selected the all-too-beautiful Diana Devereaux as the future First Lady. By that time Wintergreen was already President and he was smitten by the charms of his young secretary, Mary Turner, who among her other attractions could whip up a batch of tasty corn muffins. They were wed.

This caused a tempest in the White House. The jilted Miss Devereaux, disclosing that she was an illegitimate daughter of an illegitimate son of an illegitimate nephew of Napoleon, persuaded the French Ambassador to intervene in her behalf. Breach of promise was claimed, war with France threatened, and the President was on the verge of being impeached for not carrying out his campaign promise to marry her. At the very last moment, the First Lady danced into the Senate Chamber and announced that she was expecting a baby.

At the mere mention of motherhood, the sentimental senators forgave Wintergreen for dishonoring his campaign pledge. War with France was still in the offing, but President Wintergreen came up with a solution. He pacified the angry French by presenting Miss Devereaux to the Vice-president. He also promised to have twins—one for America and one for France.

Playing the role of Alexander Throttlebottom, the pickle salesman who much to his amazement became the Vice-president of the United States, was none other than my old friend, Victor Moore. Moore's portrayal of the candidate whose name nobody knew and the officeholder nobody remembered was so brilliant that "Throttlebottom" soon became part of the nation's political vocabulary.

He and Billy Gaxton were so great that when we played Washington they were invited into the Senate. That was my first trip to the Capitol.

Moore was perfect for the part of the useless, bumbling Vice-president—he didn't even need makeup for his role. One snowy night he arrived at the theater just in time for his first entrance. With no time to put on his stage clothes he raced onto the stage right on cue, shaking the snow off his hat and coat. The audience thought the entrance a brilliant piece of stage business.

"You know," Moore said later, "they laughed more than usual. I wonder why."

Victor Moore was the perfect innocent on and offstage. So much so that when he walked along Broadway the hawkers, who were selling everything from two-dollar watches to dirty French postcards, invariably thought he had just arrived from Hicksville. This would make him mad.

"Those guys don't know I've been in New York for forty years," he once complained to me.

My role was that of the smart-alecky press agent who guided John P. Wintergreen to the Presidency. George Kaufman, who directed the show, later expanded my part. In the second act he made me White House appointments secretary, and also gave me several musical numbers to do. Thirty-three years later, when I was running against Pierre Salinger for the Senate seat I now occupy, I jokingly pointed out that I had been a White House press secretary long before my distinguished opponent. And what's more, I would say, I had Ken O'Donnell's job as appointments secretary long before Ken did.

In *Of Thee I Sing* I danced two numbers with the lovely June O'Dea, who was married to Lefty Gomez, the star Yankee pitcher. June was a great girl, with a good sense of humor. Sometimes on matinee days I would disconcert her during a dance number by whispering into her ear, "Lefty got knocked out of the box in the sixth." Invariably June would miss the next three steps and almost as invariably she would seek retribution by pinching me.

The tryout of the show was in Boston. We knew we had a hit on our hands when the local critics went wild over *Of Thee I Sing*. The word quickly got back to New York and the show was sold out weeks before we hit Broadway.

A tryout is important. It not only gives the cast the opportunity to play together properly, but it gives the management the opportunity to iron out kinks. At the Boston opening we learned there was a dead spot in the opening of the final scene in the show. A stage carpenter named Reggie, a big red-faced fellow, made a valuable suggestion to solve the problem.

In the scene, a number of ambassadors from different countries arrived, each with a baby carriage. They were announced individually, which after a while got tedious. What Reggie proposed was that the third ambassador be announced as the envoy of Scotland and that he come on stage wearing kilts and carrying a tiny baby carriage.

"A great idea," said George Kaufman, who directed the show. "We'll do it the way he says."

Then he asked me to arrange for a two-hundred-dollar check to be given to Reggie. It was money well-spent. Reggie's idea always brought down the house. The episode taught me a lesson that has remained with me all my life: always listen to anyone with an idea. That is why I have advised my Senate aides to study all correspondence arriving at my office. You'd be amazed at how smart people are, and how anxious to help.

Once *Of Thee I Sing* was launched in New York, George Kaufman rarely came backstage. However, he would frequently monitor the show from the audience. He was primarily concerned about timing. Once you had it right, you didn't change it. An experienced, brilliant playwright, George Kaufman knew that if everyone changed the timing of one of their lines by just a few seconds, they could, without realizing it, add at least fifteen minutes of dead time to a performance. George had the show timed to go a certain length and he wanted it kept that way.

If anything went wrong, Kaufman would never talk to you about it directly. Instead he would put a note in your theater mailbox. Now it happened that Billy Gaxton fancied himself a great ad-libber. When he got bored repeating the lines of the show—which frequently happens during a lengthy engagement—Billy would nonchalantly utter some absurdity and throw everyone else off stride.

One night at the end of the first act, Gaxton found a note from Kaufman. "I'm watching the show from the back row," it read. "Wish you were here."

For a couple of weeks afterward Billy minded his manners.

As President Wintergreen, Billy was superb. He gave a deliciously accurate imitation of Jimmy Walker's platform manner. On opening night, I could see the Mayor sitting in a second row seat and laughing uproariously at Billy's antics. Close by was another public figure and one whom I greatly admired. I was happy to see that Al Smith, the 1928 Democratic candidate for President, was enjoying the show immensely.

I had become the unofficial watchdog of the cast. Too much was riding on our keeping the show going in those desperate days to permit slovenliness. We wanted this job to go on and on. So I watched the show like a hawk.

One night I noticed that the audience did not come through with the customary laugh in the big scene between the President (Gaxton) and the First Lady (Lois Moran). The next night I discovered the reason. Just as Gaxton was about to utter his big punch line, Miss Moran crossed her pretty legs under her desk where the audience could see her. As she did so, most eyes in the audience were diverted to her. No one was listening when Gaxton spoke his key line.

I asked Lois why she was giving Billy the business. Her answer was simple. She felt that Billy was upstaging her. Whenever they had a love scene together, for example, Billy would turn her around so that her back would be to the audience.

"I understand, Lois," I said. "But if we don't get any laughs we won't have a show. We'll all be out of work. So will you please cut out your monkeyshines?"

"Only if Billy behaves," she replied.

I reported Lois' complaint to Billy. He didn't take it too seriously. He said he didn't mean to hurt Lois, that his twisting her around was an old vaudeville habit. He wanted to drop the subject.

"No, Billy," I countered. "We're going to settle this business. It's urgent. If you and Lois don't cut it out the show will be in trouble. No laughs, no show."

"Now, listen here, boy," he thundered. "I'm the star of this damned show and I'll go to Hades before anyone tells me how to play a scene. And you have my permission to tell that to Miss Moran. Now get the hell out of here."

"Very well," I said, somewhat shaken, "have it your way."

That night I arranged for every man backstage to wear a Sherlock Holmes type hat. Every time Billy looked into the wings he saw one of the boys glaring at him, pipe and all. After about ten minutes it began to bug him—he couldn't keep his eyes off the wings.

"What's going on?" he demanded.

"We're just trying to keep you honest," I said.

All through his performance, Gaxton kept looking offstage only to find a Sherlock Holmes imitator glaring at him. By the time the first act was over, Gaxton had had enough.

"All right," he said. "I give up. I'll do anything you say, only get those guys with the silly hats out of here."

One of the high points of the show was an election rally supposedly taking place at Madison Square Garden. When an actor, playing the "Golden Voiced Orator from the Far West," began a thunderous harangue, a mat was hastily unrolled directly in front of him and two enormous wrestlers, each weighing at least three hundred pounds, began a burlesque wrestling match right in front of the speaker.

Believe it or not, I can still remember the wrestlers—Tom Draak and Sulo Hevonpaa. But don't ask me to pronounce their names.

The wrestling match was a very funny bit. It took about two minutes, but Tom and Sulo had to wait around most of the evening to make their appearance. To while away the time, they would imbibe a considerable amount of applejack.

I warned them they were headed for trouble. These huge men were wrestling on a very narrow bit of stage, and if they weren't careful they could easily topple into the orchestra pit.

Which is exactly what happened one night. Six hundred pounds of flesh and bone rolled over into the pit, completely demolishing the bass drum and terrifying the musicians.

I wasn't too upset about the incident, as the drummer was no particular friend of mine. Early in our engagement I had discovered he didn't like me. For that matter, he didn't like anyone. He was ornery as hell and obviously felt that he had better things to do than accompany performers on stage.

There was one particular dance number which June O'Dea and I did that would invariably stop the show, provided the music and rhythm were sharp. It was the famous "Love Is Sweeping the Country." Every performer wants to stop the show. That frequently is more important to him than a raise in salary.

But several weeks after the show opened, June and I were dismayed to find that audiences were not responding to what had been our big show-stopping number because the rhythm was soggy and the beat was flat. I looked down into the orchestra pit. Much to my amazement, I saw my pal the drummer reading a magazine as he was perfunctorily keeping time on the foot cymbal only.

I was infuriated. After the performance I sought the man out. He was an extremely tall, gawky individual, as unpleasant as they come. He quickly let me know that he was a big man around town, that he wore fifteen-dollar silk shirts (all I could afford were two-dollar shirts) and that he was head of the musicians union local, and I'd just have to get used to the way he played—and like it.

I tried to reason with him. "Now, Louis," I said, "this show means a great deal to all of us. Can't you give us a little more beat, a little more rhythm, a little more zing?"

Louis looked at me with utter disdain. "That's the way I'm going to play the drums and you might as well get used to it, buster," he snarled.

If there's one word that lights my fuse, it's to be called "buster"—especially by a *shnook*. I didn't intend to get used to it.

The next day I arrived at the theater early and waited for Louis. When he showed up, I got him aside and said, "Louis, I've got a message for you from one of my friends over on Eleventh Avenue."

Eleventh Avenue, at the time, was a really tough area and the fact was that I did have friends there. Louis knew it.

"Yeah, what's the message?" Louis asked.

"Well, this friend has heard that you aren't playing the drums as well as you could and he is terribly upset about it. He told me to tell you that if you don't shape up he's going to come over and break all your fingers. Then you won't be able to play the drums and you won't be able to scratch your head or pick your nose or even turn the pages of your lousy magazine. Do you understand?" I couldn't resist adding, "He might break your toes too."

Louis understood. Beginning with that evening's performance, Louis didn't read any more magazines and he played his instruments beautifully. And once again June and I stopped the show with "Love Is Sweeping the Country."

After one performance, I was leaving the theater through a back door when I heard a girl sobbing. I went back to find out what was going on. In a darkened area of the stage I found one of the showgirls crying her eyes out. With her was a character who was trying to get a story out of her to give to a certain columnist whom we used to call a "keyhole peeper." The girl had had an unfortunate marriage and this character was warning her that if she did not come through with the details he would circulate a vicious story about her.

That was all I had to hear. I belted him so hard that for a long time he could only look through a peephole with one eye. I also told him that if I ever caught him in the vicinity of West Forty-fifth Street, let alone the theater, I would put his other eye out of commission. In those days I was fairly headstrong and maybe even quick-tempered.

I don't recall ever seeing the man around the area again.

As a rising luminary on the Broadway scene during the early Thirties I was often called upon to do a benefit on Sunday night in behalf of some worthy cause, and you wouldn't believe how many worthy causes there were. I was only too glad to do what I could to help out. These Sunday night benefits became so numerous that some weeks there would be five or six on the same night. In later years it got to be a racket, and Equity moved in.

I have forgotten the cause for which I made my first benefit appearance, but I'm sure it was worthy. I had prepared a simple routine—tell a joke, sing a popular song and then do a soft-shoe dance.

Just before I was scheduled to go on stage, Eddie Cantor arrived. Eddie was then one of the nation's top comedians, and he was in a hurry. He had five more benefits to do.

"Can I go on right away?" Cantor asked the stage manager in his characteristically breathless voice.

"Why, of course, Eddie," the manager said and then he turned to me. "This kid won't mind, will you, kid?"

"Of course not," this kid replied.

Eddie smiled at me. "Thank you very much," he said. "I won't be too long. Oh, about three minutes."

It was more like fifteen minutes. Eddie was marvelous. But he concluded by singing the very song I had planned to sing—"It's Only a Paper Moon."

My heart sank. What was I going to do? There was no time to change my routine or music. I was stuck. I was being introduced by the master of ceremonies.

So heart pounding, I went on the stage and told my little joke. The audience was good-natured and laughed. Not as loudly as they laughed at Cantor, but they laughed. Then I did my dance. The audience applauded warmly. But I was still jittery as I prepared to sing.

Screwing up my courage, I said, "Ladies and gentlemen, it's a funny thing, but most comedians want to be singers. That goes for dancers, too. But comedians never sing a song right. Look at the way Eddie Cantor sang that song."

At which point I did a bad imitation of Cantor—popeyes and all—singing "It's Only a Paper Moon."

"That's not the way this beautiful song should be sung," I went on. "This is a ballad. This is the way it should be done."

And I began to sing the song as a ballad, all the while feeling that if there had been a crack in the floor I would go right through it—I was that nervous. Somehow I got through the number and was pleased when I received a tremendous ovation.

Since then I have played so many benefits that I long ago lost count of the number. There were many times when I didn't know the cause for which I was performing. I recall the time during World War II when Ed Sullivan asked me to show up at Madison Square Garden. As Ed's obedient servant, I arrived at the Garden prepared to put in my appearance.

The auditorium was absolutely packed to the rafters with at least 15,000 people, and as I entered there were three bands on the giant stage, all playing a medley of tunes at the same time— Harry James, Tommy Dorsey and Jimmy Dorsey. When that finished, as if things weren't already bad enough, Sullivan introduced Mrs. Jimmy Doolittle, whose husband had just led the first air raids on Tokyo. Of course, when she was introduced the roof didn't come off but it was pretty well loosened. Then Mrs. Doolittle introduced Mrs. Eddie Rickenbacker, whose husband had just been rescued from a raft after floating for over two weeks in the South Pacific. Well, I have never heard such tumultuous applause in my life, and rightfully so.

I was joining in enthusiastically when suddenly the cold hand of Fate tapped me on the shoulder and Sullivan said, "You're on next."

If I could have thought of a short route to a quick suicide, I'm sure I would have done the Dutch act at that moment. But there I was, and I had to go on. As I started up the thirty feet or more of stairs to the stage, I asked, "What kind of benefit is this?"

Sullivan said, "It's the United Jewish Appeal."

As I climbed the long flight of stairs I felt like a condemned man going up to the gallows. Suddenly the good Lord whispered in my ear and I remembered a wonderful old Jewish joke that I had heard years ago from Benny Rubin. Sullivan was in the middle of the introduction, the usual one of "star of stage and screen." By that time I had made about seven motion pictures and was fairly well-known. I began to tell the story in Yiddish.

I hadn't said five words when a lady in the front row, which was about thirty feet below me and at least sixty-five feet away, let out a scream. "And with that face yet!" she shrieked. The entire audience burst into laughter, and I was home free.

The story had to do with an elderly Jewish gentleman who was very religious. He was crossing the border between Canada and the United States at Windsor, Ontario, just after President Roosevelt had decided that nobody could have any gold. As the old gentleman arrived on the American side, the Customs officer questioned him and said, "Have you anything to declare?"

He said, "No, I don't."

The Customs officer said, "Do you mind if I look in your suitcase?"

He said, "Go ahead."

The Customs officer opened it and found four sets of solid gold teeth. The officer said, "Wait a minute—what about these four sets of gold teeth?"

The old gentleman replied, "Well, you see, I'm a very religious fellow. I have to have the four sets of teeth. One set is for *milchedig* (dairy dishes) another set is for *flayshedig* (meat dishes) and the third set is for *Pesach* (Passover)."

The officer said, "What about the fourth set?"

The old gentleman said, "Well, confidentially, between the two of us, every now and then even I like to have a little *knosh* on a piece of ham. You know how it is."

It wasn't the greatest joke ever told, but it's a pretty funny story if you enjoy Jewish humor, which I do. I told that joke to Louis B. Mayer when I got my first contract at M-G-M.

# CHAPTER 10

*Roberta*

Finally, as happens with all Broadway productions, *Of Thee I Sing* came to an end. The show had been a major landmark in my show business career. The critics had been kind to me, and I was marked as a "comer" by those who watched theatrical doings, professionally or otherwise.

So I was somewhat concerned when I was not hired to appear in the sequel, *Let 'Em Eat Cake*, which had the same producer, librettists, director and stars (except for me) as *Of Thee I Sing*.

There was a part in the new production which I thought I could do to perfection. It was the part of a wild-eyed Communist agitator. The fellow they got to play the role not only looked like a Communist, but for all I know he may have been at least a fellow traveler. He used to preach pretty good left-wing propaganda, all about how Franklin Roosevelt was a "fascist," Norman Thomas a "social fascist" and the rest of us poor benighted souls "dupes of the vicious capitalist system."

I went to George Kaufman, who was directing the show. "You're making a terrible mistake hiring this guy," I said. "I can read those lines and they'll be funny, because I'll do it tongue-in-cheek. But if he does them, they won't be funny. He looks as if he believes what he is saying. He won't get laughs, he'll get goose pimples. People will be uncomfortable listening to him." Which is exactly what happened.

Kaufman wrote me a kind letter apologizing because I was the only one in the cast of *Of Thee I Sing* who did not get a part in the new show. I wired back thanking him for his concern and asking him not to worry because I already had a job in a forthcoming production entitled *Roberta*.

As it turned out, *Let 'Em Eat Cake* folded within two weeks, while *Roberta* lasted a season and a half.

Why *Roberta* turned out to be a smash hit—although I'm glad it did—has always puzzled me. Most likely it was the great music by Jerome Kern. But the book was by general consensus uninspired. The story line was based on a novel by Alice Duer Miller, *Gowns by Roberta*.

Actually the story was about my good friend and Yale classmate, Cobbles Sturghan, who happened to be a nephew of Mrs. Miller. Cobbles had played tackle on the Yale football team and had been named an All-American. He was a huge man and the last person in the world who would ever get mixed up in the dressmaking business.

That was the kind of character around which *Roberta* was built. In the story, a big, he-man all-American fullback falls heir to his Aunt Roberta's dressmaking establishment in Paris. He falls in love with girls of various nationalities, and the big question resolved in the play is which of these girls he will decide to marry.

At the outset, I was hired to play the fullback. Julie was hired to play one of my girl friends. We had been recommended to the producer, Max Gordon, by both Harbach and Kern who had remembered our performances in the Heywood Broun show *Shoot the Works*.

But even before the show had its tryout in Philadelphia the decision was made that I was not big enough physically to play the football star. I don't believe it was my size; I think it was the size of my voice and I think Jerry Kern zinged me for the lead. I didn't blame him. You had to bug me to hear me. I needed a mike and in those days they didn't have them.

So Max Gordon brought in Ray Middleton, a huge man whose booming baritone could be heard in the far reaches of the theater.

*Roberta* didn't do too well on opening night in Philadelphia. As a matter of fact, it was pretty bad. I knew we were in real trouble when, at the end of the first act, I saw the stage carpenter go to the telephone and place a call to New York. He was already looking for another job.

I told a fellow performer, a young man from Cleveland named Bob Hope, that it looked as if we would be having turkey for Thanksgiving.

Max Gordon called New York after the curtain fell on the final act, looking for help to save the show. He finally prevailed upon a well-known play "doctor," Hassard Short, to do some quick rewriting and redirecting. The next morning Hassard Short, with a mink-lined coat thrown over his shoulders, arrived at the theater. He insisted that he would not permit Kern and Harbach around while he was working. This was unheard of but, having no choice, Gordon persuaded them to leave. Short shortened, speeded up, threw out scenes and made the show move.

There were other changes. They involved Julie and that beautiful Jerome Kern ballad "Smoke Gets in Your Eyes." The tune was introduced in the first act by Tamara, who played a Russian princess exiled in Paris. Tamara did not have a big voice. Her rendition of "Smoke" was beautiful, but she couldn't be heard.

Only when Julie and I danced to a reprise of the tune in the second act did it prove to be a show-stopper. This upset Jerry Kern who said he didn't want anything stopping the show.

After the show one night, shortly after the opening, I got a call from Max Gordon. He wanted to see me right away. I told him that Julie and I had retired, that I'd see him in the morning. No, he insisted, he had to see me right away and he would come over to the Warwick Hotel where we stayed.

Julie was in bed when Max arrived and we talked in the outer room. He looked agitated. "I don't know how to tell you this," he said. "We've got to take Julie out of the show."

"For God's sake, why?" I protested. I was the agitated one now.

"Because she's too damned good, that's why. She spoils the plot. She's taking the spotlight away from Tamara, and Tamara happens to be the star."

"That's a funny reason," I told him.

"I have no alternative."

"All right," I said finally. "If you want to fire Julie, that's your business. But I'm not going to tell her. You'll have to do that yourself."

Gordon did, and Julie, being the champ she has always been, took it fine.

"Now," said Gordon, "how about settling Julie's contract?"

"I don't know a damned thing about her contract," I said. "You made it with her; you settle it with her."

The next morning I called my old buddy Victor Moore in New York. Victor, as a board member of Actors Equity, advised me about the proper prcedures. He said that since we had rehearsed six weeks, Julie should get six weeks salary in settlement of her run-of-the-play contract.

Gordon refused to make the settlement and each week he would come back and each week Julie would tell him she would settle for six weeks salary from the time he agreed to settle. This lasted until June. This was my first real negotiation with a producer and it was an experience that served me in good stead when, years later, as president of the Screen Actors Guild, I helped negotiate contracts in behalf of thousands of motion picture people.

*Roberta* finally opened its New York run at the New Amsterdam Theater on a Saturday night in November 1933. The reviews were so-so. Curiously, even the memorable Jerome Kern melodies, including "Smoke Gets in Your Eyes," came in for a rap.

Robert Garland, writing in the *World-Telegram*, complained: "There's no tune you can whistle when you leave the theater. I tried to pucker on the one about smoke getting in your eyes, but it turned out to be 'The Last Roundup' before I reached the sidewalk."

The book of the show didn't fare much better. "As a musical comedy scribbler, Mr. Harbach is no wit," wrote the prestigious

Brooks Atkinson in the *New York Times*. "The humors of 'Roberta' are no great shakes, and most of them are smugly declaimed by Bob Hope, who insists upon being the life of the party and who would be more amusing if he were Fred Allen. . ."

That reference to Bob Hope annoyed the hell out of me. Don't get me wrong—I was also an admirer of the late, great Fred Allen. But Bob helped save *Roberta* with his extraordinary talent, despite the fact that there was very little humor in the original script. During the run of the production Hope and I kept improvising new pieces of funny business. Hassard Short had told us in desperation when he first took over the show, "Do whatever you can think of to get some laughs. As it is now, it's deadly."

Another future star I met in *Roberta* was a young saxophone player from Kankakee, Illinois. His name was Fred MacMurray and he was a member of the vocal and instrumental group known as the California Collegians presided over by Huckleberry Haines (Bob Hope). He did a ten-second imitation of Rudy Vallee singing "My Time Is Your Time," but he did it well and was such a nice guy we all loved him.

Later, in Hollywood, I helped Fred get started in pictures. I had run into the director Wesley Ruggles at a party one Sunday. He said, "I've got a great part for a young man in a picture starring Claudette Colbert. Everyone in town is working. Do you know anyone who needs a job?"

I knew many young actors who needed jobs but I could think of only one who seemed to fit the bill.

"I do know someone," I said. "He was in *Roberta*."

"Can he act?"

"I think he can. What's more, he's a hell of a nice guy."

"Have him come to see me," Ruggles said.

After all these years, Fred MacMurray is still going strong and he's still a nice guy. He is still a big draw at the box office and his television shows rate highly. Like Bob Hope, Fred will be popular forever.

Another *Roberta* alumnus who did well was the late Sydney Greenstreet. This fine character actor went on to Hollywood, where he did so magnificently in that great film classic *The Maltese Falcon.*

Ray Middleton also went to Hollywood where he did well in films. But Ray's heart was on the concert stage and he never did concentrate on motion pictures. I recall seeing him when he replaced Ezio Pinza in the role of the French plantation owner in *South Pacific.* And two years ago he came to Washington in that beautiful musical *Man of La Mancha.*

Ironically, while the men in *Roberta* went on to success, the lives of the female stars ended in tragedy. Fay Templeton had a heart attack; Lyda Roberti committed suicide, and Tamara was killed in a plane crash on her way to entertain American troops in Europe during World War II. Strangely enough, Cary Grant and I were scheduled to make that trip with Tamara, but at the last minute our routing was changed and we missed that tragedy in the Tegus River.

What with lukewarm reviews and a small advance box office sale, *Roberta's* future didn't look too good the first week. Some of us began to think of looking for other jobs. We knew we were in deep trouble when the cast got an order from Max Gordon to appear on stage following the Saturday night performance.

A despondent group of people gathered together to await the producer's appearance. When Max arrived, he stood up on a chair and he said, "We got bad notices, but we've got a great show. The critics don't know what they're talking about. We're going to be a big hit. In the meantime, I'm going to have to ask everyone to take a ten percent cut in salary."

The following Saturday night we got another notice to be on stage after the performance. Gordon was late in arriving. Ever the comic, I put on my hat and coat and a pair of glasses just like Max wore and leaped on a chair. I began to mimic Gordon's clipped manner of speaking.

"Ladies and gentlemen," I began. "We have a great show in *Roberta*. Just don't believe the notices. The critics don't know what they're talking about. We are going to be a big hit."

Everyone snickered.

My punch line was, "Now, I'm going to ask everyone here to take another ten percent cut in salary."

As if on cue, Max Gordon walked in. If looks could kill, I would have been dead. But I must say this about Max, he recovered his equilibrium quickly.

"Very funny. Very funny, indeed. But for once Mr. Murphy is right," the producer said in his clipped tones. "We have a good show, a very good show, and we will succeed. But we do have a financial problem, and as he said, I hope everybody will take a ten percent cut."

I'm pleased to say the cuts were rescinded when we began to do well at the box office. *Roberta* did have outstanding assets. It was handsomely staged and lighted by Hassard Short. And it featured (I believe for the first time on Broadway) a glamorous fashion show with gowns by Kiviette, the couturiere who designed gowns for Julie for our nightclub appearances.

What really boosted *Roberta* at the box office, without question, was its music. Despite critic Robert Garland, the Jerome Kern melodies were among his best. Besides "Smoke Gets in Your Eyes," there were such tunes as "The Touch of Your Hand" and "You're Devastating." The music caught the fancy of Eddy Duchin and he began to play it nightly at the Central Park Casino. From there the Kern melodies swept the town and then the nation via radio.

At first, the music got in the way of the book. On opening night in New York, for example, the first scene played for twelve minutes because every line was underscored musically. Within the week we got that scene down to six minutes. We knew that audiences would love the show despite its obvious deficiencies, if we could keep it moving quickly.

Bob Hope and I had a little trouble with Ray Middleton

when the show first opened. Ray, who was new to show business, had a troubling habit of killing the few jokes in the show by distracting the audience with his movements. Whenever Bob Hope or I would come up to a punch line, Ray would either light his pipe, snap his knees, blow his nose or some other damned thing. The whole point of the joke would be killed.

I pleaded with Ray to cease and desist. "Look here now," I said, spelling it out as simply as I could. "You're killing the laughs. If there are no laughs, there is no show. If there is no show, we'll all be on the bread line together."

Ray didn't seem to comprehend.

"What are we going to do with that guy?" Hope asked me in our dressing room.

"We've got to do something," I said. "We've got to teach him a lesson."

The next matinee, with the audience filled with ladies, we taught Ray a lesson. As Bob passed him on stage, he reached out and pulled out Ray's tie. Then I went by and unbuttoned his vest. Whereupon Bob pulled out his shirt. And we went on from there until he yelled quits.

"I've had enough," he said meekly. "I won't do it again."

From then on, Ray was very cooperative.

This was Bob Hope's first Broadway show. Born in London, he was raised in Cleveland and at a very early age had travelled around the country on the vaudeville circuit. As a result of working together in *Roberta*, Bob and I became close friends. In my judgment, he is not only the funniest man in show business today, but one of the great citizens of our time. I must confess, though, that I did not fully appreciate his brilliance during our early days together.

Doc Shurr got Bob a contract to make several movie shorts out on Long Island. Hope asked me if I'd like to appear in one of them. My instincts told me to thank the gentleman and decline. The shorts turned out to be pretty dreadful. I remember Walter Winchell remarking in his column that, instead of sentencing wrongdoers to thirty days, the night court magistrates ought to force them to view the Bob Hope shorts. I think the producers of those early shorts killed more fine talent than you could shake a megaphone at, but they couldn't kill Bob. He was too good.

In a way I was responsible for Bob's wonderful marriage to his beautiful wife, the former Dolores Reade, and I enjoy taking credit for bringing them together. Dolores was singing at the Club Richman. One of her admirers, Bobby Maxwell, was a good pal of mine. He had been touting Dolores' singing talents, and one night asked Julie and me to join him at the Club Richman to hear Dolores. Bob Hope was free so we took him along.

Bob couldn't take his eyes off Dolores, who sang enchantingly that night. Later all of us, including Dolores, went on to John Perona's and then Reuben's. I noticed that Bob still couldn't take his eyes off the girl. The next day, Bob said, "Gee, that Dolores is a very nice person. She's one of the most attractive gals I've ever met." A few days later Bob told me he had made a date with Dolores. Not long afterward, they were married.

Thirty years later, when I challenged Pierre Salinger for the United States Senate seat he then occupied, Dolores Hope sent a fine contribution to my campaign fund, along with a note that moved me deeply. She said she had waited all these years to repay me, in some small measure, for introducing Bob to her. She added she intended to go to church and pray for my success, and enclosed five Masses for my election.

Bob and I had one brief encounter with Communism during our *Roberta* days. We received telegrams urging us to attend a meeting after the show. We thought it was some kind of Equity meeting. The wire said the meeting was being called to discuss problems facing theatrical workers. Always interested in such problems, Bob and I decided to go.

The meeting was held at old Bryant Hall, on Sixth Avenue across the street from Bryant Park, which is just back of the Library. We found ourselves in a dimly lighted room filled with

people, most of whom we did not recognize. But we could identify the three men on the dais. One of them was the chap who
played the Communist in *Let 'Em Eat Cake*. The other two in
later years were active in the affairs of Actors Equity and the
American Federation of Radio Artists. They became well-
known for their left-wing views later on, but at that time we
didn't know too much about those things.

The smoke-filled room was stifling, and for some reason Bob
and I felt strange. The whole atmosphere struck me as being a
bit odd.

Suddenly one of the men on the dais leaped up. "Open the
windows!" he shouted.

"That's a damned good idea," Hope agreed loudly.

"Open the windows," the man shouted again. "Let the whole
world hear what we have to say. We have nothing to hide from
the exploiting class. We represent the movement of tomorrow."
And he began to pound the table.

"What's the matter with that guy?" Hope said. "No one's said
anything, and he's mad already."

The people around us looked at Bob disapprovingly.
"Shhhh," they shhhhed.

"If they open the windows, nobody will hear but the pigeons
on the windowsills," I said.

Bob continued to make acerbic comments as the man on the
dais grew wilder and wilder in his ranting against the Establishment.

After five minutes of this nonsense Bob and I decided to
leave. As we stood up and made our way to the door, we could
hear hisses and boos directed at us.

The fresh air felt good when we got outside.

# CHAPTER 11

## *Hollywood*

The way I got to Hollywood was kind of funny. My agent at the time was Doc Shurr, who had helped me get the job in *Of Thee I Sing* . Doc was a character. He always liked to have a pretty girl on his arm. His friends noticed that whoever the girl was—and he usually dated a new one every week—she wore a beautiful mink coat. Then we discovered that it was the same coat. Whenever Doc had a date he would take the coat when he went to pick up the young lady, and when he accompanied her home he would get it back. The great actor Frank Morgan used it as a sketch in the M-G-M picture *The Great Ziegfeld*.

Even in the dark days of the depression Doc was doing extremely well, and for good reason. He was an extremely capable agent, one of the best in the business. Eventually he went west where he became one of Hollywood's top representatives of talent. For years, until his untimely death, his principal client was Bob Hope.

Shurr's office in New York was located in the building housing the George M. Cohan Theater. It was a good place for his clients to hang around, particularly in the dead of winter when we had to stay indoors. On many a freezing day, Doc's office served as a haven for clients seeking surcease from the icy blasts that whistled through the canyons of Times Square. There you could pick up all the latest show news as well as jokes. Milton Berle was not invited.

We were all young guys then and we liked to gossip about our business. Occasionally we even talked about the state of the world. I don't recall many momentous things being said in Doc's office, but I do remember we had a lot of laughs. And why not? Consider some of Doc's clients: Bert Lahr, Billy Gaxton, Victor Moore, Lou Holtz and Bob Hope, among others.

One very snowy day, after lunch, I decided to drop in on Doc's office and see the boys. As I entered the building, I encountered Lew Brown of the fabulous song-writing team of DeSylva, Brown and Henderson. Brown was one of the best lyricists in the business. His credits over the years included: "That Old Feeling," "I'd Climb the Highest Mountain," "The Varsity Drag," "Life is Just a Bowl of Cherries," "Beer Barrel Polka," and "You're the Cream in My Coffee."

Lew was a nice guy, but he had one failing. He was forever telling people what wonderful things he was going to do for them, and then forgetting what he had said. As my Dad would say, "He was full of wind and high promise."

When Lew saw me on that snowy day, he could hardly contain himself. "Murph," he said enthusiastically, "I caught your performance in *Roberta*. You're simply great. Tell you what I'm gonna do. I'm gonna send you to Hollywood and I'm gonna make you a big star—a real big star."

I feigned enthusiasm. "Gee, Lew," I said, "I sure would appreciate it. Just give me an hour to pack."

Still chuckling, I entered Doc's office, occupied as usual by all the guys, busily jabbering away on matters of low moment.

"Fellows," I said, "I just dropped in to say good-bye to all of you."

"Yeah, what's up?" someone asked.

"I'm leaving for Hollywood," I replied. "I just ran into Lew Brown in the lobby and he says he's going to send me there and make me a big star."

Everybody laughed.

Hardly had the laughter subsided when the telephone rang for Doc Shurr. The call was from Hollywood. Bill Perlberg of Columbia Pictures was calling.

After Doc heard what Perlberg had to say, he began to laugh.

"I don't believe it," he said over the phone. "Well, he's here. Let me ask him."

Turning to me, Doc said, "Perlberg wants to know whether you are available for pictures."

"Would you please repeat that?" I asked, stunned by what I thought I had just heard.

I had heard right. Within half an hour I had two contracts. First I was to make a film with Eddie Cantor for Sam Goldwyn, and then I was to report to Columbia Pictures for a year's contract.

Everyone in Shurr's office was bowled over by the sudden sequence of events. They all wished me well. One remark I will never forget was that made by Bob Hope: "Murph, if it can happen to you, maybe it can happen to me." As it turned out, Hope didn't get out to the coast until a little later, but when he came, he came to stay.

I called Julie immediately. At first she couldn't believe it, but when I assured her it was for real, she was overjoyed.

I had to notify Max Gordon immediately that I would be leaving the cast of *Roberta* in June, when my contract with him expired. He was most gracious about my forthcoming departure and even gave me some friends' numbers to call when I arrived in Hollywood. He said he hoped I would do well in films.

I had long dreamed of going to Hollywood—that was the height of any actor's ambition—and now I was on my way. I had been there before. Julie and I had been in the movie capital fulfilling a nightclub engagement in 1930. The first night we were there we were drawn to Grauman's Chinese Theater on Hollywood Boulevard where Howard Hughes was premiering his picture *Hell's Angels*. This was the aviation picture to end all aviation pictures—and it was a premiere to end all premiers. The showmanship used by Hughes to sell *Hell's Angels* has rarely been duplicated. All of Hollywood seemed aglow with lights for the occasion, from the Hollywood Hills clear to the Boulevard, and literally hundreds of arc lights swept the sky in a rainbow of colors.

Like the hundreds of other fans hysterically shrieking at the sight of a celebrity, Julie and I stood outside Grauman's ogling the beautifully dressed movie stars as they rolled up in their chauffeured limousines. It was then I realized the enormous power of the screen and its hold on the imaginations of millions of people all over the world. Many years later, when I became a motion picture industry spokesman, I did all I could to help steer that power toward worthwhile ends. I think that I may have succeeded, at least to a degree. As a matter of fact, I still believe films are the most powerful influence, properly used, in the entire world.

Leaving for the coast with the knowledge we would probably be living there was not easy for either Julie or me. We had made many good friends in New York and it was difficult to leave them. But both of us realized we had to go where my career could benefit. I was thirty-two years old and Julie several years younger. We had grown tired of the rat race. We had been working hard year after year, going from job to job, but we were never able to save much money. Hollywood gave us a chance to settle down and live like normal people. We could stop being gypsies.

Under the deal worked out by Doc Shurr, I would be making seven hundred and fifty dollars a week—enormous money in those days. My dear Julie then made the biggest decision of our eight-year marriage. She decided to give up her own career and to concentrate on making a home and raising a family. Not that she didn't have movie offers on the coast. Harry Cohn, for one, was constantly pleading with her to make a screen test at Columbia, which he headed. As a matter of fact, he told me the only reason he signed me was to get Julie. But she always said no.

Julie's decision to quit and become a full-time housewife was not an easy one for her to make. She was extremely attractive, very talented and would undoubtedly have gone far in motion pictures—had she truly wanted a career. But more than anything else in the world, Julie wanted our marriage to work. She knew from the experiences of others in Hollywood that husbands and wives who shared movie careers usually had two strikes against them. For most such couples, the strains and nervous tensions of studio life often proved too much.

When you come home from a tough day of working on the set (and making movies happens to be a difficult, exacting profession) you want someone there who'll listen to your problems, not tell you about *her* problems at the studio.

In all the many years I appeared before the cameras, Julie made it a point never to come to the studio. I can think of only one time when she did, and that involved an emergency which required her personal attention. She visited the studios on two other occasions, but not to see me. Once she went over to the Disney Studios to have lunch with Mrs. Walt Disney, an old friend. Another time she visited the Metro-Goldwyn-Mayer studio in Culver City to lunch with her dear friend Joan Crawford.

One of the first things Julie did on arriving in Hollywood was to rent our first house, a beautiful, ivy-covered little place off Crescent Boulevard, in the shadow of the Chateau Marmont, the apartment-hotel where so many movie people lived. She got the place—furniture, garden and all—for one hundred and twenty-five dollars a month. Not a bad deal.

One evening Julie decided to burn the Christmas tree. The smell of pine would remind us of the East, she thought. The tree was very dry and burned faster than she had planned. The flames shot up the chimney, setting the vines covering the house on fire. I had just come home from work and was taking a shower. I heard a terrific commotion outside and people running around. I stuck my head out of the bathroom and yelled, "What's going on?" There was no response and the noise grew louder.

Now I was worried. I wrapped a towel around my middle and walked to the top of the stairs. I could hear our maid answer the phone. "I'm sorry," I heard her say, "Mrs. Murphy can't come to the phone right now. We're having a fire."

I quickly looked out the window and, sure enough, the roof of our pretty little house was on fire. I grabbed the phone and called the Hollywood Fire Department.

"Sorry, we can't come," the voice on the other end said. "You're located in Los Angeles County. You better call the County Fire Department."

Which I did, only to be told that the County Fire Department did not have jurisdiction over my house. "You'd better call the Hollywood Fire Department," I was advised.

I could hardly believe what I was hearing. Crescent Boulevard apparently was on the line between Hollywood and Los Angeles County and I had unintentionally become involved in a jurisdictional tangle. More important, my house was on fire and no one wanted to come and put the blaze out.

So, still wearing nothing but a towel, I grabbed a garden hose and climbed to the roof. By now many of the residents of the Chateau Marmont were looking out their windows at Mrs. Murphy's fire. They were to see something else.

As I hurriedly climbed out a window and went about the business of hosing down the blaze, my towel slipped off. There I was in the cool of the evening, naked as a jaybird without a bush to hide in.

I finally put out the fire and, except for my pride, the damage was minimal. Some of the neighbors gave me a smattering of applause as I climbed back in the window. I assume it was for putting out the fire.

Outside of that incident, life on Crescent Boulevard was very pleasant—until the landlord suddenly decided that the rent ought to be raised to two hundred dollars a month. Julie felt that was excessive.

"Why don't we buy our own home?" she asked. "The payments will be much less than renting."

"But we don't know how long we're going to be here," I countered. "What if my contract isn't renewed?"

"Oh, come on," she said, "let's take a chance."

There was no arguing with Julie about it. After a considerable amount of searching, she found what she wanted in Beverly Hills. It was a nice house, a little bigger than the one we had rented on Crescent Boulevard, and the price was right. Our payments amounted to one hundred dollars a month. The house had wall-to-wall carpeting, but little else. Our furniture consisted of a card table and two chairs in the breakfast nook, a bed and a dressing table in the bedroom. And that was how we lived for nearly a year.

The first Christmas we were there our friends came over with blankets and baskets of food and we had a picnic on the floor of the otherwise bare living room. Among those who showed up were Bud Leighton, Blanche Hill, the Robert Montgomerys and the James Cagneys, and there was a lot of nostalgic recalling of the good old days in New York. Bob and Jimmy had both struck it rich in Hollywood—they were two of the biggest stars at their respective studios, Metro-Goldwyn-Mayer and Warner Brothers.

When things began to go better for us financially, Julie got hold of William Haines, who was probably the most successful interior decorator in the Los Angeles area. Billy had been a top star in the silent film era and was a popular figure in the movie colony. He still is active—recently he was in the news as the decorator who helped refurbish the United States Embassy residence in London now occupied by my good friend, Ambassador Walter Annenberg.

Billy knew our general situation. He knew that we weren't wealthy, and that we intended to concentrate our financial resources on raising a family. (Julie, I'm happy to say, was about to have our first child.) Nevertheless, the first piece of furniture he brought into the house was an antique secretary which he valued at nearly a thousand dollars.

When Billy told me the price, I was nonplussed. "How do you expect me to afford a family and a thousand-dollar secretary and all the other furniture I'll have to buy?" I gasped.

Drawing himself up in his haughtiest manner, Billy said, "Mr. Murphy, you stick to the breeding and I'll decorate the house." He did, and beautifully.

On my first day in Hollywood, I was told to report to Sam Goldwyn at his studio office. I showed up promptly and was told to wait. While sitting and perusing the trade papers, I could hear someone exuberantly proclaim that "this will be the most magnificent picture, the most significant film, the most wonderful achievement of your spectacular career, one which will demonstrate your flair for beauty and taste" and so on ad nauseum. I never heard so many superlatives or high-flown adjectives.

Finally a voice broke in. "That's it. That's exactly what I want. Just tell the people the simple truth about my picture."

The second voice was that of the fabulous Sam Goldwyn.

In greeting me, Goldwyn was friendly but brusque. He had something else on his mind. "I saw you at the Richman Club some years ago and I'm still wondering," he said. "Were you the one who danced with the girl or the one who did the comedy act with that fellow?"

"I was both," I replied.

"Now, quit the kidding. This is serious."

"I'm not kidding, Mr. Goldwyn."

"My God, I've been wondering about that ever since I first saw you."

I began to work on the Eddie Cantor film, *Kid Millions,* the following day. Eddie was a delight to work with. He remembered having appeared with me at that Sunday night benefit. And he laughed when I told him the problem he had created by "stealing" my song.

The only problem was Sam Goldwyn. After my first conversation with him in his office, he seemed to be deliberately ignoring me when we happened to pass each other. I thought he was snubbing me. Worse, I felt he didn't like me and/or was dissatisfied with my work. I decided to confront him.

Encountering him one afternoon, I said, "Mr. Goldwyn, I have to talk to you."

"About what?" he said guardedly.

"I have a feeling you don't like me."

"What in the name of God are you talking about?"

"Well," I continued pouring out my soul, "you haven't said two words to me since I've been here. If you don't like my work, I'll be only too glad to let you out of the contract. The picture isn't too far along and you can get someone else to replace me. I'll give you back half of the money you paid me and I'll go back to New York."

Sam looked at me as if I had gone crazy. "Cut it out, you *meshuggener,*" he exclaimed. "Don't you understand that I'm a very busy man? Don't you realize that I'm working on my next picture? You're doing very well. Cantor likes you and the rushes are great. Now, get the hell out of here and stop bothering me."

I felt better after that, even though Sam continued to ignore me. When *Kid Millions* was completed, however, he had decided to use me in some of his forthcoming productions, although he hadn't told me about it. He instructed his production assistant, Fred Kohlmer, to get an extension on my option. Kohlmer was crestfallen. He confessed to Goldwyn there was no option and that I was scheduled to report to Columbia following *Kid Millions.* Later Goldwyn told me that he nearly fired Kohlmer over the episode.

Over the years Sam Goldwyn and his charming wife Frances became our close friends. I think Sam is proud that he was the producer who brought me to Hollywood; he has always been pleased with my success in political endeavors. The Goldwyns and the Murphys have spent many wonderful evenings together.

Sam's reputation for malapropisms, by the way, is fully justified. But he's always known exactly what he wanted to say, even though he may not always have put it into the king's best English.

A dinner party at the home of Phyllis and Fred Astaire stands out in my memory. Julie and I were there along with the Goldwyns. The three ladies were gossiping in one corner of the room while Fred, Sam and I were discussing our favorite subject—the movie business.

"Warner Brothers has a big James Cagney picture," said Goldwyn enthusiastically. "It's called  *Yankee Doodle Dandy.* It's the story of George M. Cohan and it's patriotic. I hear it's simply sensational.

"They have a great plan for its exploitation," he went on. "They plan to open it simultaneously all across the country on July fourth—Washington's Birthday!"

Fred and I didn't dare to look at each other lest we break out in gales of laughter. We managed to contain ourselves and changed the subject.

Sam Goldwyn was a great promoter as well as a fine picture maker. And as a rule, he had a lot to promote. His films were among the finest ever made. A man of great taste and integrity, he hired the best actors available and encouraged top-notch screenwriting. He had no compunctions about tearing a film apart and starting all over again if he didn't think it was right. He refused to release a picture that didn't meet his high standards. He had an instinct for greatness, an instinct sorely lacking these days among those motion picture producers who are seeking to make a fast dollar by appealing to the worst in man.

These days when I talk with Sam we both wonder what's happened to the morals of our industry. We're worried about the effect that too much permissiveness may have on our nation's future.

Sam Goldwyn was often funny without meaning to be. When I became active in political affairs, Sam asked me about the possibility of doing him a favor.

"Murph," he said, "you're in politics now and you can get things done. How about getting the road by my house shut off?"

He was referring to a cul-de-sac which divided his property from that owned by the tire magnate, Leonard Firestone, a mutual friend.

"Sam," I explained, "you and Lennie are the only ones who

own homes up there, so there really isn't any reason for public traffic on the road. The only thing is this—if they do shut off the road, it will become private and you and Lennie will have to pay for its upkeep."

"Murph," was Goldwyn's quick response, "I'd like to talk to you about a new script that I want to do." He never mentioned the road again.

I once received a phone call from Jack Mann, a friend who lived near the Sam Goldwyn home. It seemed that Sam had the habit, on returning from the studio, of getting out of his car a few blocks away and walking home, passing Mann's property on the way.

For a man getting along in years, this was a good form of exercise. One day, for some reason, Sam's kidneys weren't able to hold out long enough for him to get to his house. He had no choice but to relieve himself on Mann's holly. Mann was fit to be tied. He called me immediately.

"What am I going to do about this?" he shouted.

I thought it over. "Tell you what," I said. "If he does it again, why don't you squirt him with a hose and make it a contest?"

I never found out whether he actually did it, but I didn't hear any more complaints.

Sam was a good and tolerant man. During the making of *Kid Millions*, he made one of his rare appearances on the set. Approaching a tall, pretty, redheaded chorus girl, he inquired how she was getting along.

"Just fine," she said. "Except for one thing. This guy Sam Goldwyn keeps sending me notes to come to his office. What do you suppose that old bastard wants me up there for?"

Sam, who was then an "old" man of fifty-two, burst out into laughter. When the chorus girl finally realized whom she was talking to, she was mortified. She tried to apologize, but Goldwyn—still laughing—would have none of it.

"I haven't had this much fun in years," he said.

The girl was Lucille Ball. She had appeared in bit parts in half a dozen or so unimportant pictures. Like every bright and talented youngster in Hollywood, she wanted to be a star. Then twenty-four years old, she was afraid time might be passing her by.

I had been puzzled by Lucille's behavior on the set. During the shooting of the musical numbers, we would get five-minute breaks for a smoke or other, more urgent, duties. Lucille would invariably be late in returning. The assistant would have to call her name over the loudspeaker, "Miss Ball—Miss Ball—on the set please."

This got to be too much for the assistant director, Benny Silvie. Normally Silvie was good-natured and hard to anger, but he had had enough. Finally he told her off for holding up shooting.

I took Lucille aside. "Honey, I don't understand you," I said. "One of these days Benny will get so angry he'll fire you."

"Oh," she said, matter-of-factly, "that may be true. But one thing you can be sure of—they'll know who I am."

Seven years later, I did a picture with Lucille called *A Girl, A Guy and A Gob*. For some reason Harold Lloyd, who was the producer, began to shoot the film with only about a third of the script completed. As a result the director, Dick Wallace, and I would often sit up nights to write the stuff that would be filmed the following day.

Both Wallace and I recognized Lucille's potential as a comedienne, and we wrote her lines accordingly. She scored a remarkable success. "Lucille Ball," said a *New York Times* review of the film, "may not be made of India rubber, but she has as much bounce." From then on there was no stopping her in her rise to fame and fortune.

Lucille was grateful to me for the part I played in her much-deserved success. Unlike others in the movie business, she never forgot. She once told me, "Whenever you're out of work, if I'm working, you've got a job with me." And when that time came, I found she meant every word.

My first motion picture, *Kid Millions,* was a success and my personal notices were pretty good. I was absolutely thrilled when I read Louella Parsons' column. She wrote something to this effect: "Having just heard this new boy from New York sing, I think Bing Crosby had better look to his laurels." I wasn't sure what she meant but even to be mentioned in the same paragraph with the great Bing was quite an honor.

I was recently reminded of my singing career, the little there was of it, when George Jessel sent me the sheet music of a newly-published version of an old song he had written. Across the front page was the legend, "As Sung by Senator George Murphy."

In *Kid Millions* I sang a song with Ann Sothern, and it was quite an experience. A lot of choreography was involved. For one thing, Annie and I had to move to five different and exact positions for camera takes. The positions were marked off with chalk and the idea was for us to arrive at those places at the same time in order to fit the picture of the chorus group behind us.

Annie was wearing a big, circular, bouffant skirt and when I put my arm around her the other side of her hoop would fly up. So a man was assigned to hold it down. Because of the skirt, she couldn't see her marks, so another man was assigned to guide her feet. A third man was steering my feet, and two more were holding special lights to accommodate the cameraman. This is the way I did my first song number. It was too much.

Once, in the middle of a high C, my guide had my right foot turned outward when it should have been turned inward, and he gave it a twist that damned near broke my ankle. That did it. At the end of the number, I wired Doc Shurr:

BEEN IN HOLLYWOOD THREE DAYS AND AM
FED UP. GET ME OUT OF THIS AND INTO A
BROADWAY SHOW.

Fortunately, Doc ignored the telegram.

The "California Collegians" await the cue to begin DUNKING from George Murphy the dancing comedian.

Between scenes of the musical hit "ROBERTA" now at the New Amsterdam Theatre, New York

Stardom was about to fall on the California Collegians

With Ann Sothern, in "Ringside Maisie"

With a real champion, Joe Louis (and Leo Durocher)

With Judy Garland, "the greatest all-around talent ever in show business," and Gene Kelly

A birthday cake for the great Louis B. Mayer

In the office of F.B.I. Director J. Edgar Hoover during the filming of "Walk East on Beacon"

(Stan Creighton Photo)

In San Francisco, during one of the many great War Bond Drives

The unreleased last movie, "Talk About a Stranger," featured Nancy Davis, soon to become Mrs. Ronald Reagan.

Winning the Academy Award (with Ginger Rogers)

(Stanart Photo)

Hands and feet immortalized
at Grauman's Chinese Theatre, with Gen. Omar Bradley

Actors as politicians: the Screen Actors Guild delegation at the AFL national convention, seeking an end to the film dispute

# CHAPTER 12

## "The Black Bull of Gower Street"

Within minutes of my first meeting with Harry Cohn, the big boss of Columbia pictures, we were involved in what currently would be called a "confrontation." That's not the way to succeed in Hollywood but, in spite of warnings I had received from friends that Cohn would work me over quickly, I felt I had no choice.

I had reported to the Gower Street studios, pursuant to my contract with Columbia, on the completion of my work in *Kid Millions*. I was led into Cohn's office. There he sat behind a raised, semicircular desk. An autographed photograph of Benito Mussolini hung on the wall. Cohn made no secret of his admiration for the Italian dictator who at that moment in history had made the trains run on time and was fighting crime and hunger in his country. This, of course, was before Benito got mixed up with the German madman in World War II.

It was all rather intimidating, which was exactly the effect Cohn wanted to achieve. I must concede that Cohn's reputation as a loud, foul-mouthed tyrant did not make my first meeting with him any easier. He quickly got my Irish up.

I hardly had a chance to sit down when he said, "I don't like your name. I'm going to change it."

"What did you say?" I asked disbelievingly.

"You heard me. From now on your name will be Gregory Marshall. What do you think of that?"

"I think it stinks," I replied angrily. "There's nothing in the contract that gives you permission to change my name. I was born George Murphy and I'll die George Murphy. What do you think of that?"

"Get out of here!" he yelled at the top of his voice. "And don't come back."

"Thank you very much," I shouted.

Joe Nolan, the genial Irish studio manager, said, "Pay no attention. Harry is impetuous and you've done the right thing. He really doesn't like to be 'yessed.' "

I remained George Murphy.

Harry was not easy to work for. He assigned me to films I didn't particularly like to do. In my first assignments, I played opposite Nancy Carroll in two depressing tales, *Jealousy* and *I'll Love You Always*. Nancy herself wasn't too easy to work with. She was potentially one of the great stars, but she never quite made it—maybe because she used stage tricks instead of her God-given talents.

I never had any problems working with any other actresses, and I worked with some of the biggest. My relationships with stars like Eleanor Powell, Judy Garland, Ginger Rogers and Lana Turner, among others, were always pleasant. But Nancy Carroll was something else. She seemed to enjoy making others uncomfortable.

While at Columbia, I tried to convince Harry Cohn that my services could be used to best advantage in musical films. After all, that was how I made my reputation on Broadway. And I hadn't done too badly in my first film, *Kid Millions*.

Cohn finally agreed to hear me audition. So I booked a rehearsal hall at the studio, along with a pianist, and prepared a number. When I thought I was ready to audition for Cohn, I told the pianist, "I think I've got it right. Let's go up to Cohn's office and try it on the old bastard."

"You don't have to," Cohn's voice boomed over a loudspeaker. "I heard it and you sound okay." Unbeknownst to me, he had been listening over a concealed microphone installed in the stage.

Before long, I learned that Cohn had the entire studio wired so that he could secretly listen to everything going on in his tiny empire. Talk about Big Brother! But he made some great pictures.

Ironically, Cohn and I became good friends. Perhaps it was because I would brook no nonsense from him and didn't kow-tow to his mercurial whims. It may sound funny, but I felt sorry for this man who, born of immigrant parents and raised on the streets of a New York ghetto, managed by sheer perseverance to become a power in a tough business. Though he was tough at the studio, I always found him to be a charming man socially, with a great sense of humor.

One night Julie and I were entertaining some out-of-town friends at a nightclub on Sunset Strip. I happened to look up and see Harry come down the stairs in the company of Nate Spingold, his New York liaison and money-man. Harry waved to me and I waved back, and Harry said in a loud voice, "See this guy here. His name is George Murphy. He's the only son-of-a-bitch in Hollywood who likes me."

And why shouldn't I like him? I had finally succeeded in get-ting away from him and Columbia Pictures. In Harry's case at least, absence made the heart grow fonder.

There was a period at Columbia when I had nothing to do. I could have relaxed, reported to the studio every day and collect-ed my paycheck—but I wasn't built that way. I had to be doing something.

I got something to do when producer Henry Duffy decided to bring the New York smash hit *Anything Goes* to Los Angeles. Duffy had booked the El Capitan Theater and had to cast re-placements for such stars as Billy Gaxton, Ethel Merman and Victor Moore to play the roles they had originally created on Broadway in the Cole Porter musical. Hearing I was available, Duffy asked me to join his company and I quickly accepted the part created on Broadway by my pal Billy Gaxton.

The night before we were to open I received a phone call from Harry Cohn. I could tell immediately that he had an un-usual head of steam. Harry was never one to disguise his feel-ings.

"I hear you're going to do *Anything Goes*," he began.

"Yep."

"Who's paying you?" Cohn asked.

"You are."

"What do you mean?"

"I mean that I am under contract to you and you have no choice but to pay me whether I work or not. At the moment I'm not working at the studio."

"You must be out of your goddamn mind!" he shouted. "I'm getting an injunction to keep you out of that goddamn play." He went on like that, using obscenities that even I had never heard before.

"If you persist in going on with that show, I'll see to it you'll never work in Hollywood again," he yelled. He ranted on and on.

I didn't lose my cool because I had the studio's permission in writing to do the play. I said if he tried to stop me from going on the next night I would sue him, that Henry Duffy would sue him, that Billy Gaxton would sue him, that Ethel Merman would sue him, and that all his friends—the few he had left—at The Lambs club in New York would sue him. The conversation was heated, if not enlightening.

Harry kept bellowing imprecations. That was the night I christened him "The Black Bull of Gower Street," a description that was to follow him to his grave. Finally I banged the phone in his ear.

As I suspected, Harry Cohn's roar was worse than his bite. There were no law suits and the show went on as scheduled.

When the curtain went up opening night, who was planted in the second row center but Harry himself—beaming broadly and enjoying the entire affair.

Grantland Rice's daughter, Florence, stuck her head into my dressing room after the first act and said, "Gee, Murph, the show is going just great. You ought to see Harry Cohn out in the lobby."

"What's he doing? I asked, fearing the worst.

"Oh, he's parading up and down, taking full credit for the show and telling anyone who will listen that you're his boy and that without you the show would be lousy."

It was during this engagement that I met a tall, gangling young man named Jimmy Stewart. He frequently came backstage to wait for Shirley Ross, one of our leading ladies. Miss Ross, a lovely blonde who went on to make a name for herself in films, was definitely worth waiting for.

In those days, Stewart invariably wore a leather flying jacket, which gave rise to the rumor that he was an airport bum. That was what we called the kids who used to hang around airports to hitch rides in airplanes.

We got to talking one night as he waited for Shirley to remove her makeup and get dressed. He told me he had been graduated from Princeton University in 1932 and had almost immediately gone on the Broadway stage. He had appeared in several plays including *Yellow Jack* and had been signed by M-G-M for films.

Naturally I watched Jimmy Stewart's emergence as one of America's great stars with joy. He is one of the most decent men I have ever known.

Jimmy is modest to a fault. During World War II, unbeknownst to even his closest friends, he went downtown to an Air Corps recruiting station and, without any publicity, quietly enlisted as a flight cadet. That was the way he wanted it. But some Air Corps public relations guys heard about it and insisted that he go through the induction process again—with newsreel cameras grinding away.

I saw him from time to time during his flight training period. He was considerably annoyed about the fuss being made over his being a movie star. He wanted to learn to fly and the generals kept sending him off to make a speech somewhere to sell war bonds. Once he was even pulled out of night flying maneuvers.

"My gosh, Murph," he once told me," they're going to kill me before I even get a chance to get into the war."

Somehow James Stewart survived and today he is a Brigadier General in the Air Force Reserve and still a popular motion picture star. Whenever I am back home in California I make it a point to call on Jimmy and his beautiful Gloria. I'm proud to say they have long been loyal supporters.

From Los Angeles, the *Anything Goes* company moved to San Francisco for a short engagement. The reviews were excellent and I personally received a good press. I was a happy man, doing what I loved to do most—appearing in a great role before a live audience.

In San Francisco I met Louis B. Mayer, the production chief of Metro-Goldwyn-Mayer who was to become such an important influence in my life.

I had been invited to a birthday luncheon for the then Lieutenant Governor of California, George Hatfield. The luncheon at Jack's Restaurant had been arranged by Louis Lurie, the real estate tycoon who was active in San Francisco politics. Most of those present were also interested in politics. Since I knew very little about the subject, I said little but listened avidly.

Everyone got to feeling pretty good and there was a lot of good-natured joshing about political allegiances, what with Democrats and Republicans being represented at the luncheon in about equal numbers.

Suddenly Louis Mayer pointed in my direction and demanded to know who the silent one was. Someone said I was an actor.

"An actor?" Mayer asked, somewhat disdainfully. "Where does he work?"

"He works for Harry Cohn at Columbia Pictures."

The mention of Cohn's name struck Mayer funny. "If he works for Harry Cohn, then let him speak for Harry Cohn," he thundered.

That was a cue for a loud chorus of "Speech! Speech! Speech!"

Frankly embarrassed, I couldn't believe what was happening. My face turned red. I did rise, but all I could say was, "I know very little about politics and I'm not qualified to make a speech before this distinguished group."

"That's not good enough," Mayer said. "If you work for Harry Cohn, you speak for Harry Cohn."

Again a chorus of "Speech! Speech! Speech!"

I knew there was no way out. So I got up again. "Well, gentlemen," I said. "Since you seem determined to hear me speak for Mr. Cohn, I will try to do so in Mr. Cohn's inimitable fashion."

I paused for several seconds. A quizzical look came across Mayer's face. Then I exploded into a stream of obscenities which lasted two or three minutes. I called everyone present blankety-blank cretins and I paid particular attention to insulting Louis Mayer. Then I sat down.

By now everyone was hysterical with laughter. Louis Mayer was wildly applauding. He came over to pat me on the back. "You've got moxie," he said.

When the luncheon was over, Mayer sought me out. "What's your situation with Cohn?" he asked.

"After that imitation, I wouldn't know," I replied. I explained that my contract with Columbia had another few weeks to run.

"Would you like to work for me?" Mayer asked.

The conversation hardly seemed real. M-G-M was the giant of the industry. It made more pictures than any other studio. It had more stars than any other studio. And it paid more money than any other studio.

"I'd love to work for you, Mr. Mayer," I said.

"Well, come in and see me when your contract expires," he said.

On returning home, I discovered that my contract was to expire in three days. I laid low, not saying a word to anyone, hoping to be forgotten at Columbia. Apparently they didn't even miss me.

When the three days were over, I was a free man. Columbia had not said a word about renewing my option. I rushed over to Culver City. The thought did cross my mind that a big executive like Louis Mayer might have forgotten me, but I was wrong. Mayer welcomed me warmly and seemed genuinely pleased that I was available.

"Go down the hall and see Benny Thau," he instructed. "There will be a contract waiting for you. I suggest you sign it and report to the studio tomorrow."

The contract provided excellent terms and I signed it quickly. That began a happy and pleasant association with Louis B. Mayer and M-G-M that lasted for twenty-two years.

# CHAPTER 13

## "*Lonesome George*" *at Metro*

My first few months at M-G-M were not the most pleasant I ever spent in my life. Here I was at the biggest and most important studio in Hollywood, drawing a fairly good paycheck, which was very nice, but no one would speak to me, which wasn't very nice. I was not being given any parts and that was driving me absolutely up the wall. I was really "Lonesome George" until I met another hired hand with the same complaint—Buddy Ebsen. No one would talk to him, either, and that gave us a lot in common right off.

To while away the time, we would walk around and explore the huge Metro lot in Culver City, visiting the sound stages where shooting was going on, watching some of the most important stars in the business perform before the cameras. This, of course, did us no harm in the long run as we did learn an awful lot by observing some of the great craftsmen in action—people like Clark Gable, Joan Crawford, Bob Montgomery and Spencer Tracy.

We fooled around making up dance routines until after a while even this began to pall. We bought a couple of BB guns and set up targets on an empty stage to shoot at. Finally we invented a game where we placed empty tin cans on the handle of a shovel. By jumping on the blade we could propel the cans at least fifty feet into the air. The object was to land them into barrels or other receptacles.

We became so proficient that we set up ground rules and began keeping score. All of this fascinated the grips, electricians, carpenters and other studio workers who, when they weren't doing anything, would hang around and pick favorites. Once, while trying for a new world's distance record, Ebsen

fired a can just as Sam Katz, a major producer, walked through
the studio door. Sam nearly got beaned and that ended our
shovel-can series. Soon afterward, and this probably was a coin-
cidence, Ebsen got a small part in a Western picture and I went
back to being "Lonesome George."

One day while I was working out alone in the dance studio,
Billy Grady, the casting director, came in with a cute teen-ager,
to whom I was attracted immediately. To while away the time,
we put together a little soft-shoe routine. That's the way I met
Judy Garland.

I soon realized that some weeks before I had seen little Judy
and her two older sisters—they were called the Gumm Sisters in
those days—perform at a Sunday night benefit. The reason that
I had particularly remembered Judy was that this charming
youngster at one point in the act had climbed on top of a piano
and had done the greatest imitation of Helen Morgan singing
"The Man I Love" that I had ever seen. The scarf she used was
bigger than she was. This cute, bright-eyed, wonderful little girl
with the turned-up nose turned out to be one of the greatest
stars of all time.

Judy couldn't have been more than twelve or thirteen years
old when I met her. She was getting ready for an audition at
Metro and she was really nervous. I tried to calm her down a bit
as we were going through our little soft-shoe dance. That's the
day, too, that I met Roger Edens, one of the great musical talents. In years to come, he arranged most of Judy's songs and, in
my opinion, he should have been a producer of musical films at
Metro long before he finally was given his chance.

Judy and I became close friends. I began to call her "Grandma," a nickname she seemed to take to. After she had been
signed by Metro—Louis Mayer quickly sized her up as a potentially valuable property—I would say to Judy, "Come on,
Grandma, let's practice a little bit." We would go back to work
and try to make up some new steps with a generous assist from
Roger Edens, who would dream up new rhythms and tunes.
Those were enjoyable days.

A few years later, when Judy was one of Metro's biggest stars, I met her one day and greeted her with the usual, "Hi, Grandma."

"Uncle George," Judy said, "I would just as soon that you wouldn't call me 'Grandma' anymore. After all, I'm no longer a child."

"Of course, Miss Garland," I said. "I'll be glad to oblige."

She flushed and wrinkled her nose and said, "I didn't mean it that way. Please call me Judy."

I realized then that Judy had really grown up. In fact it would be fair to say she grew up almost too quickly, which may have been one of the reasons for all the tragedy in her life.

Her first picture for Metro was one in which I also appeared, *Broadway Melody of 1938*. Her amazing talent was apparent when she sang a special arrangement created by Roger Edens. It showed a little girl writing a fan letter in which she confessed her hopeless, adolescent love for the star of stars, Clark Gable. Her performance of this number, to the tune of "You Made Me Love You," was a real classic.

Judy became known in the trade as Metro's answer to Deanna Durbin, who was then in her heyday. She soon passed Deanna and everyone else along the way as she rose to the top of stardom. Judy was the greatest all-around talent I have ever encountered in show business. She could do anything and she did it in a way that was just—Judy.

Her next big sensation was as a gawky adolescent with a crush on another great talent, Mickey Rooney, in *Love Finds Andy Hardy*. But her greatest hit came when she was seventeen, when she played the pigtailed youngster from Kansas who was blown into fantasyland by the cyclone in *The Wizard of Oz*. It was in this film that Judy sang the song that became her trademark for over thirty years, "Over the Rainbow." It symbolized the wistful pursuit of a happiness that became, for Judy, unattainable.

Judy and Mickey Rooney were soon the mainstays of the studio. For several years their films helped keep that giant film factory afloat in a sea of increased competition. Arthur Freed, their producer, was determined to get as many pictures out of these youngsters as possible. As a consequence, both Judy and Mickey were overworked far beyond their endurance. In the late Thirties they were making three or four pictures a year with no rest in between.

Louie Mayer really loved these kids as much as if they were his own. He was terribly proud of them and their successes, but sometimes he would forget they were only children. He was forever buying them expensive things. Once, I remember, he gave Mickey a couple of fine racehorses. That afternoon I remonstrated with the boss. "I know that you mean well, but if you will permit my saying so, I don't think that's the way to handle Mickey. Number one, you're going to spoil him with too much kindness, and number two, he's not old enough yet to get mixed up with Lot Five." Lot Five was the code name for the Hollywood Race Track where, from time to time, we had to look for producers and other executives when they couldn't be located in their offices.

For little Judy it was all too much. At a time when other girls her age were having teen-age fun, Judy was constantly working—learning new songs, new dance routines, studying parts. When she was eighteen she was already seeing a psychiatrist whom she described as "an old ginker with a foreign accent." She was trying to work all day and play all night and it was beginning to tell on her.

Even more dreadful was the fact that Judy soon became addicted to all sorts of pills. She'd take stimulants during the day to keep herself awake. Then to fall asleep at night she would take depressants. Finally that great gentleman Howard Strickling, who was head of Metro publicity, convinced Mayer that if Judy didn't get a vacation and a proper rest the studio might just be minus its biggest star.

But some idiot, who shall remain nameless, thought it would

be a good idea to send Judy to New York for her vacation and, at the same time, do some promotion and publicity work. This, in my judgement, was a new high in stupidity. And the woman they sent along to accompany Judy was the worst possible choice. As a result, Judy didn't get any rest; she was staying up all night and getting involved with the worst possible influences in the big city. When Judy returned to Culver City she was more exhausted than when she had left. But it was too late. Vacation was over and it was back to work.

I had the privilege of working with Judy in several films. She was a true professional, and I recall a scene she did in *Little Nellie Kelly* that was so emotional and effective that it wrung the hearts of all those watching. Whenever I hear the song, "Oh, You Beautiful Doll," I can still see little Judy in the doll shop number that we did together. And as far as I am concerned, there will never be anything like Judy's handling of "The Bells Are Ringing," the wonderful number she did with Gene Kelly in *For Me and My Gal.*

I've always cherished our friendship. Though I hadn't seen her for some time, she called me in Washington one night some months before she died. "Uncle George, I've got some problems with my taxes," she said. I felt I was talking to the same little girl with the turned-up nose I had met thirty years before in a dance studio at Metro. This tragic little creature had made many millions of dollars, but she was a much better performer than bookkeeper and she never seemed to find the right guy to take care of her. She was flat broke.

Of course, I was happy to do what I could with her tax problems. I went to the very top to plead her case. Judy called me later to say how grateful she was for my help. That was the last time I spoke to her.

As I have already noted, my early months on the Metro lot were not the happiest for an actor who was raring to act. Despite my having been signed by the big boss himself, no producer in Culver City seemed to want to take a chance with me. I was worried, very worried. You can't stand still in show business. You move one way or the other—up or down—and I wanted to move up.

I had plenty of time to catch up with some of my old New York friends. I had great fun reminiscing with Sid Silvers, who used to be the man in the box seat who heckled that fine comedian Phil Baker. Sid and another old pal of mine, Jack McGowan, had made big names for themselves at Metro as writers of screen musicals.

McGowan also had a pretty good Broadway background. Among his other credits, he had collaborated with Buddy DeSylva in writing the book of *Hold Everything.* In his early days in the theater, Jack had been a juvenile leading man. He once had a singing role in one of the earlier *Ziegfeld Follies.* The part called for him to sit on a stage moon, about twenty feet above the platform, and sing romantically to a girl pirouetting below.

One night before the show, Jack had had a few drinks too many. He arrived at the theater, got made up and dressed in his costume, and climbed aboard his seat on the moon where, while waiting for his cue, he fell sound asleep. When the curtains parted Jack was sitting up there snoring away and the director was yelling from the wings, "Hey, Jack!" He awoke with such a start that he lost his balance, fell off the moon, and was fired. A few days later he left for Hollywood and a more successful career as a screen writer.

At one point, Sid Silvers and Jack McGowan were the hottest musical writers in Hollywood. They had developed such a reputation as collaborators that one day, as a gag, they began to ad-lib a story on the phone to Sam Katz, who produced most of Metro's musicals. They had made up some story on the spur of the moment about a dance hall with sailors and girls, and Sam got so excited that he bought the story on the phone, telling them to bring the script to his office the first thing in the morning. Well, these two clowns were forced to sit up all night and script a story. Somehow they managed to get it done.

Of course, those were the days in the movie business when you could do things like that and get away with it. A lot of the films created that way turned out to be pretty good, too.

Another Broadwayite I encountered at Metro was Alex Aarons of the producing team of Aarons and Freedley, who had hired Julie and me for *Hold Everything*. They were better known as the producers of shows featuring Fred and Adele Astaire. Alex had been brought out to the coast at an enormous salary to produce films but, like me, he wasn't getting too much to do.

Alex told me of one incident that had offended the studio brass. It seemed that Metro had placed under contract a New York actor-dancer named Clifton Webb at about one hundred thousand dollars a year, planning to make a great-lover star out of him. Only after the papers had been signed did the studio learn that Webb had some effeminate mannerisms. Now in those dear old days the general public was not yet at the point where it could accept such characteristics. The studio had a hundred-thousand-dollar problem on its hands—a lot of money, even by Hollywood standards.

The big question was how to use Webb productively. A screen test was made, and several of the top executives, including the recently-arrived Alex Aarons, examined the results in the screening room. Their worst suspicions were confirmed. Clifton's mannerisms leaped right off the screen and hit them in the eye, very definitely precluding any chance of this young man becoming the great screen lover that they had hoped for. What to do?

"You knew this fellow in New York, didn't you?" one of the executives yelled at Alex.

"Of course," Alex wisecracked, "I've known him ever since he was a little girl."

Well, that tore it completely. Alex Aarons was let go at the first opportunity and Clifton Webb, one of the nicest guys I've ever met, had to wait a few years before becoming known as one of the finest character actors in town.

I had been hanging around Metro for six months, doing little but shooting out light bulbs, jumping on shovels and collecting my paychecks. One day I received an offer from Universal Pictures to appear as the lead in what was planned to be the biggest musical ever produced at that lot—*Top of the Town.* I was so excited I couldn't sleep. But I had a problem: in order to get the Universal job, I had to get out of my Metro contract, and I had no idea of how to go about it.

By chance I heard that Nicholas Schenck, the president of M-G-M, had come out from New York on one of his periodic visits. Now I had met Schenck through my old boss, Sam Harris, in New York. Billy Gaxton and I were guests at his New York home on several occasions. I knew Nick to be a warm, understanding and sympathetic man.

I arranged to see him at his office. Schenck couldn't have been nicer. He had heard that I was now employed by his company and he knew I would do well and he was delighted. I said I was delighted, too, but I had a problem I wanted to discuss with him.

"Go ahead."

"Well, I'd like to get out of my contract."

Schenck looked genuinely astonished. "What's the trouble? Aren't you being paid enough?"

"I have no complaints about the pay. It's just that I'm not getting any work to do."

"Oh that," he said. "Don't worry about it. Out here it sometimes takes a little longer than it does in New York."

"Well, Mr. Schenck, I realize that. But I'm not getting even a nibble from the producers. Besides, if I'm here for a year without doing anything, by the end of the year they sure as shooting are going to let me go and I'll be out looking for a job with everybody saying, 'Well, Metro had him under contract for a year and he didn't do anything, so he must be pretty bad.' "

"Then," I went on. "I'll be going back to Broadway with a black eye that I haven't earned. In other words, I'll have struck out without having had a chance to go to bat. So please, Mr. Schenck, do me a favor. If you could arrange to get me my release I would be more than grateful to you."

Schenck had never had a request like that before. Usually it was just the opposite—he was badgered by people who wanted contracts. As he later told me, this was the first time in his long career that anybody had asked him to get out of a contract.

"All right, George," he finally said. "I think I understand your problem, and you've certainly made a fair case for yourself."

He gave me the release and I walked out of Nick Schenck's office feeling as if I were in seventh heaven. I was heading for my car in the parking lot, ready to drive right over to Universal, when a voice from above yelled, "Hey, Murphy!" I turned around and looked up. There on the second floor of the old Executive Office Building was the smiling countenance of Sam Katz, the executive directly in charge of making some of the biggest musicals on the Metro lot.

"Can you come up here for a minute?" he asked. "I want to talk to you."

I did as I was told. When I walked into his office Katz had a script in his hand. "Take this home and read it," he ordered. "Tell me what you think of it in the morning. You're going to star in a picture with Eleanor Powell."

Needless to say, I was startled. "But, Mr. Katz," I blurted out, "I don't work here anymore."

"What do you mean you don't work here?"

I told him the whole story of my release from Metro and of Universal's offer to give me a part in *Top of the Town* and how excited I was about the whole idea.

"Nonsense," Katz said. "Now you just sit down there for a moment."

Sam made a telephone call and the next thing I knew I was in the office of one Eddie Mannix, the studio's general manager and chief troubleshooter. Eddie listened to my story, nodded, and said, "Now George, go home, don't talk to anyone and don't do anything. Just stay home and wait for my call."

"What's this all about?" I asked.

"Don't ask me any questions. Just go home. You're going to get everything you want."

Eddie knew what he was talking about. Within two days he had worked out a deal whereby I remained under contract to M-G-M which, in turn, would lend me to Universal for several films including *Top of the Town*. And I was to get a considerable boost in salary. Who could have asked for anything more?

Well, I did appear in *Top of the Town* but, as they used to say, maybe I "shoulda stood in bed." It wasn't the greatest musical ever made. In fact it can be argued that it should never have been made at all. It had everything but a decent story line and a sense of humor, although its cast included some of the funniest people in the business—Hugh Herbert, Henry Armetta, Gregory Ratoff, Mischa Auer and Ella Logan of the Scottish burr.

The story was unbelievable. I played the part of an orchestra leader, Ted Lane, who was in love with a young heiress. This young lady had spent a summer in the Soviet Union where she had discovered culture. She wanted to bring some of it back to New York night clubs. It's funny, in retrospect, how often in those days Russia and culture were made to appear synonymous.

As Ted Lane, I disagreed with the young lady. I insisted that culture notwithstanding, there was nothing more appropriate for a bistro than the songs of Gertrude Niesen, a curvaceous chorus line and the jazzy California Collegians. We carried our debate to the public. Culture lost and I won on the opening night of the Moonbeam Roof.

Having read the script prior to shooting, I tried vainly to get some changes. I pointed out there was no continuity and little credibility. Apparently I struck a raw nerve.

"Why don't you study your part and let us take care of the script?" I was emphatically told.

I did as they suggested, telling myself that after all, it was their money. And Universal certainly poured a lot of money into the production. For example, they brought in a set designer, John Harkrider, who had had several big successes in New York. He decided to top himself with this one—he ordered a tremendous set completely wrapped in tinfoil. It was totally unmanageable and drove the cameraman nuts.

"It's very beautiful," I told the designer. "But don't you realize the dancers will tear the floor to pieces?"

"Then we'll just replace it," he said.

"But why not just paint the floor silver?"

"Because it wouldn't be as exciting."

Just as I figured, the dancers ripped the floor to shreds while they were rehearsing. That night an emergency crew was rushed in to remove all the material and paint the floor silver. About fifty thousand dollars went down the drain, and the studio heads went into a tizzy. As I said, it was their money.

Up to then I had done very little dancing in films. In *Kid Millions* I had done a brief dance with Ann Sothern, but that was all. In *Jealousy*, which I made at Columbia with Nancy Carroll, I got to box for two days with Lee Ramage just six weeks before he fought with and was knocked out by Joe Louis. In *I'll Love you Always* and *Public Menace* I didn't get to dance either. I wound up saying to everyone, "I'm a dancer. Who's going to give me a chance to dance?"

One day, while we were preparing to shoot a musical number in *Top of the Town,* someone discovered that Gertrude Niesen had forgotten the shoes that went with her costume. A messenger was sent to get them at her home. While we were waiting, I suggested that Peggy Ryan, a moppet who could dance to beat the band, and I do a little dance together.

The California Collegians ad-libbed a little music and Peggy and I ad-libbed a little dance to kill some time. The dance looked so good that the director ordered it filmed and put in the picture. This was the first chance I'd had to do what I wanted to do so badly—dance—all because Gertrude had forgotten her shoes. You never really know how to plan in Hollywood. Sometimes the best things happen by mistake.

The last scene in the movie was really something. It was supposed to take place in a nightclub setting in a superduper supper rendezvous known as the Moonbeam Roof. For some reason, the director wanted me to perform aboard a simulated moonbeam. I was hoisted forty feet above the stage by a crane. I was up there for hours. Maybe I should have stayed there, the finale was so bad.

For years L. B. Mayer would tease me about *Top of the Town*. He said it was so terrible even the extras in it could never find another job, and he wondered how I managed to survive it. I wondered too. The film, in case you're wondering, never even made the late show on television.

The first film I made on returning to Metro was a Class B mystery entitled *London by Night*. The real mystery was why it was ever made. It was filmed largely in a simulated fog which at times made it almost impossible for me to see my fellow actors. Once I had to grope my way through the fake smoke in order to kiss the girl. In those days "fog" was manufactured by shooting Nujol on an electric hot plate which threw up incredibly thick oily clouds. As a result my two fine Earl Benham suits became oil cloths, and I acquired through inhalation a slight case of diarrhea which disappeared once the film was completed.

But there were compensations—I did have top billing. I played the role of a newspaper reporter, Michael Denis, on the trail of a vicious killer dubbed the Umbrella Man in the headlines. Opposite me was a fine young stage actress, Rita Johnson, who I believe was making her first screen appearance. I would like to tell you what she looked like, but the fog was pretty bad. Also in the cast were such superb character actors as George Zucco, Eddie Quillan and Leo G. Carroll, later to make a big name for himself in *the Man from U.N.C.L.E.*

For all its shortcomings, *London by Night* was very important to me because it was one of the few films in which I actually got the girl—even though she was a bit slippery from all that oily fog by the time I got her.

My fate in all too many pictures was to play the bittersweet part of the nice guy who doesn't get the girl. In my next Metro film, *Broadway Melody of 1938,* I co-starred with Robert Taylor and Eleanor Powell. With Taylor in the picture who do you think wound up with the female? I was the guy who borrowed the money from a rich man with which to purchase an expensive costume for Eleanor so that she could make her dancing debut. After which I made my dramatic exit from her life, saying something like: "Sally, I love you very much, but you'll be much better off with him." Meaning Bob Taylor.

One night my dear wife Julie was needling me a little. "I don't understand why they don't let you get the girl once in a while," she said. "After all, you're not that unattractive."

"Honey," I explained to her, "I told them that I already had a girl at home. You're cuter than those movie girls, and you're all the girl I'm ever going to want or need."

My first film with Miss Eleanor Powell—*Broadway Melody of 1938*—was really an exciting experience. This young lady from Springfield, Massachusetts, was without question one of the finest tap dancers in the business. But I was concerned about one thing, which I explained to her when we first met. I had seen her on Broadway and in at least one film, and she always seemed to be doing the same routine. I thought in the movie we were going to do together we ought to vary the dances. "Why don't we work out some different routines?" I suggested.

Eleanor agreed and we immediately went to work practicing a waltz, a schottische soft-shoe number and then an entirely new variation of a tap dance. She was fabulous to work with, but it was awfully tough on me because here was a gal who was a thoroughly trained tap and ballet dancer while I was, as Barney Gallant had said, a reconverted halfback.

One number we were going to do together would run about seven minutes on the screen, and I was worried about shooting it. I had in mind the experience of my old friend Fred Astaire, when he and Ginger were doing "the Continental" in the film *The Gay Divorcee* at RKO Studios. In those days, of course, dance numbers were shot in one complete piece, from start to finish. I watched Fred and Ginger do "the Continental" possibly thirty times. Each take would get down to the last minute or thirty seconds and some little thing would go wrong and they would have to stop, cool off, get made up again, put on new clothes, and start all over.

This went on for several days until finally the dance director yelled, "That's it. We've got it!" I think they got it just in time, because it looked to me as if Fred and Ginger were just about ready to give up the whole thing. Of course, if they had been dancing on a stage before a live audience no one would ever have noticed the kind of minor mistakes that occasioned those retakes. But the camera is a very vicious instrument; it moves right up close. The slightest error becomes magnified on the screen.

It seemed to me there had to be a better way to shoot these long musical numbers. I went back to Metro and talked with Blanche Sewell, then the studio's top film editor of musical films. She and I finally concluded that if the sound track were used as a common denominator it would be possible to cut a dance up into several sections. The idea—then quite revolutionary—was for Blanche to splice the many segments together in the cutting room, guided by the sound track. This would, of course, obviate the problems of doing a seven-minute dance all over the stage in one take. We might have been there yet.

That night I sat down and drew a diagram for a routine that would be done on a set representing Bryant Park, just back of the New York Public Library. For each segment I mapped out special pieces of business around a park bench, near a wastebasket and then (with a thunderstorm breaking) into a park building. Then, when the rain stopped, Eleanor Powell and I would come out skipping and dancing over the rain puddles, back up to a hot dog stand and into the finish of the dance.

The diagram showed that we could do the seven-minute number in five cuts. I drew up the camera positions, where the cameras ought to be placed on dollies and so forth. With Miss Sewell's help I even suggested the lenses to be used so that Eleanor and I would be covered in full tight figures all the time.

The next morning I took the diagram to Roy Del Ruth, the director, and explained the plan for breaking up the number into five segments. Roy was one of those rare Hollywood types who never showed any enthusiasm. As I described my plan, he just stared at me. I hadn't the slightest idea whether he was for it or against it, but I kept right on talking, hoping that at some point I would evoke a response. After a while I ran out of words and began to resort to double-talk. "I thought if you moved the camera up here and dolly over there, and then moved the other camera back and into position. . ."

"Okay," Ruth interrupted finally, "if you feel so strongly about it, why don't you shoot the number yourself?"

And I did.

Of course, the camera crew was in hysterics. The idea of a relative newcomer to Hollywood advising the great Roy Del Ruth how to shoot a musical number was unheard of. The shooting schedule was called for three days of continuous work but under my direction we were able to shoot the whole number in a single day, finishing by four-thirty in the afternoon.

This new technique, I believe, revolutionized the shooting of musical numbers in Hollywood. I once figured out that if I had only one percent of the money that Metro alone saved with this procedure I would be a very rich man today. The only thing I got out of working with Blanche Sewell (and, for that matter, all she got) was the satisfaction of finding a new and better way of filming dance numbers, which doesn't always pay off at the supermarket.

Working on *Broadway Melody of 1938* was a real thrill for me. This was one of those gigantic spectacular musicals for which Metro deservedly became famous. It was exciting to watch those big numbers being filmed. Everything had to be carefully synchronized—chorus lines, the big cameras, the moving booms, the lights, the sound track, hundreds of electricians, carpenters and grips all over the stage—and all focused on the orders of the director. Everything was well-rehearsed and nothing was left to chance. The assistant director would call out, "Quiet!" and the cameras and soundtracks would begin to roll.

*Broadway Melody* was the film that made Judy Garland a star. All of us who watched her perform on the set knew immediately that little Judy had that extra something that would make her one of the screen immortals. She had that magnificent quality. Her voice could make you laugh or cry almost at the same time. There was never anyone like her.

In *Broadway Melody,* Judy did a number with Buddy Ebsen in which the lanky, rubber-legged Ebsen played a stylized chauffeur who drove the most stylized town car I have ever seen. In the number, Buddy drove up and opened the rear door of the automobile and Judy emerged. Then the two of them began to do a dance that was absolutely delightful.

Buddy and I have remained good friends all these years, and every time I see him on television in *Beverly Hillbillies,* I think of the good old days at M-G-M when nobody would speak to either one of us.

Buddy turned up in Washington back in January 1969 to entertain at the mammoth gala honoring the inauguration of Richard Nixon as President of the United States. He walked out on the stage of the Washington Armory after he had done four or five minutes to the great applause of the audience, and suggested that the Senior Senator from California join him in a soft-shoe dance. I didn't think that was the proper time and place for me to resume my terpsichorean career, but I did promise Bud that if I were re-elected to the Senate, I would "slide a little" with him on any show he selected to celebrate the event.

Two weeks after we began to shoot *Broadway Melody,* I was called to an emergency meeting of the board of the Screen Actors Guild (S.A.G.) to discuss whether we should call a strike of actors in behalf of a basic minimum contract with the studios. For a while there it seemed as if I would never get to make a film at M-G-M.

We met at the home of Bob Montgomery, the S.A.G. president and one of the best leaders the screen actors ever had. Others present, if memory serves, were Jimmy Cagney, Ralph and Frank Morgan, Lucille and Jimmy Gleason and Ken Thomson, who was then S.A.G.'s executive secretary.

The situation was touch and go. The S.A.G. desperately needed the contract and the producers were being recalcitrant. Finally, after a series of negotiations, agreement was reached. We held the first real membership meeting of the Screen Actors Guild at the American Legion Stadium in Hollywood, to ratify the proposed contract.

As we, the members of the board, sat on chairs in the boxing ring, Bob Montgomery disclosed the details of the contract to the assembled membership. The producers, at long last, had finally consented to formalize wages, hours and working conditions of actors in an orderly, decent fashion. It was terrific news for our people, who had been getting the short end of the deal for a long time.

It was terrific news to all but a handful, who loudly protested as Montgomery read the fine print. There was one actor, Lionel Stander, who could hardly contain himself. Every time Bob opened his mouth, this bushy-haired fellow would beat on the table and shake his head. I couldn't understand his behavior at all, until someone told me that Stander was one of the leaders of the "extreme left." It was my first realization that sometimes these left-wingers are not as interested in settling labor difficulties as they are in prolonging them.

*Broadway Melody of 1938* had a superb cast which included the one-and-only Sophie Tucker, Robert Benchley, Binnie Barnes, Igor Goren, Raymond Walburn, Willie Howard, Billy Gilbert (who made an entire comedy career out of sneezing) and old Charlie Grapewin. As the man once said, you don't hardly find casts like that around anymore.

The story line, if that was important, was about a race horse that we were trying to train for the Kentucky Derby in the backyards of some tenement houses in Manhattan. The set was a big one and the technical people had done a magnificent job of simulating a backyard scene with three real fences and the rest painted on the back wall. And we discovered that when Igor Goren would sing and hit a high note the horse would leap over the fences.

One day the horse got so excited that he not only jumped over the fences but headed straight for the wall. Fortunately several grips and the jockey—with disaster looming only a few feet ahead—turned the nag away just in time.

According to the script, we were supposed to take the horse to Louisville in a boxcar. So Eleanor, Buddy and I devised a routine that we thought was rather unusual. We decided to make full use of the mobility of the motion picture camera and dance all over that boxcar—inside and out—using the feed bins, buckets and other paraphernalia as props.

We were pleased with ourselves because we felt that this was the way the motion picture medium ought to be used, and that's exactly what we told the studio bosses who assembled one day to take a look at our routine before we shot it. A mock-up of the boxcar had been built on the set; the sound track was turned on and away we went with all the exuberance of three crazy kids.

Everyone seemed happy with the number, except one little man whose name perhaps intentionally escapes me. Instead of watching us perform, he stared at a stopwatch all the time we were dancing.

"It's too long," he said.

I felt like poking him in the nose. We had danced our hearts out and we knew we had done a good job. This little *nebbish,* who as I recall had been brought into the studio as a favor to someone's uncle, was making an uninformed judgment on a matter that we, professionals in the field, knew more than a little about.

Somehow I managed to contain my indignation. "May I explain something to you?" I asked.

"Yes, you may," he replied condescendingly.

"Let me put it to you as simply as possible. If a number is lousy and it's on the screen for two seconds, that's too long. But if a number is good, like this one is, it ought to be on the screen as long as the audience wants to look at it."

The *nebbish* was about ready to reply when Louis Mayer, the big boss himself, who had been watching carefully, interrupted. "I think George is right," he said. "I think the number looks fine and let's do it the way they've just demonstrated." That was the final judgment; the *nebbish,* in the tradition of the Hollywood yes-man, beamed in agreement. From then on he nearly broke his back trying to be nice to Eleanor, Buddy and me.

The number was filmed exactly as we originally planned and it worked very well on the screen. *Broadway Melody of 1938* turned out to be not only a good money-maker for Metro, but a pretty good picture to look at.

Two years later, I did *Broadway Melody of 1940,* again with Eleanor Powell. But the romantic lead was Fred Astaire and I couldn't have had tougher competition. In the vernacular of today, Fred was beautiful. He could dance up a storm, which he and Eleanor did to Cole Porter's unforgettable "Begin the Beguine." This was the finest combination of great music and expert dancing that I have ever seen.

At the opening of the film, Fred and I did a number which Cole Porter also wrote, "Don't Monkey with Old Broadway,"

which, if you will pardon my immodesty, I consider to be
another classic. It was pure, solid vaudeville, and I think it
could be televised today as an opening bit on any variety show.

In between the two *Broadways,* I made five films on "loan
out" to other studios, four of them for Universal and the fifth to
Twentieth Century-Fox. I had no idea of this "loan out" situation when I first went to Hollywood, but I soon learned. Once
you are established and under contract, a studio retains the
right to "loan" you out to another studio. In other words, Metro
had the right to sell my services for whatever it could get—but
my salary remained the same. As it turned out, I worked for Metro for nearly four years without costing them a cent.

I had no cause for complaint, however. I was being paid
regularly. Julie and I were now living like normal people in a
little house of our own and we were on our way to raising a family. Things were going very well for the Murphys.

At Universal, I appeared in *You're a Sweetheart, Letter of Introduction, Hold that Co-ed* and *Risky Business.* In *You're a
Sweetheart,* I got to play opposite Alice Faye, who was one of
the most delightful, sweetest gals I have ever known. She, in
turn, had been "loaned" by Twentieth to Universal for sixteen
days. Now sixteen days is no time at all to make a musical.
Sometimes it takes that long to rehearse a number.

The film called for three musical numbers, and we barely had
time to rehearse. Consequently, Alice and I improvised from
take to take. I did every trick I could think of—doing
cartwheels over tables, picking up lighted cigarettes with my
mouth and other kinds of nonsense. One number called for
Alice and me to dance up the proscenium arch of a theater, then
around a balcony, finally swinging down the curtain on the
other side. At the last moment we discovered that Alice was
afraid of heights. Big Dave Butler, the director, kept saying,
"Tell her she can't get hurt."

"Davey boy," I replied, "tell her yourself. If she happens to
lose her balance and fall off that balcony, she can break her

neck. So just get some nets under there and then we won't have to worry about her getting hurt."

Alice was a great trouper. Even though she was scared to death, she did the number and it turned out very well.

Incidentally, Alice and I did this sequence on the "Phantom" stage which had been constructed years before for *The Phantom of the Opera,* starring Lon Chaney. It was so old that dry rot had set in. At the end of the number, I was supposed to leap from the stage into the front row of the orchestra and seat myself. When I landed in the aisle, I went right through and completely disappeared from view. I found myself ten feet below the floor, all covered with debris. I could hear Big Dave Butler screaming, "What happened to Murphy? Where the hell did he go?" Fortunately, I didn't get hurt.

I still go by to see Alice Faye every time I get to Palm Springs, for two reasons. First, I love her dearly, and second, I always get a boot out of meeting with that wonderful husband of hers, Phil Harris, whom we affectionately call "Old Curly."

The cast of *You're a Sweetheart* included Ken Murray, who had made it big in radio; Frank Jenks, whom we called "Old Rubber Face"; Andy Devine, who I guess has entertained at least four generations of youngsters; as well as Bill Gargan, Charlie Winninger and Donald Meek. True to his name, Donny always played a meek little man. He was quite a character. He had grown up in an orphanage and had taught himself to read and write. When he was sixty-four years old he bought himself one of the classiest sports cars I've ever seen. I asked him why.

He said, "All my life I've wanted to show off in a sports car. Now I want to do it before I die." He drove that car for several years before going on to his final resting place.

In my next film at Universal, *Letter of Introduction,* I had the privilege of working with that great actor and fine gentleman Adolphe Menjou. Adolphe (or "Froggy" as I always called him) and I were allied in many good causes over the years. We both became active in Republican politics. He was one of the wisest, best-educated men I have ever known, a great collector of art objects and fine paintings and a raconteur par excellence. He was the only fellow I ever knew who could hold his own with the great George Burns in an after-dinner joust.

In this particular picture, Menjou gave an excellent portrayal of a scandalous Great Lover of stage and screen, a role obviously modeled after John Barrymore. The director, John Stahl, was a strong-willed type and it was obvious from the beginning that he and Menjou were going to have at each other all through the filming.

One scene had Menjou lying in bed, supposedly dying. Stahl kept saying, "Let's do it over again." By the eighteenth take, Adolphe was getting pretty scorched from the lights. An assistant director slipped over to the bed and whispered to him, "Don't lose your temper. You know how the old man is. He's likely to shoot this thing forty times before he makes up his mind which take he likes. Don't lose your temper whatever you do."

From under the covers Menjou said, "Lose my temper, hell! It's costing that son-of-a-bitch $167.80 a minute. I'd be glad to do this for the rest of my life at those prices."

One night we were doing a long dolly shot on the back lot. The scene called for me to walk down a street with Andrea Leeds. Seeing a billboard with a picture of her father (Adolphe Menjou) on it, I was supposed to get angry, pick up a rock from the gutter, and heave it at the billboard.

"George," Stahl told me, "here's what I want you to do. In order to be sure that we know exactly what you are doing, when you throw that rock into the darkness, try to hit the window across the street."

As we did the long take, I picked up the rock and threw it across the street and—what do you know?—I actually smashed the window. In the darkness the sound of breaking glass was clearly audible.

Stahl was amazed. "I'll bet you five dollars you couldn't do that again," he said.

"You've got a bet."

Not only did I do it again, but again and again and again. Stahl couldn't get over it. He thought it was the most amazing feat he had ever seen.

Only later did I tell him that I had sent one of my carpenter pals across the street with a hammer. Every time I threw a rock into the darkness, he smashed a window. But for a while, Stahl honestly believed he had a guy as good as a major league pitcher working for him.

Playing minor roles in *Letter of Introduction* were Ann Sheridan and Eve Arden. Ann Sheridan went on to become one of the biggest stars in the business and Eve Arden one of the finest performers in television. But the biggest scene-stealer of all was Edgar Bergen's puppet "Charlie McCarthy." Thanks to movie magic, "Charlie" seemed almost independent of his ventriloquist-master and got off some of the best lines in the picture. One thing I quickly learned in show business was that you can't compete with smart-alecky puppets, cute mongrels or dimple-cheeked children.

To this list of "uncompetables" I want to add the name of John Barrymore. Not only was he one of the great actors, but he was a fine comedian, as I discovered playing opposite him in the Universal production called *Hold that Co-ed*. The influence of *Of Thee I Sing* could be seen in the way this picture good-naturedly satirized politics. The story line was loosely based on Huey Long who, in this film, not only wanted to control the state of Louisiana but wanted to provide it with the finest football team in the nation. Barrymore played the Huey Long character, "Govenor Gabby Harrigan," who sought a United States Senate seat by promising State University a hundred-thousand-seat football stadium.

It wasn't the greatest of films, but I'm happy to report that the then usually-captious critic of *The New York Times* seemed to enjoy it: "So you'll just have to take our word that *Hold that Co-ed* is a chuckling comedy from beginning to end, with a pleasant modicum of song and dance (chiefly George Murphy's) to while away the quieter moments when Mr. Barrymore is not putting on his political circus."

For Twentieth Century-Fox I did a film with Shirley Temple called *Little Miss Broadway*. Shirley, then nine years old, had captured the hearts of film fans around the world with her extraordinary talent and charm. She played an orphan who was adopted by the hotel manager. She met all kinds of show people including Jimmy Durante and me. Also appearing in this *divertissement* were character actors as George Barkie, Edna May Oliver, Jane Darwell, El Brendel and, of course, my old bald-headed pal Donald Meek, with whom I must have appeared in a dozen or so films.

This was the film in which little Shirley and I danced together—something my political critics thought they could make sport of. As it turned out, *Little Miss Broadway* became a popular staple on the late late show and did me no harm at all when it was shown on California television prior to my 1964 race for the Senate. I hope they dust it off and run it a few times in 1970, because I can assure you it would help in my campaign for re-election.

At first I wasn't anxious to appear with Miss Temple. In fact when Benny Thau, a Metro executive, called me about it, I asked him whether he had read the script. He said he hadn't.

"Then will you please find out something about it?" I asked. "Do I have to kick her, or hit her, or shove her down the stairs? If I can be nice to her in the picture, I'll do it. Otherwise, tell them to get themselves another boy."

The next day Benny advised me that the script was okay from my standpoint. I accepted the assignment, but not without some trepidation. Wanting to know a little more about Shirley Temple, I called Warner Baxter, who had made a few pictures with the young lady. He had some bad news.

"Murph, Shirley knows everybody's part. She knows the whole script backwards and forwards, and if you make the slightest mistake she'll pick you up on it and remind you. It's got to be such a mental strain on me that I just can't make any more pictures with her."

Baxter's warning turned out to be accurate. Shirley's mother worked with her on the script, and the tiny actress knew it by heart.

In my first scene with Shirley I decided to see how she would react to some ad-libbing. The scene called for her to be seated in front of a house where I lived with one of my wealthy relatives. As I approached her, I followed the script. "What's the matter, young lady?"

"Oh," Shirley said, "I want to get in to see the man that lives there but the butler says that he's not at home."

I began to ad-lib. "You want to know something about that butler?" I asked. "He suffers from hallucinations."

Shirley's eyes popped as big as silver dollars. "Really?"

Still ad-libbing, I went on, "Yes ma'am, and sometimes he says things that you just can't depend upon."

By now Shirley was absolutely flabbergasted. Again she said, "Really?"

"Yes. How about our sneaking up to the door, giving the bell a good ring, and then slipping inside and find out whether he's really telling the truth?"

So we went up to the door and rang the doorbell. The butler opened the door and we went inside. The door closed and that was the end of the take.

Once the cameras had stopped rolling, Shirley turned to me and asked, "Where did you get that dialogue about hallucinations and how the butler couldn't be depended upon? It isn't in my script."

"Shirley, I know," I said. "It just came to me at the time. I hope it doesn't disturb you that on occasion I'll say something that isn't in the script."

She gave me a big smile. "Oh, no, just say whatever you like, as long as it makes sense."

From that day on, Shirley and I had no problems in working together.

To prepare for my dancing numbers with Shirley, I had requested a screening of the routines she had done with Bill Robinson, who was one of the greatest tap dancers of all time. I noticed that Bill liked to dance in a limited area. My technique was different. I liked to move around and use the mobility of the camera. So I asked Shirley, "Would you mind very much doing a more grown-up dance?"

"I think that would be fun," she said.

We devised a routine where little Shirley danced on a table while I moved around on the floor. It was kind of cute and, as I said, my dancing with Shirley didn't do me any harm at the polls.

One afternoon while we were rehearsing other dance numbers, there was a heavy rainstorm. Word came through that because the flooding was so bad, a lot of roads had been washed out and it was quite dangerous to travel. Shirley was an excited little girl. She called me, "Come over right away. We've got to make plans. We're going to have a big party at the studio tonight."

"What's the celebration about?" I asked.

"The flood," she said delightedly.

By about five o'clock the rains and flooding had subsided. Everyone was allowed to go home, but we held the party anyway, because no one wanted to disappoint this sweet little child.

While we were shooting this picture we learned that Mrs. Eleanor Roosevelt was coming to visit the studio. The First Lady planned to say hello to us, but because of her heavy schedule, we were warned not to hold her up in any way. Shirley was to be presented first. She was to say, "How do you do, Mrs. Roosevelt?" and then curtsy. Then I was to greet her with a minimum of words.

But when Shirley said hello to Mrs. Roosevelt, she took the First Lady by the hand and led her to her little portable dressing room. Mrs. Roosevelt was fascinated by the youngster. She had such a good time that she decided to remain past her schedule. Before long Shirley had me playing parts from *East Lynne* for Mrs. Roosevelt's amusement, and by the time the First Lady left the set, she was over half an hour late.

Shirley has come a long way since *Little Miss Broadway*. Now the wife of a California industrialist, Charles Alden Black, she has three children of her own. And she has developed into a remarkable citizen. The little girl I danced with so many years ago is now a United States delegate to the United Nations General Assembly and has proved to be one of the best diplomats we have. Shirley Temple Black has her detractors because of her movie background, just as I have, but she also has the satisfaction of knowing that most Americans love and admire her not only for what she was but for what she is.

# CHAPTER 14

### *The Labor Racketeers: "Anyone who resigns goes out feet first"*

Life in Hollywood in the late Thirties and early Forties was not just dance routines, cameras and who's your leading lady. We were trying to organize the Screen Actors Guild to help the little actors who couldn't help themselves.

At first we were fighting against the adamant opposition of the producers. But we had powerful support from some of the most important actors in Hollywood, people who didn't need the S.A.G. for their own personal gain. They could command almost any salaries they wanted. Stars like Eddie Cantor, Ralph Morgan, Bob Montgomery, Jimmy Cagney, Ronald Reagan, Walter Pidgeon, Harpo Marx, Cary Grant, Charles Boyer and Dick Powell gave generously of their time and energy to help build our union. I served on the S.A.G. board from 1937 to 1939 and then as first vice-president from 1940 to 1943. In September 1944 I was elected president and was re-elected a year later.

We were having enough problems with the producers when we learned that an unsavory pair from Chicago, Willie Bioff and George Browne—along with a collection of ex-Capone hoods—had muscled their way into the leadership of the International Alliance of Theatrical Stage Employees (I.A.T.S.E.), a nationwide projectionists' union. This union also controlled many of the motion picture crafts, and for that reason was known in Hollywood as the stagehands' union.

We in S.A.G. didn't know it then, but it later came out in federal court that Browne and Bioff were blackmailing the heads of studios into paying them huge sums of money in order to "protect" them from labor problems.

All we knew at the time was that I.A.T.S.E. was trying to gobble up our actors' union, too. This would have given Browne and Bioff a stranglehold on the entire industry. It would also have given these two shady characters a major voice in determining what you and I could see in the motion picture theaters or whether you could see anything.

Some of us in the S.A.G. leadership began to suspect something was fishy when Ken Thomson, who preceded Jack Dales as executive secretary, reported that while visiting Bioff's office he had seen a .45 automatic in an open desk drawer. We wondered why a labor leader would need such a weapon.

Then Ken Thomson and Bob Montgomery went to a meeting with Louis B. Mayer at his beach house in Santa Monica to discuss the proposed contract between the Motion Picture Producers Association and the Screen Actors Guild. When they arrived, they found Bioff among the negotiators. Montgomery took one look at this character and announced that he would return to the meeting only after the "hoodlums" had left.

Now that the gangsters had the stagecraft workers and the studio heads in their pockets, they were determined to grab control of the actors. They provided an organizing charter to a friend of theirs in New York who headed the American Federation of Actors, who in turn announced he was seeking jurisdiction over all the actors in the country—in Hollywood, New York and all points in between.

That was all we needed to know. We decided that the rumors of gangster infiltration had to be investigated. A special S.A.G. board meeting was convened at which Bob Montgomery, Ralph Morgan and I voiced our suspicions. We asked for an appropriation of five thousand dollars (a lot of money in those days) with which to conduct a special investigation. Bob Montgomery promised that if the board were not satisfied with the results of the investigation, he would personally see that the money was reimbursed.

The appropriation was granted and we hired a topflight private investigator, whose findings were even more alarming than we had suspected. That was how we first learned for sure that Browne and Bioff were shaking down studio heads by threatening strikes. These panicky executives also feared gangland violence—and well they might have. They were bluntly told that "anyone who resigns from this operation goes out feet first." So they paid through the nose.

One of the incidental pieces of information that our investigator gave us was the fact that Willie Bioff owed the state of Illinois nearly six months on an uncompleted sentence for pandering. This eventually led to Bioff's extradition to Illinois where he paid his debt to society.

When this information began to come in, the S.A.G. leadership held meeting after meeting trying to determine what course of action to pursue. Without question, Bob Montgomery is the hero of this story. He inspired the rest of us to stand up to the gangsters threatening our industry. It was no easy decision. These weren't movie tough guys; they were the real thing.

At times when I presided over these meetings, we suspected that what we were saying was somehow being transmitted to the thugs. I began to receive veiled threats. The worst concerned my children. I was warned that if I took them out on the street they would have acid hurled in their faces. This was not easy to take. But, like my colleagues on the S.A.G. board, I decided to do what had to be done.

We had help from a group of Hollywood stuntmen who volunteered to act as our bodyguards or plain muscle-men if we needed them. I will always be beholden to Cliff Lyons, Freddie Graham and the rest for their help. Mike Lally, a former tough kid from Brooklyn, would invariably be waiting when I got out of my car to attend the S.A.G. meetings. I always suspected he carried an old service .45 automatic under his coat, but I never asked him. I thought of Mike many years later while I was in Saigon and my two companions carried open briefcases on their laps in the car—with their hands inside—for the same purpose.

Bob Montgomery and a delegation flew to Atlantic City to

meet with the top leaders of the American Federation of Labor at their annual convention. All they got was sympathy. Everyone said we were right, but no one could do anything about it.

Then a group of us went to Washington to seek an appointment with President Roosevelt. Instead we got in to see Harry Hopkins, one of the President's chief advisers. Hopkins made a singular remark: "You know, individually we like some of you Hollywood people, but collectively we don't have much use for you."

I couldn't resist saying that we hadn't gone to Washington to make social contacts. If we had, Hopkins' office would be one of the last places I would have visited.

It looked as if we were getting nowhere in our struggle to get rid of Browne and Bioff. So we began to feed information about these characters to a great, gutsy newspaper columnist, Victor Riesel, who published fully-documented exposes on the B&B scheme to dominate the movie industry.

Then we realized we had the ultimate weapon—public opinion. After considerable discussion, we devised a plan whereby every performer in every theater in the country, from New York to Los Angeles, would go on strike on a selected night.

The next day we would send top stars to every big city across the nation to hold press conferences to tell our story. That story was simply that we were not striking because of wages, hours or working conditions, but because the actors of America did not want show business to be run by gangsters.

Our plan stirred up a hornet's nest. Efforts were made by studio front offices to dissuade us from carrying out our threat. Eddie Mannix, one of the top men at Metro, called me in. "Look," he said, "do you fellows know what you're getting into?"

"Yes, we do," I replied.

"You're playing with fire. These boys are tough. They'll think nothing of smashing your brains out. They've done it before and they'll do it again."

"We're aware of that."

"Then for heaven's sake cut out this nonsense," Mannix pleaded. "You're going to get yourself killed."

I don't mind telling you I was pretty scared and so were the rest, but we knew we were right. "We've made our decision, Eddie, and that's it," I said.

Never was I more proud of the acting profession than when my colleagues, despite these heavy pressures, decided to remain firm in their plan to stage a nationwide strike against gangsterism. It was a collective decision that took a lot of courage, but not one actor we called on refused us, from Clark Gable to Mickey Rooney.

The word spread through the press corps like a Beverly Hills brushfire. Preparations were underway in all the big cities.

Bioff got the message and apparently was shaken. He telephoned the S.A.G. office and asked to see us. At the time, Willie, as he was called, was living on a ranch in the San Fernando Valley which he had purchased with some of his ill-gotten gains. Led by Bob Montgomery, we drove out to the ranch in a group. This was the first time that most of the S.A.G. leaders had had a chance to see this notorious man. He didn't look terrifying. A paunchy little guy, his most outstanding characteristic was a pair of hard, pig-like eyes gleaming from behind thick glasses.

The first thing he asked was, "Are you fellows serious about this strike business? Are you really going through with it?"

"We most certainly are," Montgomery replied, adding that as far as the actors were concerned "it is going to be a fight to the finish."

Bioff looked taken aback. He couldn't believe the actors would threaten *him*. But somehow he knew we weren't kidding.

"Well," he said with a sigh, "I guess that takes care of that."

Then and there he placed a long-distance call to his cohort in crime, George Browne, in Chicago. In front of the S.A.G. group, he told Browne what had happened. Browne apparently

argued, but Bioff countered, "George, this is the end. That's the
way it's going to be. We're pulling out. Forget it!"

So the only potential strike I was ever involved in with the
Screen Actors Guild was called off. It was a strange experience
to organize a strike against gangsters instead of our employers.
Maybe we ought to organize against organized crime again—
it's costing the nation more than we can afford.

In 1941, both Browne and Bioff were indicted for extortion
and conspiracy, tried, and convicted. Bioff was sentenced to ten
years in prison and Browne to eight. Both were fined ten
thousand dollars each. Several years later, Bioff testified with
gusto in federal court against other former associates. In 1955,
while living in Phoenix under an assumed name, Willie Bioff
stepped on the starter of his car and was blown to bits by a
bomb that had been planted in the engine. As he said, "Anyone
who resigns goes out feet first."

One of the members of the S.A.G. board in the late thirties
was a young contract player from Warner's named Ronald
Reagan. I didn't know him too well at the time. But I did admire his work, particularly in *Knute Rockne, All American,* in
which Reagan played the part of George Gipp—the immortal
"Gipper" of Notre Dame football fame.

If the truth be known, I envied Reagan that part, but I must
admit he did a superb job, one that practically made him a star
overnight. In 1940, Ronald married a talented actress, Jane
Wyman, and Julie and I used to see them at parties from time
to time. In those days we went to parties for fun, not publicity,
as is so often the case today. Sunday nights we would all go over
to Ann Sothern's house where we would sing, dance or just tell
stories. I sometimes danced so much at these parties that I'd
go home wringing wet with perspiration. But I loved it. Julie
and I would do an exhibition dance, or I'd give my imitation—sometimes with Cesar Romero—of other dance teams.

Meanwhile I continued to make film after film. Back at Metro, I was assigned to something called *Two Girls on Broadway.*

I don't remember what the story was about. The producer was Jack Cummings, but you can forget that too. The main thing was that on the first day I reported for work I was introduced to a young actress named Lana Turner. I vaguely recalled having seen her dancing at the Trocadero, one of my favorite night clubs, and I asked her right off, "Would you like to do a dance number with me?"

"Oh, yes," she said eagerly.

With the help of Roger Edens, one of the finest song arrangers in the business, we put together a special number which we began to film.

During the first few days of shooting, there were very few people on the set. This was not one of those Metro spectaculars that drew curiosity-seekers from all over the studio.

When the rushes came back from the first day's shooting, however, it was a different story. Everyone at Metro was talking about this fascinating new blonde who had danced so beautifully with George Murphy. You could hardly get on the set, so many people had come to see the lovely newcomer in the flesh. And that's how Lana Turner got her big boost to stardom.

During the filming of *Two Girls on Broadway*, Lana met and began to date Greg Bautzer, a well-known lawyer who always managed to attract beautiful ladies. One day Lana and I had just finished the day's shooting and were on our way back to our dressing rooms when I said, "Lana, why don't you get hold of Greg? Julie and I are going downtown tonight to see *The Man Who Came to Dinner* and we'd like to have you and Greg join us."

"No," she said, "I'm just too tired. Greg and I are going to have an early dinner and then I'm going to go home and go to bed."

Julie and I drove downtown, saw the play and enjoyed it immensely.

The next morning when I reported to the studio, all hell had broken loose. No one knew where Lana was; she hadn't shown up for work. A few hours later the studio's spies picked up her trail and we learned why. Miss Turner had flown to Yuma, Arizona, the night before and married a fellow she had just met that day—bandleader Artie Shaw. That's how quickly things happened in Hollywood in those days; maybe they still do.

Next in line was *Little Nellie Kelly,* in which I had the privilege of co-starring opposite Judy Garland, now eighteen years old. The film, based on a musical comedy written years before by George M. Cohan, was described by the eminent critic Bosley Crowther as "A bit of Irish chauvinism." It was lighthearted and gay in spots, very dramatic in others, and included several songs from the old country inimitably sung by Judy, including one of my favorites, "A Pretty Girl Milking her Cow."

Crowther concluded his review in the *New York Times* as follows: "Let's say that *Little Nellie Kelly* is a pleasant picture for the family trade." In retrospect I can only ask, is that bad? Apparently there was a market for "family" pictures in those days. *Little Nellie Kelly* broke all box-office records wherever it played.

When the picture was being cast, Judy and I made a screen test with Barry Fitzgerald of the delightful Irish brogue. I thought Barry was fantastic. The producer thought otherwise. "You can't understand him," he argued.

"You don't have to understand him," I said. "All you have to do is watch him on the screen and you know what he's doing."

The producer wouldn't buy my argument and gave the role to Charlie Winninger. I was proved right about Fitzgerald some years later when he and Bing Crosby made *Going My Way,* one of the most popular films in Hollywood history.

Right after we finished *Little Nellie Kelly,* I was sent back to Twentieth Century-Fox to do a picture called *Public Deb No. One*—a well-meaning but rather confused story which sought to poke fun at Communism. One of the few successful films of this type had been produced at Metro the previous year. *Ninotchka* was a very sophisticated comedy, and the fact that it starred the elusive Greta Garbo did it no harm either.

Though *Public Deb No. One* had its moments, it could hardly be compared with *Ninotchka*. It was about a beautiful soup heiress, played by Brenda Joyce, who falls under the influence of a Communist butler (who else but Mischa Auer?) The resulting publicity is pretty bad and soup sales plummet. The company's future is endangered. The girl's uncle calls in the well-known social arbiter, Elsa Maxwell, played by Elsa Maxwell, who proposes to arrange one of her famous costume parties in order to take the young lady's mind off Bolshevism.

But the heiress just won't listen to reason. She even threatens to sell the soup company and turn the proceeds over to Moscow. (I thought myself that the Muscovites would have preferred the soup to the money.) I played a dashing company vice-president with a crush on the lady boss. Between my ardent wooing and the brutal Soviet invasion of Finland, the soup heiress somehow saw the light, the company was saved and the picture was finally finished—much to my relief.

I was convinced at the time that the only reason for the film was Elsa Maxwell. Darryl Zanuck had met Miss Maxwell, then at the height of her fame, and decided to build a movie around her.

The best thing about *Public Deb No. One* was that it was directed by Gregory Ratoff, who was a much finer character actor than director. Ratoff had the richest Russian accent I ever heard, with the possible exception of Sam Lyons, and his manner of speaking was so funny that I used to hang around just to listen to him. But as a director he was something else.

"Mairfy, my friend," he said to me one day, "if we don't finish this picture on schedule, Darryl Zanuck will hit me on the head with his polo mallet and I'll be a dead Russian. Will you cooperate?"

"I'll be glad to cooperate, Gregory," I replied. "If you promise to stop making long-winded speeches and keep out of the way, I'll even direct the picture and see to it that we get it in on schedule."

As a matter of fact we were three days ahead of schedule until we got to the photographing of Miss Maxwell. It took her so long to get into costume and she blew so many takes that we lost the three days. However, we finally managed to finish on schedule and within the budget and Gregory was not hit on the head.

During the filming, Ratoff and I were having lunch in the Twentieth Century-Fox commissary when another Russian, a very fine composer, who had never received the acclaim he deserved in his mother country, came in the door. Clear across the room he saw Ratoff and shouted, "Grisha, Grisha, I saw you last night at the cinema. You are the greatest actor of all times. You are the biggest star in Hollywood!"

Ratoff was visibly embarrassed. "Ssshhhhh," he whispered. "Don't be so bloody noisy!"

The little man went on shouting, "I don't want to embarrass you. You are the greatest man in the business!" Then he pulled Ratoff in close to him and muttered in Russian, "Now, you say something nice about me."

When I was sent to RKO to do *A Girl, A Guy and A Gob,* which was to be produced by the wonderful silent film star Harold Lloyd, I was very excited. I had great faith and confidence in Lloyd. Unfortunately, when I arrived at the studio I discovered that only about one-third of the script had been written. The director, Dick Wallace, and I would sit up nights writing script to be shot the next day.

In this picture I renewed my acquaintance with Lucille Ball who, when she had been a chorus girl in *Kid Millions,* had insisted she wanted to make sure people would remember her name. I not only remembered her name but her delightful sense of humor. So when Dick Wallace and I wrote the script we gave Lucille her first real chance to be funny in films.

*A Girl, A Guy and A Gob* turned out to be what some critics would refer to as a "rout." It was nothing but nonsense from start to finish, but I enjoyed my part, perhaps because I had written it myself, more than most such roles. I played a gunner's mate home on leave and ready to act like a good sailor should. Of course, Lucille Ball was the light of my life but there were all sorts of complications resulting from my pursuit. *A Girl, A Guy and A Gob* was a good picture, and it got Lucille Ball launched as a comedienne.

I did another film at RKO, this one entitled *Tom, Dick and Harry*. This was a great thrill for me since Ginger Rogers, one of my favorite people, was the female lead. Here again I was jinxed and didn't get the girl. And Ginger was definitely worth getting.

The picture had a cute, if contrived, story line involving a giddy young telephone operator—would you believe Ginger Rogers?—and three men smitten by her charms. I played Tom, the stalwart, hustling salesman who intended to sell a million automobiles in order to give the young lady anything she wants. Alan Marshal was Dick, the millionaire who already could give Ginger anything she wants. And Burgess Meredith played Harry, who said he didn't have anything, didn't want anything and all he wanted to do in life was go fishing every day.

I didn't realize it then, but in the Meredith role I was seeing a preview of the hippies of today, who don't have anything (except, perhaps, overindulgent parents), don't want anything and are never going to get anything because it's just too much trouble. Instead of going fishing every day, all the hippies want to do is to smoke a little pot and "shack up" indiscriminately.

The extraordinary thing about *Tom, Dick and Harry* was that we started to film it without having an ending to the story. We did not know who was going to get the girl. A poll was taken among the crew members, who voted overwhelmingly in favor of Tom, the hard-working all-American automobile salesman.

But Garson Kanin, the director, thought that might be too obvious a finish and decided that the shiftless character played by Meredith, the suitor who looked askance at the idea of work-ing for a living, should wind up with the girl. That's how Kanin finally filmed the ending.

Needless to say, I wasn't too happy about this *dénouement.* First of all I thought my "getting" Ginger would be the proper ending. Secondly, I felt the way it was finally filmed espoused a peculiar philosophy—namely, that you'll get what you want if you just sit around and laugh at people who work for a living.

This is not in any way to disparage Gar Kanin, who is one of the finest craftsmen I've ever had the privilege of working with. It always seemed inconsistent to me that he would make a film extolling shiftlessness or laziness, because he himself happens to be one of the hardest-working guys I've ever met.

I particularly recall one scene which pleased Kanin very much. The scene called for me to sell an automobile to Meredith. Before the cameras began to roll, Kanin had sat us both down and told us exactly what he wanted to see on film. Then he said, "There's the car. Go ahead, George—sell it to him." As the cameras rolled, Meredith and I ad-libbed the dia-logue with me delivering a very high-pressured sales pitch—the sort of thing where someone walks in to buy a car for seven hundred and fifty dollars and winds up paying thirty-seven hundred and fifty dollars for not only the car but a lot of useless accessories as well.

I never had any doubt about Burgess Meredith's being a fine actor. Though he had made a few films prior to the time I worked with him, his major reputation was developed on the New York stage. I called him the "feather merchant" because he always reminded me of a wispy little man who just came down on a moonbeam and really wasn't there at all.

He had one failing, however, that really annoyed me. He was forever showing up late on the set, keeping the cast and crew waiting for His Eminence to arrive. After awhile, I couldn't stand it any longer and I let him know how I felt. "Now listen here," I told him. "It's very rude of you to keep everyone wait-ing, especially Miss Rogers. How about straightening out?"

For a couple of days, Burgess did come in on time. Then he began to come in without shaving, and we would have to sit around and wait for him to be shaved by the studio barber.

I finally got really disgusted. In fact, I was getting angry. I called the cast together and suggested that we all stay away until we were notified that His Eminence the Feather Merchant had arrived on the set and was ready to work. A young comedian in the cast by the name of Phil Silvers said, "That's a great idea."

The next morning Burgess arrived, unshaven, at nine-thirty. There was no one on the set. By ten o'clock, when he was shaved, there still was no one around. Finally we all appeared on the set —but none of us would talk to him. He had been sent to Coventry, as the old expression goes. Two hours of this was more than Burgess could stand. He begged us to talk to him, but we weren't listening. Finally he got down on his knees and swore that he would never be late again. He was true to his word and the film was finished happily.

Burgess never took any offense at anything I said or did. He realized it was all done with good humor. Interviewed by a *New York Times* reporter later on, he was quoted as saying, "Murphy's a saint. Maybe he isn't at that. Saints, come to think of it, are pretty dull stuff. This man Murphy is a one-man Mardi Gras."

The interview was part of a feature story about my making *Ringside Maisie,* in which I played opposite another of my favorite actresses, Ann Sothern. There was a young man in the film who played the part of a prize fighter. Metro got one of the best fighters in the business to teach the young actor to box. He taught him so well that when the fight scene was being shot, and they put the young actor in the ring with a professional boxer, he got carried away and hit the real fighter on the chin, knocking him out. The young man's name was Bob Sterling and he and Ann were married right after we finished shooting the picture.

By this time I had become very involved in industry affairs. I was still active in the Screen Actors Guild and a member of the advisory committee of the Motion Picture Relief Fund, among other things. My boss, Louis B. Mayer, used to urge me to go around and talk about our industry and its problems. Once he sent me to San Francisco to speak before the United Jewish Appeal while he made a speech before the Friendly Sons of St. Patrick on St. Patrick's Day.

Interviewed by the *New York Times,* I said at the time: "I used to like to tell myself that I was on all these committees because I wanted to help out in some vague way. But maybe I was only kidding myself. The truth is I get a kick out of people."

The *Times* writer then observed: "If George Murphy gets a kick out of people, that goes for the party of the second part. His popularity is proverbial. In a town where sniping is an accepted folkway and marksmanship deadly, he is one man who isn't pulling figurative arrows out of his hide.

"On a set his dressing room is usually the center of activity," the *Times* man went on. "Here directors plot gags and new 'business' with him. Extras drop by to bum a cigarette or to have him demonstrate a particular dance step of his they liked . . . Camera crews swap laughs. Columnists look to him for quips and jests wherewith to enliven their daily stint. Boys from the publicity department arrive to whip up new angles for stories or to escort plump ladies who want George to talk on the subject, 'How I Keep My Wife and Child Contented' for the fan magazines."

That was pretty much the way it was in those good old days. But though we usually had fun making pictures, it was still hard work—particularly for the gals. They'd have to report to the studio by seven o'clock in the morning to have their hair done and get their costumes or dresses properly arranged for the day's shooting.

Generally we'd have to be on the set by nine and we would work until about one o'clock, when there would be an hour's break for lunch. The one thing that always annoyed me was waiting around for the sets to be properly lighted. This always seemed an awful waste of time to me. I would go to my dressing room, where I always managed to keep busy.

When I first went to Hollywood I would spend this time making airplane models. I suppose that at one time I had constructed a copy of every airplane ever designed.

Shooting usually finished at six o'clock in the evening. The girls would have to go back to wardrobe, get all their costumes put away, and have their hair washed and set for the next day. I'd jump into the shower, get cleaned up quickly, drive home, have dinner, study the script for a couple of hours and go to bed.

While I was working, there was little time for fun and games and Julie and I rarely went out, except for weekend parties.

Of course, when I wasn't working on a picture, things were different. Julie and I would spend a great deal of time down at the beach or over at the tennis club, and I would always find time for a game or two of golf. There was even a time when I was regarded as a golfer nonpareil by such cronies as Bob Hope and Bing Crosby.

"A Gaelic beatitude," was the way Bing Crosby described me. "Here at last is a man who can take this strange game with equanimity. He has yet to fret at missing the pellet when he swings or to swoon away when the little marble evades the cup. Very singular, yes?"

Yes, if Bing said so.

Bing and I were part of a group of former New Yorkers who came to be known around town as "the Irishmen." We used to meet about once a week in Dave Chasen's not-so-Irish restaurant. The "membership" varied, depending on who was around. Among those who showed up fairly regularly were Pat O'Brien, Spencer Tracy, Frank Morgan, Jimmy Cagney, Bob Montgomery and Billy "Square Deal" Grady, the Metro casting director.

We'd sit around and hoist a few, discussing the problems of the world and commiserating with one another about how bad it was in Hollywood and how much better it was in New York. Of course, none of us had ever had it so good. We were making more money than we'd ever dreamed of and were living high on the Hollywood hog.

Jim Cagney probably was the most affluent of us all. Early in the game he invested wisely in real estate, buying up considerable chunks of property in Beverly Hills, Balboa and even Martha's Vineyard. Most of it turned to gold.

Despite all his money, Jimmy had one peculiar problem. Because of the pugnacious nature of the roles he played in many of his films, he had developed a reputation of being one of the toughest guys in town. Actually, he was a quiet, very peace-loving guy whom I used to call, "Soft-talkin' Sam Cagney."

Because of his image, Jimmy found it the better part of valor not to frequent night clubs, which he had loved to do in New York before he became famous. He discovered that there was always a drunk who would come up and say, "I'm tougher than you. How about a fight?" This was the sort of thing Humphrey Bogart also faced in his nocturnal wanderings.

I knew a stunt man who had the same problem. He was Harvey Perry, who used to double for Cagney. Harvey, who was wont to patronize the tough bars along Santa Monica Boulevard, said he had discovered a technique to handle would-be combatants. Whenever it became obvious that someone was looking for a fight, Harvey would light a cigarette and shove it up the fellow's nose. This would give Perry time to get to his car. By the time the poor guy stopped screaming with pain, Perry would be home and in bed.

I developed another technique. I used it once on "Prince" Mike Romanoff who had gotten so enraged at Ty Cobb that he was about to take a swing at the baseball immortal. Little Mike was a tiger. Though he weighed about one hundred and twenty pounds with a rock in each pocket, he would fight anyone. As

Mike was whipping himself up against Cobb, I went over and said, "Mike, your fly is open." Mike turned red with embarrassment. "Will you excuse me?" he said, rushing out the door to adjust his clothing. That was the end of the near-battle.

When I wasn't working I spent a good deal of time at the West Side Tennis Club. In fact the members, including my pals Jimmy Cagney and Bob Montgomery, made me their president. The club, for a time one of the great institutions of Los Angeles, had been founded by Stephen Morehouse Avery, the magazine writer, and two greats in the tennis world, Frank Shields and Sidney Wood.

Victor Orsatti, who for a while was my agent, and I challenged Shields and Wood, who at the time were rated number one and two in the tennis world, to a game of baseball-tennis. This was a brand-new game conceived in the fertile minds of Orsatti and myself. The rules were simple. Shields and Wood would play conventional tennis with their rackets while we would play with fielder's mitts. We would catch the balls they would hit at us and then throw them back. We finally beat the champions six to two. They won the two games only when we couldn't catch Frank Shield's tough serve. When we caught the ball we would pitch curves at our adversaries, which were very difficult to hit back.

Later Shields and Wood took the new game to New York, where they played two top tennis players at the Racquet Club. This time Frank and Sidney wore the fielder's mitts—and they won. The game had aroused so much excitement in the little world that is New York that I understand almost two hundred thousand dollars had been wagered in Wall Street.

Somehow I always managed to keep busy, but my number one love was acting. When I wasn't working or expecting to be working soon I would almost climb the walls. Few outsiders have any real idea of how difficult most actors' lives are. Your present and your future depend on getting assignments. There is nothing more dreary than sitting around the house waiting for that telephone to ring, hoping against hope that your agent has found a good part and a good script for you.

So when I finished a film I would immediately begin to worry about my next one—what kind of part I would get and whether the picture I had just completed would make it at the box office. As they say in Hollywood, you're only as good as your last picture. If that wasn't too good, you're in trouble. You'd better find another one quickly.

Another of my between-picture hangouts in those days was Schwab's, the famous drugstore where Mervyn LeRoy was supposed to have "discovered" Lana Turner as she sat on a stool at the soda fountain, wearing a revealing sweater. At least that was the story. Whether it was true is another question.

But there is no question that the drugstore was a great meeting place and the Schwab boys—Jack and Bernard—outstanding, trustworthy people.

Let me tell you just one story. When my son Dennis was a baby, he became very ill. Our doctor was a man of high repute, but for some reason he couldn't cope with Dennis' illness. Dennis got sicker and sicker. Finally, in desperation, the physician wrote out a prescription which I took down to Schwab's to be filled.

By the time I got home, Jack Schwab was on the phone. "Look, George," he said, "I think your doctor made a mistake. If I fill this prescription, there is no question in my mind that your baby will die. Please believe me."

I believed him and changed doctors. It turned out Jack was absolutely right. That's the kind of people the Schwabs are— great people who place the obligations of their important trade above everything else in life. Believe me, I was more than pleased when the Schwabs decided to open another drugstore in Beverly Hills. It's a place I still frequently go for breakfast, particularly when I have political meetings back home. It's not only a wonderful place where you can sit and talk, but inevitably you will meet many friends whom you haven't seen for ages.

After I completed *Ringside Maisie* at Metro, I returned to Twentieth Century-Fox to star in a football comedy with Linda Darnell and Jack Oakie, *Rise and Shine,* which was loosely based on James Thurber's great story, *My Life and Hard Times.* The cast included Milton Berle, Walter Brennan, Sheldon Leonard—and, naturally, Donald Meek.

When I think back to the great talents that were used in one picture, it seems unbelievable. Milton Berle, of course, could carry pictures all by himself. Walter Brennan unquestionably is one of the greatest character actors of all time. Sheldon Leonard went on from playing heavies in motion pictures to become one of the most successful producers in television. Then, of course, there was my shiny-headed friend, Donald Meek, who seemed to go on forever.

Following *Rise and Shine* I was shuttled back to RKO for a picture called *The Mayor of Forty-fourth Street,* in which I was cast as the Mayor. The script read beautifully and we had high hopes for the project. There was an important part in the film for a youngster, who was to be about twelve or fourteen years of age—a sort of budding gangster on the way up—or down, depending on how you view gangsters.

But the actor who was hired for the role must have been an overgrown midget. He looked older than I did and he had muscles bigger than mine. When the "youngster" appeared on the screen, people just wouldn't believe he was a lad in his early teens. The credibility of the film vanished. It was panned by the critics, and justly.

What apparently had happened was that an agent had oversold the casting office on the actor in question. Agents are always exaggerating the capabilities of their clients. That's their business, of course. And if they don't get employment for their clients, they themselves are not going to get that ten percent.

Agents could be very funny without meaning to be. Once I sat in a meeting with Louis Mayer, Benny Thau and Eddie Mannix when a fairly well-known flesh-peddler, as we used to call these gentlemen, made a particularly hard sell on the merits of his client for a major role in a forthcoming production.

"This guy will be just great for the part, Mr. Mayer," the agent said. "He's been going to a gymnasium and he's built up his muscles. He's in great shape, been on a strict diet, and he looks just terrific."

Mayer listened with interest and then interrupted. "I'm sorry, but I'm afraid that your client won't be right for the part. We've changed the role. We thought we could get the character a little more sympathy by making him a very sickly, emaciated fellow."

That didn't faze the agent a bit. He leaped up as if he had been stabbed. "My client's been sick!" he exclaimed. "Terribly sick."

Turning to his client, he ordered, "Take off your coat! Take off your shirt! Wait until you see how skinny he is, how lousy he looks. Go ahead—show them! My God, he's perfect for the part. He looks like death warmed over."

By this time, we were all in hysterics and needless to say the actor did not get the part. When the actor and his agent departed, Louis Mayer, still laughing, said simply, "That's real *chutzpa!*"

Another agent story I liked was the one told me by Sam Goldwyn. It seems that this particular agent had telephoned Sam from New York about a new client. "Sam," he said, "this boy has everything—looks, talent, youth, personality. I've been sending him to dramatics school and he's a better actor now than John Barrymore. He's taking voice lessons and he sings better than Allan Jones. I've had him taking dancing lessons—he dances as well as Fred Astaire. I've treated him just like he's my own son. He's absolutely sensational. Sam, I called you up first to give you the first crack at him. I know how much you appreciate talent and I want you to have the first look at him."

"He sounds very interesting," Goldwyn said. "What's the boy's name?"

For five seconds there was a dead silence on the phone. Finally the agent said, "Sam, I'll call you right back."

When I was President of the Screen Actors Guild, I thought it would be a good idea if the S.A.G. were to franchise agents. In those days anyone could come to Hollywood and set up an agency, and some peculiar people became agents. One agency was headed by a spectacular merchant of phony oil stocks in England. Another agent had been involved in bootlegging in San Francisco. There were others with backgrounds that couldn't have withstood the slightest scrutiny.

I told our S.A.G. people we ought to franchise the agents through our Guild for two reasons: one, because we could then exert some control over their activities, and two, because the agents would benefit by obtaining some real standing in the community. The opposition was pronounced. Three leading agents called me and said, "Let's just have a little meeting and we'll work this out quietly without letting the other agents know."

"Nothing doing," I said.

I called a meeting of all the agents in town. About one hundred and twenty-five showed up. I had hired three court reporters to take down everything that was said. I began the meeting on the dot of eight by asking, "Do you agents think you should be franchised by the Screen Actors Guild?"

Well, if you had exploded a bomb on Sunset Boulevard, the reaction couldn't have been greater. I let the agents sound off one after the other until three in the morning, when I decided enough had been said.

The court reporters worked through the night transcribing all the agents' protestations. By ten o'clock the next morning, copies of the transcript had been delivered to the most important agencies in town. An hour and a half later, all five of them had called and pleaded with me not to release the transcripts to the public. Moreover, they'd asked for another meeting that very night. And that's how the agents got franchised. I've always been proud of the fact that I was largely responsible for what turned out to be one of the most productive and protective acts sponsored by our union.

In recent years, as the producers have lost control of the motion picture business, the agents have gained the upper hand. But that's another story.

# CHAPTER 15

## Louis B. Mayer

Of the many films I made in Hollywood—and I appeared in over forty-five in a career that spanned nearly twenty years—the one that disappointed me most was *For Me and My Gal.*

The film was based on an original screen story by Howard Emmett Rogers, who told me he had written it with me in mind when he asked me to read it.

"I think this is a great yarn, Murph," he explained, "and you're the guy who should play the lead."

After reading the script, I thought so too.

So I was more than happy when I learned that Metro had purchased the Rogers story. I assumed I would be assigned the major role opposite Judy Garland, who by now was one of the biggest stars in the business.

Then a strange set of circumstances intervened. A young man named Gene Kelly had made a hit in the Broadway production of *Pal Joey* and had been signed to a contract by David Selznick. But Selznick had no picture for him to do.

At the time, Mayer was trying to get Selznick to return to Metro to head up production. In order to persuade Selznick, Mayer arranged to take Kelly's costly contract off Selznick's hands. Arthur Freed, who was producing *For Me and My Gal,* gave Kelly the part that had been written for me.

Once again I was relegated to the part of the *shnook* who never gets the girl. Needless to say, I was disappointed. I'd begun to develop a phobia about this state of affairs.

As *For Me and My Gal* got under way, however, I realized there was something basically wrong with the new story line. The hero now played by Kelly was no hero. He was a draft-dodging vaudevillian who, to keep out of the Army, went so far as to slam a trunk lid on his finger in order to become physically disqualified for service. I thought this didn't make too much sense and I mentioned it to Arthur Freed. After all, we had just undergone the trauma of Pearl Harbor and Americans generally weren't cottoning to draft evaders. Besides that, Kelly, in the script, stole a song from a girl. Not a very appetizing character.

By now resigned to the role of the "other guy," I did my best in the limited part. I was happy that at least Gene, Judy and I did the final number together.

The day after the sneak preview, which I did not attend, I encountered Louis Mayer at the annual Metro golf tournament. There was something on his mind and I instinctively knew what it was.

"How was the preview—how was Judy's performance?" I asked, trying to break the ice.

"She was simply magnificent."

That I already knew. She couldn't be bad if she tried. The word had gone around about Judy's magnificent handling of such ballads as "Smiles," "After You've Gone," "Till We Meet Again" and "Oh, You Beautiful Doll."

"But," said Mayer, "you spoiled the picture."

I was surprised. "How did I do that?"

He explained that about eighty-five percent of the preview cards submitted by the audience following the sneak preview contended that I should have gotten the girl and not Gene Kelly.

"You were right about the script," said Mayer. "Now we've got to do a repair job and make a hero out of Kelly."

On his orders, the entire cast of *For Me and My Gal* was recalled for what turned out to be twenty-one days of retakes. Two big scenes were added to make Gene a hero. The toughest part for me to take was when they shot the whole finale over again—without me.

This really upset me because everyone involved—including Mayer—conceded that I had done a more than adequate job. It wasn't pleasant to discover that my efforts had wound up on the proverbial cutting room floor. But that's Hollywood, as I used to tell fledgling actors when I was president of the Screen Actors Guild.

"Don't come out here with a weak heart," I would warn the new kids. "It's a tough, heartbreaking business. You've got to be able to take it."

They came rushing out to Hollywood, long on ambition and short on talent and luck, hoping to make it big but unable in many instances to get through the front gate of a studio. The movie business can be cruel.

For those who made it, there were many rewards, not the least of which was the pay. While I couldn't describe myself as the highest-paid actor in the business, I did pretty well under my contract with Metro. At the beginning, I did have one complaint. It was an old studio custom to pay you on a weekly basis for forty weeks instead of fifty-two. As a result, most actors were in fine financial shape at the end of the fortieth week but the following twelve weeks without pay would usually create financial problems.

Deciding this made no sense, I approached one of the executives about changing my contract so that I could be paid every week of the year.

"Impossible. It's against tradition."

That really provoked me. I went directly to the top and, after explaining my predicament, asked, "Mr. Mayer, do I have to live with tradition?"

"I don't see why," he replied. He arranged that I be paid weekly—a privilege (if that was what it was) which at that time was extended to only one other employee—Greta Garbo.

I tell this story not because it was tremendously important (except to me) but because it provides some insight into the kind of man Louis B. Mayer really was. I am aware, of course, of some of the derogatory things that have been written about this man, particularly since his death in 1957. Some of the stories about him undoubtedly are true. Mayer was not the easiest man in the world to get along with. But he knew what he wanted and what he wanted most was to make fine films.

Besides that, Louis B. Mayer was one of the great men of his time. Certainly he was one of the outstanding figures in his industry—even his most ardent critics would admit that. Under his personal direction the finest movies were produced with taste and distinction. Mayer always insisted on perfection. If something went wrong, as in the case of *For Me and My Gal,* he would reshoot entire segments of a production, no matter what the cost. He was in many ways like that other great film-maker, Samuel Goldwyn, who had great taste, judgment and a talent for making fine films.

Mayer was without question the greatest developer of star talent. Name one important movie star of the years gone by and he or she was probably on the Metro payroll. I was master of ceremonies that day in February, 1949, when Mayer gathered together on a huge sound stage fifty-eight of his stars and feature players including a collie dog. The occasion was the twenty-fifth anniversary of the founding of what became the biggest studio of them all. Metro was a city within a city. It had its own police and fire departments, a hospital and a power plant that could service ten thousand people. There was even a school so that kids like Mickey, Judy, Liz Taylor and Freddie Bartholomew would not be listed as truants.

At that silver anniversary party, Louis Mayer had asked all of us under contract to join him for a group picture. And what a picture that was! In it were Clark Gable, Greer Garson, Joan Crawford, Judy Garland, Deborah Kerr, Spencer Tracy, Ava Gardner, Esther Williams, Katharine Hepburn, Gene Kelly, Bert Lahr and Jennifer Jones. Also Walter Pidgeon, Wallace Beery, Fred Astaire, Frank Sinatra, Robert Young, Ethel and Lionel Barrymore, Ann Miller, Errol Flynn, Janet Leigh, Mario Lanza, Red Skelton, Jeanette MacDonald and Lassie the collie.

And front and center sat Louis B. Mayer, beaming proudly.

Mayer had a right to be proud. He had brought together what was undoubtedly the greatest assemblage of talent ever seen in the entertainment world. More important, Mayer had accomplished much for his industry, his community and his nation.

I am still proud to have been associated with this great human being. As I have suggested, he was a major influence in my life. Essentially he was a simple man with a simple philosophy. Once he handed me a card on which was printed a poem which he said expressed his views of life. The title of the poem was "The Man in the Glass." I never did find out who wrote it. But the first and last stanzas went like this:

When you get what you want in your struggle for self
And the world makes you king for a day
Just go to a mirror and look at yourself
And see what that man has to say. . . .

You may fool the whole world down the pathway of years
And get pats on your back as you pass
But your final reward will be heartache and tears
If you've cheated the man in the glass.

In reaching the heights of an extraordinary career, I don't believe Louis Mayer ever "cheated the man in the glass." It was a career that began in 1885 when he was born of impoverished Jewish parents in Minsk, Russia. At an early age his parents brought him to Saint John, New Brunswick, where his father became a not-too-successful scrap metal businessman. Louis took over the junk yard while still in his teens, and began to make impressive deals. Chance and imagination led him into the then-fledgling motion picture business when, at twenty-two, he purchased a "store show" in Haverill, Massachusetts, and made a go of it. From then on there was no stopping young Louis.

Metro-Goldwyn-Mayer came into being in 1924 and Mayer

took control of all production. From the beginning, he concentrated on attracting the finest talent money could buy. He had so many high-priced stars under contract that it was impossible for anyone outside Metro to make an important film without borrowing someone from Mayer's glittering roster. And every time a Clark Gable or a Greer Garson was borrowed, Mayer would get something he wanted back in trade—which was another reason that Leo the Lion roared so defiantly for so many decades.

When that shaggy lion flashed on the screen to signal the beginning of an M-G-M picture, audiences knew they were in for a treat. Not always, to be sure, but Metro had a better average than most studios. Under Mayer's tutelage, Metro always aimed at quality in its productions. At the silver anniversary gathering Mayer told his assembled salesmen that he would resist efforts to slash costs of producing films. "Anyone can make pictures for less money," he said.

For years Mayer had given orders to his story department to try to buy as many best-selling books as possible, no matter what the price. He believed that, despite all the star values he could add to a production, basically the play was the thing. He also had an excellent sixth sense about what kind of stories would interest the public. Most times he came up with winners.

By and large Mayer's judgement on most matters was excellent. His was the final word on any of the tough decisions that had to be made at the studio. He was truly the boss. He had an understanding with Nick Schenck that the company president remain in New York and worry about sales while Mayer took care of production on the coast.

There were rumors that Schenck and Sam Katz had conspired to take away some of Mayer's command when Schenck turned up at the studio, allegedly to take charge. Mayer immediately took off for Europe for an extended vacation. By the time he returned, there was virtual chaos at the studio. Production was at a standstill. All of the big stars had been loaned out to other companies. There was hell to pay all around. Eventually Mayer straightened out the mess, but he had made his point. As he used to tell me, "When you have a tough fish to catch, let him take plenty of line before you hook him. Let him run with it a bit—he may get tired."

Louis Mayer's friends were not confined to the industry. He was intimately associated with people in all walks of life. Two of his closest friends, in fact, were the late Francis Cardinal Spellman of New York and K.T. Keller, board chairman of the Chrysler Corporation. Spellman was a prince of the Catholic Church, while Keller was a Thirty-second Degree Mason. Mayer, of course, was Jewish. Yet these three men, despite differing faiths, were more than friends. They were, in many ways, more like brothers. They tried to see each other as often as they could, and they were always in touch by telephone. They counseled together on all important matters.

Mayer and Keller jointly contributed generously to purchase a pair of magnificent bronze doors for Saint Patrick's Cathedral in New York. There was only one problem, as Spellman informed his two benefactors at dinner one night at Mayer's home in Beverly Hills. It seemed that the relief figures on top of the doors had begun to attract the pigeons, which had a tendency to perch on the figures and generally mess things up in front of the beautiful church.

As Mayer later told me the story, K.T. Keller told Spellman he had a solution. His Eminence was definitely interested. "Yes, what's the solution?" he asked.

"Make it legal for Catholics to eat pigeon on Friday," deadpanned Keller.

Still another story Mayer told me about the Cardinal revealed the intimate relationship that existed between them. It seems that a well-known bishop in Los Angeles had passed away and Mayer thought he might put in a good word for a young priest whom he knew, as a possible successor to the departed.

Mayer flew to New York and immediately called at the Chancellery, which is back of the Cathedral. Hardly had the movie magnate sat down when the Cardinal said, "He's too young, Louis."

"Who's too young?" Mayer asked in surprise.

"Now, Louis," Spellman said, "we can't have any dissimulation between two good friends, particularly in this house. I know why you are here. The young man is a fine priest, but he's still too young. You see, in your business, Louis, you get young people under contract for a year or two, or perhaps five years. But in my business it's different. We get them for life and we move them along slowly, deliberately so, in order to make sure they are prepared and capable of handling more important jobs."

This was one of Mayer's favorite stories and he must have told it to me a dozen times. And every time he'd tell it, he would finish off by asking, "Murphy, how do you suppose he knew what I had in mind when I went to see him?"

It was a good question. The Cardinal was an amazing man.

I got to know His Eminence during the Korean War. He would stop off in Los Angeles for an evening or so with Louis Mayer before taking off for the Far East to spend Christmas with American troops stationed there.

On a few of these occasions I had the great honor of driving the Cardinal to the airport. Knowing of my interest in sports, His Eminence would regale me with tales of his athletic prowess as a youth. "You know," he once told me, "if I hadn't entered the priesthood, I might have been one of the great third basemen of all time." Then his kindly countenance beamed a big smile.

Once we arrived at the airport to find a most solicitous airline executive awaiting the Cardinal. "Your Eminence," he began, "I'm wondering whether your party will need any extra seats."

"No, I don't think so," said Spellman. "I'm not a very big man. I don't think I will need more than one seat."

In those years, the Cardinal would go off to the fighting fronts all by himself, carrying a little black bag containing the tools of his trade and radiating his wonderful faith and jolly wisdom. As a morale builder he had few competitors. He and Bob Hope were in a class by themselves.

Cardinal Spellman did not permit his friendship with Mayer to influence his principled objections to motion pictures that he considered indecent. In 1941, His Eminence publicly condemned a Metro film, *Two-Faced Woman,* for containing several suggestive scenes. He wrote to "Dear L.B." explaining his reasons. But this minor contretemps never upset their deep friendship.

In retrospect the film, which incidentally was the last one in which the Great Garbo appeared, was mild as compared with the filth being poured onto the nation's screens today. I often wonder what the good Cardinal—or even L.B. Mayer—would have thought if they had lived long enough to see brazenly advertised in the nation's press the public screenings of such outright pornography as *I Am Curious, Yellow.*

I knew I had really arrived at Metro when I found myself being invited to Mayer's annual Christmas luncheons in the executive dining room. Only Mayer's closest friends and top stars were asked to come to these prestigious affairs. I found myself in such splendid company as Spencer Tracy, Clark Gable, Joan Crawford, Greer Garson and Katharine Hepburn.

Usually the toastmaster on these occasions was one of the top executives, Harry Rapf. Harry had been with the company since it was founded, but by this time he had seen better days. One Christmas when Rapf got up to begin his introductions, it quickly became apparent that the Christmas cheer had gotten to him already. He got upset and burst into tears, fighting to control himself but unable to do so. The moment was terribly embarassing for all present.

But Mayer had had enough. "Harry, please sit down!" he barked. Then turning to me, he said, "Murphy, take over!"

Never at a loss for words, I told a few jokes and tried to restore the festive spirit of the occasion. Mayer was pleased. That's how I became the official toastmaster for all of Metro's functions.

Poor Harry Rapf—he just couldn't get along with his associates. In 1941 he was named executive manager of a Metro unit which produced a better grade of so-called B pictures. As the unit's producer, Mayer named a young writer, Dore Schary. Within eighteen months, the unit produced such remarkable low-budget features as *Joe Smith, American; Journey for Margaret; Lassie Come Home,* and *The War Against Mrs. Hadley.*

By this time, however, Rapf was shouting at everyone in the unit. Schary, having had a bellyful, offered his resignation to Mayer. On hearing the reasons, Mayer called in Rapf and, after giving him a brutal tongue-lashing, fired him. Schary, who had watched all this, went to the men's room and threw up. He didn't like Rapf but he didn't want him dismissed under such circumstances after all his years with Metro. The following day he asked Mayer to reinstate Rapf. Mayer told Schary he was too softhearted—a "boy scout."

After being fired, Rapf picked up his personal things and drove directly to the Hillcrest Country Club where he knew he would meet a lot of Mayer's buddies. Looking pale and haggard, he told everyone in sight about his misfortune. "My good lifelong friend, the man I love like a brother, has just thrown me out of the studio," he moaned to anyone who would listen.

"It isn't that he fired me that hurts," he went on, tears streaming down his cheeks. "I have done very well and I have lots of money. But when my poor old mother hears what Louis has done to me, the shock will kill her."

As Rapf expected, Mayer's friends began calling him and Mayer was heard to say, in an angry voice, "Harry's mother will have to die some day, but why in hell does he have to blame it on me?" Mayer, however, caved in under the pressure. He reinstated Rapf.

Some years before, I had had my own personal run-in with

Rapf. He had informed me he was going to make a film with an Ice Follies group and he wanted me to star in it. First he wanted to know whether I could skate. I told him that while I was no fancy Dan on ice, I had skated as a kid in Detroit.

"Fine," he said, "I want you to start practicing with the group on the skating rink they're building on Stage Fifteen. Get in shape for the picture. Don't worry too much about the fancy skating. We'll use a professional in the long shots and cut you in for the close shots."

I hardly knew how to thank Harry. At that point I was between jobs. So I went down to the rink every afternoon and practiced until I was quite proficient on skates. I did so well that I could finally perform the fairly intricate swing waltz with the group. I was feeling pretty good.

Until one day when I dropped into the studio barber shop for a trim. The shop was always a good place to pick up news on what was going on around the studio. This time the news floored me. The barber happened to refer to an ice-skating picture that had been under production for the past two weeks.

"What picture?" I asked, somewhat dismayed.

"Oh, it's something called *Ice Follies of 1939*."

"Who's in it?"

"Joan Crawford and Jimmy Stewart."

I raced out of the shop to seek confirmation. As usual the barber was accurate. The part Harry Rapf had promised to me had gone to my good friend, Jimmy Stewart. I was so angry that if I had run into Rapf just then I would have shortened his somewhat elongated proboscis for good.

After cooling off a bit, I went to see Eddie Mannix and explained what had happened. Mannix called in Rapf, who said, "Honest to God, I haven't determined what part George is going to play in the picture. As soon as I find out, I'll let him know."

I never did learn what part I was to play. The picture was completed without me. Which actually was no tragedy, because in spite of Crawford and Stewart, *Ice Follies of 1939* turned out to be a bomb.

On one occasion I saw Rapf getting his comeuppance. While I was working in a film Rapf was producing, a young lady, who was dating Jimmy Dorsey at the time, had an unfortunate habit of coming to work late. Rapf decided to tell her off. He waited for her one morning and when she finally showed up, he said to her in a loud voice, "Young woman, do you realize how much money you have been costing M-G-M by showing up late?"

Without blinking an eye, she replied, "Mr. Rapf, did you ever figure out how much it costs M-G-M for you to be on time?" With that she got into her car, drove off, and that was the last we saw of her.

Eddie Mannix was one of those sympathetic executives to whom everyone went with their problems. He was a diamond in the rough, having been in his youth a bouncer at the Palisades Amusement Park when it was owned by the Schenck brothers, Nicholas and Joseph. He was in on the formation of Metro-Goldwyn-Mayer and over the years had become a smooth troubleshooter for the studio.

From time to time Eddie would ask me to straighten out some problem or other. One such problem was being created by Richard Brooks, a very fine director who used to vent his frustrations by cursing people out on the set. During the making of one film, Brooks literally blew his top because the lighting was not satisfactory. The crew was threatening to drop a heavy lamp on his head.

"Would you do me a favor?" Mannix asked me, explaining the problem. "Brooks likes you and he'll probably listen to you. Would you go down to the set and have a little talk with him?"

So I did. Taking Brooks aside, I told him what the crew had been saying. He couldn't believe it. "I know you really don't mean to say those things," I went on. "But be smart. Call the whole crew together and give them a blanket apology for anything you might say that might be misunderstood. Two things will happen: you may save five days on the shooting schedule and it may help save your life."

"I guess you're right," Brooks said. He did apologize to the crew in advance. And he did save time on the shooting schedule. And he didn't get a broken head.

By this time I myself had become some sort of troubleshooter for the motion picture industry. I say "some sort of" because I was never officially designated as that. Nor did I receive any financial rewards for my services which at times were quite considerable. The only money I was making came from my acting career.

It all started when Mayer discovered that I "had a way with people," as he put it, and that I could handle audiences of all kinds. One day he showed me some newspaper clippings about "dirty" films. By today's standards these films were fairly innocuous. Anyway, the exhibitor was rallying support from his colleagues around the country on his proposal that actors be licensed on a morals basis. The issue was to come up at an exhibitors meeting in Atlanta.

Both Mayer and I agreed that the licensing proposal was absurd and unworkable. "I know it doesn't stand a chance of being legislated," Mayer said, "but the exhibitors do have a right to have their questions answered. Would you go to Atlanta and represent the industry?"

The Atlanta session was somewhat tense. I answered every question raised by the angry exhibitors. On the main issue I said they shouldn't judge all of Hollywood by some of the names making news that year—the Errol Flynns and the Ingrid Bergmans.

I conceded that our business—like any other business—had a few bad apples. The difference was that in show business the "bad apples" were unduly publicized. "But," I went on, "most of the people in the industry are decent, hard-working citizens. They just don't have the time to play around." And I cited examples of long-married couples and the various good works they and others were performing for their communities and the nation.

I must have done pretty well with the exhibitors, because the licensing proposal was quickly forgotten.

I recall another meeting with a group of about fifty Baptist ministers in Birmingham, Alabama, who had voiced similar complaints about the industry. These good pastors just didn't like anything about Hollywood—the headline-making proclivities of some stars, the Communists, the drinking in pictures.

On the drinking scenes I couldn't help but agree with the ministers. I blamed it on the directors who were too lazy to think up any other kind of business than having two people sipping the brew as they played a scene. Yet, I went on, it was natural in *real* life, so it would be unnatural if it weren't demonstrated at times in *reel* life.

This didn't satisfy the ministers at all. They just wanted all drinking scenes abolished from the screen. They contended that such scenes were making drinking socially acceptable and leading to excesses in their communities.

"Gentlemen," I said, "as I walked over here from the hotel, I passed at least fifteen liquor stores. They all looked relatively new and prosperous. Obviously quite a number of people in this town are drinking whiskey."

The ministers laughed. They had gotten the point. But I wasn't home free yet. Much to my amazement, the good pastors raised still another issue. After a while I realized this may have been their real beef. They wanted to know why whenever there was a religious part in a film it was usually filled by an actor playing a Catholic priest or Jewish rabbi.

I was dumbfounded. I had never heard the religious issue raised as far as Hollywood was concerned. I hemmed and hawed for a few moments, trying to think of a suitable reply. I realized that Hollywood had enough problems without my getting the industry involved in some sort of religious dispute.

So, drawing a deep breath, I began by pointing out that Hollywood was not trying to sell the public on any particular religion. Our job was to provide entertainment to a public which is composed of many faiths, and that we were trying to do that without giving offense to anyone.

"The reason producers use priests and rabbis," I went on, "is because they are easily recognizable as men of the cloth by their dress. Priests wear turned collars and rabbis—at least the ones of the Orthodox persuasion—frequently have beards and wear *yarmulkes*."

"But if you fellows go out and get yourselves uniforms," I concluded, "I can assure you I will find you parts in our films."

That did it. Everybody laughed and applauded. I was home free at last, even though I remained a bit shaken.

All of which reminds me of a story which tells a good deal about Hollywood and religious differences. The story—and it is a true one—involves the late W. C. Fields, whose comic genius only recently has come to be universally recognized, largely by the younger generation.

Fields was having an argument with two executives at Universal and, as a consequence, he refused to show up at the studio to begin a film.

"I'm through with those two so-and-sos," he told a director friend. "It proves what I've always told you—you can't do business with Jews."

The director was aghast. "It just so happens," he told Fields, "that both those men are Roman Catholics."

"So what?" Fields replied. "I've always known Catholics are the worst kind of Jews there are!"

Getting back to Louis B. Mayer, there is one thing about this great man that ought to be stressed. He deeply believed that the United States was the greatest nation on earth, and his belief was based on the fact that people like him—foreign-born and of a faith that had been persecuted for centuries—could rise to such spectacular heights. "Only in America" was an adage with

him long before Harry Golden made it famous among his
*goyisher* readers.

Working with Mayer in community activities, I came to realize the importance of promoting brotherhood among peoples of
various religions and races. Mayer naturally was interested in
Jewish affairs, and from time to time I would work with him in
this area. My own support of the great country of Israel stems,
in some measure, from my friendship with Mayer. President
Nixon, aware of my pro-Israel sentiments, was good enough to
invite me to the White House state dinner honoring Prime
Minister Golda Meir of Israel in the fall of 1969. It was a night
L.B. Mayer would have enjoyed.

Like the rest of the nation, Hollywood has come a long way
in the field of black-white relations. There was a time when the
movies did not present Negroes with dignity. Negro leaders had
good cause to resent this. To L. B. Mayer's credit, he recognized
the problem and carried on a largely unpublicized crusade to
prevent offensive characterizations.

It was not always easy. Film-makers were just as subject to ir-
rational prejudices as other Americans. Fortunately they have
learned that black people are Americans with the hopes and aspirations of other Americans. They want a piece of the action
and, more and more, they are getting it.

Who would have thought not too long ago that one of the
screen's biggest stars would be a black man named Sidney
Poitier? And deservedly so. He is a fine performer.

Long before it became fashionable I was sensitive to the
problems faced by the Negro in a white society. As head of the
Screen Actors Guild and, later, as president of the Motion Picture Industry Council, I worked on projects designed to
promote Negro aspirations in our industry. I have long been
sensitive to slights—intentional or otherwise—directed towards
our black fellow citizens.

I'll never forget one embarrassing scene during the filming of

*This Is the Army* in 1943. This was the screen version of the brilliant World War II stage success produced by Irving Berlin with an all-Army cast.

The episode occurred during the filming of the finale—a huge scene involving hundreds of people singing Berlin's classic "This Is the Army, Mr. Jones." The film was being shot on the biggest set on the Warner Brothers lot at Burbank, and cameras were mounted on huge cranes to shoot the intricate movements. Sound equipment was everywhere. The set was brilliantly lighted.

The director was the late Michael Curtiz, a wild Hungarian about whom there were as many stories as there are about Sam Goldwyn. He was one of the finest picture makers in the business.

Assuring himself that the cast and technicians were ready, Curtiz ordered the cameras to begin rolling. The ubiquitous booms began moving into position as a chorus of singers entered.

"Bring on the white soldiers!" Curtiz bellowed. (The Army, like all the military services, was still segregated even in World War II.) The white troops entered in full formation. Then Curtiz said; "Bring on the nigger troops!"

I blanched. "Hold everything!" I demanded.

"What's wrong?" Curtiz asked.

"Mike," I explained, "you just don't use that word. It's offensive to Negroes and it's offensive to me. From now on call them 'colored troops.' "

Curtiz looked genuinely astonished. "I didn't mean anything by it," he apologized. "I just didn't understand."

I guess he didn't.

Once again Curtiz bellowed his instructions. The cameras began to roll. "Bring on the white soldiers," he ordered. Then he shouted, "Bring on the colored niggers!"

I threw up my hands in despair. What do you do with a crazy Hungarian who doesn't know any better? I knew he didn't understand what he was saying. But any ethnic slight—no matter how unintentional—can hurt deeply, as I carefully tried to explain to him after that day's shooting.

Along with most others in the cast of *This Is the Army,* I gave my services. I was glad to do so—it was the least I could do for the war effort. All profits from the film—and it turned out to be an enormous moneymaker—went to Army Emergency Relief. There couldn't have been a better cause.

Incidentally, a young lieutenant was detached from active military duty with the Army Signal Corps to appear in the film. His name was Ronald Reagan.

By this time I was active in all sorts of war connected work. Later I became more and more involved in public relations assignments for the industry. Probably the kindest description of my activities was given by Bob O'Donnell, a major movie exhibitor in Texas.

"Murph's a one-man bucket brigade," Bob said.

And there were many occasions when I did have to trot out the bucket.

Though I was never paid for these endeavors, I must confess to having enjoyed the work. I knew I was doing a necessary job, one for which I was well-qualified. And in the back of my mind I realized that this was the sort of thing I would like to be doing once I was too old to be dancing with lovely gals like Eleanor Powell.

Little did I realize in those days that my extracurricular activities would lead me to the United States Senate.

# CHAPTER 16

### *War and Politics:*
### *"George, you'd better take over."*

It's not easy to change your politics, but in 1939, after considerable reflection, I became a Republican. And it was one of the leading Democrats in the nation who, perhaps unwittingly, convinced me I had made the right decision.

Until 1939, I was what you might call a dormant Democrat, faithful to the party of Woodrow Wilson and Al Smith in a perfunctory way. Most of the Irish, particularly those on the Eastern Seaboard, were Democrats. It was largely a question of inheritance. Grandfather Long, for example, had been a Democratic member of the Michigan State Assembly.

Most of the other members of my family and most of our friends considered themselves Democrats. So I was one too.

Most of the political figures whom I came to know in my early days in New York—Jimmy Walker, Al Smith and the great James Farley, among others—were Democrats. I guess it just seemed that people of this political persuasion were more attractive, more fun, and more my type in those halcyon days. The Republicans looked to be a little bit stuffy. The few Republicans I knew were hardworking, responsible citizens, but—for me at least—the Democrats seemed to have more excitement and style.

But I had become disenchanted with some of the excesses of the New Deal following the re-election of President Roosevelt in 1936. One of the many things that troubled me was the President's plan to "pack" the United States Supreme Court because he did not like the manner in which the highest court in the land had ruled on some of his ill-conceived legislation. Fortunately, an outraged Congress put an end to that incredible scheme.

259

Ironically, it was a long conversation with Supreme Court Justice Frank Murphy that convinced me I had done the right thing in switching to the Republican party. I say "ironically" because Frank Murphy not only was a top Democrat but a confidante of President Roosevelt.

Justice Murphy, who as far as I know was not related to me, had been an old friend of the family back in Detroit. He had had a brilliant career in American politics—Judge of the Recorder's Court, Mayor of Detroit, Governor-General of the Philippines, Governor of Michigan and then Attorney General of the United States. We had our talk about seven or eight months after he had been named by F.D.R. to the Supreme Court. It was then that Murphy disclosed to me that the President had asked him to return to his job as Attorney General, apparently because Roosevelt was unhappy with his successor. Murphy, however, decided not to do so.

While Murphy was Governor of Michigan, the nation witnessed the first major strikes in the automobile industry. Plants and machinery were destroyed. Mob violence was stirred up by a new and dramatic use of propaganda in the news media. Everything was carefully orchestrated until, eventually, the most important industrial city in the nation was in shambles. By finally settling the strike of the fledgling United Automobile Workers of America, Governor Murphy became the most talked of public figure in the country. There was even talk of "Murphy for President in 1940!"

In my casual correspondence with "cousin Frank," I never detected any overwhelming desire on his part to run for the Presidency. Of course, it became a dead issue when he was named to the Supreme Court.

Actually when Justice Murphy came to California late in 1940, he wanted to talk to both Julie and me. Frank had always loved Julie and admired her for her good judgement and common-sense attitude towards things. Unfortunately, on this particular day Julie had something going on at the house—one of the many community projects she was involved in.

So Murphy and I repaired to the home of an old friend of the Justice's, Dick Richards, who owned a Los Angeles radio station. Richards, incidentally, later on became a target of the left wing. In a widely-publicized campaign aimed at destroying him, he was accused of having sought to exercise controls over some of the left-biased news reports being broadcast over his station. There was a lawsuit which cost Richards over a million dollars and which eventually gave him a heart attack.

It was obvious from the start of the conversation with Frank Murphy that the Justice was sorely troubled, which caused me great concern because I knew very well the intimate nature of Frank's relationship with President Roosevelt. Like Harry Hopkins, he had easy access to the President and was a frequent visitor and respected advisor. As a matter of fact, Frank Murphy had made this long trip to California on a special mission for the President.

As I recall the mission, Murphy, who had a commission in the state guard, had been sent out to take a look at a place near Indio, California, as a possible site for large-scale tank maneuvers. It was on the basis of Frank's report that the President gave the go-ahead signal to build what became known as the Desert Training Center. This, in turn, became famous as the place where General George Patton trained his tank corps.

One of the things troubling Murphy was the progress of the war in Europe. This was just three days after the German *Luftwaffe* had begun to pound the British industrial city of Coventry to bits. We were not yet in the war, but many of us in the United States felt that the fate of Europe and our own country was intertwined.

"Do you think that the British can hold out?" Murphy asked me.

"I do think so," I replied.

"Why?"

"Well, Julie and I lived in England for nearly a year and we got to know the British fairly well. They are a strong-willed and determined people, and while they might keep getting knocked down by air raids, I think they'll keep getting up until somehow they find a way to win through."

"George, don't kid yourself," Murphy said. "The British can't last three weeks and that's official. That's right from the horse's mouth."

As long as I live, I will never forget how shocked I was on hearing these words. One of the highest officials of the United States Government was saying that the Nazis, who had already overrun much of Europe, were about to conquer the British Isles. The thought was too much to bear.

Well, it didn't happen, thank God. Later I learned who had been the source of this defeatist propaganda and was feeding it into the highest echelons of the Government. The "horse's mouth," I believe, was none other than Joseph P. Kennedy, our Ambassador to the Court of St. James's, who was making no secret of his sincere belief that, no matter what our country did, there was no way of stopping the Nazis.

The war situation wasn't the only thing troubling Murphy. He began to talk about events in Washington, events about which he had firsthand knowledge, and about personalities in and out of the news, people whom he knew intimately. He made his uneasiness clear about certain political and ideological pressures which he claimed were being exerted in Washington.

He named some powerful persons who he felt were seeking to influence the White House in a wrong direction. He confirmed the fears that had been troubling me for some time— that there were powerful forces seeking to promote Socialism or some other form of centralized government.

Among other things Murphy told me was that, as Attorney General, he had prepared cases against Seymour Weiss of New Orleans, Mayor Frank Hague of Jersey City, the Kelly-Nash machine in Chicago, and the Purple Gang of Detroit which had begun to move to the West Coast. He said he had worked for months with J. Edgar Hoover on these cases, but that President

Roosevelt had called him to the White House and had ordered him to hold off prosecutions. Then Murphy was appointed to the Supreme Court.

Murphy mentioned that Roosevelt was pressuring him to resign from the Supreme Court and return to his post as Attorney General.

"Well," I asked, "doesn't that mean that the President wants you to prosecute those cases?"

Murphy said he didn't think so because most of those whom he had wanted to indict were important figures in the Democratic party.

Then he talked about Felix Frankfurter, his colleague on the high court. "Felix is one of the most powerful men in the country," Murphy said. He said the White House was heavily populated with Frankfurter's proteges, who had an inordinate influence on American policies.

There were other people who caused him concern. For example, he spoke of the nation's archives, and the effect that a wrong person in charge of the archives could have on the writing of accurate history.

Though I did not agree with many of Murphy's rulings in the Supreme Court, I've always held him in high regard. Incidentally, my first venture into public political life came as a high school student when my chum Frank Nolan and I hit the hustings in behalf of Murphy, then seeking his first political office. At one rally near the old Ford plant in Hamtramck, Michigan, Murphy spoke for about fifteen minutes and nobody seemed to understand what he was talking about. Small wonder—the audience consisted largely of recently-arrived Polish and Hungarian immigrants.

Nolan and I managed to circumvent the language barrier by singing a few songs and doing a couple of Irish jigs. The crowd liked the performance and that was the first time I realized the part show business could play in politics.

Years later I found myself entertaining at a Democratic din-

ner at the Ross-Fenton Farms in New Jersey. My good friend
Jim Farley, who had just been appointed Postmaster General of
the United States, was the guest of honor. It was no secret that
Jim was there to organize the Jersey Coast for the Democrats.
Until that time, Jersey had voted Republican fairly consistent-
ly.

Other dignitaries at the dinner included Governor Harry
Moore and Mayor Frank Hague of Jersey City. And there were
scores of the underlings who always flock to such gatherings.

Jim had come down from New York accompanied by that
fine actor Eddie Dowling. But just as dinner was over and the
program of speeches was about to begin, Dowling was nowhere
to be found. Jim Farley turned to me and said quietly, "George,
you'd better take over."

When I became active in the Republican Party, that became
my lot. I have been known as the "take-over" guy, the M.C. at
thousands of functions, always willing to do what I could to
come to the aid of a party whose basic philosophy I believe in so
strongly.

In 1940 I helped organize the Hollywood Republican Committee, one of whose purposes was to "combat the general belief
that all Hollywood actors and writers belonged to the left
wing." Another reason was that the Democrats had launched
the Hollywood Democratic Committee, and I thought we ought
to have a two-party system in our town as well as in the rest of
the nation.

One of my colleagues in this venture was Morrie Ryskind, my
old playwright friend from New York who co-authored the
book of *Of Thee I Sing*. Like me, Morrie had been a Democrat
but hadn't liked what he was seeing in the New Deal. So he
turned Republican about the same time I did.

About this time a new political luminary flashed across the
political scene. Wendell Willkie had also been a Democrat but
he had turned Republican in time to win the G.O.P. nomination for President. Robert Montgomery, who knew and liked

him, had been touting Willkie's virtues among Hollywood
Republicans for a long time. Bob convinced most of us that we
had no alternative but to get on the Willkie bandwagon. "Win
with Willkie" became our rallying cry.

At least one prominent Hollywood Republican had his
doubts about "the barefoot boy from Wall Street," as Willkie
had been labeled by the Democrats. And that was my old boss,
Louis B. Mayer, whose perspicacity in political matters could
rarely be faulted. Mayer thought that Willkie was trying "to
out-Santa Claus Santa Claus" and that if people are only provided a choice between "the original Santa Claus and a road-com-
pany version, they sure as hell are going to select the original
Santa Claus," namely Franklin D. Roosevelt. And that's exactly
what the people did.

But Wendell L. Willkie was the Republican candidate and
we in Hollywood had little choice but to give him our all-out
support, hoping against hope that he could somehow overcome
the well-entrenched Roosevelt. We organized "We the People
for Willkie" at a meeting in the little rose garden of the Beverly
Hills Hotel. Present, besides myself, were Bob Montgomery,
Ralph Morgan, Ginger Rogers and her mother Lela, Adolphe
Menjou, Irene Dunne, Ward Bond, Morrie Ryskind and several other brave souls.

I say "brave souls" because it did take a little nerve in those
days of New Deal hysteria in Hollywood to espouse a
Republican candidate, even one of liberal credentials. But we
did manage to get something started and at one meeting we
managed to sign up over two hundred supporters from the industry who pledged to work actively for our candidate.

Our stars had to take rebuffs and embarrassments in order to
promote the Willkie candidacy. One group consisting of Ginger
Rogers, Bob Montgomery and Morrie Ryskind decided to carry
the message into a Negro neighborhood in Los Angeles. On
their way to a church where a rally had been scheduled they
were stoned and rotten-egged. Ginger and Bob were very big

stars at the zenith of their fame, the kind of names that could have packed Madison Square Garden. Yet when they arrived at the church they found only a dozen or so in the audience.

As Morrie Ryskind later told me, "I had been under the impression that because of the Civil War, most Negroes were Republicans. Was I ever naive."

I guess back in 1940 most of us were naive. We couldn't understand why, because we were opposed to the re-election of Franklin Roosevelt to a third term, we suddenly became "isolationists," "appeasers" and "pro-Nazi." People were choosing up sides as if their political opponents were mortal enemies, and wounds were deep and long-lasting.

I remember the particularly tragic case of a noted Beverly Hills throat specialist, Dr. Harold Barnard. He had closed up shop to travel with Willkie, who was given to hoarseness. When this outstanding doctor returned after several weeks with the Republican candidate, he found that many of his Democratic patients had decided to seek other doctors. He had a terrible time rebuilding his practice. These were emotional days indeed.

The pro-Nazi charge leveled against our Willkie group was particularly dishonest and infuriating. All of us involved in the Hollywood campaign were firm foes of all kinds of totalitarianism, whether of the right- or left-wing varieties. We were more knowledgeable on the subject, perhaps, than some of our opponents who, though they described themselves as anti-Nazi, frequently overlooked the complicity of Communism in the rise of the Hitler menace. This was during the period of the Soviet-Nazi pact, when Stalin embraced Hitler and vice versa. Yet the naiveté of some liberals towards Communism was appalling. I began to suspect they were operating under a kind of double standard.

I had long been obsessed by the knowledge that Nazism boded danger not only for the United States but for all mankind. A lot of well-meaning people considered me a little silly when I

sounded the tocsin about the menace represented by a funny little man with a Charlie Chaplin mustache named Adolf
Hitler.

But I was one of those Americans who had read Hitler's *Mein
Kampf* and felt he meant what he had written. I had picked up
a paperback edition in a Beverly Hills bookstore and read it
twice. Julie also spent time with it. We talked it over and
agreed that Hitler and the evils he represented were no
laughing matter.

A little while later I was in New York on some show business.
I stopped off at one of the town's watering spots, where I encountered Ed Sullivan, then mainly famous for his *Little Old
New York* column in the *New York Daily News*. After the usual
show biz chitchat, I began to discuss *Mein Kampf* and Hitler.

Ed was amused. "Oh, you Hollywood crusaders," he scoffed.
"You people out there take everything so seriously. That Hitler
is nothing more than a little punk."

"No, Ed," I countered. "You'd better read *Mein Kampf* very
carefully. I think this little punk, as you call him, means business. I think he intends to put his words into action. And I
think if we have any sense we'd better do something to stop him
before he begins to wreak great destruction in the world."

Ed was way ahead of most Americans in recognizing the
dangers of totalitarianism, whether of the brown or red varieties. He has used his powerful voice to promote good patriotic
causes on many occasions since. I've known him a long time and
have always been happy about his remarkable success in television. His Sunday night variety show reflects the best there is in
the entertainment world.

Probably the most important insight into Nazism I received
during the thirties—at a time when there were still people who
thought they could "do business with Hitler"—came from a
conversation I had with Lowell Weicker, a dear old friend from
Yale days. Lowell, who was Ted Weicker's younger brother, had
been studying the chemistry and manufacturing of pharmaceu-

tics in Germany. His father's firm, E. R. Squibb & Sons, was training him to take over the business. When he came back from Germany he had alarming news.

He told me of being invited to a dinner which was attended by the leading lights of the Nazi hierarchy—Von Ribbentrop, Admiral Raeder, Von Neurath, Kepler and Krahnefeus, among others. It was a pleasant dinner and afterwards everyone went to Admiral Raeder's apartment in Berlin for a nightcap. By this time everyone was talking frankly about their government and its plans.

The year was 1937; all the world was wondering what Hitler and his cohorts were planning. Lowell listened and what he heard was chilling. The Nazi big shots openly discussed the forthcoming war. The fact that an American was present did not deter them at all. They boasted that they planned to invade Czechoslovakia the following year, then Poland and Holland.

Weicker asked a pertinent question: "What do you think the United States will be doing when all this takes place?"

Von Ribbentrop, who was to become Hitler's Foreign Minister, replied, "The United States will do nothing. You Americans will take so much time debating what to do that the war will be over before you can make up your minds."

When Lowell told me this I was horrified. It was proof positive that the goal of Nazi Germany was war and conquest. I realized, too, that Von Ribbentrop's comments on American irresolution were not all that farfetched. Anyone who read a newspaper in those days knew that our military posture was weak, that an unreasoning pacifism was eating at the very vitals of the nation's will to resist. College students were publicly taking oaths to the effect that they would never, never, never fight for their country. Antiwar and so-called "peace" groups were mushrooming. The picture looked bleak indeed.

Still another insight into Nazi intentions was provided me by Louis B. Mayer who, because of his close contacts with Jewish leaders, was being kept informed of the plight of the Jews in

Germany. Long before most of the world had heard about concentration camps, Mayer had received firsthand accounts of Nazi atrocities. Thanks to Mr. Mayer, I early realized the necessity of a homeland which could harbor in safety the remnants of European Jewry. As a United States Senator, I have been in the forefront of efforts to preserve the integrity of the tiny nation of Israel, beset from all sides by Soviet-sponsored Arab enemies.

I was pleased when the *B'nai B'rith Messenger,* the leading Anglo-Jewish weekly in Los Angeles, commented about me in its January 9, 1970 issue: "When Zionist leaders called on him in Washington several months ago they were amazed at Mr. Murphy's knowledge of the history and of the development of the State of Israel. When he speaks of the Middle East, he does so as both student and as a Senator."

Despite Louis Mayer's doubts about Wendell Willkie, he did what he could once the man from Indiana began to campaign. He encouraged me in my extracurricular work for "We the People for Willkie." Our little group began to pick up steam and we attracted a lot of newspaper coverage.

One of the strange things about Louis Mayer was that despite his tremendous dislike of President Roosevelt, he still maintained great respect for the office. Through the grapevine Mayer had learned that F.D.R. was terribly ill. He said, "Roosevelt is still the President and he should look as good as possible when he makes public appearances." As a consequence, Mayer dispatched expert makeup, lighting and camera men to the White House whenever Mr. Roosevelt asked for them.

To counteract our efforts, leading Hollywood Democrats, who had formed a rival organization, tried to become as active as we were. Their leaders included Melvyn Douglas and his wife Helen Gahagan Douglas, Fredric March, John Garfield, Edward G. Robinson and a few others.

As the national campaign increased in tempo, the rhetoric of both the Hollywood groups escalated. The mimeograph machines in our respective headquarters ground out press releases. There were noisy charges and countercharges.

Our battle of words created so much interest among the public that the Democrats suggested a debate be held in the Hollywood Bowl between our two groups for the benefit of people in the motion picture industry. We accepted the proposal with enthusiasm. Soon ground rules were being discussed. The decision finally was made that there would be six people from each side—all well-known personalities—to argue the relative merits of their candidates. About sixteen thousand to eighteen thousand people were expected to fill the Bowl.

Maybe we showed too much enthusiasm at the idea, because as time went on, we heard less and less from the Democrats, until they decided that the event was much too important for just local consumption. They suggested that the debate be broadcast nationally over a radio network. We once again agreed enthusiastically. And we also agreed to put up half the money for the broadcast.

Believe it or not, that was the last we ever heard of the debate. For some reason the Democrats dropped the idea like a hot potato. They never gave us an explanation that made sense. All we could do on the Republican side was to accuse our political foes of being chicken. And while that made news locally, I'm afraid it didn't get many votes for Willkie.

We naive Hollywood Republicans kept dreaming that somehow our standardbearer would catch on with the public, overcome F.D.R.'s advantage as the incumbent, and take the lead. At times we thought Willkie was scoring points.

The war issue became a major one during the campaign. Willkie began appealing to isolationist sentiments by asking crowds across the nation whether his opponent's "pledge for peace is going to last longer than his pledge for sound money."

Poor Wendell never had a chance. Roosevelt came back with this historic utterance: "I have said this before and I shall say it again and again and again: Your boys are not going to be sent into any foreign war."

A little more than a year later the nation was at war and our boys were on their way to save Europe for the second time in my lifetime.

On December 7, 1941, I drove down to the beach with my three-year-old son, Dennis, in my brand-new Ford station wagon. As he played in the sand and I watched the waves roll in from the Pacific, I heard a bulletin on the radio saying that Pearl Harbor had been bombed. It is difficult now, three decades later, to describe the jumble of emotions that beset me. All I can really remember is that I picked up Dennis and quickly drove home.

By the time I reached the house, Julie was already at work for her country. At that time, Julie and two other civic-minded women comprised the Red Cross Motor Corps in the Los Angeles area. And on that "day that will live in infamy" Julie was quickly alerted by headquarters to begin hauling medical supplies from Red Cross warehouses in Los Angeles to Fort MacArthur.

Julie immediately pressed me into service. All night long, we drove back and forth from the warehouse to the old fort delivering supplies. What shocked me that night was the fact that Fort MacArthur—located on the point near San Pedro—was without the most rudimentary necessities one would have expected to find on a military post.

To say that they were unprepared for war would be the understatement of the century. They had literally nothing. Military hardware was virtually nil. There were two old antiaircraft guns down on the point, both so primitive that I believe they couldn't have fired a shell more than two hundred feet. A fifteen-inch railroad gun stood just behind the mess hall. A few days later someone had the bright idea of cleaning it up and trying it out, just in case of a Japanese invasion. When the weapon was fired, the blast knocked down two shacks and shifted the foundation of the mess hall at least fifteen feet. That was the last time they fired that railroad gun.

Our great nation would have been helpless had the Japanese been able to attack the mainland. If there is anything to be learned from Pearl Harbor, it is simply that the United States should never again let itself be caught defenseless.

Unfortunately there are those in the Congress today who sincerely believe that military primacy is an unnecessary luxury. They have not been convinced by the lessons of the past, including Pearl Harbor. They still don't seem to understand that a strong military establishment in America is the best possible insurance for world peace.

As long as I can raise my voice in Congress, I will never agree that we should be disarmed—either laterally or unilaterally—until we are certain that all nations in the world have not only agreed in principle but will give proof of their honest desire to join in complete disarmament.

Our defenselessness in those early days of the war led to the spread of hysterical rumors, particularly on the West Coast. One sad, still-troubling consequence was the suspicion directed against our fellow citizens of Japanese ancestry that they might constitute a possible Fifth Column. Only after the war did we learn that the Japanese-Americans were as loyal to this nation as any other group of citizens. By that time it was too late. The Japanese-Americans, deprived of their Constitutional rights, had been rounded up and relocated in "safer" areas in the country.

Most of my friends in Naval intelligence and in the military never agreed with this procedure. Ironically, one of those most insistent on this extraordinary treatment of the nisei was none other than my good friend, then Attorney General of California, Earl Warren, who later was to become the Chief Justice of the U.S. Supreme Court. Also ironic was the fact that the *bete noire* of so many of my liberal friends, J. Edgar Hoover, was the one man in those troubled years who raised his voice against the relocation of the Japanese. President Franklin D. Roosevelt refused to listen to the Director of the Federal Bureau of Investigation, and "relocation" became national policy under the New Deal.

Just lately there have been some suggestions that maybe some of those concentration camps would be used once again for those who would violently dissent from some of our government policies. I am pleased to say that I was a co-sponsor, along with Dan Inouye and others, of a bill to see that these camps will be completely dismantled so they can never be used again.

Well, we were at war by this time, and Julie and I threw ourselves into war work. Julie, a wonderful organizer, was in charge of handling the first shipload of evacuees from Pearl Harbor to arrive at San Pedro. It was a tough job that called for placing the evacuees on all sorts of transportation in order to get them to their respective homes as quickly as possible, and finding food and housing for them until they were on their way. It was a crisis situation and Julie worked at it around the clock with little sleep for three days running. As always, she got the job done and with dispatch.

After Pearl Harbor, I seriously considered entering one of the services. Though I was forty years of age, I felt I could be useful somewhere in the military. I had a wonderful job figured out for myself in the Navy. It was to go from ship to ship to explain to the skippers how important a motion picture film record of actual battle conditions could be in future military action. It would have been an exciting job, and I was anxious to do it, but the top brass thought I was a bit overage and I was turned down.

I did have the opportunity to go into the Army, and I was very sorely tempted. I could have gone in with the rank of Lieutenant Colonel in charge of all Special Services, because the General in charge in Washington, while an excellent artillery officer, had no knowledge of Special Services. He kept me around his office for three days trying to convince me that this would be a wonderful job for my talents and background, but I was advised by a close friend that I could do much more for my country in this area as a civilian.

My old Navy friend, Harvey Haislip, explained, "As a civilian, Murphy, you can get things done as quick as a flash, but once you put on that uniform you'll have to go through channels just like all the rest of us. For a guy of your temperament, it could be very, very frustrating."

My major activity in the war effort was as head of the Hollywood Victory Committee which arranged for thousands of motion picture people to make personal appearances at military bases around the world. None of them were paid. All went as volunteers and the job done by the actors of Hollywood during the war is one I will always be extremely proud of. We supplied over eighty-five thousand free play dates in the Army camps of the world—not just for the Americans but for our Allies as well.

Adolphe Menjou, who had been in World War I as a captain, spent four months in North Africa with a troupe and then another several months in the British Isles just before the invasion of Normandy. Pat O'Brien, Bob Hope and hundreds of others went to far-off places like India and China.

Probably the most magnificent volunteers were the three gallant gals who started the whole thing—Martha Raye, Kay Francis and Carole Landis, who toured military bases as the first visiting troupe and went into the most difficult areas. Martha Raye, as courageous as ever, is still at it, making tours to all parts of Vietnam to entertain our troops.

I heard her one night on television giving a report on her last trip to Vietnam, I wish she could tell all the people the true story of what the American military are doing there and of the great courage and morale of our troops, who have been sent off to fight a strange war that they dare not lose but have not been permitted to win.

Besides helping map out the tours for the Victory Committee, I spent as much time as I could on the road entertaining troops.

A theater man in Portland, Oregon—Ted Gamble—had done such a fine job of selling war bonds that President Roosevelt put him in charge of the entire program, in spite of the fact that he was a Republican. Ted was a close friend of mine, and whenever he got an exceptionally difficult area to work he would call me and I would be on my way. I used to spend four and five nights a week trying to sleep on airplanes or trains getting from one part of the country to another.

At the end of the war there was a big dinner in New York to celebrate the success of the war bond tours, and I was asked to be the master of ceremonies. The Grand Ballroom of the Waldorf-Astoria was decorated on one side by a facsimile of a war bond. The chairman was Spyros Skouras, whose accent was as rich as Gregory Ratoff's and just as Greek as Ratoff's was Russian. Bob Hope used to say that though Skouras had been in America for forty years, he spoke English as if he were coming next week.

Looking up and down the dais that night, I didn't sense much wit or humor among the bunch, and when I was introduced by Spyros Skouras in his rich dialect there was only perfunctory applause. I waited until it was absolutely quiet and said, "Now, ladies and gentlemen, I will translate what Mr. Skouras has just said." That broke the ice and from then on we had a pleasant evening. Even Henry Morgenthau made a little joke, which after all was not really in his line of business.

During these days there were a number of guys from our bunch in Hollywood who were making names for themselves in the service. One of the outstanding wartime records was made by Bob Montgomery, whom I had known since our school days at Pawling. In the midst of a brilliant acting career, Bob enlisted in the American Field Service and drove an ambulance in France during the time of the Nazi blitz.

Bob had been making a film in London in 1940 when he enlisted. There were cynics back home who insisted that he had done it for publicity. I remember talking about this with Bob's commanding officer, Don Coster, who remarked that Bob had gone about obtaining publicity in a pretty odd way, since it meant lying on his belly in a ditch on a French roadside while scores of Stukas strafed the area with real—not picture—bullets.

Coster also told me about the three days when the entire provisions of the ambulance outfit amounted to three chocolate bars which Bob had thoughtfully brought with him, along with a few bottles of very bad French wine which a storekeeper had left behind in his mad dash to depart ahead of the Panzer divisions.

Following the fall of Paris, Bob somehow made his way across France into Portugal, where he was fortunate enough to get the last seat on a Pan-American Clipper bound for New York.

The year was 1940 and our nation was not yet at war— officially. On his return to Los Angeles, Bob told me of his overwhelming concern for the future of the nation in a world dominated by the Axis powers. Between us we even formulated a plan to follow isolationist spokesman around the country, answering their arguments. We felt that the nation was in jeopardy and we had better arm ourselves and get prepared for war as quickly as possible, if for no other reason than "no one has ever been known to pick a fight with Joe Louis."

During this time only a few of his close friends knew that Bob was going to school at night preparing to take examinations for a Navy commission. In 1941 he finally was commissioned as Lieutenant (junior grade) Henry Montgomery, Jr., his real name, in the United States Naval Reserve. You can imagine the surprise when it came out that Henry Montgomery was really Bob Montgomery, the noted film star.

Again there was a great deal of scoffing on the part of the cynics. Montgomery's first assignment was as Assistant Naval Attache in London and the cynics spread the word that it was a social position. What they didn't know—and what Bob himself refused to publicize—was that he spent two months on British destroyers hunting submarines in the North Atlantic. At the same time he flew with the Bomber Command over occupied Europe and even made a trip on a British motor torpedo boat because he wanted to find out what made those little powerhouses tick.

Later he was named a liaison officer between the U.S. Navy and the British Admiralty. When he returned home, he was assigned to the White House.

But the motor torpedo boats had made a big impression on him. This was understandable, since his one luxury in life had been fast cars, usually semiracing jobs which would have been more appropriate on the Indianapolis Speedway than on the boulevards of Hollywood. In fact, it got to the point where the only two people who would ride with him were Jimmy Cagney and myself. We did so at our own risk.

When the first motor torpedo (PT) boat school was organized in Newport, Rhode Island, Bob put in a request for transfer from the White House to the school. The request had to be approved by President Roosevelt. There was some question whether the President would permit him to leave. Bob was scared stiff when he went to see the President about getting the necessary papers signed.

I was in Washington at the time, and I waited for Bob to return from that appointment. When I saw his beaming countenance I knew he had succeeded in getting his dream assignment. When he finally calmed down, Bob said the President had told him, "Bob, you are doing exactly what I would like to do if I were a few years younger. Good luck to you, and go up there with my blessing."

Bob saw action at Guadalcanal and in the Marshall Islands, and in the invasion of Normandy he was on the first destroyer to enter Cherbourg Harbor. By this time he was a Lieutenant Commander and was awarded the Bronze Star for "meritorious achievement" on D-Day. Late in 1944 he returned to Hollywood where, still on active status, he recuperated from attacks of tropical fever.

His first film following his return to Hollywood was naturally
*They Were Expendable*, the brilliant dramatization of William
L. White's best-selling book on the PT-boat crews. And who do
you suppose would direct a film like that? None other than his
good friend John Ford, who later attained the rank of Admiral
in the United States Navy Reserve, one of the great directors of
all time and one of my closest friends throughout the years.

# CHAPTER 17

## *The Communists: Using "Muscle"*

Not only did the Screen Actors Guild conduct a successful fight against labor racketeering, but I am proud to say that our union also took the lead in combating a very serious Communist party effort to infiltrate the motion picture industry.

For a time the Communists and their fellow travelers nearly succeeded in capturing several labor union and guild organizations of those employed in the industry, which would have given them control of what could have been a powerful propaganda instrument. They were militant, clever, well-financed and, as we discovered in the post-war years, most proficient in the arts of character assassination, destruction by rumor and the application of guilt by association. The real party members were as vicious, evil and intellectually dishonest a lot as I have ever encountered. Thank goodness there weren't too many of this type.

Fighting Communism was not easy. It was a terribly complex and sensitive business. A lot of good people, particularly those of honest liberal persuasion, just didn't want to believe what we knew to be true about Communist machinations in our industry. Not that they were at all sympathetic towards subversive activity or dictatorship. Far from it. They just thought that people like Bob Montgomery, Roy Brewer, Morrie Ryskind and I were somewhat "tetched in the head" and saw Commies under every bed. I never saw one under a bed but I have recognized a couple in plush offices, fancy limousines and at some of the gayest champagne parties in Hollywood.

In the early days some people felt we were exaggerating the Red menace. One of these was my close friend Ronald Reagan, who has never made any secret of his once-naive sentiments.

Ronnie was an honest liberal, a gung-ho labor man, and a supporter of any organization that would guarantee to work for peace, decency and freedom.

In his own words, Ronnie in the mid-forties was "a near-hopeless hemophilac liberal." As he put it in his autobiography, *Where's the Rest of Me?*, "I was not sharp about Communism; the Russians still seemed to be our allies. There were as yet no rumbles of the plans the Russians had for the capitalism which had saved their hides on every front. In that era, the American Communists were high on the Hollywood hog, but only by reason of deception. Most of us called them liberals, and, being liberal ourselves, bedded down with them with no thought for the safety of our wallets."

These are honest words, and Ronald Reagan is an honest, sincere man who has always had a deep, abiding concern for social problems. When I tried to tell him about Communism and the extent of its infiltration into our industry he frankly thought that I was trying to convert him to becoming a benighted Republican.

Honestly, that was not my objective. My main aim at the time was to unite Hollywoodians of all political philosophies, as long as they were antitotalitarian, against the increasing encroachments of Communism. Eventually, I am happy to report, Ronald Reagan discovered that I wasn't too far off the mark. Although he remained a liberal, he became increasingly anti-Communist. And of course, as time went on he did decide that the Republican philosophy was more in keeping with his own. The rest is history still in the making.

As Ronnie put it in his book: "George Murphy was a worthy successor to Bob Montgomery [as S.A.G. president] and equally aware of the strange creatures crawling from under the make-believe rocks in our make-believe town. I owe a great deal to this cool, dapper guy who had to deal with me in my early white-eyed liberal daze. There were some of our associates, I'm sure, who believed I was as red as Moscow, but Murph never wavered in his defense of me even though I ranted and railed at him as an arch-reactionary (which he isn't)."

I could completely understand Ronnie's point of view, because I myself had gone through a period of uncertainty, as did so many others. For a while I wasn't too certain about Whittaker Chambers because the Alger Hiss affair was so shocking it made credibility difficult. I've since learned better.

When I first went to Hollywood, for nearly a year I regularly had lunch with a most attractive and intelligent man. You can imagine my shock when I learned that he was one of the top Soviet agents in the Los Angeles area. A capable assistant to a studio head also finally publicly confessed his role in the Communist movement. No, it wasn't too easy in those days to separate the wolves from the sheep and many good people were temporarily fooled.

I wasn't fooled too often, however. I had known J. Edgar Hoover for several years before coming to Hollywood and I was familiar with the magnificent work of the F.B.I. in combating Communism. Moreover, I was far more interested in studying Communist programs and tactics than most of my fellow actors. For a time, I even looked at the *Daily Worker*, which was sent to me free when I became active in the Screen Actors Guild. I began to study anti-Communist literature. One book that had an important effect on my thinking was Eugene Lyons' *The Red Decade* which cited chapter and verse on how the Communists were able to lure celebrities into their nefarious "front" groups.

I also watched the Communists operate during the period of the Soviet-Nazi pact, when Stalin embraced Hitler. For twenty-two months, the left-wingers preached a rigid isolationism to the American people and, in effect, sought a Nazi victory in Europe. Their chief slogan was: "The Yanks Are Not Coming!"

Then came June 22, 1941. Hitler, who, I learned later, had never really trusted Stalin, doublecrossed him, sending his jack-booted legions blitzkrieging into the Soviet Union. Literally overnight, the Communists and their multitudinous "peace" fronts became the noisiest warmongers and began shouting "The Yanks Are Coming!" It was probably the most remarkable political turnabout that I have ever encountered in many decades of observing Communist shenanigans.

Those in Hollywood and elsewhere who had preached peace and disarmament the loudest, now yelled like demons for a "Second Front." I remember hearing a news commentator ask Charlie Chaplin if he considered the American invasion of North Africa a second front, and Chaplin answered, "If it is satisfactory to Premier Stalin, it's satisfactory to me." Such was the confusion of those days.

Then came the formation of the Hollywood Intertalent Council to coordinate the joint war efforts of the writers', directors' and actors' guilds. On paper, this seemed like an attractive idea. A war against Hitler and the Japanese war lords was being fought, and the very least that creative people could do in those desperate days was to unite our varied talents in behalf of freedom.

But a few of us became suspicious early in the game. There were certain people in our town who often seemed more intent on helping the Soviet Union than in defeating our enemies. Once the Council was launched Bob Montgomery and I began to sense something wrong. The statements of the Council's leadership were so slanted that I felt the S.A.G. was involuntarily becoming involved in a standard Communist front operation. Montgomery and I went before the board and, after a bitter fight, got the S.A.G. leadership to agree to continue with the Intertalent Council only if it took both an anti-Communist and anti-Nazi stand. We suggested that, among other things, the Council would publicly avow that "we would jointly oppose all enemies of America from within and without, whether they be Nazi, Fascist or Communist."

When the S.A.G.'s Jack Dales put it up to the Intertalent Council that way, the whole thing collapsed like a struck set.

"Now that I look back," Dales told the *Saturday Evening Post* in 1955, "Murph was aware of what was going on much faster than the rest of us."

Even before the war ended (and in defiance of the labor movement's no-strike pledge) a series of major strikes broke out as Hollywood unions vied with one another over jurisdictional matters. Between 1945 and 1947, these strikes cost our industry at least one hundred and fifty million dollars, while over eight thousand workers lost over nine million man-hours and some twenty-eight million dollars in wages.

All the available evidence suggested to the S.A.G. leadership (I was president at the time) that the bitter struggle had been created by neverending Communist efforts to seize control of the entire movie business. In effect, the jurisdictional disputes were between the Communist-infiltrated and anti-Communist unions.

Chief sponsor of the left wing effort was the Conference of Studio Unions (C.S.U.), a newly-formed organization made up of unions representing the painters, set designers, sign writers, screen cartoonists and office employees. From the beginning, it was obvious that the C.S.U.'s design was to replace I.A.T.S.E— the so-called stagehands—which by now had gotten rid of its gangster influences and under the leadership of Dick Walsh had become a strong force for Americanism in Hollywood. In turn, the C.S.U. was headed by Herbert K. Sorrell, a large, muscular man who also headed the local painters' union.

A complicating factor was the Carpenters Union, a legitimate organization which had its own jurisdictional squabbles with the I.A.T.S.E.

But basically the fight was between Herb Sorrell's C.S.U. and Dick Walsh's I.A.T.S.E. And we in S.A.G. had reason to believe that Herb Sorrell was in some way under the control of the Communist Party. In February 1946 we learned, not to our surprise, that there was in existence a Communist party membership card bearing the signature of one "Herbert Stewart." A

California State Committee hired two top handwriting experts
who compared this signature with the admitted handwriting of
Herb Sorrell. The experts testified that both handwriting
samples were the work of the same man.

In March 1945 Sorrell selected Warner Brothers Studio for
the strike, largely as a matter of convenience. It was in Burbank,
where they had a very small police force, and its physical setup
was ideal. It had one main entrance gate as against the several
entrances at most other studios, and its location was away from
congestion.

The picket lines were formed and the entrance gate was
blocked off. When a court ordered a reduction in the number
of pickets, the C.S.U. got rough. They brought in "the muscle"
and dozens of workers were injured. Longshoremen were in evidence; clubs, chains, bottles, bricks and two-by-fours were used;
police cars were tipped over. A real labor war had broken out in
Hollywood.

A few members of the Screen Actors Guild demanded that
our union endorse the strike and honor the picket line by refusing to go to work. To ascertain the wishes of the general membership I called a meeting at the Hollywood Legion Stadium
where we heard Sorrell of the C.S.U. and Walsh of the
I.A.T.S.E. We gave them each half an hour to state their case
and then sent out a secret ballot.

The membership voted overwhelmingly—over ninety-seven
percent—not to join the strike. Our duty to the Guild was clear
and we on the Board set about carrying out the wishes of the
members.

Our people wanted to work, so we helped keep the studios
open. We arranged for the transportation of our actors and actresses through jeering picket lines. Many of them were pretty
scared of the violence around them, and I could hardly blame
them. All that any of our members needed was a face damaged
by some crazed picket and his or her motion picture career
would probably be over.

A couple of funny situations were connected with the strike. One of the S.A.G. board members was also an officer in the State Guard, and he was sent by his Commanding Officer to Warner Brothers to see whether a state of riot existed. As he went through the small picket line in front of the Administrative Offices a woman suddenly fell to the ground, screamed and hollered, and swore he had knocked her down, punched and even kicked her. Like magic, ten witnesses appeared who said they saw him do it and the poor man was to be sued for $50,000 damages, which he didn't have. This was his story as he told it to Jack Dales and me. We sent him home with a sedative and Jack said to me, "You don't seemed concerned."

I told him that I wasn't concerned and that he shouldn't be either. "They've made a mistake. They picked on one of their own boys and you will never hear another word about it." And we never did. There was no law suit, no trial and I guess no injury to the woman who said she had been punched and kicked.

Another funny episode occurred when the leftist-led Longshoremen arrived at the Warner Brothers Studio in trucks. One picket objected because he thought they were Teamsters. "What did you expect them to come in—boats?" shouted a burly picket captain.

In early 1947, the Senate Fact-Finding Committee on Un-American Activities of the California Legislature had this to say about Herb Sorrell: "Under ordinary circumstances, he would be a very unimportant individual. He probably might have developed into a very good house painter. He is, personally, a likable fellow. He probably doesn't like journeyman painting, and his frustration and sense of guilt are compensated by the hearty back-slapping bestowed upon him by the Communist hierarchy. He is inclined to grow more arrogant as his defiance for law and order goes unpunished. He pictures himself as a professional revolutionist leading the downtrodden proletariat (in this case the highest-paid workers in the world) on the barricades, resisting the oppression and tyranny of the industrial barons."

Sorrell knew early in the game he wasn't kidding me. He knew that I knew what he was and we managed to get along. At least we were able to communicate. He had been a wrestler at one time, but now had gone to fat, and I would jokingly say to him, "Herb, I wish you were the heavyweight champion of the world, because if there is one guy in Hollywood I could lick, it's you."

After I said this the third or fourth time, I think he began to believe it. I was in my early forties at the time and in pretty good shape. I began to believe it, too. Anyway, Sorrell always handled me with kid gloves. My only objective in talking to him at all was to try to end the chaos and turmoil and try to restore some order and good sense to our industry.

At any rate, we repeatedly offered S.A.G.'s good offices to try to mediate the jurisdictional tangle. We came close to finding a solution on several occasions. But our well-meaning efforts failed, often at the very last moment. I realized then that sometimes a settlement is not really the objective of troublemakers—they want problems, not solutions.

For example, one Sunday afternoon with representatives of all unions present, Sorrell agreed to our proposed terms to settle the dispute. It was typed and signed for delivery. But the next day Sorrell turned up at our S.A.G. offices and, like a little boy who has been scolded by his father, said, "I'm sorry, but I can't stick with the agreement I made yesterday."

That brought home to me one pertinent fact; that it is virtually impossible to make a deal with someone allied with the Communists. Such people have to take orders; they can't make deals on their own. As the California Fact-Finding Senate Committee put it in its 1959 report: "The Communist party working in Hollywood wanted control over everything that moved on wheels. . . . They soon moved Communist units into those unions having jurisdiction over carpenters, painters, musicians, grips and electricians. To control these trade unions was to control the motion picture industry."

In September 1946, I knew something had to be done to break the deadlock. Because of Sorrell's intransigence, it looked like the strike would never end unless it was on his terms.

I made the suggestion to the board that the S.A.G. fly some of our top stars to Chicago where the American Federation of Labor was holding its national convention to plead for a system of impartial arbitration of jurisdictional disputes. The violence had by now spread to other studios.

An S.A.G. delegation consisting of Dick Powell, Edward Arnold, Walter Pidgeon, Jane Wyman, Ronald Reagan, Alexis Smith, Robert Taylor, Gene Kelly and me flew to Chicago. Bob Montgomery flew in from New York where he was directing a play.

We tried to contact William Green, the president of the A.F. of L., and other top leaders, but none of them would see us. Once again it became obvious that we actors would have to go it alone. And once again we decided to use our public opinion "muscle." We made a newsreel telling exactly why we had come to Chicago and what we hoped to accomplish. Then we threatened to send top stars to every city in the country to discuss and show films of the violence outside our studio gates.

Our threats worked like magic. We were immediately invited to dinner by none other than William Green himself. Green, ostensibly one of the biggest men in the labor movement, was pathetic. He literally wept before us. "What can I do?" he asked us. "The A.F. of L. is a federation of independent unions and I have no power to control them."

When we returned to Hollywood we thought we had failed. The old-line labor leaders refused to end their quarrels over jurisdiction.

Then the Sorrell people launched a propaganda campaign against Ronnie Reagan, Eddie Arnold and me as "scabs" and "producers' stooges." They were invitations to violence and the three of us conducted ourselves appropriately. We didn't walk down dark streets alone at night. We all had a feeling of *déjà vu*.

It was like being back in the Browne and Bioff days again.

At a membership meeting held at the Legion Stadium after our return from Chicago, the Sorrell forces managed to convince a few innocent souls to carry the ball for them. Katharine Hepburn, for example, had been prevailed upon to read a speech which was, almost word for word, a copy of a C.S.U. strike bulletin that had been issued a few weeks before.

Another innocent was that fine actor, Edward G. Robinson, who also got up to appeal for peace in the labor movement. Later I asked Eddie, as warmhearted a human being as I have ever known, whether he had written the speech, which followed the Sorrell line. "No," he told me, "they gave it to me." Years later, Eddie Robinson learned to his horror who "they" really were and has made amends by performing many good anti-Communist deeds.

One actor, Alexander Knox, who had played Woodrow Wilson in a Darryl Zanuck film about the World War I President, tried to ridicule our efforts in Chicago. I must say his speech was original and, at first, he got a lot of laughs. But the assembled members had second thoughts. Catching on quickly to his hidden purpose they began to shout angrily at him to sit down. "What would you have done?" some yelled at Knox. In the language of *Variety*, Knox "laid an egg." He was booed off the platform.

The S.A.G. leadership (Reagan was now our president) had won an important test. The actors held firm against selling out to Sorrell and his comrades. Finally, when responsible labor leaders endorsed the position of I.A.T.S.E., the C.S.U.-sponsored strike sort of fizzled out. But great damage had been done and many fine workers never got back into the industry.

The Communist party had lost a major battle, but the war continued on other fronts. Then came the stormy "Hollywood hearings" in the fall of 1947, at which testimony before the House Un-American Activities Committee (H.U.A.C.) sketched in the extent of Communist infiltration and influence in the

motion picture industry as well as its staggering financial contributions to the party. Incidentally, a member of H.U.A.C. was
a young Congressman from Whittier, California, Richard M.
Nixon, then in his first year in the House of Representatives.

The Communists, however, did a magnificent job in
befuddling the real issues in the public mind. They set up a
"front" organization—The Committee for the First Amendment—which somehow made it appear that most of Hollywood
was opposed to the H.U.A.C. hearings. A planeload of glamorous stars were sent to Washington, where they made great
headlines in the *Washington Post* trying to explain that the
"witch hunt" against Communists somehow threatened their
freedoms. I will not name the people who got involved in these
Communist-sponsored activities only because most of them now
realize that they had been duped. They were used, just as many
youngsters are being used today, confused by slick half-truths
and responding to carefully created slogans and false-premised
objectives.

A group of us who had been fighting the Communists in our
various craft groups was subpoenaed to testify before the House
Committee. The pressures that were mounted against us were
enormous. The Communists and their "liberal" friends began
to call us "Fascists" or "crackpots." The Congressmen, including Dick Nixon, were labeled "witch-hunters and Gestapo."

My argument was that there were, indeed, "witches" in
Hollywood.

The pressures nearly got to my dear friend, Ronnie Reagan,
who at the time was President of the S.A.G. He didn't enjoy
having old friends in the acting profession sidle up to him and,
with sheer hate on their faces, sneer, "Fascist!"

The one thing I had learned about the "liberals" was the fact
that most of them are probably the most unliberal and intoler-
ant people on earth. Unless you agree with them, they'll try to
destroy you. And I have often felt their lash. But once you make
up your mind to fight for freedom (and that means being anti-

Communist as well as anti-Fascist), you've got to learn how to take it. The situation reminds one of the more recent Free Speech Movement, in which only radicals are permitted free speech.

Reagan was particularly forthright before the Committee in describing how, only weeks before, he had been hornswoggled into lending his good name as a sponsor to a questionable enterprise. His testimony is interesting because it demonstrates how the Commies operated at the time, and probably still do.

"I was called several weeks ago. There happened to be a financial drive to raise money to build a badly-needed hospital in a certain section of town—the All Nations Hospital . . . I was called to the phone. A woman . . . told me that there would be a recital held at which Paul Robeson would sing and she said that all the money for the tickets would go to the hospital and asked if she could use my name as one of the sponsors.

"I hesitated for a moment because I don't think that Mr. Robeson's and my political views coincide at all and then I thought I was being a little stupid because here is an occasion where Mr. Robeson is perhaps appearing as an artist and certainly the object, raising money for a hospital, is above any political consideration . . . I have contributed money myself. So I felt a little bit as if I had been stuffy for a minute and I said, 'Certainly, you can use my name.' "

Reagan continued: "I left town for a couple of weeks and when I returned I was handed a newspaper story that said that this recital was held at the Shrine Auditorium in Los Angeles under the auspices of the Joint Anti-Fascist Refugee Committee. The principal speaker was Emil Lustig. Robert Burman took up a collection, and remnants of the Abraham Lincoln Brigade were paraded to the platform.

"I did not, in the newspaper story, see one word about the hospital. I called the newspaper and said I am not accustomed to writing to editors, but would like to explain my position, and the editor laughed and said, 'You needn't bother, you are about the fiftieth person that has called with the same idea, including most of the doctors who had also been listed as sponsors of that affair.' "

Then Ronnie was asked: "Would you say from your observation that that is typical of the tactics or strategy of the Communists, to solicit and use the names of prominent people to either raise money or gain support?"

"Yes sir," Ronnie replied, "I think it is in keeping with their tactics."

There is nothing a good Commie activist enjoys more than a friendly humanitarian who wants to help his fellowman, particularly if he is rich and doesn't know the score.

Ronnie's testimony was largely about the S.A.G., of which he was President, and the struggle our union had waged against the Communist-inspired strike led by Herb Sorrell.

The questioning was largely done by a committee investigator named H. Allen Smith, a former F.B.I. agent who today is a ranking Republican member of the House of Representatives, representing the Twentieth District of my state.

As an investigator, Smith had done a remarkable job in Hollywood, rounding up some of the biggest names in our business as "friendly" witnesses. He assured us that we would only be asked to testify about what we knew as facts and not about hearsay. And he kept his word.

Among these witnesses, besides Reagan and myself, were Bob Montgomery, Adolphe Menjou, James K. McGuinness, Robert Taylor, Morrie Ryskind, Gary Cooper, Leo McCarey, Walt Disney and Louis B. Mayer.

Leo McCarey, who testified the same day I did, was very amusing on the subject.

"Were *Going My Way* and The *Bells of St. Mary's* two of the most popular pictures that you have produced?" Leo was asked.

"According to the box office, they were both very successful."

"They did very well?"

"Yes, sir."

"How did they do in Russia?"

"We haven't received one ruble from Russia on either picture."

"What is the trouble?"

"Well, I think I have a character in there that they do not like."

"Bing Crosby?"

"No, God."

My testimony, like Reagan's, was largely about the S.A.G. and the Sorrell strike. I pointed out that over ninety-seven percent of our membership voted to continue to work in the struck studios.

"Were there any attempts from within the Screen Actors Guild to change the guild's policy?" investigator Smith asked me.

"Yes," I replied, "there was some disagreement, not very much. . . Some people thought, and there was a great campaign put on to the effect, that we were crossing picket lines where brother unionists were out on strike. There were throwaways which called Mr. Arnold, Mr. Reagan and myself 'scabs.' Actually we felt we were not going to work to take another man's job, which is what a 'scab' really is, I believe." Of course, we were perfectly right in going to work when our union had decided not to join the strike.

"As to the people who took that position, I think some of them did it sincerely," I said. "I believe, however, there may have been a few who were taking advantage of the situation, if possible, to create greater turmoil within the industry."

Smith then asked me: "Leaving aside for the moment the Screen Actors Guild, do you feel there is any Communism in the motion picture industry?"

"Yes," I said, "there is Communism in the motion picture industry, as there is in practically every other industry in our nation today. . ."

"Have you ever been called upon to give lines in a picture which you felt were Communistic?"

"No, I have not."

"Supposing you were called upon to give such lines, what would be your position?"

"I am afraid, as they say in the theater, I would dry up. I wouldn't read the lines, nor would I play the part if I considered the part to be one that spread Communist propaganda."

"Do you feel that if things continue as they are the Communists might gain enough strength to control the industry?"

". . . I don't think the Communist party is in any particular hurry to achieve its aims. I think to look for direct Communist propaganda in pictures at this particular moment might be a mistake. However, I believe we should be on our guard lest the infiltration that is taking place reach a point where the screen may be used in a manner inimical to the best interests of our country."

Actually there had been some pretty pro-Soviet scenes inserted into pictures, but these were always excused as being a part of the war effort—to bring us closer to our allies, the Russians. The production *Mission to Moscow* was a glaring example of what our Government had asked the industry to do. And it was a glaring failure at the box office—even in Moscow.

There was one exceptionally moving moment during Bob Montgomery's testimony. This fine citizen was asked his "opinion regarding Communism."

"Mr. Chairman," Bob replied, "in common with millions of other men in this country in 1939 and 1940 I gave up my job to fight against a totalitarianism which was called Fascism. I am quite willing to give it up again to fight against a totalitarianism called Communism."

The audience spontaneously broke into applause.

It had been a harrowing experience for most of the "friendly" witnesses. That evening some of us ate dinner on the third floor of Harvey's Restaurant before taking the ten o'clock flight back to the coast. We were going over the day's proceedings when Quentin Reynolds, the magazine writer, came up and asked whether he could join us.

Reynolds, who was writing a piece about the Hollywood hearings, was not known to be very sympathetic to our cause. In fact, when we had testified earlier in the day, we had noticed that Reynolds sat with some members of the press identified to us as extremely leftist and hostile.

Leo McCarey told Reynolds, who had had one too many before he arrived, that he was not welcome. I thought Reynolds was on the verge of a crying jag. "What's happened to me?" he moaned. "What should I do?"

"Go to a Turkish bath," Leo told him, "and get boiled out for a couple of days. Then get yourself a rocking chair and sit on top of the Pacific Palisades and look at the Pacific Ocean for a while. Maybe you'll get yourself back on the beam."

Reynolds began to cry and walked away. I never saw him again. This is just one example of the confused bitterness engendered in those days by the all-out Communist effort to capture the movies—an industry which Stalin himself had declared an important propaganda weapon.

That the Communists failed is a measure of the good sense of the American people who made it clear in many ways that they wanted no part of subsidizing through their ticket purchases the "swimming-pool proletariat" in their revolutionary cause.

It is also a measure of the courage of those prominent Hollywood people who refused to give up the fight against subversion, despite all sorts of pressures brought against them. I have already named a number. There were many others—Ward Bond, Ginger Rogers, Charles Brackett, Ida R. Koverman, Charles Coburn, John Wayne, Art Arthur, John Ford, Bob Arthur, Clark Gable, Fred Niblo, Jr. Pat O'Brien, and Sam Wood.

Some of those who testified before the House Un-American Activities Committee found themselves the victims of a reverse "blacklist." Morrie Ryskind, one of the best writers of screen comedies, couldn't find work. Jim McGuinnis, a top Metro executive, was let go. And Adolphe Menjou, one of the finest actors in the business, was having his difficulties.

The naiveté about Communism and Communists, even among those who should have known better, was absolutely unbelievable. Louis Mayer, for example, once asked me about a certain writer. I said I didn't think well of him. An hour later, Mr. Mayer called me and said, "This man is no Communist."

"How do you know?" I asked.

"Well, I asked him and he told me so," was Mayer's reply. And then he realized how stupid he had been. The fact was that the writer in question had been publicly identified in Congressional hearings as a leading left-winger.

On January 16, 1948, several months after our appearance in Washington, the United Press reported from Budapest that the Communist Minister of the Interior Laszlo Rajk had ruled that films featuring Robert Taylor, Gary Cooper, Adolphe Menjou, Robert Montgomery and George Murphy would no longer be permitted on Hungarian movie screens. The dispatch quoted the Government spokesman as saying the action was taken because the actors involved had "expressed hatred of our 'peoples' democracies' when testifying in a Congressional investigation of Hollywood." The fact was that none of us had even mentioned the "peoples' democracies" in our testimonies.

Ronald Reagan was mortified because his name had been left out. But he made up for it. Under his leadership, the S.A.G. did more to purge its ranks of actors who were of uncertain allegiance than ever before.

In 1953, the S.A.G. membership voted overwhelmingly in behalf of a bylaw which would require anyone seeking membership in our union to sign the following statement: "I am not now and will not become a member of the Communist party nor of any other organization that seeks to overthrow the Government of the United States by force and violence."

The bylaw was proposed by a special committee made up of Ward Bond, Frank Faylen, Glenn Ford, Frank Lovejoy, Walter Pidgeon, Ronald Reagan and George Murphy as chairman.

It was significant, too, that when the Federal Government

passed a law making it mandatory for all officers of a union to take a loyalty oath, two members of the S.A.G. board handed in their resignations.

My last official act as president of the Guild was to change the bylaws on the question of a quorum. Until then, the bylaws required that only fifteen percent of the membership be present to legally conduct business. This meant that any group maintaining tight discipline over three hundred members would be able to control policies of our forty-five-hundred-member organization. Over the opposition of the so-called "liberal group," we managed to change the bylaws so that all matters pertaining to S.A.G. policy had to be voted in a secret ballot by a majority of the members.

Usually the Communists obtained supporters by appealing to idealistic convictions such as anti-Nazi sentiments. But not always. One of my colleagues testified that he had joined the party because he got to sleep with prettier girls. Another got his membership card because, he said, his lawyer had advised it. Still others joined because it meant they could get better acting and writing assignments from left-wing studio higher-ups.

Whatever the reasons, the Communist party became a major threat in the motion picture industry. Fighting Communists was not easy, nor was it pleasant, but it had to be done. It still has to be done—and not only in Hollywood.

# CHAPTER 18

*1948: Big-Time*
*National Politics*

I got my first taste of big-time national politics in 1948 when I attended the Republican National Convention in Philadelphia as a delegate committed to the Presidential aspirations of Earl Warren, at that time Governor of California.

Warren had been a good Governor. First elected on the Republican ticket in 1942, he did so well that four years later he won in both the Republican and Democratic primaries and was elected as a bipartisan candidate.

Still, some of us active in Republican affairs felt that the Governor was excessive in extolling "nonpartisanship" in the administration of state affairs. With the resurgence of national political rivalries, this "nonpartisanship" was drawing considerable criticism in Republican quarters as sort of short-selling of party principles.

In the fall of 1947, a new Hollywood Republican Committee had been formed to spearhead a drive to put the motion picture business into the Republican column in the 1948 Presidential campaign. At the first meeting, I was elected president and Bob Montgomery, first vice-president. I made a short speech whipping the troops into action.

"For too long a time a vociferous minority has misled the public into believing that the majority of Hollywood actors and actresses are radicals, crackpots or at least New Deal Democrats," I said. "We will do all in our power to dispel this impression."

Our officers included Walt Disney, Charles Brackett, John Arnold, Bert Allenberg, Sue C. Weiss, Eve Parshalle, Herbert Preston, Ida R. Koverman, Leo McCarey, Adolphe Menjou, Ginger Rogers, Morrie Ryskind and Lewis Allen Weiss.

Among charter members were Bing Crosby, Fred Astaire, Dennis Morgan, Joel McCrea, Randolph Scott, Dick Powell, Robert Taylor, Barbara Stanwyck, Harold Peary, Mary Pickford, Buddy Rogers, Penny Singleton, Harriett and Ozzie Nelson, Jeanette MacDonald, Gene Raymond, Sam Wood, Edward Arnold, Walter Pidgeon and William Bendix.

It was before this distinguished group that Governor Warren finally renounced the "nonpartisanship" which had been both a boon and a problem to him in California.

As chairman of the meeting, I introduced the Governor and was happy to hear him say something nice about the Republican party. After all, if a man wants to be the Republican candidate for President, he ought to sound a bit partisan.

The Governor also emphatically assailed Communism, derogating any appeasement of the Soviet Union as foolish and futile. He endorsed inquiries into Communist infiltration in the United States and he pleased his audience of motion picture notables with the suggestion that "for every Communist or fellow-traveler in your industry, there are literally thousands of men and women who abhor Communism."

The Governor certainly knew the score then, and many of us went all out for him when he sought the Presidential nomination. Accompanied by Julie, I went to Philadelphia determined to do what I could for his cause.

We had been invited by our good friends, the Batsons, to stay with them in a Main Line house they had rented for the week and to use their chauffeured limousine. Lucy and Lee knew we weren't the richest kids in town; they thought they would save us from having to pay hotel bills and, at the same time, provide us pleasant surroundings away from the downtown convention tumult.

Julie and I truly appreciated their offer but, as I explained to "Bat," we had not come to Philadelphia for a rest. We had come to work hard for our candidate and to do what we could for the

Republican cause. As it turned out, the Batsons spent most of their time at the Warwick (where we were stopping) along with the Len Firestones and other California friends.

On the first day of the convention, we drove to the hall in Batson's limousine. But there was no place to park. A top police officer was about to shoo us away when I yelled out that I was Mike Murphy's son.

"Oh," the officer said, all smiles. "You're all grown up now. What can I do for you?"

"Can you find a place for this rich man and his chauffeur to park?" I asked.

"Of course, George," he said and he arranged to make room for the Batson limousine. Batson was absolutely astonished. He hadn't realized how popular my father had been in Philadelphia.

Lee Batson, who was a generous contributor to the Republican party, for some reason wanted very much to consult with Earl Warren, who was also staying at the Warwick. When "Bat" tried to reach him on the phone one day, he was told that the Governor was in a conference and could not be disturbed.

"I wonder who the Governor is talking to," Batson said to Len Firestone. "Gee, it must really be important."

By this time Batson had discovered that the bathroom of the room Julie and I were occupying was just across the areaway from the Warren suite. So they rushed upstairs to our room and tried to make out who was talking to Warren. Using a pair of field glasses, Batson quickly found out.

"My God," he gasped. "Warren is talking to Murph!"

And so he was. Warren and I were talking about the need for some demonstrations in the Governor's behalf. All over downtown Philadelphia there were parades of highly flushed and starry-eyed young Republicans carrying banners, behind brass bands, for the other Presidential contenders—Robert Taft, Harold Stassen, Thomas E. Dewey and Arthur Vandenberg. Warren had nothing going for him in the hoopla department.

I pointed out that all the contenders were arranging to have demonstrations in their behalf on the floor of Convention Hall. Warren confessed he didn't know how to go about it. I told him that a police official I knew from the old days had told me that for a few dollars we could get all the demonstrators we wanted to yell and parade around the hall when the Governor's name was placed in nomination.

"I assure you, Governor, that you won't be embarrassed," I said.

"If that's the case, then go ahead," he replied.

I also prevailed on the Governor to ask Irene Dunne to make one of the speeches nominating Warren. At first Irene wasn't too willing. She said she didn't have the time to memorize a speech and she wouldn't want to read one because she would have to put on her glasses.

"Listen here," I said, "when Irene Dunne, one of the most glamorous ladies in the world, is introduced, she's going to get a tremendous amount of applause. And at that moment you will reach into your bag and take out your glasses. You will make a big thing of it. Don't try to hide them. Lift them up and blow on them as if they're dusty. And when you place them on your nose, just like any other woman in the hall, I will guarantee you even greater applause."

Which is exactly what happened. Miss Dunne is an enchanting lady and she played her role perfectly.

All I can really say about our demonstration on the convention floor was that we had one. Standing on the rostrum, I led the "We Want Warren" chant. Irene Dunne stood behind me briefly but fled from the harsh lighting. The organ pealed and the noise was loud, but I must concede that neither the delegates nor the galleries seemed visibly moved.

The most spectacular demonstration was mounted in the early hours of the morning by the supporters of Harold Stassen. I watched in amazement as hundreds of Stassenites put on a show which for sheer theatre, variety and duration had—according to veteran observers—never been matched. For the first time in over four hours of speeches and demonstrations, all the delegates were compelled to sit up and take notice.

The galleries were packed with partisans of the Minnesotan and they joined in the ear-shattering chant of "We want Stassen!" There could be little doubt that the Stassenites stole the show on nomination night. Stassen looked like the man to beat.

But it didn't mean a thing. Tom Dewey was nominated for President and he chose Earl Warren as his running mate.

Up to that point Stassen had not been able to move anywhere in Philadelphia without an entourage of noisy, shiny-faced, eager young people in tow. The beaming candidate obviously loved the adulation. Suddenly he was a beaten man. There were no crowds around him. His countenance reflected the bitterness of having lost a hard-fought campaign.

When I saw him later walking through the revolving door of the hotel, alone and dispirited, my heart went out to him. I asked Julie to wait for me, and I went over to greet Stassen, shake his hand, and take him to the elevator. I did not have the heart to see him walk through the lobby alone. He was very grateful. He thought he had at least one friend left in the world.

It wasn't that I was that much of a friend. I just knew that politics, like show business, can be a cruel profession. The humiliation of defeat can be devastating. I've seen big stars become "bums," in the eyes of their colleagues, after they suffered a series of failures.

Seeing Stassen in such a sad condition reminded me of the time that I arrived at the Ziegfeld Theater on West Forty-second Street too early to get made up for my performance. As I sat around talking with the guard at the stage door, I noticed a woman who looked vaguely familiar. Her clothes were in disarray and she looked as if she had been on a three-day drunk.

"Who's that woman?" I asked the guard.

"Why, that's Dolores." he replied.

"It can't be!" I exclaimed in horror. Dolores had been one of

Flo Ziegfeld's most glamorous show girls. She had had such beauty, such grace, such presence that all she had to do to stop the show was walk across the stage in one of those fabulous costumes Joe Urban or some other great designer would whip up for the Follies' girls. Now the glamor and excitement that had enveloped her were gone—she aroused only pity.

What always troubled me about Harold Stassen was that he never learned to get off stage. He had had his day in 1948 but he kept coming back onto the political stage every four years to suffer humiliation after humiliation. The crowning indignity came at the 1968 Republican Convention in Miami Beach when Stassen couldn't even muster a handful of supporters for a demonstration after his name had been placed in nomination for the Presidency. That was truly a pitiful sight.

I also ran into Will Hays at the 1948 convention. He was the so-called "czar" of the motion picture industry. I had met him once before with Louis Mayer. Hays had been Chairman of the Republican National Committee in 1920 and as a reward for his services in that year's Presidential election campaign, President Harding appointed him Postmaster General. In 1922, Hays resigned to become president of the Motion Picture Producers and Distributors of America and brought about the establishment, by the producers themselves, of a code of motion-picture censorship. Hays became widely known for his stringent enforcement of the code. He always remained a major force in Republican circles.

Hays remembered having met me with Mr. Mayer and he couldn't have been nicer. "George," he said, "have you ever thought about becoming active in politics?"

"No, General," I replied, "I've never given it much thought."

"Well I think you should give it considerable thought. You certainly seem to have a flair for it."

When word of what Hays had said reached Ida Koverman, Louis Mayer's secretary, she nearly flipped, she was so pleased.

"You know, George," she said, "you do have a flair for politics."

Miss Koverman was much more than a secretary to Louis Mayer. She was a trusted confidante and an extremely capable adviser on political affairs. A dyed-in-the-wool Republican, Ida was cognizant of party affairs from one end of the country to the other. She taught me a great deal about the basic principles of political action which has stood me in good stead all through the years, particularly when I ran for office. I've often thought how happy she and Mayer would have been had they been around when I was elected United States Senator.

Among my assignments during the Dewey-Warren campaign was a speaking trip to Lake County, Indiana, an industrial area which included the city of Gary. I asked some film luminaries to accompany me but Buddy Rogers, who was married to Mary Pickford, was the only one who could find the time. Buddy and I knew we were headed for territory traditionally unfriendly to Republicans. It didn't make us feel any better to be told by the local Republicans: "You guys must be crazy. Those steel workers will run over you and flatten you like bent tomato cans."

All I could say was: "Well, we promised to come out here and campaign and we're going to do the best we can."

Buddy and I were provided a flatbed truck with a loudspeaker on the rear end, which we backed up in front of the gates of the steel mills in the area. Much to our amazement, we began to draw crowds of between three and four thousand workers. True, they came to hear us more out of curiosity than political sympathy, but at least they listened to our Republican message. Even when the rain was pouring in bucketsful one day, we drew an audience of twenty-five hundred from an afternoon shift.

Occasionally we would be heckled. We didn't mind; it only made it more interesting for the onlookers. We always had the same retort: "This is a free country. If you disagree with what we are saying, and if you have something to say, you can use this microphone to say anything you please, as long as you let us finish."

Not once did any heckler avail himself of our invitation.

The Republican County Chairman was a wonderful little Irishman who couldn't believe the crowds we were attracting. One night he came into my hotel room and announced, "I've just made a bet on you."

"What about?" I asked.

"Some of the guys were saying that you don't have the guts to make a speech at the Teamsters Union hall tonight. And I said that a guy with the name of Murphy is afraid of nothing."

"If you think it'll do any good, I'll go there."

The little Irishman jumped up and down. "I knew you'd go," he said, laughing, "I knew you'd go."

We went. The teamsters had taken over a private house and had converted the basement into a kind of recreation hall. When I entered, my heart leaped into my mouth. I had never seen bigger men in my life. Every mother's son of them must have weighed at least two hundred and fifty pounds. In those days, they didn't have power steering and you had to be a well-built guy to be able to haul those trucks around, particularly those big trailer jobs.

There were about forty of these giants peering at me—some grimly, others grinning—as I entered. I immediately walked to the bar where a great big guy slapped me on the shoulder and almost knocked me to the ground.

"What you wanna drink?" he demanded.

"Who's the boss around here?" I asked.

"I am," the man said.

"Then what do you drink?"

"Why you wanna know?"

"Well," I said, "if you don't know what's good to drink at this bar, maybe these guys ought to get a new boss."

Since it wasn't customary to challenge the big guy in his own place, everybody laughed and we got off to a good start.

About a half hour later, after we'd downed a couple of drinks, the boss said, "I hope you're not going to hang around too long."

"Why shouldn't I?" I asked.

"Cause if you hang around this town for a couple of weeks, I'm afraid you'll be the boss of this joint and I'll be back pushing a truck again."

Everybody laughed again.

The thing I have always remembered about these teamsters— all hard-working and hard-drinking citizens—was that they were about the nicest and politest group I have ever addressed. Sure they were all Democrats, but they listened to everything I had to say. They wanted to know why I was working so hard for Dewey and what the Republicans had ever done for the working people.

I'm sure most of them disagreed with me profoundly, but there was no rudeness nor rough stuff, such as we have lately come to expect from those young militants, particularly on the nation's campuses, who come to meetings not to learn but to disrupt with violence if need be. Take the Free Speech movement which, I'm sorry to say, began at a university in my state. The record clearly shows that the proponents of this movement want free speech only for themselves—not for anyone with whom they disagree.

The Republicans didn't carry Lake County, but they came closer to doing so than they ever had before, and I would like to think that Buddy and I may have had something to do with it. Before we returned to the West Coast, the little County Chairman gave us each a pint of rye whiskey that had been bottled in the spring of 1913.

"I've saved these bottles a long time," he said. "Both of you have added such pleasure to my life that I want you to have them."

I have never asked Buddy what he did with his pint, but I

was so proud of this particular gift that I still have it intact. Every now and then I look at the bottle, one of the many souvenirs in my Beverly Hills den, and think back to those wonderful few days in Lake County.

Things looked pretty good for Tom Dewey throughout most of the campaign. The polls showed him an easy winner and he was already picking his Presidential cabinet. All of us Republicans in Hollywood were overjoyed at the prospect of a Republican in the White House and an end to sixteen years of what we called "Democratic misrule."

I found our candidate to be a very sensible man. Some of our Hollywood people had asked him to pledge the formation of a cabinet post for Arts and Letters. "Now stop and think," Dewey said. "Do you people really want that? If we do set up such a cabinet post, an entire department will be formed. And do you know what that department will be doing? It will be examining your pictures and reading your books and the next thing they'll do is start telling you how to make your pictures and how to write your books. If you really want that kind of setup, that's fine. But otherwise I would suggest you forget about creating a cabinet post for arts and letters."

Our people decided he was right.

Dewey's opponent, Harry S. Truman, was scheduled to campaign in Los Angeles on September 23, 1948, but it was difficult to find much enthusiasm for the President, even among the movie people traditionally aligned with the Democrats.

I ran into George Jessel in front of the Thalberg Building in Culver City, and he showed me a telegram which he had received from President Truman. It read: "Please meet me at the train. Looking forward to seeing you." Jessel did not look too overjoyed.

"You're going to meet the President, aren't you?" I asked.

"You must be nuts," Jessel replied. "That bum's all washed up."

Which reminds me of another Jessel story. For a time George

couldn't get work. Growing despondent, he announced to all and sundry that he was thinking about suicide. George M. Cohan, who was sick in a hospital, called Jessel and asked him whether he had written his obituary yet. Jessel said he hadn't thought of it.

"Why, that's ridiculous," said Cohan. "A fellow as important as you ought to have a properly prepared obit. Why don't you come over to the hospital and we'll work on it together?"

Jessel went over to the hospital and he and Cohan worked on the document for an hour or two. Finally Cohan said, "Why don't you read it and let's see how it sounds." Jessel got up and began reading. As he read, he got more enthusiastic. "My God," Jessel said, "this is too damn good for an obituary. This stuff is good for at least two television shows. I'll see you later."

Jessel's attitude towards Truman was indicative of the way most Hollywood Democrats felt about the President. Very few celebrities were on hand when he arrived to campaign in the Los Angeles area.

Tom Dewey was scheduled to speak at the Hollywood Bowl the following night. We had booked the Bowl for two nights in order to give Leroy Prinz a chance to rehearse a show we planned for the Dewey rally. Leroy was a World War I flyer who had become the top dance director at Warner Brothers Studio. I have never got involved in a big political meeting since unless I had Leroy's help—there is no one like him.

We heard that the Democrats were having trouble getting a hall in which to have Truman appear. Being a younger and more naive man than I am now, I thought it would be a nice gesture—particularly since the President of the United States was involved—if we would invite the Democrats to use the Bowl on our rehearsal night and we would make other arrangements for our rehearsal. That way the President would have a proper place to appear.

Instead of getting a kind thank you from the Democratic National Committee, half an hour later they put out a press release charging that the rich Republicans had rented all the big halls in Hollywood in order to prevent the President from getting a meeting place. I considered this a pretty low blow, even from the Democrats.

What I didn't know was that the Democrats had already rented Gilmore Stadium for their Truman rally. But the Democratic coffers were so bare at that time that they didn't have enough money to pay for turning on the lights.

So I couldn't resist another friendly gesture. I didn't think it was good for the President of the United States to address an audience in the dark, so I called my good friend and solid Republican, Charlie Skouras, and suggested that he might put up the money to turn on the lights. Charlie, I am glad to say, did it. For which, incidentally, no one ever thanked either him or me. Since that time I have been very wary of making kind political gestures to Democrats during any political campaign.

Truman spoke before ten thousand people in Gilmore Stadium, and the next night Dewey addressed about twice that many in the Hollywood Bowl. The Hollywood notables introduced to the Dewey audience included Gary Cooper, Jeannette MacDonald, Charlie Coburn, Ginger Rogers, Frank Morgan and a whole host of others.

That night at the Bowl, Leroy Prinz rushed up to me and said, "I've got something very exciting."

"What is it?" I asked.

"A live elephant!" he exclaimed. "It's got a big sign on one side that says DEWEY and another on the other side that says WARREN."

"What are you going to do with him?" I asked.

"March him through the crowd and up on the stage."

"How does he get on?"

"I hit him in the rear end with this club—and he walks on, of course."

"Well," I said, somewhat taken aback, "how does he get off?"

"Oh," Leroy said, "that's up to the elephant."

I was scared to death until that elephant had completed his political chores and was returned to his truck.

Four years before, the meeting for Tom Dewey had been held in the Los Angeles Coliseum. With Cecil B. DeMille in charge of the overall production, we had a great line-up of Hollywood stars and the largest crowd I'd ever seen at a political rally. But Tom Dewey made one of the dullest speeches I've ever heard. He broke the first rule of show business—he bored the audience. What the crowd had wanted to hear was Tom Dewey, the exciting, alert District Attorney who had smashed Murder Incorporated in New York City. What they heard that night was not a hard-hitting, no-holds-barred candidate, but a man trying to be a statesman before the votes were even counted. This was a vital mistake and it cost the Republican ticket heavily.

However, in 1948 Dewey's speech in the Hollywood Bowl was a particularly effective one. He spoke about Communist activities both at home and abroad; it was his first major address of the campaign on this subject. Twice in the course of his speech, Dewey assailed the President for having characterized Congressional exposure of Communists in government positions as a "red herring." Truman's statement, Dewey said, encouraged the Communists and brought despair to those resisting Red propaganda abroad.

It was a speech that particularly pleased those of us in Hollywood who were waging a bitter struggle against Communist infiltration of our industry.

At Earl Warren's request, I put in a lot of time setting up rallies and meetings for the Republican Vice-presidential candidate. For Warren's rally in New York, I arrived in town three days ahead and discovered that even then New York people resented us yokels from California. The New Yorkers had scheduled the worst possible time for a Warren rally—registration day—and they had arranged to have him speak in a highly inaccessible theater down on Fourteenth Street.

Why I didn't get ulcers during those few days I'll never know. I argued with the New York Republicans until I was blue in the face. For several days I lived on chopped egg sandwiches and malted milks. And I began to feel weary for the first time in the campaign.

Warren came to town and didn't do too badly. But he was worried—he was scheduled to cut through Pennsylvania and his speechwriters had failed to come up with anything fresh in the way of material.

"I need some new speeches," he told me. "Got any ideas?"

I did have an idea. I telephoned my old pal Henry Taylor who, at the time, was broadcasting brilliant fifteen-minute commentaries on radio for General Motors. Henry not only said the right things but his views were based on a profound knowledge of the situation and years of personal observations both at home and abroad. And he wrote with a beautiful economy of words.

As I knew he would, Henry rushed over with about thirty of his commentaries. I took the transcripts to Warren and suggested that he put some of them together and, with a little rewriting, he would have himself a fine speech. He did. The interesting thing about all this is that Warren agreed with most of what conservative Henry Taylor was saying in those days. What happened to Warren in later years would be a subject for another book.

The campaign was then in its closing weeks and I was so exhausted that Fred Waring suggested I spend a weekend with him at an old inn he had purchased at the Delaware Water Gap.

"That's exactly what I need," I told Fred. "One weekend away from the pressures and I'll be my old self again."

I arrived at the inn on a Friday night and in that good mountain air I got the best night's sleep I'd had in months. The next morning I felt like a new man. I had a big breakfast and played eighteen holes of golf.

Then the phone rang. It was a call from Herbert Brownell, Jr., who was managing the Dewey campaign. Could I come to his home outside Washington for an important strategy meeting the next day, which was Sunday?

"If you need me, I'll be there," I said.

Actually I was flattered to have been invited. This was the first time that members of the Republican Establishment had thought of me in any terms except as a performer or a producer of rallies. Apparently they wanted my advice on policy matters.

Borrowing one of Fred Waring's cars, I drove all the way to Brownell's home in Virginia. I even arrived on time—an unusual achievement since I invariably get lost on long trips.

By now the Brownell mansion had become famous because the noted New York lawyer had purchased it in anticipation of the election of Tom Dewey as President. There were about eighteen men sitting around in chairs in the living room when I arrived. Earl Warren greeted me effusively. The others, mostly older party leaders, nodded perfunctorily. Once the meeting got under way, a few dozed off. I thought to myself then that if the Republicans were ever to succeed they would have to rid themselves of these anachronisms.

The meeting was a kind of last roundup two weeks before Election Day. Brownell asked everyone present to speak their piece. Everyone did and it was cut-and-dried stuff for the most part. Then Brownell pointed to me and asked, "What do you think?"

"Well, Mr. Brownell," I said, "let me say first of all that I am honored to be here and I don't feel qualified to give an opinion. I'm just the guy who carries out orders."

"You must have some opinion," Brownell said. He was right, and I did not need to be coaxed any further.

"As a matter of fact, I do have an opinion."

"Then present it to us, please," Brownell said somewhat impatiently.

"There's an old American custom," I said, "that if someone stands in front of your house for five nights in a row and calls you every obscenity in the book you have no alternative but to go outside and punch him in the nose, hit him with a broom or call the police. If you don't hit back, the other guy will win by default. And that's how I think this campaign is going."

Everyone present picked up their ears. One man even stopped snoring. They all knew that I was referring to the no-holds-barred, "give 'em hell" campaign being waged in desperation by Harry S. Truman.

"President Truman is running around the country calling the Republicans every name in the book," I went on. "Most of what he is saying just isn't true. I think it's time that somebody got up and called him a liar."

"George," Brownell interrupted, "we just don't want to get into a gutter fight with Harry Truman. That's exactly what he wants us to do."

"But meanwhile, he's getting away with lies and distortions," I said. "It's about time that somebody took him on and quickly, or his 'give 'em hell' technique may well cost us the election."

Everyone looked taken aback. No one had even considered the possibility of a Republican loss that year.

At this point Earl Warren arose and said, "Herb, I think George is absolutely right. I think one of us has to take on the President. If Tom doesn't want to, I'll do it."

Now everyone seemed to want to get into the discussion. Herb Brownell asked for silence. "Let's all calm down," he said. "I've got something here which will show why we can't rock the boat at this late stage of the campaign."

Brownell reached into his pocket and pulled out a sheet of paper. The paper contained the figures of a secret poll taken by the Republicans which showed Tom Dewey so far out front that he could never be defeated by Harry Truman. Smiling benign-ly, Brownell read off the figures. This was the first time I had ever heard of such a thing as a political poll.

"You see," he said, "there's no need to worry. We've practical-ly won this election."

I think I was the only one in that room who didn't believe it.

My doubts were reinforced when, on my way back to California, I stopped off in six different cities. I could sense that the mood of the people was shifting away from Dewey to Truman. For one thing. Truman was playing the underdog and was swinging away at Dewey with both fists. What he was bellowing about didn't make much difference. People were saying that that gutsy little man from Independence, Missouri, was putting up one hell of a fight. And people admire fighters, especially when the odds look stacked against them.

On the way home I sent telegrams to Brownell, repeatedly urging him to get Dewey to stop acting like a statesman and more like a fighting candidate. Dewey had delivered a rousing speech in Oklahoma City and I suggested that he repeat it several more times. Had he done so, I think he might have swung the election.

This was not just hindsight. I had told Dewey before that he was projecting himself as too nice, too perfect and too smart. A remark attributed to Alice Roosevelt Longworth described Dewey as resembling "the little man on the top of the wedding cake." It was an apt description.

"Why don't you spill some gravy on your vest and brush it off?" I proposed to Dewey one day. "It will make you look a little more human."

I also suggested that he not act like such a "smarty-pants" on television when he was under questioning. He not only knew all the answers—sometimes he seemed to know the questions even before they were asked.

"Take your time answering," I said. "The audience will appreciate a fluff once in a while."

I pointed out that many topnotch jugglers, when doing their act, will deliberately miss a trick in order to get the audience rooting for them. When they finally manage to do it right the audience goes wild with excitement.

This is a stratagem I learned from that great performer, Jack Donahue, whose dancing I had so much admired as a youth. I used to go and watch him regularly. After a while I noticed that he missed the same step at each performance. One night I approached him and said, "Mr. Donahue, I notice that you miss the same step every night. Why don't you practice and do it right?"

"Irish," he said, "I'm doing it wrong deliberately. That's the way I get sympathy from the audience. When you miss a step, you're doing it exactly the way they would do it and that puts them right up there with you. And if you don't have them up there with you, you've got very little going for you. Never be too perfect."

I've never forgotten that sage piece of advice. I've tried to apply it in my several careers, including politics. I think it works.

Whether I convinced Thomas E. Dewey I don't know. But he and I have remained good friends through all these many years. I have never had any regrets about working in his behalf. I still believe that Dewey would have been one of our greater presidents.

Election night 1948 found us at one of the great houses in Hollywood, the Greystone Manor, attending a dinner party given by those delightful hosts, Lucy and Lee Batson. They had invited a group of about twenty good Republicans to share in what most of them expected to be good tidings. I myself was hoping against hope that my political instincts had gone awry.

After dinner, Bat and I left the party and went into the music room where we poured ourselves two scotches-and-sodas. It was about eight o'clock Los Angeles time and we turned on the radio. After we'd listened to the returns for about five minutes, I said, "Bat, I think Dewey has had it."

"I'm afraid you're right," he agreed.

I didn't finish my drink and, perhaps for the first time in his life, neither did Bat. I got up, picked up Julie, drove home and went right to bed. The next morning we learned that Harry S. Truman had been elected.

Later Joe Schenck told me that the day after Truman's victory he had received a telephone call from fellow-producer Sam Goldwyn.

"We've got to fly to Washington," Goldwyn said agitatedly.

"What for?" asked Schenck.

"We've got to see President Truman."

"What for?"

"What for?" Goldwyn repeated. "To give him some money so he'll know we're for him!"

Well, as that movie columnist says, that's Hollywood.

# CHAPTER 19

## *The Eisenhower Campaign*

Not long after the disastrous 1948 Presidential election, Louis Mayer asked me to drop by his office. He had received a call from Eric Johnston, head of the Motion Picture Association in Washington, asking whether I would be available to stage the Republican party's first Lincoln Day box supper in the nation's capital.

The price of admission was to be one dollar and the idea was to change the image of the party from a rich man's organization to one that more ordinary people could identify with.

At first, I must confess, I was not too anxious to fly East. I had only recently come through a tough campaign and was frankly eager to get back to making films and seeing a little more of my family. Besides I was still active in a multitude of other activities including the Screen Actors Guild, which has always been important in my life.

But Mayer would brook no objections. "George," he said in his quiet, authoritative way, "I think you'd better go and see what you can do."

Once again I was forced to tell Julie I would be going away—this time, however, for just a few days. By this time Julie had become used to my sudden departures, and I must say she was a good sport about my extracurricular activities. Occasionally she would joke, "If you don't get away from some of these committees, I'll divorce you." But there was one thing she never objected to, and that was my work for the Republican party.

I arrived in Washington on a Thursday. The box supper was scheduled for the following Monday at the Uline Arena. They had sold only two hundred tickets at this point. We had half an hour of radio time and my job was to arrange the broadcast as well as a program at the Arena for the rest of the evening.

The first meeting was held at the apartment of Senator Owen Brewster of Maine at the Mayflower Hotel. There wasn't much time and I hadn't flown all those miles to argue with anyone. I got right down to brass tacks.

Usually a political broadcast in those days involved a long-winded orator who would frequently force the listener to change stations. I proposed that we use nine Republican Senators and nine Congressmen, each of whom would talk for only one minute or less on some pertinent subject.

"It just can't be done," I was told.

Senator Taft was one of the disbelievers. "How can I say anything worthwhile in one minute?" he asked.

"Senator," I said, "all you have to say is something like this: 'I've been accused of having written a slave labor law. All I can tell you is that after one year of this so-called slave labor law there are more people at work under higher salaries and better working conditions than ever in the history of our country.'

Though Taft and his Congressional colleagues were doubtful, they were game enough to try out what this crazy actor from Hollywood was proposing.

I had a little more difficulty selling the idea of hiring Fred Waring to provide the music for the rest of the program. The Republican leaders thought the fee—I think it was about seventy-five hundred dollars—was too steep. Actually Waring was charging the rock-bottom minimum for his huge contingent of musicians and singers.

"Why Waring?" I was asked.

"Simply because we don't have time to put a program of entertainment together and Fred can do ten minutes, a half hour or two hours, if necessary. I have no idea what is going to happen Monday night and we need Waring for insurance."

Still kicking like steers, the leadership reluctantly agreed that I could hire Waring. Fortunately, he was available.

Meanwhile the Washington press corps had learned that this Hollywood character was in town and all sorts of stories about what I was doing began to circulate around the rumor-ridden town. I made a big mystery of what I was about and that only helped the publicity.

The Republican leaders had hoped for about three thousand people at the Uline Arena that Monday night. Instead, eleven thousand showed up. We ran out of box suppers, but no one seemed to mind. The half-hour broadcast went off better than any of its participants expected, even though—because the cheering and applause took so much time—poor Joe Martin couldn't make the final summation.

The show did a great deal to lift the spirits of the Republican leadership and rank-and-file at a time when, following the 1948 defeat, it looked as if our party was finished for a long time to come. It was so successful that from then on I became, in effect, the Ziegfeld of the Republican party.

Between the end of World War II and 1952, when pressure of public relations work and political commitments brought about my retirement as an actor, my movie roles—mostly for M-G-M —varied widely in character. I had finally broken away from musical parts and was playing straight roles.

One of the better roles I had during this period was that of "Pop" Stazak in the Dore Schary production of *Battleground*, which the hard-to-please Bosley Crowther of the *New York Times* described as "the best of the World War II pictures that have yet been made in Hollywood." Bob Pirosh, who had participated in the Battle of the Bulge, had written the screenplay, giving the story extraordinary authenticity. Bill Wellman, who directed, did a tremendous job of making all the action—and there was plenty—plausible. He also had a great deal to do with the script, adding a couple of good scenes for me.

*Battleground* had an excellent cast that included Van Johnson, Ricardo Montalban, John Hodiak, Marshall Thompson, Don Taylor, James Whitmore and Leon Ames. It also included thirty-two paratroopers of the original 101st Airborne Division, all of whom had jumped in Normandy on D-day.

One day we were on the drill field rehearsing a scene with these veterans when Billy Wellman, who had been a flying sergeant in World War I, began riding me to beat the band. He just refused to stop picking on me. At about five o'clock in the afternoon, I finally blew my stack and grabbed him by the lapel.

"Now, listen here, you gray-headed bastard," I shouted at Wellman, "if you have one more word to say to me in that tone of voice I'll knock you flat as a mackerel."

Still seething, I went home. As my anger waned, I began to feel ashamed of myself for having lost my cool. I called Bill to apologize. "Bill," I said, "you know you rode me pretty hard today. I lost my temper and I'm sorry. It won't happen again."

"Oh, that's all right." Wellman laughed. "I just wrote a scene for you in the picture in which you are supposed to get so mad at a guy that you try to kick his brains out. You're always such a nice guy that I didn't know whether you could play the scene or not."

That had been Bill Wellman's way of testing me. As it turned out, I played the scene very well.

There were many great scenes in *Battleground*, but one that remains fixed in my memory was based on that thrilling moment at Bastogne when the Germans who surrounded the Belgian town sent over an emissary to request the surrender of the besieged GI's. The reply of the American general was a firm "Nuts!"

Wellman wanted to make certain that the actor who played the general was in the right mood when he uttered that unforgettable and historic riposte.

I was talking to him in a corner when the actor made his way towards us. "Watch this," Bill whispered to me. "I'll show you how to get an actor into the right mood to play this scene."

"Sir," the actor said to Wellman, "may I ask you a question?"

Wellman, who was almost as good an actor as a director, feigned indignation. "Can't you see that I'm in an important conversation, you stupid bastard? Hasn't anyone ever taught you any manners?"

The poor actor got so angry that he couldn't get over it for several hours, and that was how he played one of the key scenes in the film. He was absolutely masterful—thanks to Bill Wellman's unusual facility for getting the best out of an actor.

There was another good scene—one that was completely wordless. The story called for German planes to drop leaflets over Bastogne urging the beleaguered GI's to surrender. I quietly picked up some of the leaflets and walked away—and everyone knew where I was going.

*Battleground* was the film that introduced Denise Darcel in a bit part which mainly consisted of wiggling her derriere. When Denise was first introduced to Wellman, he said, "She looks just great. She looks like a good, husky, big-busted French gal—one that could really withstand the bombardments of the war."

After she had been approved, the casting director took her away for about two hours. When Wellman sent for her, she returned wearing a fancy hairdo that couldn't possibly have been on a woman's head in a war-ravaged area.

Wellman was really angry—and he wasn't acting. He picked up a bucket of water and, after drenching Denise with it, threw some dirt on her. Then he took a long look at her and announced, "Okay, gentlemen, Miss Darcel is ready for her scene."

Denise was a great sport. Except for her, the cast consisted entirely of men. She took a lot of ribbing, but she was good-natured about it. The scene she played, as seen through the eyes of Van Johnson, will always be one of the classics of the screen.

Technically, *Battleground* was a fine picture. People just didn't believe that we'd shot at least seventy-five percent of that film indoors. To be frank, when they cooled the stage down to forty degrees for the sake of realism, even I had trouble believing we were indoors.

Another role I enjoyed playing was that of Inspector Belden of the Federal Bureau of Investigation in *Walk East On Beacon*. This was a particularly fine film, produced by Louis de

Rochemont in semidocumentary fashion, about the difficult spadework which the FBI does daily in protecting the nation from Communist espionage. The excellent screenplay by Leo Rosten was based on a documented story written by J. Edgar Hoover himself.

Aside from some scenes in Washington, most of the film was shot in Boston, not in facsimile sets built in Hollywood. It captured an air of reality which brought kudoes from most of the critics with one not-so-significant exception, Art Shields of the *Daily Worker* . The Communist critic termed the film "evil, grim and stupid." His comments, needless to say, were not unexpected.

I liked what the *Boston Herald* had to say editorially about *Walk East on Beacon* . "What makes it important above the ordinary suspense plot is that, without hysteria, flag-waving or editorializing, it points out that danger can lurk under the most ordinary exterior, in the most innocent-appearing places and behind the most average facts. It reminds us, more eloquently than sixteen superstar-studded productions, that the preservation of our way of life is everybody's business and that eternal vigilance is the price of safety."

I wish there were more films of this type being made today.

I also played the boss-frightened father of Elizabeth Taylor, then fifteen, in *Cynthia* and the husband in a domestic triangle in Arch Oboler's *The Arnelo Affair*.

In *Big City* , which Joe Pasternak produced at Metro, I portrayed an Irish Catholic policeman who joins a Protestant clergyman (Robert Preston) and a Jewish cantor (Danny Thomas) in adopting a waif, played by Margaret O'Brien.

I even played a newspaperman in one of six little short-story dramas that comprised *It's a Big Country* , which was produced by Dore Schary as an entertaining tribute to the greatness that is America. Bosley Crowther called my performance "credible" and coming from a newpaperman that was high praise indeed.

*It's a Big Country* was also memorable for me because it gave me the opportunity of playing a scene with the immortal Ethel Barrymore. I had long been one of Miss Barrymore's greatest admirers. To actually appear with this gracious lady was one of the most exciting experiences I ever had in show business. She was all that the critics ever said she was, and even more. She was an absolute delight to work with.

The last film I made was for Metro in 1952. But I'm afraid the only reason *Talk About a Stranger* may be of interest is that in it I appeared opposite a very lovely young actress named Nancy Davis. Today Nancy is better known as Mrs. Ronald Reagan.

After we read the script of *Talk About a Stranger,* Nancy and I talked it over and agreed it wasn't very good. We tried to persuade the studio to shelve the project, but to no avail. The finished product was so horrible that I don't think it ever was released. Every year since then, around Christmastime, I have promised Nancy that I would get a print and run it—but thus far she has been spared that pleasure. I do hope that the Democrats don't get hold of the film and run it on the late, late show during my 1970 campaign. It might be more than I could overcome.

Nancy met Ronnie about the time we were making *Talk About a Stranger*. Ronnie had succeeded me as president of the Screen Actors Guild and it was in that capacity that Nancy paid him a visit. She was repeatedly being embarrassed by the fact that "Nancy Davis" kept popping up on Communist front lists, and she was receiving invitations to attend radical meetings. This was difficult to bear since Nancy was decidedly anti-Communist. At director Mervyn LeRoy's suggestion, she sought out Reagan for his counsel. Reagan not only straightened out the matter but a year later he married the girl.

There were many occasions in the ensuing years when I was tempted to try television acting. I had had some experience in radio. Among other things, I had been the master of ceremonies of the Motion Picture Relief Fund radio show which raised enough money to build our Actors' Home in the Valley.

Once I got a very excited call from Lew Wasserman, who was then the number one man at Music Corporation of America (M.C.A.), asking if I would read a script. I said I would be glad to do so. Before you could say Harvey Snodgrass three times, the script was delivered to my door. After reading it through, I phoned Lew and said, "Yes, I think I would be very interested in this particular series."

"That's just great," Wasserman said. "I'll get on it right away."

That was the last I heard from him. Two days later I went over to the M.C.A. office and asked what had happened. They said they weren't sure. I suggested that they call New York, which they did. On the other end of the phone was a vice-president of one of the top networks, who said politely, "Murphy is not acceptable to our network because of his political activity."

Later I was barred from working on two other TV shows because of the objections of this particular gentleman. The fact that I was being "blacklisted" because of my political beliefs did upset me for a time, but there was little I could do about it. I was always amused by the caterwauling of my liberal friends whenever they discovered that some radical or other could not get a job in Hollywood. Very few of them ever had any compassion for those on the other side of the political fence who faced the same problem.

At any rate, I'm sorry that the network gentleman kept me out of television, because had I done the three series I would have been a very rich man today and wouldn't have to worry so much about paying the bills. On the other hand, had I not been "blacklisted," I might have ended up in television and not in the United States Senate. And I'd rather be where I am.

Just before I decided to run for the Senate, one of my favorite writers at Universal called me about a television series in which he thought I would fit very well. I went over to the studio and had lunch with him. After we discussed the series, I asked him which network he had in mind and he told me.

"Sorry," I said, "it's no good. I'm barred from that network."

"George," he replied, "I just don't believe it."

I assured him it was no figment of my imagination. He asked me whether I would mind if he checked out my story.

"Of course not," I said, "Go ahead."

My writer friend called me back three days later. "I'm stunned, but you're right," he said. "That guy in New York said he won't have anything to do with you."

Apparently the antagonism this network executive felt towards me because of my politics had lasted all those years.

I had one other chance to appear on television. I was offered the part of the doctor in the television version of *Peyton Place*, which turned out to be a mighty profitable series for Twentieth Century-Fox. I decided to turn down the offer because I had heard it was a pretty dirty book and, at that point in my life, I thought I'd rather not get involved in projects of that nature.

On another occasion, too, I guess I was a "square." I had been asked to play two weeks in Las Vegas for more money than I had ever been paid in my life. But I decided that wasn't right either. I explained that I didn't think I should be shilling for a gambling joint and I thanked them very much. The only time I ever appeared in Las Vegas was to make a speech at the Knife and Fork Club, which has nothing to do with the gambling fraternity. Maybe it was just as well.

Even though I stopped making films, I remained with M-G-M, working full time as the studio's "official ambassador," representing the studio at exhibitor's conventions and speaking before groups such as the PTA. Because of my close associations with labor, I was also appointed liaison between Metro and the unions. Since I was now representing management, I was forced to resign my membership in the Screen Actors Guild. But I have always maintained strong ties with the S.A.G. and its leaders. And I still proudly carry my membership card in the Guild.

After what amounted to a power struggle with Dore Schary, my dear friend and mentor Louis B. Mayer resigned as head of the studio in 1951. Mayer's departure was a blow to me, and I made no secret of my feelings. Nevertheless, despite our differing political philosophies, Schary and I got along very well. Schary, of course, was as well-known in Democratic councils as I was on the other side.

He was quoted as saying of me: "I've known George since I wrote a *Broadway Melody* script for him back in 1939. In that time he has brought more dignity than any other one person to our business. He's never been afraid to say exactly where he stands. When he was once warned that all actors get criticized for taking a political position, he just said, 'I happen to be a citizen before I am an actor.' There haven't been enough guys like that in Hollywood. He would be a first-class man for anybody's side."

But I was on the Republican side and I devoted what time I could to that cause. In 1952 I had helped to stage-manage the Republican convention held in the International Amphitheater in Chicago. It was one of the most exciting conventions I have ever attended, featuring as it did an epic struggle for the Presidential nomination between the two giants of the Republican party—Dwight David Eisenhower and Robert Alphonso Taft.

As a member of the California delegation, I was pledged to vote for Earl Warren at the convention. But I never considered the Governor as a serious contender, even though he did himself.

The night before I left for Chicago, Louis Mayer asked me over to his house. He was an ardent Taft supporter and he began to preach the virtues of the man from Ohio.

"I agree with you one hundred percent about Taft," I told Mayer. "He would make a great President. My only question is whether he can win. The Republican party needs a winner. That's why I'm for Eisenhower."

These were also the sentiments of our new young Senator from California, Richard M. Nixon, whom I had known and admired ever since his first try for political office in 1946.

Nixon was a powerful voice in the California delegation that went to Chicago in 1952. Because of the unit rule requirement, all members of the seventy-man delegation were committed to Warren's nomination until he released us. But Nixon had sent out about two hundred letters to the California delegates and alternates asking who they thought would be their choice if Warren did not make it. The replies confirmed Nixon's belief. Most of the replies said Eisenhower.

Warren was fit to be tied. Nixon had been in Chicago a week before the convention began as a member of the platform-writing resolutions committee. On July 4 he flew to Denver to board a special train bringing most of the California delegates to Chicago. Warren called Nixon to his headquarters in the front car and began to denounce him for the letter. He said that if Nixon didn't recall the letter, he would destroy him politically.

"Now look here, Nixon," he ended, "after all I've done for you—"

"Earl," Nixon replied, "you've never done anything for me or anyone else in politics, so let's get that straight."

And that's how the famed feud between Warren and Nixon began. But time has a way of softening antagonisms. I was reminded of this at the dinner President Nixon gave in honor of the retiring Chief Justice in mid-1969. Present were most of the members of the Supreme Court and the President's Cabinet and their ladies. I was particularly honored to have been the only non-Court, non-Cabinet member there. I've often wondered why I was invited—maybe it was because, aside from the President himself, I was the only one who knew the whole story.

On my first day of the 1952 convention in Chicago, I reported to Mrs. F. Peavey Heffelfinger, a national committeewoman from Minnesota who was chairman of the Entertainment and Decorations Committee.

A charming lady, when she saw me she gave me a big hug and a kiss and said, "I'm so glad you're here." And that was the last time I saw her.

From then on I was on my own, and it wasn't easy. One of the first problems to arise was the tickets. It seemed that despite all the months of planning that went into the convention, someone had forgotten to have the tickets printed in a union plant. They arrived at our headquarters in the Stevens Hotel (now the Conrad Hilton) by the many thousands without the union "bug." This was tantamount to political suicide among union voters so we had them hurriedly redone in several union plants.

Then there was the problem of getting entertainers. Very little had been done before I arrived on the scene, and the matter was dumped in my lap. There was no program, no budget, and very little hope, but somehow I managed to get some excellent talents to appear at the convention.

The nicest tribute I received for my efforts came from the aforementioned Mrs. Heffelfinger. Talking to Dorothy Brandon of the *New York Herald-Tribune*, the lady from Minnesota described me as "that wonderful man who calms turbulent theatrical temperaments and gets our shows on the platform through sheer muscular endeavor. . . . George Murphy is the littlest man at the convention—he is humble, helpful and hefty. Why, he isn't above hauling chairs, checking on choir aggregations and finding a secluded resting place for our great soloists before the opening ceremonies. He's the man who thinks and does everything."

The truth is that I couldn't have done anything without the help of a lot of other "little" people who were always there when I needed them. When things were really rough they would restore your faith in humanity. They were there to work for a cause they believed in and not for any personal gain.

Sure, there were plenty of aggravations. I remember one man who was in charge of distributing the tickets. This poor fellow later had a heart attack and I've always thought it was because of the emotional strain he endured at the convention. I learned quickly that if you let things prey on your mind there is no place you can lose your cool more quickly than at a political convention.

A thousand and one things can go wrong and you've got to try to stay on top of them. For example, before the convention began, I paid a visit to the Amphitheater to test the sound equipment. The chief electrician, a bit annoyed, told me not to worry, that everything would be fine. I wasn't satisfied and I insisted on a test.

It turned out that my fears were justified. The speakers were so placed that the delegates in the first fifteen rows—the most important people at the convention—would not have been able to hear any of the proceedings. On my instructions, the electricians worked all night placing speakers under the stage.

Would you believe that eight years later at the Republican convention in that very same hall we had the same problem? "Now fellows," I told the electricians who had welcomed me warmly, "don't you remember what happened eight years ago?" Glumly they proceeded to work all night again.

At the 1952 convention I got a kind of new insight into the character of Earl Warren. He was a hopeful man who felt that if there was a deadlock between Eisenhower and Taft, the convention would turn to him as the Presidential candidate. And the California delegates, the great majority of whom were for Eisenhower, were bound by an election law that required us to vote for Warren until he freed us to do otherwise.

When the balloting began, it was obvious that despite the well-fought efforts of Taft and his delegates the convention was moving inexorably to nominate General Eisenhower. During the balloting I was sitting just behind Warren and Senator William F. Knowland.

Most of the seventy-member California group was waiting impatiently for the Governor to release us so we could vote for Ike. When it was obvious that the horse race was over, Warren told Knowland to grab the microphone and ask to make the Eisenhower nomination unanimous. But it was too late. I think it was Arkansas that beat us to the mike. Warren had waited too long.

All this made President Eisenhower's appointment of Earl Warren as Chief Justice in the fall of 1953 all the more puzzling to me. A lot of people criticized the appointment as a "political payoff." I doubt it. Warren had done very little for the Eisenhower cause. All I could find out about the nomination was that it apparently had been recommended by my good friend, Herb Brownell, who was then the Attorney General of the United States. Herb was and is a great lawyer, but in this case I didn't quite understand his reasoning.

Herb Brownell was a key figure in "selling" Eisenhower on Dick Nixon as his running mate. Except for some die-hard Warrenites, who accused Nixon of having "double-crossed" the Governor to obtain the number two spot on the Eisenhower ticket, most of us from California were overjoyed at the nomination. These very same Warrenites then began to spread rumors about a "secret fund" supposedly established by Nixon supporters. These rumors reached the ears of certain newspaper correspondents, and by mid-September the "Nixon Fund" sensation dominated the headlines and nearly threatened to ruin Republican chances that year.

The stories broke as Dick Nixon was about to board a train to campaign through California. I was standing next to him when word came of the controversy already raging back East. From then on the pressures for Nixon to resign from the Republican ticket were enormous. The one thing I learned from this most unpleasant episode was that Nixon is not a quitter. This was one of Dick's "six crises" and he came through with flying colors.

There were two other attempts to smear Nixon—one about the furniture in his home and another that implied that he was owned by the oil industry. Needless to say, there was no truth at all to any of these tales.

I first got to meet General Eisenhower several weeks after the convention at an election rally at the Pan-Pacific Auditorium in Los Angeles. I was in charge of the rally.

Mamie Eisenhower introduced me to her distinguished husband. "Oh, there's Murphy," she said on spotting me. "My mother says you're the finest fellow for getting a lady down the stairs that she ever met."

Mrs. Eisenhower was referring to the time I accompanied her mother, Mrs. Doud, down a steep staircase in order to get her out of the convention hall without being trampled by the crowds.

The Pan-Pacific rally went off like clockwork. Actually there were two rallies. Inside the auditorium some seven thousand partisans were gathered to cheer Ike to the rafters. Outside, and for this innovation I took full credit, I arranged for the General to address some fifteen thousand people gathered in a parking lot. Eisenhower ad-libbed his outdoor speech and I think it came off much better than the prepared speech he delivered inside.

Eisenhower was that kind of man. When he ad-libbed, he spoke from the heart and wasn't mouthing words prepared by speech-writers. True, he occasionally got his syntax mixed up, but the people couldn't have cared less. They loved him. They trusted him and believed in him—and they elected him.

Eisenhower was so pleased with his Pan-Pacific appearances that he made inquiries as to who had made the arrangments. He was told it was George Murphy. The next day I received a call from one of his aides who said the General wanted me to join his campaign tour.

"As much as I'd like to," I said, "I'm afraid that I can't. I'm still under contract to M-G-M."

At seven o'clock the next morning, I got a call at home from the big boss in New York, Nicholas Schenck.

"George," said Schenck, "I want you to do something for me. Pack your bag and come to New York immediately. Report to the Commodore Hotel. You are assigned to General Eisenhower for the duration of the campaign. Help in any way you can."

Shortly after I arrived at the Commodore, where the Republican campaign headquarters was located, I was taken in to see Eisenhower who quickly got to the point.

"I want you to arrange all my rallies," he said.

"Anything you say, sir," I said, "but only on one condition."

"What's that?"

"Please don't make any official announcement. In every town there are at least two or three groups already at odds with each other about how to run a meeting. Just let me go into a city quietly and have a free hand. If I get into any trouble and need you, I will call you to bail me out."

"Agreed," the General said, shaking my hand.

And that was the way I worked throughout the campaign, preceding Eisenhower wherever he went, arranging rally after rally, seldom seeing the candidate or even talking to him, but somehow getting the job done. All I can say is that the General was happy with the results. Being a military man, he most of all valued good timing, and that was what he usually got.

The final rally of the campaign was to be held in Boston Garden. This was the big one since it also involved a national hour-long television program which was to feature the Eisenhowers and the Nixons. I went to Boston several days before the rally.

There I learned that Senator Henry Cabot Lodge, who had done so much to encourage Eisenhower to run for President, was himself headed for defeat in his re-election campaign at the hands of a young Congressman named John F. Kennedy.

I also learned that the Kennedy forces were moving heaven and earth to win over Senator Joseph McCarthy's large number of followers in the state.

Going to Cabot Lodge, I suggested that if he wanted me to, I would talk to Joe McCarthy about coming into the state and making speeches in his behalf.

"But," said Lodge, "I don't always agree with McCarthy."

"Neither do I," I said, "but you want to get elected, don't you?"

"Of course I do. What will Joe say?"

"Anything we want him to say. I think you'll find him cooperative."

In those days I found McCarthy completely cooperative and had no doubt that, no matter what his private feelings about Cabot were, he would have come into Massachusetts to help him. After all, both men were Republicans.

"It's your choice whether you want to return to the Senate or not," I went on. "Eisenhower will be elected and he will most certainly need another voice in the Senate."

"Let me think it over," Lodge said.

He thought it over and decided against it. When he told me the next day, I said, "Cabot, you're going to lose the seat."

That's what happened. The bulk of the McCarthyite vote went to Jack Kennedy and the rest of the story is history.

There were a lot of problems connected with putting on that rally at the Boston Garden. About three bickering groups, each with its own idea of how to run things, finally got together at my urging. My big problem was a Wild West rodeo show that was to close the previous night. There were two feet of dirt on the Garden floor, dozens of horses and cattle, and last but not least, Leo Carillo.

"Can you cut your performance short tonight?" I asked Leo. Leo was obliging. Though a good Democrat, he generally supported Republicans, particularly if he thought they were going to win. He had always been a great fan of Earl Warren's.

At about one a.m. the next morning the bulldozers were busy and we began moving in our own paraphernalia. One basic problem was the pungent aroma left by the animals. We brought in some huge fans to blow the stuff out. By the time the rally started the Garden smelled a little more like a political arena.

But my troubles weren't over. By six o'clock the Garden was nearly packed. I had hired half-a-dozen vaudeville acts to keep the crowd amused, but the electrician wasn't there to turn on the microphones. Someone had told him to come in at seven-thirty. When he did finally arrive, he couldn't get the mikes to work properly.

Meantime the large group of entertainers, headed by Fred Waring, was stranded in New York. We had chartered an airplane to bring the group to Boston. The plane was scheduled to leave LaGuardia Airport at four-thirty p.m., but it was still on the ground an hour later because of pouring rain and poor visibility in Boston. Finally the plane took off and the microphones at the Garden began to function properly, and my vaudeville acts kept the crowd happy until the big show arrived.

My final problem was with Senator Henry Cabot Lodge.

"Cabot," I said, "the General will be upstairs in the Garden Club. When he leaves there, I will give you a hand signal and you just say, 'And now, ladies and gentlemen, it is my privilege to present the next President of the United States, General Dwight David Eisenhower.' "

"My dear Murph," Lodge said. "If you don't mind, I would like to read a short introduction which I have written. It's kind of precious to me—"

"Now, Senator," I said, "I've been doing these rallies for a long time—"

"Well, Murph, I do feel I have to insist on reading the statement."

Shrugging my shoulders, I said, "Okay, you do it your way, but don't say I didn't warn you."

The original plan was to have an hour and a half of political speeches before the Presidential candidate arrived. I said it was too much and succeeded in cutting the verbiage down to two twenty-minute segments. The rest was entertainment. The huge crowd packing the auditorium was waiting to explode.

General and Mrs. Eisenhower and their party had hardly left the Garden Club upstairs when the crowd knew they were coming. How they sensed it I'll never know. The crowd started to roar. The noise was deafening.

And there was poor Cabot Lodge at the microphone trying to read from a paper in front of him. The crowd just didn't want to listen. Finally I went over to the Senator and said, "Cabot, I don't think you have to say anything. They know the General is in the hall."

"I guess you're right," Cabot said with a happy, good-natured smile.

It was truly an exciting night, and it was over before I realized that I had completely forgotten to eat for forty-eight hours.

All the months of campaigning ended at the stroke of midnight. I had planned to take the first plane back to New York, but General Eisenhower asked me to join the rest of the staff on the campaign train. We left Boston about one o'clock.

Instead of going immediately to their bedrooms, as they had during all those hectic weeks of travel, the General and Mrs. Eisenhower came to the conference car where all the staff and the entertainers had gathered.

"I understand," the General said, "that before I arrive at a meeting you people provide great entertainment and whip up enthusiasm. Could you show me what you do?"

So we restaged what we had done at the Boston Garden several hours before. Bob Montgomery made a short speech, and Fred Waring and his orchestra, as well as several singers, provided the entertainment. I told a couple of "Eisenhower stories"— ones I had used in the camp shows—and the General responded with a few stories of his own. This went on for at least three hours and the General seemed to have the time of his life. Dawn was breaking when we arrived in New York. Before that day ended, Dwight David Eisenhower was elected President of the United States.

The Republicans, having been out of power for twenty years, prepared to go all-out on a big bang-up Inauguration celebration. I was promptly named director of entertainment, and once again my headaches began. I flew to Washington and found myself quartered in a couple of bare, beaverboard rooms in a crackerbox eyesore on Pennsylvania Avenue left over from World War II.

"Murphy's madhouse" was the way my good friend Bill Henry of the *Los Angeles Times* described my place of work. Bill came over to interview me just as I was nearing the end of my inaugural chores. With just hours left to go, crisis after crisis developed. And I was in the center of the storm, hoping that my sanity would hold out until it was all over.

Bill Henry wrote: "George Murphy, fortunately, has long years of physical accomplishments to his credit and with the good athlete's ability to relax, he seems to be holding up remarkably well despite the harassments of the job and the lack of anything resembling real rest. George has been through this sort of thing in fair weather and foul and he manages, somehow, to preserve a sense of balance."

The demand for tickets was so great that I found myself masterminding three inaugural balls with six dance bands. The President-elect promised to attend both, and kept his promise.

For one of the balls we came up with the idea of having a "grand march" or "grand promenade" lead by some two hundred of the top socialites in Washington. Leroy Prinz was assigned to getting the thing into shape. It wasn't easy. At one point Leroy asked Mrs. Marjorie Post, in his most polite way, to move on cue to the music. He explained to her that in the old days, when he was directing chorus girls for Ziegfeld, he had issued such orders a little differently.

"How did you do it in those days?" Mrs. Post asked.

"I would have yelled, 'Get your rear end over there in a hurry and get moving to the music,' " Prinz said.

Mrs. Post, fascinated by this bit of show business lore, laughed uproariously. "That's the funniest thing I ever heard," she said.

One result of that episode was that Leroy got a column in the society section of the *Washington Post* which he's never forgotten.

In addition I had to plan the Inaugural Festival at the Uline Arena. I had almost no problems with the fine entertainers I invited. They were willing to do their best for this historic occasion. My problems were with the managers and press agents. For example, some chap from New York was terribly upset because he didn't think his ballet dancers were getting a good enough spot. He was so mad that he said he'd only bring half as many dancers and they would dance only half as long. I said to myself that was just dandy, since it made it all the easier to cope with an already overlong list of entertainers.

As it was the Festival ran for four hours, twice as long as I had planned. But the audience seemed happy. Among the stellar personalities making appearances were Yehudi Menuhin, Ethel Merman, Edgar Bergen, Marge and Gower Champion, Dorothy Shay, Sid Caesar, the De Marcos, Jarmila Novotna, Fred Waring, Abbott and Costello, William Gaxton, Irene Dunne and, again and again, the production team of Leroy Prinz and George Murphy.

One entertainer who did not appear was my good friend George Jessel. George had called me repeatedly and asked to be invited for the Inaugural celebration. "After all," he pointed out, "I am the toastmaster general of the United States." But I pointed out that he was closely identified with the Democrats and that he had had many opportunities to come to Washington under Presidents Roosevelt and Truman. "I think it's time to give some other people a chance," I told him. But it was like talking to the wall.

When President-elect Eisenhower appointed a plumber as

Secretary of Labor, Jessel sent me a wire: "If Eisenhower can appoint that bum, you certainly could use me." He kept right on calling until the Inauguration was finally over.

After the Inauguration I returned home to resume my work at Metro as well as my extracurricular activities which by now included membership on the Republican state central committee. In October 1953, Governor Warren was named Chief Justice of the Supreme Court, and Lieutenant Governor Goodwin Knight became Governor. A. Ronald Button, the Republican State Chairman, was made a national committeeman. One day I received a telephone call from "Goody" Knight. The new Governor tersely told me that, after meeting with both Vice-president Nixon and Senator Knowland, he had picked me as the new State Chairman.

When I hesitated, being somewhat overwhelmed, Knight said bluntly, "George, you've got to take it. You're the only guy in the state that nobody's mad at!"

# CHAPTER 20

*I win the*
*battle against cancer*

The big problem I faced as Republican State Chairman was a divided party. California Republicans were split on ideological as well as geographical grounds. Liberals contended with Conservatives and Northerners with Southerners.

By all accounts I was fairly effective in reconciling the various factions at least for the duration of the 1954 election campaign. I was even given credit for having made a major contribution to the triumphs of Governor Knight and Senator Thomas H. Kuchel. It wasn't that I necessarily agreed with everything these gentlemen said or believed. They were our candidates and I did all I could to help get them elected.

But I faced an even greater problem as a human being. None of my colleagues, either at Metro or in Republican headquarters, had the slightest idea that I was fighting the biggest battle of my life.

Some months after the Eisenhower Inauguration I developed a hoarseness in my throat. I thought I had laryngitis and began to gobble cough drops by the handful. They did no good. The hoarseness not only persisted, but it got worse.

Finally I paid a visit to my dear friend, Dr. Harold Barnard, the ear, nose, and throat specialist in Beverly Hills who has looked after many movie people for years. Dr. Barnard, incidentally, was the physician who closed up shop in 1940 to take care of Wendell Willkie's throat condition during the campaign.

Barney looked at my throat several times. One night he telephoned me after I had gone to bed. "I've been concerned about your condition for some time," he said. "I want you to fly to Philadelphia in the morning and see Dr. Louis Clerf at Jefferson Hospital. He's the best in the business and he will be expecting you."

The next morning, after a sleepless night, Julie and I packed our bags and flew to Philadelphia where we checked into the Warwick Hotel. I reported to Dr. Clerf at the hospital and he immediately began to examine my throat. I could see right away that this world-renowned surgeon was worried. He gave it to me straight—he had discovered several nodes on my vocal chords which could be cancerous. He wanted me to check into the hospital that afternoon for an operation the next morning.

I was semiconscious as I was wheeled into the operating room. It was necessary to keep me breathing through the throat while the bronchoscope, a narrow tubular instrument, removed the suspected tissues—not the most pleasant experience in the world. I couldn't help but think while I was lying on the surgical table that the operation ought to be filmed for the benefit of medical students all over the world. Dr. Clerf is probably one of the best men in his field in the world—he must have saved thousands of lives with his skill. Someday I hope to see that this film is made.

Even worse than the operation was waiting the few days for the outcome of the biopsy. The day I was called in to learn the results I sat next to a man who had lost his entire voice box. That was hardly reassuring. Growing more tense every minute, I said a prayer or two. When the doctor called me in, he came right to the point: the results were not good. The tissues that had been removed from my trachea had proved to be malignant.

The news came with cold, chilling impact. It was as if a ton of soft snow had dropped right on my head. For about fifteen seconds I just sat in shock. Then I began to think: sure, cancer of the throat is horrible—that poor soul waiting outside has lost his larynx. Still, many people have conquered cancer. Why can't I?

"You have a good chance," I heard the doctor saying. "I think that I got it all out in the operation. But to make doubly sure we'll have to give you deep X-ray treatments for the next thirty days."

That afternoon Julie complained of a pain in her wrist. She thought she might have gotten it by carrying her own bag when she moved from the Warwick to a hotel closer to the hospital. I scolded her for not getting a bellboy, but she said she had been in too much of a hurry.

The next day the pain got a little worse and, in fact, penetrated her elbow. That was the beginning of the arthritis that was eventually to cripple my wife. I have always believed, whether medical evidence supports me or not, that the shock of hearing that I had cancer threw her metabolism out of gear and brought on the arthritis.

Whatever caused it, the fact was that while her condition was getting worse I was gradually getting better. After thirty days of intensive treatment, Dr. Clerf was satisfied that the operation had been in time. Julie and I returned to Beverly Hills.

I returned to a normal life but my Julie, usually busy with a thousand and one things, was for all practical purposes incapacitated. She was being treated with cortisone, a new drug about which very little was known at the time. The reaction she got from cortisone was just dreadful, and her condition worsened.

I was absolutely at wit's end. In desperation, I called Dr. Verne Mason, who had the reputation for being the finest diagnostician on the West Coast. "I know this is probably unethical, but I just don't know what to do," I told him. "Would you please take a look at Julie?"

Verne did, and he was horrified by Julie's condition. He said she must be taken off cortisone immediately or she would die. The shock of taking her off the drug might kill her too, but there was a chance it wouldn't.

Julie was removed to Good Samaritan where she was taken off cortisone and given heavy dosages of aspirin. The terrible pain and suffering that she underwent just about broke my heart. There was so little I could do to help her.

Julie insisted on returning home to be with her dogs and things. And when Julie insists, if I can arrange it she usually gets her way. Once home, she was forced to stay in bed. The slightest movement, even to sit up for breakfast, resulted in excruciating pain. I can remember many, many mornings when I would lie awake and almost hate to see the dawn come up because I knew it meant that Julie would awaken to more pain.

Often on those terrible mornings the horror of it all would hit me so badly that I would seek solace in the quiet and solitude of the Good Shepherd Church with a rosary that my friend, Father Patrick Peyton, had once given me. Invariably my few moments in church would bring me peace of mind.

That rosary never failed to remind me of the Family Rosary Crusade which Father Peyton founded. I was at Metro, shortly after I had forsaken acting for public relations, when this big, handsome, red-faced priest came in to see me. He was deadly earnest about his mission.

"I want to get on the radio," he said. "I was told you could help me."

"Sorry, Father, but I've had very little experience with radio. I don't think I know anyone connected with broadcasting except performers."

I was about to usher the good priest out of my office when suddenly it occurred to me that I did know someone in the broadcasting field—a very nice man named Lou Weiss.

"Wait a minute," I told him. I called Weiss and told him of Father Peyton and his mission.

"Bring him right down," Weiss said.

I drove the priest to Weiss' office and within half an hour an agreement was reached whereby Father Peyton went on the air regularly with the famous theme of his crusade, "The family that prays together stays together."

Sitting in my Senate office in Washington many years later, I reached into my pocket and discovered that Father Peyton's rosary was broken. I decided to take it to the jeweler's and get it repaired. Strangely enough, the next morning I received a letter postmarked Peru from Father Peyton, whom I hadn't heard from in some time. It read: "Dear George. I thought it might be possible that your rosary is wearing out and I thought you might like some extras. I remember you in my prayers." But I'm still using the original rosary—it means a great deal to me.

When Julie became ill, we decided to send our son Dennis, then fifteen years old, to a prep school back East. We thought it would do the youngster good to see another part of the country. We selected the Gunnery School in Washington, Connecticut, whose headmaster, Ogden Miller, was one of the finest educators I have ever met.

For Dennis it was indeed a new world. At first he was amazed that his schoolmates, particularly those from the East, "did not know the difference between a shark and a porpoise." But he quickly discovered that the Eastern kids knew a lot of things he didn't know. I think my son returned home with a better education and a much greater tolerance for people who didn't always think about things the way he did. He also got a taste of the New England that had meant so much to his forefathers.

Like most Murphys, Dennis excelled in athletics. He learned a new game, soccer, and did so well that he was made captain of the Gunnery team. And though he had never seen a racing shell before, he made the crew. This was rather exceptional since no one was supposed to be allowed to join the crew unless he had been rowing for three years. Dennie did it the first year.

The Gunnery crew was so good that they beat all the prep school competition and even got to the semifinals in the Olympic trials at Syracuse. Here, of course, they were racing against college crews. This was a great day for the Murphys and we were all on hand. It was a close race and as the shells neared our vantage point my little girl, Melissa, ran the last two hundred yards along the shore with the boats. When it was announced on the public address system that Gunnery had come in second,

Missy kept right on running. It took me about an hour to find her. She was perched up in a maple tree crying her heart out. She said she had climbed up there so no one would see her crying. She was heartbroken that Dennie and his crewmates hadn't won.

I tried to console her. "Honey, they did the best they could. That's all you can expect. You've got to learn that your side can't always win."

Four years later, Dennis and three pals from Menlo Preparatory School won the small college championship with a shell loaned to them by Jack Kelly, Grace's father. I'm sure that had Dennis gone in the singles he would have made the Olympics.

Dennis had a buddy, Donnie MacFadden, who was about as adventurous a youngster as I've ever met. Donnie discovered that if he tied a rope to a tree outside the balcony of his bedroom window he could swing out over the freeway. But that wasn't enough for Donnie. He decided he could have much more fun if he did it with no clothes on. You can imagine the amazement of the early morning motorists on their way to work when they suddenly saw the skinny frame of Donnie MacFadden flying across the road in mid-air. The sight stopped traffic on Sepulveda Boulevard all the way to the Valley.

Then there was the time Dennis and Donnie borrowed our stationwagon to go on what they described as "a little trip." The next thing I heard they were up in Wyoming. During the trip they stopped off to fish in a stream. Both were dressed like young cowboys with Donnie MacFadden sporting a .22 Frontier model pistol on his hip.

A farmer approached and told them that no fishing was permitted there. Words were exchanged and Donnie took out his gun and gave it a spin like Wyatt Earp, firing two shots in the air. Whereupon the farmer picked up a .22 rifle and shot Donnie right through the shoulder. So the boys didn't fish there.

Missy, born in September 1943, was five years younger than her brother. Both of them had gone to public school in Beverly Hills. It was a well-run school, one of the best in the country. At

PTA meetings there were more movie stars than could be found at a good-sized premiere.

There was only one problem with the school. My kids didn't learn to read well. A lady who specialized in reading at eight dollars an hour finally taught them. I am still struggling with this problem on the Education Committee of the U.S. Senate.

Later Missy went to Marlborough School, a private girls institution in Los Angeles with a reputation for turning out proper young ladies. When Missy was about twelve, Julie insisted that I get her a horse. Julie had been a fine horsewoman as a youngster in Detroit—she came from a horse-loving family—and she wanted her daughter to experience the joys of riding.

My two girls drove me crazy looking for and at horses. I finally purchased a quarter horse from a one-armed cowboy named Freddy Bales. Bales was an amazing fellow. Despite his physical disadvantage, he had a three-goal handicap in polo. How good a cowboy he was I can't say, but he was a mighty rough character on a polo pony.

As it turned out, he had sold me a pretty rough animal. This was a fine-looking roping and cutting horse but apparently the mare had been treated badly because she could not abide people near her head. I took my problem to an old Englishman who operated a stable for youngsters and he told me not to worry. "Horses and children have a way of getting along together, so don't worry about it," he said. He was absolutely right. Within two weeks, Missy had that mare following her around like a big collie. Missy became quite a proficient rider, winning all the barrel races up and down the Imperial Valley for four years.

When she was older and went away to college, we retired the mare to Walt Disney's ranch. Missy makes a point of seeing her whenever she comes in to visit us from Denver where she is now a housewife with two children of her own. She has two dogs that are nearly as big as the horse, and I'm sure in another year or two I'll be shopping for horses again for my granddaughters.

Politics claimed both George Murphy and Shirley Temple (with the late Sen. Everett Dirksen)

January 19, 1953: The Inauguration Festival

Goldwater, Nixon, Murphy, Eisenhower

(Rothschild Photo)

October 15, 1969: At his testimonial dinner, with Gov. Reagan and Bob Hope

# CHAPTER 21

## *"The Ziegfeld
of the Republican Party"*

In 1956 I was once again tapped to coordinate the programming of the Republican National Convention, this time at the Cow Palace in San Francisco. The renominations of President Eisenhower and Vice-president Nixon were pretty much assured—the only fly in the ointment was a "dump Nixon" movement launched by that perennial loser Harold E. Stassen.

This time Harold wasn't promoting himself. His candidate for the Vice-presidential nomination was Governor Christian Herter of Massachusetts. What made Stassen's "Open Convention" crusade all the more ludicrous was the fact that Chris Herter, at Len Hall's invitation, had already decided to make the nominating speech for Nixon.

At the President's suggestion we put a time limit on nominating and seconding speeches at this convention. The only fellow who broke the rule was Stassen who, unable to think of enough to say, said the same thing several times.

For the most part the convention proceedings ran like clockwork. The only untoward incident involved a delegate from Nebraska, Terry Carpenter, who was a Stassen supporter. When Stassen finally announced his support of Nixon, "Terrible Terry" refused to give up the "dump Nixon" banner. He got up and nominated "Joe Smith" for Vice-president. That caused a tremendous commotion on the floor as TV and other newsmen converged on Terry for interviews. The questions went like this:

"Who is Joe Smith?"

"A friend," Carpenter answered.

"What does he do?"

"He works."

"At what?"

"Different things."

"Where?"

"Oh," replied Carpenter, "in different places."

The press, always on the lookout for something unusual, just loved the twenty-four-hour emergence of "Terrible Terry" Carpenter.

Permanent Chairman Joseph W. Martin, who was presiding over his fifth Republican Convention, was scared stiff of "Terrible Terry." "You don't know that man," Martin whispered to me. "He will do anything to create a scene."

Which was exactly what he was doing at that very moment, holding forth, surrounded by a crowd of newsmen, getting far more attention than Governor Herter who was trying to make a speech. I did something then I had never done before (or since) at any political convention. I left the rostrum and made my way over to Carpenter. He was having the time of his life. He was the center of attention.

Some newspaper and television commentators reported that I "assailed" or "threatened" Carpenter and implied that I used bad language. That's nonsense. All I did was say to the man, "Hey, Terry, you're disturbing the Governor. Now you don't want to be rude. So how about letting me give you a fine big caucus room all to yourself where you can conduct a press conference properly."

"Sure, Mr. Murphy," said Carpenter. That was the extent of our widely-publicized altercation. I took him gently by the arm and we left the hall together. As far as I was concerned, "Terrible Terry" was now "Amiable Terence."

Actually, a more anxious moment occurred because of an open microphone in the sound control men's cubbyhole downstairs. All of a sudden we could hear their conversation on the public address system while a clergyman was delivering the benediction. Though it was reported there was no swearing, there was plenty from me. I grabbed the phone and told those guys to switch that blankety-blank mike off.

A tough problem was presented by the mid-hall television tower that blocked the vision between the Chairman and the band at the other end of the hall. Only my gesturing from a wing of the rostrum (telephone contact was too slow) kept the two ends coordinated—at least most of the time. I used to get kidded about my communication system but we managed to keep things moving and usually on schedule.

The entertainment was for the most part excellent. Among those who made appearances were Wendell Corey, Perry Botkin, Dennis Morgan, Irene Dunne, Ethel Merman, Jane Powell, John Charles Thomas, Gene Archer, Patrice Munsel, Lucille Norman, Nat "King" Cole, Allan Jones, Brian Sullivan and Irving Berlin.

Berlin, who wrote the 1952 campaign song "I Like Ike," led the singing of his new campaign song "Ike for Four More Years." Another highlight was Ethel Merman's singing of a parody of Berlin's "Alexander's Ragtime Band," with lyrics I helped whip up.

Following the nominations of Eisenhower and Nixon, I again took to the campaign trail. Reports from Texas indicated that the Republican team was a few points behind. Jeannette Mac-Donald, Gene Raymond, Ward Bond, John Wayne, Irene Dunne and I spent three days in cities like Dallas, Austin and Fort Worth, and I think we helped turn the Lone Star State around at least three percentage points.

Then we did a show for a Nixon rally in Harrisburg, Pennsylvania. The performers included Lee Bowman, Cesar Romero, Abbott and Costello, and two or three others besides me. It was a great show, but our chartered plane was grounded because of fog and we couldn't get to New York where we had other commitments the next day. We hired cars and stopped at every Howard Johnson restaurant along the way, giving impromptu performances for the Republican ticket at each stop. Abbott and Costello were particular favorites. Whether we picked up any votes that night I don't know. But it was for a good cause and we had lots of laughs.

In January I took Dennis and Melissa to the Eisenhower-Nixon inaugural festivities (which once again I directed) and they had a ball. As I was busy almost every moment, I turned the kids loose and they visited places in Washington that I have yet to see.

I'll never forget Missy the night of the Inaugural Ball. She was then all of thirteen and dressed in a beautiful evening gown. Some old duffer wearing an ill-fitting full-dress suit (it looked as if he had picked it out of the corner of John Barrymore's dressing room) stepped over and asked, "Young lady, would you care to dance?"

"Thank you very much, sir," Missy said. "I never dance with older men." She put a freeze on this old geezer that should have lasted him until midsummer.

President Eisenhower had asked me to take charge of the Inaugural arrangements. I met with him on the lawn just outside his White House office and we talked for about fifteen minutes. As we talked, the President kept swinging his golf club and hitting balls down towards the fountain. As always, Sergeant John Moaney was close by, this time shagging balls.

That was the only time we ever talked about the arrangements. "Mr. President," I said in accepting his assignment, "all I ask is that if I get into real trouble I'll be able to call you."

"Of course," Eisenhower said. We shook hands and I bade him farewell. I never needed to call him.

By this time my relationship with the President had become a warm one. He seemed to like me and, as far as I was concerned, he was one of the kindest men who ever lived. Whenever I ran into him while I was visiting in the White House, he would invariably ask, "George, where've you been?" It was a friendship which I will cherish for the rest of my days.

Though I never presumed on that friendship, I never hesitated to talk to the President when it involved the interests of the party. There were a few occasions when I served as a go-between between the Republican National Committee and the White House.

On one such occasion I was talking to Len Hall, the Republican National Chairman, who informed me that the President had decided not to address the annual Lincoln's Day box supper. He wasn't even going to attend.

"Why not?" I asked.

"Because, I'm told, the General thinks he's made too many speeches. He's tired of them."

"But that doesn't make sense—the President not showing up at this important affair."

"I agree. But there's little we can do about it."

"Oh yes, there is," I said, and that afternoon I went over to the White House.

As was my wont whenever I hoped to see the President without an appointment, I hung around the office of his marvelous secretary Mrs. Ann C. Whitman. When the President would pop his head into the office, he would ask, "Where've you been, George?"

Sure enough, that's how it went on this particular day.

"Mr. President," I said, "may I see you for a moment?"

"Of course, George."

Once in his office, I came right to the point. "Why aren't you going to this Lincoln Birthday thing?"

Eisenhower looked astonished. "What thing are you talking about?"

I explained.

"You may not believe this, George, but as far as I know I've never been invited."

This time it was I who was astonished. "Somebody obviously goofed, Mr. President." Which, as I learned later, was exactly what had happened. There had been a complete breakdown in communications between Republican headquarters and the White House.

"Sir," I went on, "your presence is absolutely necessary for the event."

"Do I have to make a speech?" he asked.

"Not unless you wish to—you are the President, you know," I said. "You could just greet the people."

"What else will happen?"

"Well, since this is a Republican function, there will be speeches by four senators and four congressmen," I explained.

"Now wait a minute," the President gasped. "Did I hear you correctly? Am I supposed to follow eight long-winded orators?"

"Sir, they won't be long-winded."

"George, you don't know my friends on the Hill."

"I can assure you, Mr. President, that the speeches will be short and to the point. They will be limited to five minutes each."

"How can you be so sure?"

"I will write all the speeches."

"George," the President laughed, "you continue to amaze me. How long should I talk?"

"That's up to you—you're the President."

The President then wanted to know who the senators would be. I went over the names with him. He reared back when I mentioned John Bricker, the distinguished Ohioan whose "Bricker Amendment" was being vigorously opposed by the White House.

"Now, wait a minute, George," Eisenhower said. "Don't you read the papers? Don't you know I'm having a fight with Senator Bricker?"

"Sir," I replied, "you're not in a fight with the Senator. You are having a disagreement with him over his amendment. That's a big difference. After all, you're both on the Republican team."

The President smiled. "I guess you're right."

I hesitated telling Eisenhower the name of the last senator, but finally I blurted out the name of Joseph R. McCarthy.

The President leaped up as if someone had just touched him with a hot poker. "Now that's really going too far," he said sternly.

"Maybe it is, sir," I said quickly. "But it's time this whole Mc-Carthy business was put in proper perspective. It's gotten out of hand and is demoralizing the Republican party. Besides that, it's dividing the American people when you need everyone's support."

"Well, I'll have to talk to Sherman Adams." He asked the Presidential Assistant to come in.

When Adams came in he was also taken aback when I named Joe McCarthy. But he didn't say no. "What will McCarthy say?" Adams asked me.

"He'll say what I want him to say."

"Do you trust him?" Adams asked.

"Sir, in my few dealings with McCarthy, I've found him to be absolutely trustworthy."

"I'll have to think it over," Adams said.

About two hours later, Adams telephoned me. "Okay," he said, "you can have McCarthy on the program."

Greatly elated, I rushed over to Len Hall's office. I informed the genial Chairman of what had transpired, adding, "This is the greatest thing since canned spaghetti."

"It would be except for one thing," Len said. "You can't have McCarthy. I've assigned him to make a speech in North Caro-lina."

"Then cancel it, Len," I insisted. "Send Meade Alcorn or anyone else, but keep McCarthy here. I'll get Joe to say that Eisenhower is the greatest President ever. That will help get the McCarthy thing cooled off and maybe bring peace to the Republican party."

"I'll see what I can do," Hall said.

I never did find out what transpired behind the scenes but I suspect that some of the party's leading lights considered their judgements better than mine. In any case, the idea of having McCarthy on the same program with Eisenhower was squashed.

President Eisenhower, however, was simply magnificent in his short speech to the faithful. He spoke off-the-cuff and with great eloquence. He said something that has stuck with me all these years. These were the President's words: "So that here we have really the overall philosophy of Lincoln: In all those things which deal with people, be liberal, be human. In all those things which deal with the people's money or their economy, or their form of government, be conservative—and don't be afraid to use the word."

Then came the Army-McCarthy hearings. Unfortunately they were to dominate the headlines for many bitter weeks, relegating the President and what he was doing to the back pages. The amazing thing is that today most people don't even remember what the McCarthy hearings were all about.

One night shortly after the hearings started, I had dinner with Ed Birmingham, a very close friend of Eisenhower's whom I had met in the course of the 1952 campaign. Both Ed and I were upset at the way the hearings were going and I said, "We ought to figure a way to get this mess settled and get it off the front pages. The hearings are serving no useful purpose. Instead they are only confusing and disgusting the American people."

Ed and I also concluded that all sides in the complex dispute—Joe McCarthy, the White House, the Army and the Senate leadership—would like nothing better than to end the hearings, provided that a suitable face-saving formula be devised. After a discussion that lasted long into the night, Ed Birmingham and I came up with a three-stage plan.

Stage one called for the President to announce that because of the great public interest he was personally going to take a first-hand interest in the hearings and, after finding out exactly what was going on, make a complete report of the facts to the American people.

Once the President had become involved, stage two would come into play. Senator McCarthy would announce that since the President had taken over he would retire from the investigation and transmit all the pertinent documents in his possession to the White House. He would say that he was completely satisfied that the President could and would properly settle the entire affair.

The third stage of our plan called for the voluntary resignations of both Roy Cohn, as McCarthy's counsel, and Boston lawyer Joseph Welch as Special Counsel for the Army, giving as the reason personal incompatibility or some other excuse. Both had engaged in personality clashes which had helped enliven the television coverage but certainly did not help the public understanding.

Finally, after several months had passed, the man who had been ground up in all of this, Robert T. Stevens, would resign as Secretary of the Army. I was convinced that Stevens had been led into a situation that he didn't fully understand and therefore would welcome a way out. By this time, hopefully, peace and calm would be re-established and the entire matter dropped from the nation's front pages.

These were very delicate matters of state and the entire plan hinged on whether the President would accept it and agree to make the first statement. The question was how to bring our idea to his attention without any public announcement.

Suddenly an idea came to me. Why not take the plan to Dr. Milton Eisenhower who, I knew, was scheduled to see his brother in the White House that coming Monday?

I telephoned Dr. Eisenhower at Pennsylvania State University, of which he was then President, and asked for an appointment that Sunday. Dr. Eisenhower graciously consented to see me.

Driving up to Pennsylvania, I met with Dr. Eisenhower for two hours, carefully going over the Murphy-Birmingham proposal. He thought it was an excellent idea, but he raised some questions. He wondered whether we could trust McCarthy. I assured him we could, that the Senator was well aware of the tremendous beating he was taking in the communications media. As for Roy Cohn, I had no doubt he too would see the wisdom of the plan. And I was certain that the message could be gotten through to both Joe Welch and Secretary Stevens. Ed Birmingham had assured me he could handle those gentlemen.

Dr. Eisenhower said he would discuss the proposal with the President the next day and let me know what the decision was. I carefully explained that I would proceed only if the President so desired, and that I would await word from him.

Well, I waited and waited and waited to hear from Dr. Eisenhower. I waited an entire week before I was forced to return to the coast. I never did get a message of any kind from Dr. Eisenhower. Birmingham and I wondered whether I should reestablish contact with him. I decided that it would not be proper. I just assumed the President opposed the plan. The McCarthy hearings continued interminably and finally came to a dismal end.

Roy Cohn resigned to go back to New York. Joe Welch returned to his Boston law practice and a small part as a judge in the Otto Preminger film, *Anatomy of a Murder*. Secretary Stevens resigned to return to his textile business in New York. And Joe McCarthy died.

I always wondered just exactly what went wrong. A lot of hard thinking went into this plan and at the time we thought it might provide a solution for one of the most embarrassing problems ever faced by the Eisenhower Administration. But nothing had happened. Why?

Many years later, after President Eisenhower had left the White House, he and I played golf a few times in Palm Springs. Once after a game and a drink, when he was walking me to my car, I couldn't resist. I asked him if he had ever heard of our plan and told him how important it seemed to us at the time. He had never heard of it. Apparently Milton Eisenhower had completely forgotten to discuss it with his brother or maybe he just didn't think it was a good plan. Sometimes such small things may have such large effects on historical developments.

After the Eisenhower Inauguration festivities in 1957, I returned to the West Coast and was elected President of the Motion Picture Industry Council (M.P.I.C.), succeeding Ronald Reagan. This is a group of labor and management representatives whose job it is to set public relations policies for all the major studios.

Almost immediately I was plunged into a new kind of battle for me, this time against the so-called scandal or smut magazines. These were publications which concentrated on publishing outrageous stories about movie stars. Their only purpose seemed to be the exploitation of the weaknesses, mistakes and possible indiscretions of a few. Perhaps blackmail was also involved, I don't know.

As I said at the time: "This industry relies to a large degree on public good will; obviously any scandal has a harmful effect. It's up to the industry to prove that we are, in the main, good citizens with good morals.

"Years ago, when Communist agents first attempted to creep into our industry in order to use our screens for propaganda, actors and actresses decided that these people were not only un-American but also unwelcome and destructive. . . . Now it seems that a new immoral type of parasite is attempting to gain a foothold in our industry. I refer to the so-called scandal magazine. . .

"Where these evil people have come from we do not know. However, in the short time that they have been in our midst we find them disgusting, destructive and unwelcome. It is for this purpose that a special meeting of the Motion Picture Industry Council has been called."

At the meeting, of which I was the chairman, it was decided that a permanent committee be organized to combat the smut-peddlers. Besides myself, the committee included Ronald Reagan, Lou Greenspan, Ken Englund, Sam Engel, Mendel Silberberg, Maurice Benjamin, Marvin Faris and Steve Broidy. We immediately took the offensive, launching a series of public relations and legal maneuvers which ultimately led to the demise of the scandal publications.

I also served as a vice-president of the Motion Picture Academy of Arts and Sciences—the organization that annually hands out "Oscars" to deserving folk in all areas of the industry. For years a few of us had felt that the Academy should have its own theater, equipped with the most modern projection and other theatrical features. Jean Hersholt and I decided to do something about it.

We met with theater operator Charles Skouras, and among the three of us we made a deal to buy a theater from Skouras for the Academy. Then we had to figure out how to pay for it. We sold bonds to raise the cash and retired the bonds by renting the theater to the studios for previews. All of us got our money back within three years, and I never enjoy a movie as much as I do in those surroundings. My only sorrow is that Jean and Charles are not around to enjoy the fruits of their efforts.

This theater was the source of another labor fight for me. The head of the union was a tough cookie who wanted to put two projectionists in one booth when all we needed was one man. This would have cost us an extra ten thousand dollars a year which we couldn't afford. I finally solved the problem by removing three seats from the theater. Under union rules, we did not then need the extra projectionist.

For many years I served as chairman of the Hollywood Coordinating Committee, which during World War II, the Korean War and afterwards, sent players to hospitals, camps and overseas installations to provide entertainment. Only the good Lord knows how many volunteer performers were sent out under the direction of the Committee. They were in the many thousands.

Today that great tradition is being carried on by that grand trouper, Bob Hope, in his Christmas shows on the battlefronts. Still others who deserve honorable mention are Johnny Grant, a Los Angeles disc jockey who was always available for assignment anywhere and has possibly made more overseas appearances than anyone else, and such fine performers as Martha Raye, Ina

Balin and Raymond Burr, who have made many trips to Vietnam with little publicity.

Only once did we have any trouble with a performer on any of these trips. An attractive young lady named Terry Moore had been quoted in the press as saying that in her forthcoming tour of Korea she intended to take off everything the weather would allow. The flak from outraged parents and church groups was earsplitting.

I talked to Miss Moore before she left and she assured me that she would be circumspect and not wear the bikini in question. But once she arrived in Korea it was a different story. The word came back that Miss Moore had, in fact, performed in the mini bikini. Sensing a good story, the press boys demanded to know whether I would have the young actress "ordered out."

Of course I was shocked, and I certainly didn't want to be responsible for anything offensive being sent out of Hollywood. But I announced that since Miss Moore was in Korea it had become a problem for the local Area Commanders and that I had no intention of asking anyone to send her home. I said that if the Army couldn't take care of Terry Moore, they'd have a hell of a time with the Koreans. But the way it came out in the newpapers it looked like I had demanded that Miss Moore return home.

I was deeply touched when I was presented with a special Academy Award in 1951 for "services in correctly interpreting the film industry to the country at large." About the same time the National Conference of Christians and Jews honored me for "outstanding work in promoting understanding among peoples." The awards have been many and varied over the years, and they have all reflected my deep concern not only for my industry but for the future of my country.

I have also had more than my share of critics. At the time I received the Academy Award, a "frustrated star"—as he or she was described in the *Saturday Evening Post*—was quoted as saying: "Leave it to that flag-waver to cop himself an Oscar by just being for American motherhood and deep breathing!"

An amusing line, but hardly an accurate portrayal of the many activities that had me hotfooting around the countryside, local, national and international, in behalf of good causes at a time when I could well have been relaxing in my Beverly Hills home or out playing golf.

I've never been one to sit idly by when there was work to be done, whether it was to prevent juvenile delinquency or to promote the Boy Scouts. In 1953 I produced and directed a film of the International Scout Jamboree at Newport Beach, which was subsequently translated into seventeen foreign languages and shown in more than one hundred foreign countries as well as in every state of the union. For this project I received the Silver Buffalo Award, the highest national award that can be given by the Boy Scouts.

Of course, all this time I was still working for M-G-M as an actor, dancer and a public relations executive. I helped launch the studio into television in 1954, by serving as director and master of ceremonies of  *The M-G-M Parade* . In the first sequence, we ran a film clip from *Broadway Melody of 1940* that showed Fred Astaire and me doing a dance together. "It had a haunting quality," wrote TV critic J.P. Shanley in the *New York Times*. "In fact, it was pretty delightful."

Actually,  *The M-G-M Parade* was a badly conceived project and should never have been done. After I discovered that an agent had sold NBC something he couldn't have delivered, I objected. As a result, I was fired from the show and George Jessel replaced me. The show closed the following week.

After twenty-three years of association with Metro, I resigned my position with the giant studio in 1958. I felt I had no choice. A stockholder's suit had been initiated with the objective of restoring my old boss and dear friend, Louis B. Mayer, to his former position. Some people in management felt I might be in cahoots with Mayer. When such suspicions were raised, I went to the big boss, Joe Vogel, and told him what he could do with his company and my contract. I also told him Metro was headed for disaster. Unfortunately, I was right.

Soon after I left Metro, I got a call from Desi Arnaz, president of Desilu Productions. "Hey, amigo," he said, "I just bought RKO. Come on over and help me run it."

The next day Desi and I walked around the studio, which had been shut down for a time. Moths literally were flying around the offices. That night I had dinner with Desi and his wife, Lucille Ball, one of the most wonderful people in show business. The next morning I signed on as a vice-president of their television film empire. I was to get a broad education in the wiles and ways of the television industry.

In helping get the studio into operation, I had to announce a decision which caused sorrow among movie fans around the world. Tara, the hollow mansion that was built for *Gone With The Wind,* was being dismantled. But not destroyed—we made a deal for the graceful building to be reassembled in Atlanta, Georgia. What had always interested me about Tara was that many people thought it was typical of Southern antebellum architecture. Actually, in accordance with the Margaret Mitchell novel, it was built to look like an Irish mansion. It was a beautiful building and we hated to part with it, but Desilu needed the room for TV production.

The idea had been brought to us by Robert Troutman Jr., who headed a group that wanted to reconstruct Tara in Atlanta as a tourist attraction. The last I heard, the group had been enjoined from doing so and the bricks, lumber and original mortar of Tara were still in storage somewhere.

I spent two good years at Desilu before deciding to resign. There was a clash of personalities at the studio which wasn't working out too well for either Desi or me. I wanted to form my own public relations company and had several projects in mind.

I wanted to offer to other industries the experience and skills of the motion picture industry.

Desi and I parted on the best of terms. We were both opposed to Castro and the Communist regime he had foisted on the island of Cuba. Desi knew a great deal about Fidel. His father had been Mayor of Santiago where Fidel had spent his youth. When it was announced that Fidel would meet with Richard Nixon, I telephoned the Vice-president and arranged for him to get a background briefing on the Cuban dictator from Desi's father. This was when the *New York Times* was still referring to Castro as the George Washington of Cuba.

Some months later Nikita Khrushchev came calling on Washington. President Eisenhower proposed that Bob Mathews of the American Express Company and I accompany the Soviet dictator on a trip around the country, but the State Department nixed that idea.

This was the trip in which Khrushchev made a big stink about not being permitted to visit Disneyland while in Los Angeles. The truth was that the visit was cut out of his itinerary on orders from the Soviet secret police for security reasons. Walt Disney told me he would have been more than pleased to have the Soviet party visit his pride and joy.

Khrushchev met with Eisenhower at Camp David. Dick Nixon, who was there for lunch, later told me a story which was very revealing of the Soviet mind. The Vice-president, seeking to inject a little levity into the otherwise heavy proceedings, said something to this effect: "Mr. President, in Russia there is a very good custom which we ought to adopt. When a man is forty years old, he takes four weeks vacation. When he is fifty, five weeks vacation, And when he is sixty, six weeks vacation and so on."

"Yes," said Eisenhower, "that's a pretty good idea. But no matter where you go on vacation here, the darn telephones will ring and they'll manage to find you."

Whereupon Khrushchev, somewhat nettled, arose and said, "Mr. President, we Russians appreciate the fact you have many telephones in America. But I want you to know that in a very short time we in Russia will have more telephones than you."

A few days after I left Desilu I was offered a job with the Technicolor Corporation. A new management consisting of Pat Frawley, Ed Ettinger and Mel Jacobs had taken over. None of these gentlemen had had any experience in motion pictures and, because of my extensive background in various phases of the industry, they wanted me to come aboard. Since I was still interested in launching my own public relations firm, I agreed to work for Technicolor on a part-time basis.

Before long the part-time became full-time and I was soon named vice-president as well as a director of the corporation, working very closely with Ed Ettinger. The company did very well under the new team, doubling its business every year for three years. The stock rose from three to twenty dollars in a very short time.

In 1960 I was once again called upon to take charge of programming and staging of the Republican National Convention, this time in the International Amphitheater in Chicago. The Democrats had already nominated John F. Kennedy for President in the Sports Arena in Los Angeles.

And once again I was back on the rostrum coordinating the proceedings in order to get the maximum benefit out of the all-pervasive television coverage. The entertainers who volunteered included Wendell Corey, Gene Archer, Efrem Zimbalist Jr., William Lundigan, Brian Sullivan, Patricia Morrison, Louis Sudler, Allan Jones and Edgar Bergen. They did a great job in helping to keep the program moving.

I should say Edgar Bergen and Charlie McCarthy, with Edgar playing a Democratic straight man to his dummy, who proved to be a Republican.

"I just can't forget what the Democrats have done for America," Bergen said.

And Charlie McCarthy retorted, "Well, you shouldn't. You're still paying for it." That was funny then but it's not so funny anymore—it's serious.

One of the wittiest speeches was delivered by Thomas E. Dewey. The New Yorker kept the audience in stitches as he assailed John F. Kennedy for having classified himself with Napoleon, Alexander the Great and similar statesmen in defending himself against attacks upon his youth.

Dewey asked why Kennedy had neglected to compare himself with Julius Caesar and Hannibal. "Did he omit Hannibal because he crossed the Alps with a herd of elephants?" If Tom had exhibited this sense of humor in 1948, he would have been elected President.

Behind the scenes, meanwhile, Vice-president Nixon flew to New York to meet privately with Governor Rockefeller. The result was a document which became known as "the Compact of Fifth Avenue." Conservative Republicans were up in arms. Len Hall was shocked. Senator Barry Goldwater, responding to the enthusiasm of a young Republican group clamoring for the Arizonan's candidacy, termed the fourteen-point document a "surrender" to the liberals and "the Munich of the Republican party." The fat was in the fire.

When I read the text of the "Compact" I wondered what the furor was all about. If anything, the new document was even stronger on national defense than anything previously recommended by the platform committee. For example, this statement was added: "Swift technological change and the warning signs of Soviet aggressiveness make clear that intensified and courageous efforts are necessary, for the new problems of the 1960's will of course demand new efforts on the part of our entire nation."

I could hardly have argued with that. It wasn't so much what was said that was troubling, but the manner in which the document was prepared.

At any rate, Goldwater's name was put in nomination by

Governor Paul J. Fannin of Arizona and properly seconded. Then Barry did something characteristic of this great and humble man. Hardly had the seconding speeches ended when he appeared at the back of the runway to announce his withdrawal. He appealed to his supporters to "give these votes to Richard Nixon" and asked conservatives around the country to vote Republican in the fall. He became nine feet tall in a matter of seconds, and I will never forget the surge of emotion that greeted this genuinely generous gesture.

The demonstration that followed the nomination of Richard Nixon was one of the best I have ever witnessed at any convention. As soon as Governor Mark Hatfield of Oregon had placed the Vice-president's name in nomination, I turned my back on the delegates and motioned towards Manny Harmon, the orchestra leader. The band struck up and Bill McMains, the two-hundred-pound organist, attacked the keyboard. I signalled LeRoy Prinz, the Hollywood dance director whom I had placed in charge of "floor movement," who was stationed in the balcony. On a signal from him, Prinz's lieutenants, scattered about the floor, stood up and the demonstration was on.

It lasted for eighteen minutes, and was well worth all the hard work. As I told the press on the last day of the convention, "We've been here night and day for four days. This will be my last convention for sure."

But wouldn't you know—eight years later I was back doing the same job, this time in Miami Beach where once again the Republicans nominated Richard M. Nixon for President.

During the Kennedy years I did several closed-circuit TV dinners for Republican fund raising. One, in February 1962, stands out in memory. The program called for General Eisenhower to speak from the Olympic Auditorium in Los Angeles and Dick Nixon from Fresno.

I was having lunch with the General and Charles Jones of Richfield when a call came in. Nixon was "flat on his back" with a virus infection and the Republican National Committee, which was sponsoring the affair, did not know what to do.

"Somebody's got to get to Fresno in an awful hurry," I told my luncheon companions. "That whole program is carefully planned. We just can't take the Fresno segment out at the last minute."

Eisenhower and Jones looked at me quizzically. "Yes, we know," they said, almost in unison. "And we know who is going—you!"

"Now, gentlemen," I blurted out, "wait a minute."

"There's no time to wait," Eisenhower said. "You'd better get going."

Getting to Fresno took a minor miracle. No plane had landed at the airport for two days—the fog was that thick. I hired a plane, and after interminable circling the pilot finally found a hole in the famous tule fog and zoomed in for a landing. Once we got on the ground it was impossible to see fifty feet ahead. It took us thirty minutes to find the terminal building, where a car was waiting to speed me to the dinner.

No one at the dinner had a copy of the speech Nixon had prepared, so I had to write one quickly and read it with a stopwatch. The timing had to be perfect because of a simultaneous switch of about three thousand circuits down the line.

Little did I realize when I stood in for Dick Nixon that two years later I would be running for public office myself.

# CHAPTER 22

*1964: "Boy did they
laugh when I decided to run"*

Boy did they laugh when I decided to run for the United States Senate. And I'm not sure I blame them. It was hard for many of the political pros to believe that a former song-and-dance man who'd always lost the girl to his best friend in the movies would even contemplate winning election to that most august of legislative bodies.

One political pro thought otherwise. His name was George Murphy.

From the start, the Democrats considered me a pushover. And why not? With a four-to-three edge in Democratic voter registrations among California's seven million voters they figured that any presentable candidate would knock me for a loop. Besides that, they had President Johnson in the White House and Pat Brown in Sacramento, not to mention a well-organized party in the state.

For years I had been a favorite after-dinner speaker at Republican gatherings. I had been active in Republican circles, both local and national, for nearly two decades. Though I had never been good at mathematics, chemistry or physics, I loved history and those who made it.

Along with this political background, I had been active in the Red Cross, Boy Scouts, Community Chest, National Conference of Christians and Jews, and had received awards from a raft of other organizations during my many years of public service. Meanwhile, I had moved from the sound stages into the business offices of the motion picture industry.

Most important, I had worked all my life with people and I knew all kinds of people. As I told a newspaperman around that time: "I consider myself something of a human engineer. I've done a lot of things in my life, and I have had a broader chance to study people in general than anyone I know. I've lived in every kind of place from a comfortable home in Beverly Hills to a fleabag in Hell's Kitchen. I've worked in speakeasies and in big corporations and everything in between—coal mines, garages, studios and factories. I think I know what the people look for in a candidate. I think I know what they want."

In other words, I was not just a former actor who had danced with Shirley Temple in *Little Miss Broadway*— although that did not hurt me in the slightest when I finally got my campaign under way. I hope I'll have Shirley's help when I run again this year.

It was shortly after the tragic assassination of President Kennedy when I first thought seriously of running for office. I had been invited to address a Republican women's luncheon in Long Beach. The chairlady was my good friend Gladys O'Donnell, who later became president of the National Federation of Republican Women's Clubs. These ladies were as enthusiastic—and effective—a group as I have ever seen.

About six hundred of them listened to my ideas and solutions regarding the evils of big government and the necessity for greater decentralization in the affairs of state. I embellished my remarks with references to a foreign policy which had brought us into crisis after crisis climaxed by our involvement in Vietnam. I spoke about the tax policies which would inevitably destroy the American middle class—the backbone of our great nation. And I said that while I was absolutely for helping those who couldn't help themselves, I did not believe in making a political instrument out of such antipoverty efforts. I thought this was immoral, and I still do.

In short, I preached what I considered sound Republican doctrine—or better still, just sound American doctrine.

The response was overwhelming. As the kids say today, the vibrations were good. Everything I said was greeted with an enthusiasm rarely engendered by my previous oratorical efforts, and I had the feeling that the things I was saying were really on the political beam.

Finally, during the question period, one lady arose to ask why I did not consider running for the Senate. There was earsplitting applause. I don't know to this day whether or not she was a plant.

"Frankly," I said, "I hadn't thought about it."

"Well," the lady said, "you ought to start thinking about it."

When the renewed applause subsided, I picked my words carefully. "Let me say this," I said slowly and seriously, "if you ladies will back me and get out and work for me, I might very well decide to run for the Senate."

And that's how my major venture into politics was launched. From that luncheon on, I gave the idea great consideration. I mentioned it to my good friends Leonard Firestone and Freeman Gosden. Both thought I ought to look into the matter further. They weren't hysterical over the idea, but at the same time they didn't oppose it. Gosden called me three days later and gave me my first encouragement. He said the more he thought about it, the better he liked it.

I made some personal inquiries into whether voters would accept an actor running for office. Remember, this was quite unusual at the time, long before Ronald Reagan or Shirley Temple had decided to enter politics. The word came back to me that I had a pretty fair chance. After all, people remembered me from all those old movies, many of which were playing on late, late television. And I had never played a bad guy. I had always been a good guy—that was my so-called "image."

I found that my biggest support would come from the ladies, the ones over thirty-five. They are real workers. If they like you, they'll swarm all over the neighborhoods like a pack of busy beavers—and they get the job done.

The next time I seriously discussed the subject of becoming a candidate was at a luncheon in Palm Springs attended by former President Eisenhower, Herbert Hoover Jr., Leonard

Firestone, Justin Dart, Freeman Gosden, Lee Batson and Walt Disney.

When I concluded my presentation, Justin Dart, who was head of the Rexall Drug Company, raised an objection. "George, that sounds like a pretty far-out idea," he said. "After all, you have never run for public office. I'm your friend but—"

I was about to respond when General Eisenhower broke in. Pointing to Hoover, the General said, "Herbert's father had never run for public office and neither had I, yet we both managed to become President of the United States on our first try." He paused, then asked, "Any other objections?"

There weren't any.

"All right then," I said finally. "I am now a candidate for the Senate."

At that everyone in the room, led by Dwight D. Eisenhower, came over to shake my hand. "George," the General said, "I know you'll make it. You can count on me for anything."

Ike proved as good as his word. From then on the former President, a wintertime California resident, always referred to me as "my Senator"—at a time when few other Californians thought I had a chance.

It was my dear Julie who gave me my strongest encouragement. When I broached the subject to my wife, she said simply, "I'll make you a deal. If you will promise me that if you lose, it won't break your heart, then it will be okay with me."

"It's a deal," I said. "I have no idea whether I'll win or lose, but honestly, all my instincts tell me that I can win it."

"Then go ahead."

Before making my official announcement, I talked to several people who reportedly were interested in seeking the Republican nomination. One of them was oil man Joe Shell, who had contested Richard Nixon in the 1962 Republican gubernatorial primary and had lost to the former Vice-president. That battle had left bitter wounds in Republican ranks which I think contributed to Nixon's defeat that year.

Joe Shell emphatically told me he had no interest in the Senate contest. But some weeks later he suddenly had second thoughts and became interested. He told me he had decided to run for the Senate after all and advised me to withdraw. By this time I had announced and was running, and I was honestly amazed at his turnabout.

"That's silly, Joe," I told him. "If I didn't think I could beat you in a primary I wouldn't have entered in the first place." That cooled Joe off and he never did enter. This year he has promised me all the help he can give.

Then I flew to Washington where I talked to Senator Thomas H. Kuchel of California regarding his possible support of my efforts in our state.

I felt I had a right to Kuchel's endorsement if for no other reason that I had gone out of my way to work in his behalf eighteen years before when he ran for State Controller. In fact, I had raised some money and had gone on the radio denouncing some Democratic skullduggery designed to hurt Kuchel.

The man who had been State Controller for many years had died. Some smart manipulator had discovered someone with the same name and had persuaded him to run, hoping to fool the voters. This made me angry and I exposed the ploy. In my broadcast I said over and over again, "Remember—the man you should vote for is Tommy Kuchel. The other man died. You say Kuchel's name like 'people.' Kuchel—people. People—Kuchel." Kuchel got in by a thin margin, and he gave me credit for helping him win.

When I went to see him in 1964 to ask his endorsement, Tom was reticent. "I'm not certain as to your positions on some major issues," he told me. "So I am going to send you some questions to answer."

"Fine," I said.

Some time later, I asked Tom again whether or not he intended to endorse me. "You never answered the twenty questions I sent you," he replied.

I was absolutely astonished. I had never received the questions, and I told the Senator so.

"But if you give me the questions now, I will reply to them," I said. I never got the questions, nor did I get his endorsement.

I was in pretty good company, however. Two years before, Kuchel had refused to endorse Richard M. Nixon when he ran for Governor of California, and he later refused to back Ronnie Reagan when he ran for Governor. I have never quite understood Kuchel's reluctance to help other Republicans. I think it was an unfortuante mistake that contributed to his eventual defeat by Max Rafferty in the Republican primary in 1968. A Democrat named Alan Cranston now occupies the Kuchel seat.

As soon as the period of mourning for President Kennedy was over, I officially announced my candidacy. I did this in three cities in one day. Flying down to San Diego at dawn, I told of my plans at a breakfast session there. I returned to Los Angeles for a press conference before noon, after which I flew to San Francisco. I was seeking to counter the natural rivalry that exists between Northern and Southern California. I knew I was going to need all the help I could get, and I didn't want any of my cohorts to be wasting their time in that old North vs. South rivalry which should have disappeared years ago.

When I announced my candidacy I had no organization to speak of or even a headquarters. It wasn't that I was naive. I just didn't have any money. But something Walt Disney had said to me at that luncheon in Palm Springs had impressed me no end.

"Murph, I have an idea that if you can just talk to enough people, you can get elected," Walt had said. And I had the greatest respect for his judgement and instinct. So my son Dennis and I got into our little stationwagon and began driving and talking to whoever was willing to listen. We concentrated on the women's groups.

Meanwhile, Julie and Mrs. Robert Arthur (she had been Irving Thalberg's secretary at Metro and is a wonderfully bright gal) went looking for a headquarters. Thanks to a real estate man who was a friend of ours, George Elkins, they got a small store on Canon Drive in Beverly Hills at a very low rent as our base of operations.

There was not a stick of furniture in the store. It was completely empty. But Julie came up with another bright idea—she was full of them throughout the campaign. She called Lillian Disney and some other friends and explained our predicament. Within two days these gals had outfitted the store with furniture, red-white-and-blue bunting, and even a couple of desks. Thanks to Julie, Lilly Disney, Goldie Arthur, Mary Ryskind and others, the Murphy-for-Senator headquarters was in business.

Not long afterward a San Francisco financier, Leland Kaiser, announced that he too was in the race for the Republican nomination. I flew to San Francisco and had lunch with Kaiser, whom I found to be an agreeable gentlemen. I told him quite frankly that I did not intend to campaign against him personally, that I could see no reason why I should waste my time and effort campaigning against another Republican. I said I planned to campaign against the Democrats exclusively, concentrating my fire on Governor Pat Brown and his record and, of course, the Democratic Administration in Washington.

Whereupon Kaiser said he didn't intend to attack me, but instead would concentrate his fire on the Democrats, too. In this way, he said, we would both display our wares and let the people make their choice.

Kaiser was as good as his word, and after I won the primary he threw his full support into my campaign, made a substantial contribution and was very helpful in other ways.

There was another contestant whose name I have forgotten. A former Governor of a Midwest state, he had moved to Long Beach, where he had become involved in some plans for a world's fair.

When a newspaper reporter asked me about my primary opposition, I replied, "Lee Kaiser is a fine person, a good citizen."

"But what about that other fellow?"

"Oh," I said, "I don't know too much about him except that I understand that the people where he used to live not only don't want him back but they don't even want him to fly over."

That was about the only remark I ever made about that gentleman, and as far as I know he never really filed for the office.

During the primary campaign I got my earliest firsthand look at the manner in which a nationally televised news show sometimes operates. I am referring to NBC's Huntley-Brinkley Report. I was greatly honored to learn one day that David Brinkley had flown out to cover what was becoming "the most talked-of senatorial campaign." He turned up one day with a camera crew at a luncheon meeting in the San Fernando Valley where I was scheduled to address about three hundred and fifty women. The problem was that every seat had been taken and there was no room for either Brinkley or his camera crew. The fact that the great Brinkley wanted in did not impress the ladies, who told him frankly that they couldn't have cared less. I was upset because I felt the publicity might help me, but I was too smart to argue with the girls.

I told Brinkley that I planned to speak at still another ladies' meeting, this one in Pasadena, that afternoon, and that he would be made welcome. I was again hopeful for the television "break." But Brinkley arrived just as I had concluded my speech. Once again I hadn't dared to suggest that the ladies change their schedule. When they said, "You're on!" I was "on."

"That's a real shame, David," I told him. "Look, I'm speaking tonight at the Roosevelt Hotel in Hollywood. I'll hold up my speech until you get there."

"That sounds great," Brinkley said.

I arrived at the hotel just in time to see Brinkley walking out of the lobby. Why he was leaving I never did find out, but the noted TV newscaster never did get to see or hear me.

Apparently it didn't matter. The next night there was David Brinkley on the tube pontificating on what the California race was all about. I must concede he was very good. He even gave *me* the impression that he had been observing me all the previous day. He gave an excellent rundown on what I had been saying and the manner in which I was running my campaign.

Meanwhile, a battle royal was shaping up on the Democratic side. At stake was the seat held by Senator Clair Engle, a Democrat who because of serious illness was not able to run for re-election.

First to announce for the Democratic nomination was State Controller Alan Cranston, then one of the kingpins of the California Democratic Council (CDC), a statewide volunteer group whose views on domestic and foreign affairs were usually left of center. Cranston also had the important backing of Governor Brown.

But there was no love lost between Brown and Jesse Unruh, better known as "Big Daddy" who, as Speaker of the State Assembly, was one of California's most power-hungry Democrats. Anyone Brown wanted, Unruh automatically opposed.

Unruh's choice was Pierre Salinger, who had won a modicum of fame as press secretary to President Kennedy and, temporarily, to President Johnson.

There were some complications. After all, Pierre had himself stated in the summer of 1963 when asked if he were interested in running for Congress in California: "My home's in Virginia. There's no way I could run for public office in California."

But one day in March 1964 Pierre marched into President Johnson's office and announced he was resigning then and there as the White House press secretary. The President apparently was taken aback but he recovered quickly and dictated a "Dear Pierre" letter thanking Salinger for his services.

Within hours, Pierre flew to San Francisco where, in the dead of night, he registered at the Fairmont Hotel on Nob Hill. The next day he rounded up sixty-five friends to sign his nominating petitions. With less than two hours left before the deadline, Salinger filed for the Democratic primary at the Registrar of Voters at City Hall.

It was a very surprising move, to say the least, one that set my chances back a little. But when I saw news photos of Pierre leaving the San Francisco airport in a Rolls Royce, smoking a big cigar, I felt better about the whole thing. This was not good "image-making."

The extraordinary manner in which Salinger had entered the race in itself became a campaign issue. I never permitted the voters to forget all the juicy details.

Some of my best ammunition against Salinger came from the Cranston camp. All I did was arrange for someone to monitor the statements of both Democratic contenders and keep track of what they said about each other.

At one point Salinger accused Cranston of having hustled campaign contributions from tax assessors whom he had appointed as State Controller. That got to be pretty bitter. Finally both candidates publicized an agreement whereby the primary winner would pick up a share of the loser's campaign deficit. Pat Brown loved this arrangement until he discovered it might be illegal.

My research on Salinger was kept to a minimum; in the fall campaign I just "borrowed" what Cranston had said about him.

Cranston's backer, Pat Brown, really exploded when Salinger announced his candidacy. According to the Governor, Pierre was "a political rookie" who knew next to nothing about the problems of the state.

But for a "rookie," Salinger quickly developed a campaign organization that blanketed the state. His picture was on every billboard and his bumper-stickers—"P.S. I love you."—were everywhere. That took money, plenty of money. The Cranston people began wondering out loud where all the dough was coming from. I wondered, too.

I also wondered where my money would come from. During the primary I spent very little. But the campaign itself necessitated greater expenditures. In all, I believe we spent less than three hundred and fifty thousand dollars to win the Senate seat. It was said to be the cheapest campaign for such a high office in the state in fifty years. That wasn't by choice. We just didn't have the money, and we were forced to get along on what we had.

One reason for our difficulty in raising money was the bitter primary struggle between Nelson Rockefeller and Barry Goldwater for the loyalties of California voters. In that contest money was being spent on all sides as if it were going out of style. There was very little left over for me. Another thing, not too many Republicans in those early days thought I had much of a chance to win anyway, so why throw away good money? At this point I was quoted at 20 to 1 in Las Vegas.

But some friends came through when I really needed them. I was particularly grateful to Walt Disney, whose wise council was of invaluable help. It was really fascinating to see how needed funds were gathered. My finance committee was very generous. I got a call from Dick Buck, an old friend from my days at Bache & Co., and a sizeable check followed the call. The Class of 1925 at Princeton remembered I had had some athletic skill in the old days and they took up a collection and sent it in. People I hadn't seen in years helped. It was one of the most gratifying experiences of my life, to learn how many friends a fellow has when he needs help.

Salinger and I won our respective primaries and then the campaign began in earnest. Salinger launched his race with what most experts regarded as a substantial lead. The first poll taken after the primary had Salinger beating me by seventeen points—a formidable lead.

Still I wasn't worried. Dennis and I continued to travel around the state talking to people and frequently, in my case, signing autographs.

I always remembered Julie's Law: "A tired candidate is worse than no candidate." What she meant was that every day at five o'clock, no matter what we were doing, we were to quit and take a two-hour rest until seven o'clock. So wherever Dennis and I were—Bakersfield, Fresno, Chino, Watsonville or any other of several dozen other towns—we would quit at five. I would go to our motel and get right into bed and rest while Dennis would scout the town and bring back information. Then I would get up, take a shower, get into fresh clothes and begin the evening's activities ready to go the full distance.

I guess that by the end of the campaign I must have made at least two thousand speeches and travelled many thousands of miles. Yet because of Julie's Law, I felt better at the finish than I had at the beginning of the campaign. I've always pressed this advice on my political friends. I remember one time when Ronald Reagan got himself into hot water at a press conference because he was overly tired. During one of those sessions when newsmen were badgering him as they love to do, Ronnie answered a question less effectively than he usually does. I knew he was upset and I called him immediately. Before I could say a word he popped, "I know—I was tired. It won't happen again."

"Remember this," I told him, "you must not let yourself get tired. You've got to stay sharp. The people really are not interested in whether you're tired or sick. In politics, you're supposed to be at your best at all times."

I ran what was described by reporters as a relatively sedate campaign. Soon after the primary, my good friend Robert H. Finch kindly consented to become my campaign coordinator. He handled all matters at headquarters with the finesse that he had acquired in Washington as the top aide to the then Vice-president Nixon and later in Nixon's 1960 campaign. His advice to me was always to the point and he worked long hours in my behalf. I will always be grateful to Bob, and I was pleased that I had a chance to help him when he ran for Lieutenant Governor in 1966.

It was Bob Finch who first introduced me to Salinger. Bob and I had had lunch at the California Club, and as we were leaving we ran into my portly opponent. "Hello Pierre," Bob said, "do you know George Murphy?" For some reason Pierre seemed to juggle his cigar, almost dropping the stogie. Maybe he was nervous. "How do you do?" he finally said.

At my headquarters a fine group of young men and women had been mobilized to work on the campaign. As a result of their efforts, speeches were written and position papers were prepared. Occasionally I would use some of this material as advance handouts to the press. But most frequently I would get up before audiences and talk extemporaneously with just a few notes that I had prepared for myself. I don't like to read canned speeches. I do better talking from notes.

The biggest compliment I ever received was from an elderly lady at a Hollywood meeting who came up to me after one of my extemporaneous talks and said, "You know, Mr. Murphy, it's wonderful the way you say things. You make important problems sound so simple that even I can understand them."

The campaign took a sharp turn after the death of Senator Clair Engle. Governor Brown, who by now was reconciled to Salinger and was even calling him "the rookie of the year," appointed him to fill out Engle's term as Senator. The idea was that Pierre's incumbency would help him in his race against me.

I thought so, too. And I yelled like hell. I challenged the appointment as illegal. I pointed out that California law clearly stated that the Governor could only appoint an elector, that is, someone who had lived in the state at least a year. Salinger had come to reside in California only within the last few months. Therefore, I said, it was an illegal appointment. Pat Brown thought so too, but added that since Attorney General Stanley Mosk said it was all right, he guessed it might be legal.

I flew to Washington and spoke to Senator Everett Dirksen,

and explained the problem to him. "I will help you if I can," the Minority Leader said. Several other Republicans offered to help, and they did raise objections on the floor of the Senate.

But the Senate voted to seat Salinger conditionally pending a hearing by the Senate Rules Committee on objections raised by the appointment. I appeared before a subcommittee accompanied by Bob Finch, who was acting as my council.

"The law is very clear," I told the subcommittee headed by Senator Claiborne Pell of Rhode Island. "It says that the Governor in the event of a vacancy may appoint an elector of the state to fulfill the unexpired term caused by the unfortunate death of Senator Engle. The man who is appointed (Salinger) is not an elector of the state of California, and, therefore, we take the position that the entire action should be nullified and the Governor's decision should be vacated before the matter is brought to the attention of the U.S. Senate."

Two days later the Democratic-controlled subcommittee ruled in Salinger's behalf. But we had gotten the point across to the people back home—namely that Pierre Salinger was a "carpetbagger" and that there was some question about the legality of Pat Brown's appointment.

The campaign was interrupted by the national conventions. Ours was held in San Francisco and I was overjoyed at the prospect of not having to stage-manage the affair. I got to wear a big gold badge that read simply "CANDIDATE."

Still not many of my fellow Republicans believed I had a chance to defeat the formidable Salinger. They thought I was fighting a lost cause. Only Ev Dirksen seemed optimistic when I ran into him in Convention Hall. "My goodness, George," he said, "you're even beginning to look like a senator. I think you'll surprise everyone and make it."

President Eisenhower gave me a tremendous boost. He and my pal Freeman Gosden cooked up a luncheon one day in my honor. With their endorsement, all the important Republicans knew I was a real candidate. The publicity was magnificent, and from that day on, things began to move. We were on our way.

It was obvious to anyone with any political savvy at all when the delegates gathered in San Francisco in early July that Barry Goldwater was going to emerge as their choice for President. Governor William Scranton of Pennsylvania was making a last-ditch effort to convince the delegates that Goldwater's nomination would be a tragedy for the party.

I talked to Senator Hugh Scott of Pennsylvania, one of Scranton's more ardent supporters, begging him to get the Governor to make a graceful exit before the wounds deepened among the delegates. I pointed out that Goldwater was a cinch for the nomination and what was now needed above all else was party unity. I have always believed that most disagreements among Republicans were not that deep and that, as a rule, they usually resulted from conflicts in personality.

Unfortunately, the convention proceeded—and ended—on a note of internecine bitterness.

But I had my own campaign to run. My basic aim was to unite California Republicans, regardless of how they felt about Goldwater, behind my candidacy and to win over as many Democrats as possible to my banner.

It was difficult to campaign against Salinger simply because he had no political record in California. He had been a newspaperman and magazine writer before being tapped by Robert Kennedy in the fifties to work for a Senate Investigating Committee. In 1960 Pierre had become John F. Kennedy's press agent and followed him into the White House. After the tragedy in Dallas, Lyndon Johnson kept Pierre on as press secretary. But life with Lyndon apparently was not as much fun as life with the Kennedys. There was never any question as to where Salinger's loyalty lay, and I've heard it said that LBJ was glad when Pierre decided to run in California.

Happily, the campaign never got dirty. Oh, some of the Salinger people had sought to link me with right-wing extremists who wanted not merely to impeach Earl Warren but to hang him or who believed that Dwight D. Eisenhower was some sort of unwitting dupe of the Communist conspiracy. That, of course, was the biggest joke of the campaign. If there is anything I will treasure for the rest of my days, it is my friendship with the late President, whom I consider to have been one of the greatest men of our times. With regard to Earl Warren, I was shocked at some of his court decisions but his impeachment never occurred to me.

Much to my amazement, I discovered that one of Tom Kuchel's staff members was travelling about the state claiming that I was refusing to take a position on the Birch Society and other so-called controversial issues.

I telephoned Kuchel. "Now listen, Tom," I said. "A man from your staff has been running around the state making vicious remarks about me. He has been visiting newspaper offices and passing along false stories. I don't know his purpose. I just want you to know that because of this I will not communicate with you again during the campaign. If I do it will look like I am trying to make a deal with you and that I will not do. I would like your help but I will make no deals. I will add only one thing—I'm going to win this one with or without your help. So you will have to decide on your own what you intend to do."

That was the last time I spoke to him during the campaign. Even after I was elected we never became very close. I have never understood Tom Kuchel.

Following my election I ran into my friend Phil Gibson who was then the Chief Justice of the Supreme Court of California. Gibson, a Democrat, said, "You know, George, you amaze me. You've never done a bad thing in your life. We went through your record with a fine-tooth comb—"

I stopped him right there. "Phil, I'm shocked," I said. "Do you mean to tell me that you, the Chief Justice, lowered yourself to exploring the life of an opposition candidate to try to find dirt?"

Phil turned scarlet. I was embarrassed for him and I think he was embarrassed for himself. Digging up information about your opponent is an old story in politics, but I honestly never expected a respected jurist to involve himself in such an undertaking.

At one point in the campaign, a member of the Salinger entourage asked me if we had any information on the Democratic candidate.

"Quite a bit," I replied. "I've got a book of material about two-and-a-half inches thick. But most of what's in it I'll never use—unless your man forces me to."

I have often said that I could either waltz or wrestle, and though I'd rather waltz, I'd wrestle if I were forced to. Fortunately, as I have noted, the campaign was generally conducted on a high level. Personal charges were few and far between, on either side.

For example, there had been stories circulated about a member of Pierre's family. In fact, one man offered to make a very substantial contribution to my campaign if I used what he called fully-documented material on the matter.

"I'm sorry," I said. "I can't use your material. I'm running against Pierre Salinger and not against any member of his family. I certainly could use your contribution, but if that's what I would have to do to get it, then I'll have to forego the pleasure."

I did nip in the bud one serious attempt by the opposition to embarrass me. Someone had placed a pile of viciously racist pamphlets on the literature table in the reception area of our headquarters. Fortunately, someone on my staff had the presence of mind to call me immediately. I knew exactly what had happened. I remembered all too well the 1960 campaign when anti-Catholic literature was planted in several Nixon-for-President headquarters and the cry went out from the Democrats that the Nixon people were spreading bigotry.

To forestall any possible newspaper repercussions, I had my

people immediately telephone the principal newsmen and ask them to meet me at my headquarters.

"I know someone is going to feed the story of how my headquarters is supposedly distributing scurrilous literature," I told them. "I want you to know that I had no knowledge of this, no connection with it, and would never dream of circulating such vicious stuff. Someone—and I honestly don't know who—planted this stuff for obvious reasons."

All of the newsmen, including Dick Bergholz of the *Los Angeles Times,* wrote fair stories. Not that I've always received fair treatment from Bergholz. He is a very fine writer but his views are sometimes tainted by his political biases. His lack of objectivity when it came to Dick Nixon's 1962 gubernatorial campaign was pronounced. When I launched my own campaign two years later, I had made up my mind that no matter what Bergholz said or did I was not going to be disturbed. I told my staff, "No matter what Bergholz writes, we love him dearly," reminding them of the old saying: Don't waste time fighting a newspaper unless you own another newspaper.

On one issue I did have considerable difficulty with the press. The issue was Proposition Fourteen, a measure which called for the repeal of the Rumford (Fair Housing) Act. Rumford was a very bad bill which had been pushed through the legislature late at night, but it had a civil rights label. Subsequently Proposition Fourteen, a repealing amendment, was placed on the ballot. This went too far in the opposite direction—it not only cured the illness but killed the baby, you might say. So when I was asked my position I said that I refused to take one. I refused to choose between two extremes, neither of which I agreed with.

"But that's no position," a bird dog of a newsman insisted in Fresno one day. "I've got to know your position."

"I've told you my position," I said, "which is simply this—if I may paraphrase Gilbert and Sullivan—'I have chosen to take a position which is no position.' "

The newsman insisted that I explain myself. He not only insisted, he demanded.

"I demand to know how you are going to vote when you enter the voting booth."

For once I could hardly contain myself. "Young man," I said, "in the United States of America we have something called a secret ballot and, frankly, it's none of your damned business how I personally vote on any issue."

The newsman dashed off to write the story. My press aide, who had turned white and nearly fainted dead away, said, "George, I think you've just blown the election."

But as it turned out, my remarks were carried all over the state and they probably got me more votes than any other issue in the campaign. At least Pierre Salinger, who had come out strongly against repeal of the Rumford Act, thought so. He later conceded that his position cost him heavily at the polls.

But the real issue was not the Rumford Act or any other synthetic sociological proposition. I believe that I had expressed the sentiments of the great majority of Californians who resented the fact that they were being asked to choose between two extremes. Most Americans are not extremists; they are essentially moderate people and I think they want their legislative representatives to act moderately.

One thing the Salinger forces tried to use against me—and it backfired badly against them—was the fact that I had been a song-and-dance man. Oh, did Pierre laugh it up before audience after audience about my being an "ex-hoofer" unworthy of a Senate seat.

"It would take Murphy six years to find the bathroom in the Senate Office Building," he said. He nearly split his sides laughing whenever he said it. Apparently Salinger, who had ostensibly been occupying a Senate suite for several months, did not realize that, like every other Senator, he had bathroom facilities right in his own office.

I never made any bones about having been a hoofer. I had danced with some of the greatest stars of our time and I said so, and I was not the least embarrassed that I had been one of the best in my trade. I was taught when I was very young that if you did your job well, you were okay, no matter what your job.

"Believe me," Pierre told an Oakland gathering, "come Election Day this performance will win no Academy Award."

Yet Salinger himself went in heavily for Hollywood talent to promote his cause. He staged a big fund-raising rally at the Hollywood Palladium, recruiting dozens of stars to bring out the crowds. Among them were Gene Kelly, Janet Leigh, Andy Williams and Dan Blocker, who plays "Hoss" in the *Bonanza* television series. Earlier Salinger had used Dean Martin's home for a fund-raising party. As far as he was concerned it was all right to use stars, but wrong to be one.

My people played the same game. They borrowed John Wayne's house in the Valley for a big party. The Duke had a big lawn and the party was to be held outdoors. But the tickets were over-subscribed. There was room for only five hundred people, and eight hundred had paid to come. There was a big to-do which was brought to my attention. "No sweat," I said. "We'll have two Saturday parties."

The second Saturday proved a problem for me. I had been booked to speak elsewhere that day. So I rented a helicopter which took me to the first engagement where I made my speech. Then the helicopter landed right on the hill of the Wayne property. That turned out to be a real fun party. Some of my oldest friends in the film business were there—Buddy Ebsen, Walter Brennan, Cesar Romero, Lloyd Nolan, Lee Bowman and, of course, "Duke" Wayne himself.

After I made my little speech, we all sang songs and finally someone asked, "How would you girls like to kiss Cesar Romero?" The girls got all excited and Brennan said they had to ante up one dollar each to buss the tall, dark and handsome Romero. Some even paid a dollar each to kiss Walter Brennan, so great was the hysteria. Others paid to kiss the other stars present. I went home that night with two big grocery sacks crammed full of dollar bills. I think I collected about eight hundred bucks. With my limited financial resources that didn't hurt a bit.

Wherever I went, I talked issues. I talked about inflation and high taxes and how old folks on fixed incomes were being hurt by continuing rises in the cost of living. I discussed the problems of working people and pointed out that I had been a working man myself. I stressed the need for improved law enforcement. In agricultural areas, I took a stand favoring the *bracero* program, under which fruit and vegetable farmers could hire immigrant workers from Mexico.

I likened the war in Vietnam to the Korean conflict, explaining how our policy-makers in the White House and State Department had muddled the issues. And on one major state issue—that of water—I called for desalinization as a major solution to the problem. This was at least six months before President Johnson set up a commission to investigate the desalting of sea water, and I sent the President a telegram thanking him for joining me in the effort.

I also kept hitting away at the thesis that Salinger was part of a Kennedy plan to grab control of several vital Senate seats and thereby create a power bloc that could influence key votes in the Senate. Besides Salinger, Bob Kennedy had entered the New York race; Ted Kennedy was running in Massachusetts; John Glenn in Ohio; and Sarge Shriver in Illinois.

I also kept repeating Pierre's own words about his entry into California politics: "I arrived in San Francisco at one-thirty a.m., took a room at the Fairmont Hotel, and signed up to run for the Senate the next afternoon." Then I would say, over and over again, "Pierre is not really a carpetbagger—he came in such a hurry he didn't even bring a bag."

Of such things are campaigns made and it rarely changes. You point with pride and you view with alarm.

Basically, however, Pierre and I were running two different types of campaign. As a writer described our barnstorming in *The Road to the White House:* Salinger "is a chubby five-foot-seven, somewhat Santa Clausian, even in his expensive suits, a cigar-chewing exponent of the hard sell. Murphy dresses like the very model of a man of distinction and always looks fit. His campaign was conducted in a relatively sedate manner while Salinger used helicopter, automobile, airplane, an outmoded narrow-gauge train, folk-singers and a jazz band. At one point Salinger's supporters conducted a 'swinging affair with Pierre' at an old lakeside mansion in Oakland. On the top floor was a group of folk singers, on the main floor a jazz band, in the basement a record player rocking with the Beatles and on the lawn a combo tooting some old favorites. Four bars were in operation. Murphy, meanwhile, used the soft sell, talking quietly and mixing easily with crowds . . ."

What I was really trying to do was shake hands with as many Californians as possible. I never hesitated to stop and listen to a voter with a complaint. For a few days I surprised early-morning commuters by boarding trains on the San Francisco peninsula and interrupting their card games and newspaper reading. Sometimes I would wake up people and say, "Hey, I'm George Murphy and you'd better vote for me or you'll never sleep on this train again." Everybody took my campaigning in good humor.

According to a *New York Times* dispatch, my opponent "replied . . . with plans to help cablecar operators turn a car around at the turntable at Powell and Market Streets in downtown San Francisco and campaign aboard it up to Nob Hill. The idea was promising but a cable broke earlier in the afternoon, throwing the whole system out of service."

Another thing happened that day that helped me. As Pierre opened his office in San Francisco in a store on the ground floor, a great banner about a hundred feet long dropped from a window on the seventh floor spelling out MURPHY. This had

been put together by Ed Slevin and my staff by tying six
bedsheets together, each with one letter of my name. Naturally,
we stole Pierre's publicity.

One of my major problems was to win over Democratic votes.
That was urgent because I needed to obtain at least seven
hundred and fifty thousand Democrats on my side in order to
break even. Y. Frank Freeman, who once headed Paramount,
and a lawyer, Z. Wayne Griffin, were very helpful in forming a
committee called Democrats for Murphy.

One day another dear friend, Walt Disney, called me and
asked whether it would help my campaign if he announced for
me. "Help?" I exclaimed. "Well, it won't get me more than
three hundred to four hundred thousand votes." I think that a
candidate can be helped enormously when he's endorsed by
someone of the stature of Disney, Bob Hope, Bing Crosby,
Cesar Romero, or Duke Wayne. Let the other side parade the
"swingers" as being in their corner—I'll take the solid citizens
of my town anytime.

As October rolled around I began to feel in my bones that I
was narrowing the gap and that I would overtake Salinger in
the stretch. Salinger had launched his campaign with what
many of the experts had termed an almost unbeatable lead but
he began to slip in the polls.

I got a shot in the arm with the entry into the New York
Senate race of Robert F. Kennedy. This revived the "carpetbagger" issue. "Why vote for a man who can't vote for himself?"
became one of the hard-hitting slogans of my campaign.

If there was a turning point in my favor during the campaign,
it may well have been the "Great Debate" in which I participated with my rival. At first I wasn't too happy with the idea of
a face-to-face confrontation with Salinger on statewide television. I remembered only too well what that first television
debate had done to Dick Nixon in his 1960 race against Jack
Kennedy. I did not want to put my whole future on the line

with a single television appearance. Salinger was a glib, fast-talking "snow man" and had a lot of experience in the hard sell of
the Kennedy and Johnson Administrations.

Nevertheless, after consultations with Bob Finch and other
advisers, I felt that like Nixon in 1960, I had no alternative but
to meet my adversary head-on. But I had talked to Nixon about
that Kennedy debate and I had learned at least one major lesson
from that misfortune. Nixon had campaigned almost to the
moment he entered the studios and his fatigue showed up on
millions of television sets.

What I did was cancel all weekend appearances and concentrate on the debate itself. And I did what Jack Kennedy had
done in 1960. I brought together some experts from the communications media who fired all sorts of questions at me, the type
of questions that might be asked during the debate. Among
those who participated were Dick Moore, a television executive;
Sandy Quinn, a public relations man borrowed from a Los Angeles firm; Ky Jorgensen of a local advertising agency; Ed Ettinger, a colleague from Technicolor and several others.

If my answers to their questions weren't any good, we would
work on rephrasing them. We worked on every conceivable
topic that could possibly come up. By the time I entered the
studio for the debate I was primed for any possible surprise.
More important, I was feeling pretty relaxed and well-
prepared—so relaxed that I drove over in an old shirt and a
pair of slacks. Pierre and I greeted each other warmly, but I'm
sure he was wondering whether that was the way I was going to
appear on camera. I didn't disabuse him of the notion.

I went to the makeup room where I was made up and where I
put on a blue suit. When I returned to the studio, Pierre looked
astonished. "You've changed your clothes," he remarked.

"Yeah," I said, "I always wear blue for a *bar mitzvah*."

I could see Pierre was getting nervous. Apparently he wasn't
in the mood for socializing. He was obviously "uptight" as the
kids say nowadays. So I went right ahead.

"I see you've lost a little weight."

"Oh yes," he said, "I guess I must have lost about twelve pounds."

"Don't worry," I told him, "on you it doesn't show."

Now he was really nervous. That made me feel a little better as we were asked to step behind our respective podia. I began to feel the tension mounting in the studio. Once I got going, I quickly took the offensive and tried to put Pierre on the defensive.

At one point, Salinger began to name-drop, and I decided to outdo him at his own game. One exchange went like this:

*Salinger:* I have conferred with Secretary of Defense McNamara. I have conferred with Senator Magnuson, the chairman of the Senate Commerce Committee . . . I had a call this morning from Secretary of the Interior Stewart Udall . . .

*Murphy:* I know, for instance, Senator Dirksen quite well . . . J. Edgar Hoover, and the rest.

*Salinger:* As Mr. Romulo told me—you know General Romulo?

*Murphy:* Very well.

I was telling the truth—I did know Romulo better than Pierre did.

Salinger repeatedly accused me of agreeing with Republican Presidential candidate Barry Goldwater on a number of issues including California's water problem.

"You're assuming things that aren't true," I said. "Goldwater is the head of the ticket and I respect him as head of the ticket—but I don't agree with him on all issues. I reserve the right to disagree . . . on civil rights for one thing, on California water for another . . ."

Each time Pierre tried to hook me, I was able to shake loose and put him on the defensive again.

Then came an interesting exchange, in light of more recent developments. After citing events in Vietnam and the Gulf of Tonkin, I said, "The people want to know what's happening in Vietnam."

Salinger responded: "I think the war in Vietnam can be won. I think we must help Vietnam to win that war . . ." (In recent years, Pierre apparently has had a change of heart about Vietnam. He has been in the forefront of so-called antiwar movements.)

What Pierre couldn't explain was why we were not permitting our troops to win and win quickly, which I have always thought would have saved thousands of lives and billions of dollars.

As the debate went into the closing minutes, I had run out of things to say. So I "graciously" announced that I would permit my distinguished opponent to use the one-and-a-half minutes that were left to make up for the extra time I had used during the discussion.

Salinger froze. Recovering quickly, he began a discourse on his close association with the late President Kennedy. Then he realized he had made a mistake. Only moments before I had charged that Pierre had no experience in or knowledge of the state's problems and that he was running on the basis of the Kennedy name and apparently was not competent to stand on his own feet.

It was too late, and Pierre knew it was too late. You could see what we used to call the "flop sweat" breaking out on his forehead. He left the studio in a huff.

Then he did something that was uncharacteristic of the former Presidential press secretary. He showed annoyance with the waiting reporters. He lost his temper, and with it perhaps the election.

When I came out, I did my best to be "charming George." I answered all questions including the obvious one as to who had won the debate. "I don't know," I said. "We won't know until Election Day—which is the only thing that counts."

The fact was that I did know. The only thing that really troubled me in the closing weeks of the campaign was the size of Lyndon Johnson's vote. I knew Barry Goldwater was in trouble and that could only hurt my chances.

On Election Day I drove over to Andy Devine's home in Balboa and sat around his house and dock and just talked. Buddy Ebsen and Dick Richards, who runs the Richards Market down there, came over and we went over to the golf club for lunch. There is very little you can do on the day the people are casting their ballots, except wait. It was without question the longest day I've ever spent.

In the evening Julie and I went downtown and spent some time at the Ambassador Hotel watching the returns. About midnight Los Angeles time (which is three a.m. back East) Huntley and Brinkley were saying something to the effect that Murphy was now some two hundred thousand votes ahead and had a fifty-fifty chance of winning. At that point I already knew I was the winner because the only votes not tabulated then were from Orange County and the San Diego area where I had great strength. These were Republican strongholds.

So about 12:15 a.m. Julie and I went home to get some much-needed rest and to wait for the final count.

The official totals showed that the old song-and-dance man beat unlucky Pierre by more than two hundred and sixteen thousand votes while Lyndon Johnson was carrying California by nearly one million three hundred thousand.

Whenever I run into either Chet or David, I never forget to ask, "When are you guys going to concede?"

# CHAPTER 23

## *The United States Senate*

And so on January 4, 1965, I was sworn in as a member of the United States Senate. You can't imagine the excitement and the confusion, but the thrill of putting my hand in the air and repeating the oath of office was worth all the trouble and the hard work of the campaign.

The oath was administered by the veteran Senator from Arizona, Carl Hayden, and when I said "I do" I was officially one of the two senators representing the most populous state in the Union. Ours is a state which has all the problems you can think of. And if anyone thinks that the life of a senator is one of ease and relaxation, let me persuade him otherwise.

My days are long and my hours uneven. Generally I get through at about seven or seven-thirty in the evening, and when I leave for home my secretary always has a bulging briefcase of personal mail that has to be signed and gotten out by the next morning. I get an average of twelve hundred letters a day—probably more than any other senator—and each one of my correspondents expects an answer. How my staff manages to get their work done with such dispatch still bewilders me.

When I first entered the Senate, my old friend Y. Frank Freeman, the former president of the Motion Picture Producers Association, advised me to "be sure to get to know Senator Dick Russell of Georgia." I did, and found him to be one of the wisest, most respected and kindest men ever to serve in public office. When he speaks the Senate listens. Of course, I had known such senators as Everett Dirksen, Karl Mundt, Hugh Scott and Carl Curtis for many years, and I knew from the beginning that I could depend on these fine Republicans for guidance.

Another old friend was Senator Harry Byrd, Sr., and I had
been in Washington only a short time when he invited me to
visit Winchester, Virginia, in order to crown the queen of the
annual apple festival. That this great man would so recognize
me was like being given the Good Housekeeping seal of approval. That approval was of tremendous help in my early days and
I now prize my close friendship with Byrd's son, Harry Jr., who
succeeded him in the Senate.

I tried to get to know my colleagues in order to learn their
ways, their thoughts and philosophies. The bulk of them are
fine lawyers. Many have been governors of their states. Others
have been congressmen. As a group they are outstanding and
frankly, I used to wonder whether I would be able to hold my
own for my home state in such distinguished company.

After the swearing-in, we got down to work. Among other
things, committee assignments were handed out. As I told my
colleague from New York, Senator Jack Javits, while I had the
greatest respect for the seniority system, my constituents in
California had, in effect, told me to go to Washington to
"work," not "wait."

"Jack," I went on, "if there are times when I seem to be ignoring some of the old protocol, please forgive me. There is so
much work to be done and so little time to do it."

Javits, who is a sort of maverick himself, didn't disagree.

I was assigned to the Labor and Public Welfare Committee,
Chairman of which was that fine old Irishman from Michigan,
Senator Pat McNamara. I had known Pat in the past and, in
fact, I had helped a Republican who had campaigned against
him unsuccessfully. Pat and I had one thing in common. We
were the only members of the Labor Committee who had ever
been members of labor unions.

In the early meetings of the Labor and Public Welfare Committee, I discovered that the Democratic members had a
troubling habit of not attending in person but rather sending in
their proxies to the Chairman. This annoyed me so much that I

said to the Chairman, "Patrick, I have an important amendment that I would like to get into the labor bill, but I'll be darned if I'm going to bring it up against a pocketful of proxies. I believe my amendment deserves to be heard by the members on your side of the table."

Pat was somewhat taken aback. I went on: "I hope they'll all be here tomorrow to give me the same courtesy that I have extended to them. If they are not going to be here then I'll go before the TV cameras out on the Capitol steps and tell the people in Bakersfield, Fresno, San Diego, and Long Beach why I haven't brought my amendment up before. In order to make the case complete, I'm going to name those fellows on your side of the table who don't show up."

Old Pat chuckled, said, "I'll bet you'd do it, wouldn't you?"

And I replied, "I sure would, Pat."

The next day, as a result of the Chairman's urging, the entire Committee was present. I proposed my amendment and it was accepted. It was an amendment that would seek to take politics out of the poverty program. I believe if we had gotten the Murphy amendment through the Senate many more poor people would have benefited than have from the tremendous sums of money that have been wasted in the so-called "war on poverty."

One of the first votes that I cast in the Senate had to do with a proposal to allocate seventy-five million dollars to purchase wheat for Egypt's Nasser. Senator Javits turned around and asked me, "How are you going to vote on this, Murph?"

I told him, "Jack, I am committed. When I campaigned in California I said I wouldn't give Nasser or Sukarno or any other of those phony little dictators four dollars of American taxpayers' money."

I voted against the amendment then, and I will continue to vote against aiding Nasser or any of his kind today.

When I first came to Washington, everyone wanted to have a

look at the movie-actor-turned-Senator. Invariably, people would ask, "How do you compare working in the Senate with working in Hollywood?"

Facetiously, I used to reply, "It's pretty much the same. The only difference is that the sets are much larger in Washington and the budgets are far greater than Hollywood could ever afford—even on one of those spectaculars."

One lady asked me why I had considered running for the Senate. I told her in pseudo-seriousness that, after my long and varied career, I couldn't think of anything else to do for a finish. Actually, I ran because I thought that I could better serve my nation and my community in the Senate than I could working in community affairs as a private citizen.

Of course, there aren't any other senators who have appeared in films that, though of somewhat ancient vintage, are still being shown on late-night television. I suppose that's why, unlike most of my esteemed colleagues, I am so immediately recognizable.

I must confess I do have considerable competition in such widely-publicized figures as Senators Edward M. Kennedy and Eugene McCarthy, both of whom, because of their considerable good looks, could have done well in show business. In recent months, Ted Kennedy has been busy running for re-election in his home state of Massachusetts, while Gene McCarthy apparently is not spending as much time in politics as he is writing poetry. I'm told Gene is a mighty fine poet. Perhaps my friend from Minnesota has finally found his true vocation.

I have a lot going for me in the Senate besides my show business background. Everything I've done in my life ties in with my Senatorial duties. One morning, for example, there was an executive session of the Armed Forces committee at which eight top-ranking Air Force officers were talking on highly secret matters. Two of my Senate colleagues were completely bewildered by the technical testimony.

"Let me help you gentlemen a little," I said. Then I explained the complicated testimony in as simple terms as possible.

When I'd finished, an Air Force General asked me in astonishment, "How did you know that?"

"Well," I said, "in spite of the fact that everyone thinks of me as that nice young man who danced with Shirley Temple, the fact is that I spent several years at Yale studying engineering. I've managed over the years to keep informed on technological innovations."

In a sense, therefore, my varied background may have given me a slight edge over my colleagues, most of whom have spent their adult lives immersed in law books.

"In five months," *Life* reported in May 1965, "Murph has made a favorable impression on colleagues." A little while later, the late Edwin A. Lahey, then chief of the Washington bureau of the *Knight Newspapers,* wrote: "Murphy is all business. His credentials as a U. S. Senator are respected by his colleagues." And in May 1967, Clayton Fritchey described me in *Harper's* as one of several senators working their way into the Senate's inner club, that little group of influential solons who supposedly make the organizational wheels go around.

Well, nobody has told me whether or not I've been admitted into "The Club" but I have been lucky in managing to get things done. One reason is that, from the beginning, I tried to learn how the Senate functions. Another reason is that I've always managed to maintain mutual respect and good relations with colleagues on both sides of the aisle, even those with views I may disagree with most vigorously.

Take my good friend, Senator Jack Javits of New York, who has occasionally berated me for being "conservative" in my approach towards certain issues.

"Jack," I told him, "I don't know exactly what that word 'conservative' means. Just show me where I'm wrong; don't hurl words at me."

Javits looked at me with a twinkle in his eye. "We don't know what to do about you," he said.

Happily, I was also assigned to the Public Works Committee at a time when it had just begun to delve into the problems of air and water pollution. At one of our early meetings I said to our Chairman, Ed Muskie of Maine, that for many years I had watched a very smoky dump in the southwest section of Washington, not too far from the Capitol itself, that was without question polluting the air as fast as anything I had ever seen. I proposed we discover who owned the dump. Much to my amazement, the information came back that it was owned by the federal government. How long had the dump been polluting the air? I was told twenty-five years.

So my first proposal to the Public Works Committee was that the federal government itself begin to combat its own pollutions.

Not long afterward I went down to the Potomac River to observe a demonstration of what was purported to be a machine that could be useful in desalinization. In my opinion the machine was not too effective. But what shocked me was the sight of the filth in what once was the beautiful Potomac. As I told someone at the time, "You wouldn't dare to go water-skiing in the river, because if you happened to fall in, I'm sure things would be growing out of your ears by the time you got to shore."

With the help of the Committee, I succeeded in getting the Murphy Amendment into the Air Quality Act of 1967, which gave California the right to have stricter automobile standards than any other state in the Union—this over the strenuous objections of the Detroit automobile manufacturers.

In Detroit, I pointed out to a representative of the Big Three manufacturers that the industry must begin to construct their automobiles with a due regard for the problems raised by air pollution. I was pleased to note, shortly after our visit to Detroit, an announcement that not only the automobile industry but the tire makers and the oil men at long last had come to realize their responsibility in combating the problems for which they were primarily responsible.

Again my show business background helped me tremendously. In order to obtain support for the Murphy Amendment, I made one appeal on a single television station in Los Angeles. As a result I received three hundred thousand pieces of mail which I brought to Washington by truck and had photographed in front of the Capitol. I'm certain that this had some effect on the votes of many of my colleagues on both sides of the aisle.

I am still amazed by the number of things the Government should have taken care of years ago, which only now are coming to our attention. Of course, there are some brand-new problems. The one concerning me most is what to do about solid waste material. This unquestionably is one of the problems we will have to face up to pretty quickly if man is going to continue to inhabit the earth.

Freshman senators, of course, are expected to stay quiet and be respectful during their apprenticeship, and I had every intention of following tradition. But a crisis developed in my home state when Secretary of Labor W. Willard Wirtz agreed to end the importation of supplementary harvest workers who used to come into California from Mexico—the braceros. Wirtz said that this additional labor force was unnecessary. By boosting the minimum wage, he hoped to attract a flood of domestic urban unemployed onto the farms. Theoretically it sounded like an excellent idea, but practically, as anyone who had any experience around the farming area knew, it just wouldn't work.

California's fruit and vegetable crops began to suffer vast losses because there were no field hands to do the harvesting, and the prices of these products began to soar in the marketplace. I watched fields of strawberries being plowed under because their owners could not hire enough harvest hands. Later on, I saw many thousands of tons of tomatoes rotting in rows because no one was around to pick them.

So I made speech after speech on the Senate floor calling on Secretary Wirtz to rectify his mistake. I assailed "the whimsical dictatorship of theorists who simply do not understand what is going on on our farms." I added, "The design of disaster continues toward its inevitable final impact which will hit not only the farmers and the economy of my state, but the pocketbooks and food budgets of all the housewives in the nation along about next November."

That's exactly what happened.

I might say that I was most capably aided in these efforts by Senator Spessard Holland of Florida. Floridians were suffering from the same kind of "Wirtz disease" as Californians.

I couldn't get any satisfaction from Willard Wirtz, despite my feeling that I had proved to him the absolute necessity of the braceros. I have always felt that Wirtz was carrying out a promise he had made to organized labor, and that the entire exercise was part of the effort to force the organization of all farm workers in the country.

Moreover, I was certain that President Johnson was not getting correct information on the subject. I made several efforts to see him at the White House. One day, in desperation, I said to my dear friend from Florida, former Senator George Smathers, "When you go over to the White House tonight to have your evening highball with the President, will you please tell that big-eared so-and-so that if he doesn't let me come over and help get this thing straightened out, I'm going to take the state of California away from him."

I never did get in to see the President, and you may notice that we now have a Republican Governor in California and, for that matter, a Republican President in the White House.

The President did speak to me briefly on the farm labor problem, during the signing of a bill at the White House. I had come up in the reception line with other senators and, as the

President shook my hand, he said, "George, you don't like my Secretary of Labor."

"No, Mr. President."

"Why not?"

"Sir," I explained, "he has an unfortunate habit of changing the rules in the middle of the game, and that can become very annoying."

"Well," the President said, "I wouldn't be too tough on him if I were you. Do you remember the old Mosaic law?"

"No, Mr. President, I don't.

"It goes this way, George, 'an eye for an eye and a tooth for a tooth.' "

I got the implication immediately. "Mr. President," I said, "You will have to understand that I've been around the track three times and I am on the back nine now, and I'm expendable. Also, I am in the habit of doing what I think is right and I guess I am just too old to change."

The President smiled and said, "Thank you very much, George. Nice to have seen you."

"Thank you, Mr. President. It's been a great pleasure to have seen you."

That was the last time I ever got to talk about the farm labor problem with President Johnson.

Another early lesson about my fellow senators came in an exchange with one of my liberal Republican colleagues for whom I have great respect, Senator Clifford Case of New Jersey. I noted that he and I seldom voted together, and I suggested that possibly he had information on which he based his votes that I didn't have. Or, I said, it might be the other way around.

"Anyway," I went on, "why don't you and I sit down, just the two of us, and discuss all these things some night?"

He looked at me for a long minute and asked, "Did you ever go to a Jesuit school?"

"Yes, I did."

"Well," he said, "that will be about enough of that." And he walked away.

I still don't understand what Case meant by his question. Maybe he just didn't trust Jesuit logic. Or maybe he didn't think I had any information that might be of use to him.

One of the most amusing and exciting nights I ever spent came at the end of my first session. It was very late and we were waiting around for a bill to come over from the House. One of my colleagues had gone to a cocktail party where he apparently had overestimated his capacity. On his way back to the Chamber someone said something that made him very angry at some of his Democratic colleagues.

As the evening wore on, I went over to bid my Democratic friend goodbye and to thank him for the many kindnesses he had shown me during the session. For some reason, my remarks triggered his resentment against his Democratic colleagues, and he leaped to his feet and tried to get the floor. I immediately realized that he had overcelebrated at the cocktail party and so I grabbed him by his coattails and pulled him back into his seat. He would have none of it and was back on his feet, shouting, "Mr. President!" Once again I pulled him down.

When he went up the third time, I got some help from Senator Smathers and my old schoolmate, Senator Stu Symington. The three of us finally got our distinguished colleague out of the Chamber before he said anything that he might have regretted the next day.

The colleague in question has always appreciated my imposing my judgement on him at that particular moment. Later, when we were on the verge of being concerned about a filibuster, this colleague gave me a great deal of excellent advice on how to conduct one if we had to.

I enjoyed my relations with the two Kennedy brothers, Bob and Ted, very much from the time I arrived in the Senate. My

father and their grandfather, Honey Fitz, had been good
friends, having met while they were youngsters in Boston. I had
also known their brother Jack, who had been a frequent visitor
to Hollywood both before and after he became President. I used
to kid a good deal with Bob and Ted, especially about the extent of their publicity. I used to promise to make remarks about
them from time to time to make certain that their names would
be kept before the public. They would laugh and enjoy the
joke.

I also pointed out that if they had read Irish history they
would have discovered that the Murphys always preceded the
Kennedys in any of the important functions in the old days.

On a few occasions some of my fellow senators found it difficult to remember the state from which Bob Kennedy had been
elected. There was the occasion, for example, when Bob rose in
his seat only to be recognized by the presiding officer, Senator
Joseph Montoya, as "the Senator from Massachusetts."

"Mr. President," Bob said, "will the record show that it is the
Senator from New York?"

Early in my Senate career, Ted Kennedy had the questionable pleasure of proposing the name of his father's faithful political retainer, Francis X. Morrissey, for a federal judgeship,
despite the fact that both the Massachusetts and the American
Bar Associations had dubbed him as distinctly "unqualified."
Extensive hearings had been conducted by the Judiciary Committee and more information being developed made it clear
that Morrissey was not going to make it.

While the hearings were going on, Bob and Ted Kennedy
stopped by my seat in the Senate Chamber and asked, "Are you
going to give us a vote on Morrissey?" I said I hadn't made up
my mind.

"You know, George, he's your type of fellow. He started from
nothing and is a self-made man, raised himself by his own boot-
straps. And he's a family man."

I said that was excellent and that was the kind of fellow I

liked, "but I am afraid that I will have to read the Committee report before I make my final decision."

A couple of days later, the two brothers approached me again and asked, "Well, have you made up your mind on Morrissey?"

I said, "No, I haven't."

"We want you to know he is a good Catholic and a good churchman. He goes to communion regularly and he is your kind of guy. We'd like to have your vote."

"Well," I said, "his strong religious beliefs won't hurt him, certainly, but I haven't made up my mind yet, nor will I until I finish reading the record."

A few nights later, I did stay up to read the entire report and reached my conclusion. At noontime, when the Senate went into session, I stopped Bobby and Teddy as they came in and said, "Fellows, did Morrissey go to Mass this morning?"

Bobby asked, "Why do you want to know?"

"Well, today is the day he is going to need it because we are going to vote on him."

Morrissey's religious inclinations never did get to help him because we never got to vote on his nomination.

In a very emotional speech, Senator Ted Kennedy advocated Morrissey's appointment and then, in the same speech, removed his name from contention. I thought it was a very wise move, even though it went against one of the old Irish sayings, "Better to have fought and lost than never to have fought at all."

In another amusing episode in 1966, when Ronnie Reagan was running for Governor against Pat Brown in California, Senator Ted Kennedy flew out to campaign for the incumbent. Bobby asked me one day, "How did Teddy do while he was in California?"

"He did just fine," I said, "Reagan went up three points in the polls while he was out there."

Later on, Bobby Kennedy informed me he was going out to California to campaign for Brown and he wondered whether I would be out there to greet him when he arrived. I said that I would be glad to if he would give me three minutes on his program.

"What do you want the three minutes for?" he asked.

I replied, "The Murphys could always handle the Kennedys in three minutes."

Anyhow, Bobby flew out and after he was in California for two days, I couldn't resist the temptation. I sent him a telegram reading, "Keep it up. You are doing much better than Teddy. Reagan has gone up seven points since you've been in the state."

When Bobby came back to Washington, we had a good laugh over the telegram.

At one time, Bobby did have a minor objection. "Murph," he said, "when you make political speeches you are always cracking jokes about me."

"Bob," I replied quickly, "that's good for you. I'm keeping your name before the people so they won't forget you."

"If you don't mind, would you let me take care of that myself?"

"All right, Bob, if that's the way you want it. But if they forget you, remember it's your fault, not mine."

I really got to know Bob Kennedy very well when our Subcommittee on Migratory Labor held hearings in California. We worked together closely at this time and later I sent him all the information I could obtain on the farm labor program in my state. I also tried to explain the complexities involved in the problems, but I don't think I had much success in convincing my colleague from New York.

Of course, I was terribly shaken by his assassination. A very brilliant career was cut short before it really got started. We disagreed on many subjects, but I had the greatest respect for him and his capabilities. I think that he returned the confidence.

One of the terrible things about the assassination was that it provided one more piece of evidence of the obvious irrationality that is beginning to pervade our society. Many of my liberal friends maintain that we are really a violent society, and I am forced to agree. But, according to my observations, a considerable amount of the contemporary violence seems to stem from extreme left-wing sources. After all, I cannot help but remind them of the fact that Lee Harvey Oswald was not a right-winger. He was an avowed Communist and a misfit. Sirhan Sirhan, who killed Bob Kennedy, was another who had been affected by Marxist hate propaganda.

The Black Panthers, who store arms and ammunition in their pads and who preach violence and assassination of all those who disagree with them, have adopted the Maoist line. The Weathermen faction of Students for Democratic Action, whose proudest achievement thus far seems to have been running riot in the streets of Chicago, is openly dedicated to the violent overthrow of our form of government.

Yet there are leading opinion-makers who close their eyes to all of this and, in the name of civil liberties, condone, in effect, the kind of license that inevitably will destroy all freedom-loving Americans, whether they be liberals, middle-of-the-roaders or conservatives.

This is exactly what has happened on some of our nation's campuses where fanatical revolutionaries have shut down classrooms, beat up opponents, bombed buildings and even burned books and manuscripts.

Unfortunately, the beginnings of this campus revolt have been in my state. This is one California product I would rather not have seen exported. There is little doubt in my mind that these school disruptions are part of a carefully-prepared plan to disrupt eventually the government itself.

As an unequivocal believer in free speech, I am the last person in the world to advocate the suppression of dissent. After all, as a Republican since 1939, I have often voiced a minority view myself. But dissent and disruption are two different things. We must make that emphatically clear to those who advocate change.

Neither am I arguing that our system and institutions are perfect. Far from it. That is one reason why my Senate colleagues and I spend many long hours wrangling over legislation. In our own way we are constantly voting for change. We may not always agree, but paramount in our minds—whether we be Democrats or Republicans—is the national interest.

Though we may not be perfect as a nation, I know from the traveling I have done around the world that we have achieved a greater degree of perfection in a free society than any other system devised by mankind.

Campus disruptions were the subject of a speech I delivered on the floor of the Senate on May 1, 1969. In part, I declared: "I recall the trouble which started at the great university at Berkeley, one of the outstanding universities in the world, and then the troublemakers came in. There was something called the free speech movement. Free speech—free speech for themselves. Anybody else who wanted the right to speak would be hooted down, booed down. Realizing their positions could not stand exposure to the light of reason and debate, they resorted to the picket line and to violence and destruction.

"We had a similar experience recently at San Francisco University.

"Governor Reagan told me that the admission of the troublemakers there started when a group came into the dean's office with knives in their hands and made certain demands. . .

"I was glad to hear a reference today to the unfortunate emphasis on the part of the news media. I know it makes a better picture in the newspapers to see somebody jeering or yelling. It is a much more exciting story than to tell the story of the good, run-of-the-mill student, of the good, ordinary student.

"I know something about this. In my former vocation as an actor in Hollywood, some of my friends of the press would come to me and say, 'Murphy, why don't you get into some trouble, so that we can give you some publicity?'

"I always said that I was not interested in getting into trouble; that I was more interested in doing my job to the best of my ability. I believe that that is the feeling of the great majority of students in the universities today. I see no reason why the one or two percent should be permitted to interrupt the intellectual advance of the other ninety-eight or ninety-nine percent who want to go to school and learn and get on with the job of helping to make this a better Nation and a better world in which to live. Do not the vast majority of the students deserve the opportunity to go to classes and secure an education without being exposed to the destructive and dangerous disturbances of a small minority?

"Dr. Hayakawa has done a magnificent job at San Francisco University. We say it is magnificent because he did what was obvious. He demanded that the rules be obeyed; and, with the help of the great Governor of California, he has made a nation-wide reputation. . .

"I have asked a simple question of ten reputable lawyers. I am not a lawyer, but I know something about the law. I have asked ten reputable lawyers, "Is there a special set of laws that applies only to people who are outside the campus, who are not part of the academic community; or are the people on the campus supposed to live by the same laws that apply to the rest of us ordinary citizens?"

"They all have answered that there are not two sets of laws; that if I, outside the campus, break a window or throw a Molotov cocktail or forcibly hold a man against his will, certain rules and laws apply. I recommend that the same laws should be applied to those on the campus, unless I have been misled, unless there are special restrictions of which I know nothing. . .

"Dr. Hayakawa has told me, also, that the students are not completely to blame; that, in his experience, members of the faculties have told the students to go out and join in the mischiefmaking, join in the troublemaking, join in the disruption, and 'If you don't you'll flunk the course.' This is shocking. Were I the head of a university, any faculty member who recommended breaking the rules or breaking the law in such a manner would be fired."

Following my speech, our Minority Leader, that great patriot Everett Dirksen, introduced a resolution calling for a "comprehensive study and investigation of campus disorders." That investigation is continuing.

Late in 1969 Everett Dirksen passed away, to the great loss and sorrow of his country and his party. Watching and listening to this great man from Pekin, Illinois, had been one of the high points of my life in the Senate. He stood head and shoulders over most of his colleagues in his great depth of experience, his wealth of understanding, his exquisite use of the language, his well-trained legal mind, which were accompanied by a sense of balance, a sense of humor and unrestrained self-confidence.

If there is such a thing as an Inner Club in the Senate, I think that Dirksen, along with Dick Russell and one or two others, would have been on the Board of Directors. His counsel and support were sought on both sides of the aisle, and it is a matter of record that a major Civil Rights Bill was finally written in an acceptable form in Dirksen's office. Without his help it is doubtful that it would ever have been voted into law.

I will always remember the evening when the Republican leadership was about to reply to Lyndon Johnson's State of the Union message in a half-hour television program. Surprisingly, only hours before the show was to go on the air several leading Republicans were invited to the White House for a briefing. Vietnam, of course, was developing into a sticky mess and we thought there must be something new in the wind to be invited in such a hurried fashion.

The briefing was given by Secretary of Defense Robert McNamara and his staff. They were there with all of their usual charts, some of which we had seen before. I couldn't help but notice that while this rehash of a bunch of familiar McNamara statistics was going on, President Johnson kept his arm around Everett Dirksen's shoulders. From time to time, the President would signal to a White House steward who would immediately bring Everett another drink. I have never been certain whether President Johnson was just being hospitable or whether he was trying to get Everett overtrained for the TV program he was going to do as soon as he left the White House.

None of us Republicans learned anything new from the McNamara briefing. I felt that Ev Dirksen could have used the time to better advantage in preparing for his TV performance. The first part of the Republican telecast went fairly well. Towards the end, Congressman Gerald Ford was forced to carry the major share of the load when Senator Dirksen became visibly tired and was not his usual bright, animated and vivacious self.

The following year, a group of younger members of both the Senate and the House of Representatives came to me and said they felt there ought to be others besides Dirksen and Congressman Gerald Ford to speak for the party in the forthcoming telecast.

I went to Dirksen and told him that I would be less his friend if I didn't report this rather widespread feeling.

"What do you think?" Everett asked in his forthright manner.

"I think these young fellows ought to be given a little exposure," I replied.

"That's fine with me," he said. "Do you have any ideas on how to handle it?"

"What I thought we might do is use nine or ten of the new people with a couple of attractive ladies and put on an hour's show," I explained. "We could break it up into short segments and let each individual Congressman or Senator cover one subject or topic."

"That sounds excellent," said Dirksen. "Why don't you put the thing together?"

I did and, from all accounts, the hour-long Republican reply went well indeed. It gave the American people an opportunity to see and listen to some very attractive newcomers who, of course, weren't done any harm by nationwide exposure on the tube.

My own relations with President Johnson were always pleasant. In 1967, in fact, the President invited me to become a member of the special bipartisan commission to observe, at first hand, the Presidential elections in South Vietnam. I told the President I would be happy to serve, but only if I could visit any part of the country I wished, talk with anybody I pleased, and be permitted to give my own report under any conditions I chose when I returned home.

It was an exciting trip, and I am glad I went. There were a few scary moments, but I was very lucky. In the tiny town of Tuy Hoa a bomb had unquestionably been intended for me. Because I had stopped to have a cup of tea with the headman of the village, I was five minutes late—and missed the explosion.

One thing that troubled me greatly on my return from Vietnam was the knowledge that pronouncements by a few senators were being used by Hanoi to convince its people that the American war effort was about to collapse.

This is not to slight in any way the patriotism or deep-seated concern for their nation's security of any of these senators.

"But the fact is," as I told Wayne Morse of Oregon, "your words and those of several other of our colleagues are being used by the enemy as propaganda material. And I'm sure you don't really want anything you say to be used against the best interests of your country."

"Of course not, George," Morse said.

"Perhaps you ought to get up and make such a statement," I suggested.

"That's a good idea," he said.

Unfortunately, Wayne never got around to making that statement. It might have helped him in his 1968 quest for re-election. But I'll say this about Wayne's position on Vietnam. He was one of the first to voice his doubts about the growing American involvement and, in fact, was one of two Senators who voted against the Tonkin Bay Resolution which authorized the original involvement. The other Senator, Ernest Gruening of Alaska, also went down to defeat.

One of my unforgettable Senate experiences was a field trip in April 1969 to explore the educational conditions of Eskimo children in Alaska. The trip was arranged by Senator Ted Kennedy as Chairman of the Indian Education Subcommittee, and I was a little concerned over the way in which our hearings would be conducted, since I had had some experience with such junkets in the past. I agreed to go along only if the hearing would be carefully organized for the purpose of actually gathering information and not aimed at getting publicity for anyone. I made it abundantly clear that if I found the latter to be the case I would not participate in the Subcommittee hearings.

When I got on the plane to fly to Alaska with my fellow senators I discovered that this was one of the most carefully-planned excursions that I had ever seen put together. It was done with much more precise care and craftsmanship than the old motion picture publicity junkets in which we'd go out with a lot of stars to storm the country to introduce a new film.

First, I discovered that there were some twenty-five special writers aboard the plane, all covering what would normally have been considered a routine investigation. The three television networks were represented by camera crews. There were also a number of staff people, most of whom seemed to be concerned only with the care and comfort of Ted Kennedy. It had all the trappings of a Presidential campaign.

On arriving in Alaska we learned that the *Chicago Tribune* had published a confidential staff memorandum to Kennedy which outlined methods for garnering political capital from the tour. Among the conclusions suggested to the Senator from Massachusetts was that the "native population" (Indians, Aleuts and Eskimos) were the victims of "economic exploitation" by "the small white minority."

I immediately got together with my Republican colleagues, Henry Bellmon of Oklahoma and William Saxbe of Ohio, and we decided that very little practical usefulness could be served by our remaining with the Subcommittee. Before we returned to Washington, I issued a statement:

"After one day with the Subcommittee, I came to the conclusion that what started out to be a fact-finding trip on the serious situation involving the educational welfare of the Alaskan natives has been turned into an unfortunate political publicity junket at the taxpayer's expense.

"After visiting native villages and the town of Bethel, I have concluded that this entire trip has been 'overarranged,' to the point that in my opinion the primary purpose of the project was destroyed.

"I have no intention of wasting my time or the taxpayers' money on trips of this type either now or in the future. I will return to Washington so that I can get back to perhaps less spectacular but at least more productive duties."

Senator Kennedy, wearing a button proclaiming "Eskimo power," was left to carry on the inspection trip alone.

On one or two occasions I have tangled with my good friend, Chairman J. William Fulbright of the prestigious Foreign Relations Committee. From time to time the Senator from Arkansas inveighs against what he considers to be the inordinate influence of the Pentagon in the shaping of our nation's policies.

After listening to him on one occasion, I declared that if the diplomats had performed their duties in peacetime nearly as well as the military people had in wartime, we wouldn't have half the problems our nation is facing today.

One of the things that has galled me for some time—and I'm not easily galled—has been the facility with which some senators and leading opinion-makers have misrepresented President Eisenhower's views warning against the so-called "industrial-military complex" in this country.

What those who demonstrate this rare affection for the words of Eisenhower have failed to do is provide the rest of the Eisenhower quotation. This I did in a Senate speech on June 19, 1969 in which I spoke in behalf of the Anti-Ballistic Missile system proposed by President Nixon. I could never fully comprehend the furor which the President's proposal aroused. It was not a new idea. In fact, it had first been officially proposed by Secretary McNamara on September 18, 1967 in a San Francisco speech and its opponents at that time were few in number. Somehow, after being advocated by a Republican President, it became the subject of loud and clamorous debate.

At any rate, this is what the late President Eisenhower also said in the "farewell" speech he made when he left the Presidency: "A vital element in keeping the peace is our military establishment. Our arms must be mighty, ready for instant action, so that no potential aggressor may be tempted to risk his own destruction."

He continued: "We face a hostile ideology—global in scope, atheistic in character, ruthless in purpose, and insidious in method. Unhappily, the danger it poses promises to be of indefinite duration. To meet it successfully, there is called for, not so much the emotional and transitory sacrifices of crisis, but rather those which will enable us to carry forward steadily, surely, and without complaint the burdens of a prolonged and complex struggle—with liberty the stake."

In other words, as I said on the Senate floor, "we cannot progress in the fight to achieve a better life for all Americans unless we are free to operate within a framework of security and safety which can be provided only by our great military, scientific and technical strength—not to make war, but to guarantee peace."

Some of the criticism directed against the ABM verged on the ludicrous. I sat through long hours of testimony on the subject as a member of the Armed Services Committee.

I especially recall the testimony of a former adviser to the late President Kennedy. In my examination, I asked him if he knew whether the Russians had their own ABM system. He said he did. I then asked him if he knew that their system had been deployed for three years. He said he knew that. And he conceded that the Russians had experience in this field we did not possess.

"Then," I asked, "what about their ABM?"

"It's a bunch of junk," he replied.

"Do you know that for a fact?"

"No," he said, "that is my opinion."

"Is your opinion based on scientific knowledge?"

"No, it is not," he said. "It is my opinion."

Unfortunately, he was often quoted as an expert. I have reason to believe he just didn't know what he was talking about. He is only one of the self-opinionated "experts" who, operating from ideological biases rather than with facts, seek to influence the nation. That they are likely to cripple the national defenses, should they be successful, does not seem to trouble them at all. They are willing to take their chances in a world in which the Communist superpowers have made no secret of their ultimate aim—namely, the "burying" of the free world. They argue that such talk is part of the "mythology of the cold war."

They conveniently forget that the cold war is quite real in Berlin, in Korea, in Vietnam, and in other places around the globe. They ignore the fact that the Soviets have not noticeably changed their objectives at all. And unfortunately, their propaganda is having an effect on public opinion.

Another lamentable political attitude is that the pouring of billions of dollars into sociolgical experiments somehow will make all such federally-sponsored programs work. The truth about some of these programs is shocking. The bureaucrats running them quite often have no idea of what is being done with the money in the field, and it is very frustrating to try to find out what is happening.

You could never get many real answers from someone like Sargent Shriver when he was head of the Office of Economic Opportunity (O.E.O.) Trying to pin Shriver down in a Committee session was next to impossible. The fact that scandal after scandal has erupted in the poverty program has never surprised me. As one observer put it, "Poverty is where the money is."

My argument is not with the stated aims of the "war on poverty." My argument is with the ill-conceived programs that just haven't worked. As a result, endless billions from hard-pressed taxpayers have gone down the drain and have created problems in places where none existed. The tragedy is that the poor people, who had been led to expect so much by the overblown rhetoric of the poverty warriors, have not benefited as they should have.

Six top men from the Department of Education once appeared before our Education Subcommittee. This is an area the people of California are particularly interested in, so I asked these gentlemen how long certain experimental programs were continued before they decided whether to go ahead with them or scrub them. They just didn't know. I asked whether they could list for the Subcommittee some of the programs that were "ongoing" at the moment. No, they said, they couldn't. Even Bob Kennedy was shaken by the testimony, or lack of it. He could hardly believe that these were men sent over as "experts" to enlighten us.

I believe in spending money on limited programs that have a chance of succeeding. In my first term as Senator, in the field of education alone, I successfully pushed through the Dropout Prevention Program amendment, aimed at keeping in school one million youngsters who normally drop out each year. I coauthored the 1967 Bilingual Education Act which is giving Mexican-American children the opportunity to be educated in Spanish before first becoming fluent in English.

I drew up legislation establishing Model Vocational School and Skill Centers, prototypes for improving vocational education. And I co-sponsored President Nixon's emergency legislation to help needy students stay in college with guaranteed loans. These are not pie-in-the-sky efforts. They are realistic and practical programs which are already highly successful.

For these efforts I was awarded the Distinguished Service Award of the National Education Association. And President Nixon, although feeling early in 1970 that the Labor-HEW appropriations bill was too high, singled out my dropout prevention program in his compromise message to the Congress and, in fact, requested an increase of my program by ten million dollars.

One project that has generated national interest was the one in Texarkana, where the school districts of this Texas and Arkansas border community have called on private industry in an effort to raise basic levels of potential dropouts. The school system has entered into what is called a "performance contract" with a private corporation to bring potential dropouts up to grade level in academic performance. As the name of the contract implies, the companies must perform or they do not get paid.

The Texarkana project is experimenting with a system of rewards and incentives for students. For example, successful students will receive coupons redeemable for merchandise and students who successfully complete two grade levels of achievement will receive transistor radios.

Much has been written about the crisis in urban education, but I believe I have done more than just talk about it. My Urban and Rural Education Act, enacted by the Senate, provides additional resources for needy urban schools so that the quality of education of their students may be improved. I sincerely believe that the majority of Americans support such legislation to bring about educational improvements for all students, particularly minority youngsters, which is the approach that I advocate rather than wasting so much time and spinning so many wheels on the artificial and unwise policy of bussing students hither and yon.

I used to greatly enjoy the gatherings of the Republican Coordinating Committee. General Eisenhower was the Chairman of the group that included other Presidential candidates— Dick Nixon and Tom Dewey—governors, members of the National Committee and the Republican leaderships of the House and Senate.

At these productive meetings, a series of position papers were presented for discussion and debate. If accepted, they were released and presented to the public as party positions. Most of the documents were exceptionally well-written and documented. They served the Republican cause well.

One such paper was presented on the complex problems of the Middle East. A few senators were hesitant about accepting it, believing that the paper was tilted in favor of one side of the Israeli-Arab argument.

Normally, any such objections meant the end of the document. But I felt there was a lot of good material in this one that could be so reshaped that it would obtain the approval of the objectors. I asked permission to rework the document for presentation the next morning.

That night I went to work, along with Bryce Harlow, who today is one of President Nixon's top men, and Kent Crane, who is on Vice-president Agnew's staff. Working far into the night we came up with a document that, we felt, contained ideas which if implemented, might well solve some of the frictions in the Middle East.

For example, we envisioned the building of two atomic reactors to be combined with desalinization plants that would provide enough fresh water to make a garden spot out of the Sinai Peninsula. It was our belief that if the people who live in that barren land could get water, they could accomplish what Californians have done in both the Imperial and Cochella Valleys. And if they were busy growing badly-needed food, they might have less time or inclination for fighting.

The next afternoon I received a telephone call from General Eisenhower. He said that President Johnson had called him to ask that we refrain from releasing our paper lest it interfere with some of the things he was trying to do in the Middle East.

"It's too late," I told General Eisenhower. "We've already released the paper. Everyone approved it. It has gone."

To make certain that the Israelis knew about our document, I asked two close friends of mine from Los Angeles, Taft Schreiber and Holmes Tuttle, both good Republicans, to take it to the Holy Land on their forthcoming visit. Before they left, I arranged for them to spend several hours being briefed by Admiral Lewis L. Strauss, who had originally envisioned the idea of using atomic reactors in the Sinai Peninsula.

The Israelis, I later learned, were most interested in and pleased with the plan. Unfortunately, the Arab reaction has been practically nil. I still think it's a good, workable and practical program and I would like to see President Nixon work for its implementation. I sincerely believe that if all the people of the Middle East, no matter what their religious and cultural differences, could be taught to work and live together, with plenty of food for all, an awful lot of problems that have been stirred up by the Soviets would disappear. At least, I'm hoping.

In August, 1966, I underwent surgery on a vocal chord which the doctors thought might have contained a malignant growth. Ever since, because of a scarred vocal chord, my voice has sounded like Andy Devine's—that dear friend even offered to lend me his orchestrations. When I returned to the Senate, I asked the consent of my colleagues to violate their rules by using a microphone and portable amplifier. Jack Javits was so impressed with the results that he later suggested that amplification equipment be installed for all senators, who have traditionally enjoyed the privilege of not being able to hear each other speak very clearly.

Using my mike, I said, "I would like to be a co-sponsor of such a measure."

As a matter of fact, one day in a colloquy one of my colleagues complained that I had a distinct advantage with my darned mechanical device.

When I was in charge of programming for the 1968 Republican convention in Miami Beach, I was taking a dip in the hotel pool when a little old lady came up to me and said, "Excuse me, but didn't you used to be George Murphy?"

"Yes."

She leaned over and whispered, "You sound sexier than you used to."

Unfortunately, wild rumors concerning my health did spring up from time to time—avidly circulated by some Democratic newsmen who always seem to feel that if a Republican holds an elected office he's just holding it for them temporarily until they can find a Democrat to replace him.

One Sunday afternoon while I was walking my two dogs—a beagle and a Shetland collie—around the block in Beverly Hills, a car pulled up to the curb and a nice-looking gentleman jumped out. Before I could recognize him, he asked, "How do you feel?"

"I feel fine," I said.

"No really, how do you feel?"

"I feel just great."

"Honest to God?" And his face fell. It was my old friend, former Governor Pat Brown.

The rumor got into the press through Pat's office that I would never return to Washington following my 1966 operation. I was supposed to have been a terminal cancer case. I think I am the liveliest terminal case that Pat Brown will ever see.

Feeling that my constituents were entitled to a full account of the state of my health, early in 1970 I spent five days at the esteemed Scripps Clinic in La Jolla, undergoing extensive medical tests. A complete copy of my medical examination was released to the press. In it, Dr. Edmund L. Keeney of the clinic wrote: "In summary, the findings of this extensive physical survey disclose the patient to be in excellent health."

The Scripps' specialists also informed me that, because of my background as a dancer and an athlete, I had the physiology of a forty-five-year-old man.

As a matter of fact, I do feel twenty years younger when I campaign across the length and breadth of my home state. I enjoy it. My only regret is that my dear wife has not been fully able to share the great joys I have experienced in recent years. But Julie is still the boss. She keeps herself informed and lets me know, almost daily, how she feels about the issues. And most of the time I find that her instincts are far better than the studied conclusions of the professionals.

A great comfort to Julie have been our two dogs—Mr. Biggs, the beagle, and Revel, the Shetland collie. Both seem to have an instinctive understanding of their mistress' plight. She spends so many lonely hours crippled by arthritis, and they have been boon companions. Every morning and afternoon about forty to fifty doves feed outside her bedroom window. These feathered creatures have been a particular joy to Julie, who watches them roost in the nearby trees.

It hasn't been easy for Julie, but she has faced her vicissitudes with incredible courage. To me, she will always be the beautiful young lady who launched her dancing career with me in a chop suey joint on upper Broadway. And she will always be my strongest campaign booster.

As I campaign, I can't help but be thankful that both in Washington and Sacramento two dear friends are in power. I have always had faith in Dick Nixon and Ronald Reagan, and I know they have faith in me.

President Nixon was kind enough to say: "For over twenty years I have known and respected Senator Murphy, both as a loyal friend and supporter and as a strong and effective spokesman for the principles of the Republican party. All Californians can be proud and thankful for the job George Murphy is doing for the state and the nation . . ."

And Governor Reagan said: "George Murphy and I have been close personal friends for many years, a background that has brought a working partnership between Washington and Sacramento. It is paying daily dividends in progress for California. It's good to know that when I call on Washington, Senator Murphy is there to answer . . . and to help."

As I look at the calendar, I realize the time has come to put a staff together for the 1970 campaign. I do not as yet have any idea as to who my opponent will be, but that is comparatively unimportant. I intend to run on my record, which I believe to be one of considerable achievements.

And I'm absolutely certain that when I make my first campaign visit to San Diego or Long Beach or San Francisco or Sacramento or Fresno, a nice little old lady will come up to me and whisper, "Say, didn't you used to be George Murphy?"

# Index

Boyle, Johnny, 122
Brackett, Charles, 294, 297
Brandon, Dorothy, 328
Brandwynne, Nat, 111
Branigan, Eddie, 33
Brendel, El, 214
Brennan, Walter, 237, 390
Brewer, Roy, 279
Brewster, Owen, 318
Bricker, John, 356
Brinkley, David, 378, 397
*Broadway Melody of 1938*, 203, 208, 326
*Broadway Melody of 1939*, 193
*Broadway Melody of 1940*, 209, 364
Broadway Rose, 122
Broidy, Steve, 361
Brooks, Richard, 252
Broun, Heywood, 58, 105, 150
Brown, Lew, 160
Brown, Pat, 371, 377, 379, 380, 383, 410, 426
Browne, George, 219, 222, 288
Brownell, Herbert, 310-11, 330
Bubbles, John, 49
Buck and Bubbles, 49
Buck, Dick, 381
Bull, George, 129
Burnham, Sadie, 34
Burnman, Robert, 290
Burns, George, 2, 212
Burr, Raymond, 363
Butler, Big Dave, 210
Button, A. Ronald, 338
Byrd, Harry, Jr., 400
Byrd, Harry, Sr., 400

C

C.D.C. *see* California Democratic Council
C.S.U. *see* Conference of Studio Unions
Caesar, Sid, 337
Cafe de Paris, London, 97
Cagney, James, 56, 165, 168, 207, 219, 233, 234, 235, 277
California Club, 383
California Democratic Council, 379
Camp, Walter, 6
Cantor, Eddie, 145, 161, 219
Carillo, Leo, 333
Carlisle Indian School, 10
Carpenter, Terry, (Terrible Terry), 351-2
Carpenters Union, 283
Carroll, Earl, 116
Carroll, Leo, G., 202
Carroll, Nancy, 184, 201
Case, Clifford, 407
Castro, Fidel, 366
Cavallaro, Carmen, 112
Central Park Casino, New York City, 109, 155
Chambers, Whittaker, 281
Champion, Gower, 337
Champion, Marge, 337

Chaney, Lon, 211
Chaplin, Charlie, 267, 282
Chasen, Dave, 233
*Chicago Tribune*, 2, 418
Civil Rights Bill, 415
Class of 1925, 381
Clayton, Jackson and Durante, 123
Clerf, Louis, Dr., 339-40
Club Gallant, 56
Club Richman, 70, 157
Cobb, Ty, 234
Coburn, Charles, 294, 308
Coca, Imogene, 106
Coconut Grove, Los Angeles, 129
Cohan, George M., 2, 134, 168, 226, 307
Cohn, Harry, 162, 183, 185, 188
Cohn, Roy, 359-60
Colbert, Claudette, 153
Cole, Nate "King", 353
Coleman, Emil, 51, 54, 79, 98, 111
Columbia Pictures, 160, 167, 183, 185, 188, 201
Committee for the First Amendment, The, 289
Commodore Hotel, New York City, 332
Communism, 157-8, 226, 254, 266, 279-96
Compton, Betty, 103
Conference of Studio Unions, 283-8
*Connecticut Yankee, A,* 133
Content, Harry, 110
Connolly, Bobby, 88
Convention Hall, Philadelphia, 300
Cooper, Charlie, 40
Cooper, Gary, 291, 295, 308
Copacabana, New York City, 55
Corey, Wendell, 353, 367
Costello, Lou, 337, 353
Coster, Don, 276
Cow Palace, San Francisco, 351
Crane, Kent, 424
Cranston, Alan, 376, 379, 380
Crawford, Joan, 163, 191, 244, 249, 251
Crosby, Everett, 70
Crosby, Harry Lillis, (Bing), 70, 82, 116, 171, 226, 233, 292, 297, 393
Crowther, Bosley, 226, 319, 322
Cuba, 366
Cummings, Jack, 225
Curtis, Carl, 399
Curtiz, Michael, 257
*Cynthia*, 322

D

*Daily Worker*, 281, 322
Dales, Jack, 220, 282, 285
Darcel, Denise, 321
Darnell, Linda, 237
Dart, Justin, 374
Darwell, Jane, 214
Davis, Meyer, 76
Davis, Nancy, (Mrs. Ronald Reagan), 323
DeMarco, Tony and Renee, 25, 48, 84, 116, 337

433